fine Cooking
In Season

Your Guide to
CHOOSING & PREPARING
the Season's Best

Editors & Contributors of **Fine Cooking**

The Taunton Press

The Taunton Press, Inc.

63 South Main Street

PO Box 5506,

Newtown, CT 06470–5506

email: tp@taunton.com

Editor: Martha Holmberg
Copy editor: Li Agen
Indexer: Heidi Blough
Jacket/cover design: Chalkley Calderwood
Interior design: Chalkley Calderwood
Photographers: Matthew Benson except pp. 294–305, 306 (right),
307–309 Scott Phillips © The Taunton Press, Inc.; p. 306 (left) Steve Hunter © The Taunton Press, Inc.

Fine Cooking® is a trademark of The Taunton Press, Inc.,

registered in the U.S. Patent and Trademark Office.

Special thanks to Melissa's and Stonegate Farm for supplying produce for use in the photography.

The following names/manufacturers appearing in *Fine Cooking In Season*
are trademarks: Best Foods®, Carr's®, Coleman's®, Droste®, Eagle®,
Fruit-Fresh®, Grand Marnier®, Hellmann's®, Lee Kum Kee®, Maytag®,
Ortega®, Pepperidge Farm®, Pyrex®, Sugar in the Raw®, Tabasco®

Library of Congress Cataloging-in-Publication Data

Fine cooking in season : your guide to choosing and preparing the season's best / editors and
contributors of Fine cooking.
    p. cm.
 Includes index.
 ISBN 978-1-60085-303-6
1. Seasonal cooking. 2. Cookbooks. I. Taunton Press. II. Taunton's fine cooking.
 TX714.F5644 2011
 641.5'64--dc22

             2010047357

Printed in the United States of America

10 9 8 7 6 5 4 3 2 1

Contents

Spring 4

Early Summer 44

Late Summer 100

Fall 168

Winter 254

Introduction

At *Fine Cooking*, we shop almost every day. We shop for the *Fine Cooking* Test Kitchen, where we test every recipe that runs in the magazine, and we shop for ourselves and our families. For us, food shopping isn't a chore but a pleasure, even an adventure—one that can consume the better part of the weekend. It's not unusual for us to make trips to the grocery store, a farmer's market, maybe an ethnic market, possibly a big-box store, and occasionally a specialty foods shop over the course of those couple of days. We're tireless when it comes to finding the best ingredients to cook with, and we're devoted to cooking with the best of what's in season.

Of course, we're not the only ones with a passion for seasonal produce: Our readers are just as crazy as we are about fresh, locally grown fruits and vegetables. They come to us for shopping hints and buying advice, storing information, and preparation tips. And they come to us for recipes that make the most of the season, highlighting peak produce in unique and delicious ways.

Which is how this book came about. With more than 106 issues of the magazine under our collective belts, we've gathered and researched reams of information about every kind of fruit and vegetable, from apricots to winter squash, edamame to tomatillos. For us, this book was an opportunity to share the most interesting things we've learned about more than 90 different kinds of produce, along with our favorite fruit- and vegetable-centric recipes from more than 16 years' worth of seasonal cooking. And we've organized all this information by season because cooking with foods at their seasonal peak is the best possible way to ensure real flavor (by way of example, consider the weak and watery taste of a February tomato up against one pulled from the vine in late summer). And when you try to keep your shopping both seasonal *and* local, you've done both yourself and the planet a favor, since locally grown produce doesn't need to be transported from one side of the country to the other.

Our story begins in spring and continues through the summer months and into winter. As the produce changes, so do the recipes and the many ideas for what to do with your farmer's market finds. We've got recipes for every meal of the day, from breakfast (Blueberry Muffins with Cinnamon Crumble, p. 51) to dessert (Rhubarb-Raspberry Galette, p. 27). And we've got tips on how to choose the best produce and how to keep it fresh. In addition, you'll find information on preserving a variety of fruits and vegetables, along with some new ways of thinking about what goes with what (think apricots with Mediterranean herbs like rosemary and lavender). All in all, this may well be the only guide you'll need to cooking in season.

—Laurie Buckle
Editor, *Fine Cooking*

Spring

Asparagus officinalis and cvs.

Asparagus

One of the first tender vegetables to arrive after a long winter of roots, tubers, and braising greens, asparagus gets an enthusiastic welcome from cooks each spring. Its long, elegant shape, nutty-grassy flavor, ease of prep, and versatility make it a favorite from breakfast to dinner.

asparagus is growing in popularity, as is purple. Know that white asparagus (prized in Europe) can be stringy, and purple varieties lose their color when cooked, reverting back to dark green.

KEEPING IT FRESH

Stand asparagus bundles in a jar with about an inch of water and refrigerate. Cook asparagus within 2 days for the best flavor.

PREPARING

To prepare spears for cooking, grasp in the middle and bend the spear until it snaps; it will break naturally at the point where it starts to get tough and stringy. Save the fibrous ends to make an asparagus soup base or toss in your compost pile. If the asparagus is thick-skinned or fibrous (take a small bite to test), peel the spears from just under the tip to the end of the stem.

HOW TO USE IT

Asparagus is truly versatile and is happy in a number of preparations. Steaming whole spears brings out subtle, vegetal notes. Roasted or grilled asparagus deepens its nutty, sweet flavor. Sliced and sautéed asparagus is perfect in side dishes, pastas, frittatas, and casseroles. And whole asparagus spears are beautiful on a crudité platter. If very fresh and tender, serve them raw; otherwise steam lightly and chill.

PICKING THE BEST

Commonly sold in bundles of about 1 pound, asparagus is often displayed standing upright in a tray of water, which helps to keep it fresh. Choose fresh-looking, firm spears with tight tips. Check the cut ends of the stalks; they should be moist, not dried out. Many people think thin spears are more tender than fat, but asparagus of any size can be sweet and tender as long as it's fresh. Most asparagus is green, but white

PRESERVING OPTIONS

Pickling asparagus is easy and it makes a delicious addition to green salads, potato salads, and Bloody Marys. To freeze asparagus, blanch it for 3 to 4 minutes before freezing in zip-top freezer bags.

DID YOU KNOW? White asparagus isn't a different vegetable, it's just grown differently. To produce white asparagus, the stalks are mounded with soil to keep sunlight out. As the spears develop in darkness, they don't produce chlorophyll, so they never turn green.

RECIPES

Grilled Asparagus with Fresh Tarragon Mayonnaise

SERVES 4

1 large egg yolk, at room temperature, or pasteurized egg product

½ cup extra-virgin olive oil; more for grilling

2 teaspoons minced shallot

2 teaspoons minced fresh flat-leaf parsley

1 teaspoon minced fresh tarragon

1½ teaspoons fresh lemon juice

½ teaspoon kosher salt, plus more as needed

1½ pounds asparagus, trimmed

Make the mayonnaise: Put the egg yolk in a small bowl. Add a few drops of lukewarm water and whisk well. Begin adding the olive oil in a very thin stream, whisking constantly. When the sauce thickens and forms a creamy emulsion, you can add the oil a little faster. Whisk in the shallot, parsley, tarragon, and lemon juice. Season with the salt, adding more to taste. If needed, whisk in a few drops of water to loosen the mayonnaise until it's spoonable, not stiff.

Prepare the asparagus: Bring a large pot of salted water to a boil over high heat. Add the asparagus and blanch for 1 minute for small spears or 1½ minutes for medium spears. Using tongs, transfer the asparagus to a bowl of ice water. When cool, lift the spears out of the ice water and thoroughly pat dry.

Prepare a hot charcoal fire or heat a gas grill. Put the spears on a rimmed baking sheet or platter. Drizzle with 1 tablespoon olive oil, season with a generous pinch of salt, and toss with your hands to coat the spears evenly.

Position the grill grate as close to the coals or heat source as possible. Heat the grate and then arrange the asparagus on the grate directly over the heat with all the tips pointing in the same direction. (Be sure to arrange the asparagus perpendicular to the bars so the spears don't fall through.) Grill, turning the spears once with tongs, until they're blistered and lightly charred in spots, about 3 minutes total. Transfer to a platter and serve immediately, passing the mayonnaise separately.

Asparagus, Goat Cheese, and Bacon Tart

SERVES 4

5 slices bacon

1 shallot, finely chopped

1 bunch asparagus (about 1 pound), tough ends trimmed and cut into 1-inch pieces

½ pound puff pastry, thawed if frozen

½ pound soft goat cheese

Salt and freshly ground black pepper

1 large egg yolk mixed with ½ teaspoon water

Heat the oven to 450°F.

In a medium frying pan, cook the bacon over medium heat until crisp, about 8 minutes. Transfer to paper towels. Pour off all but 1 tablespoon of the bacon fat from the pan. Add the shallot to the pan and sauté for about 1 minute. Add the asparagus and cook over medium-high heat until the asparagus is crisp-tender, about 5 minutes. Remove the pan from the heat. Crumble the bacon into tiny pieces and mix it with the asparagus and shallot.

On a lightly floured piece of parchment, roll out the pastry to a 10x16-inch rectangle. Transfer the pastry and the parchment to a baking sheet.

Using your fingers, pat the goat cheese onto the pastry, spreading it as evenly as you can and leaving a 1-inch border around the edge. Sprinkle the asparagus, bacon, and shallot mixture evenly over the goat cheese. Season with salt and pepper.

Brush the edge of the tart with the egg wash. Bake until the pastry is golden brown, 20 to 25 minutes. Let cool slightly and serve warm.

Other recipe ideas

LEMON-NUT ASPARAGUS SPEARS Sprinkle roasted or grilled asparagus with finely grated lemon zest and crushed toasted nuts (walnuts, pine nuts, or almonds work well).

PASTA WITH LEMONY SAUTÉED SHRIMP AND ASPARAGUS Blanch 1-inch asparagus pieces, then sauté with some peeled and deveined shrimp, minced garlic, and strips of sun-dried tomato. Finish with a little grated lemon zest and a squeeze of lemon juice and toss with any small pasta shape.

Vicia faba and cvs.

Fava Beans

Favas are nutty and slightly sweet, with just a touch of bitterness and an intriguing hint of cheese flavor. Cooked until tender, they turn buttery and can be added to soups, salads, or pastas, braised as a side dish, puréed for a dip, or eaten plain out of hand as a delightful snack. Favas—also called broad beans—are a bit of work, but their rich and complex flavor is so delicious, they're worth the effort it takes to shuck the floppy pods and then peel each bean.

PICKING THE BEST
Choose heavy, brightly colored pods that show bumps from the beans inside. Avoid very large beans, which can be starchier than the tender and sweet small to medium beans.

KEEPING IT FRESH
Store the fava pods in a plastic bag in the crisper section of the refrigerator right away. The pods will keep for 5 to 7 days. Store cooked and peeled favas in the refrigerator for up to 5 days at most.

PREPARING
Grown in large, fleshy pods that have a thick, cottony lining, each flat fava is encased in a pale, fairly thick skin, which becomes thicker and more bitter as the favas grow larger. Except when the favas are very young (½ inch or smaller), these skins should be removed. Start by removing the favas from the pods. Next, blanch the favas in boiling water anywhere from 30 seconds to a minute, to soften the outer skins; drain and run under cold water to cool. Grasp the fava between your fingers with the slightly flattened end facing up, and with the thumbnail of your other hand or a small paring knife, tear into the skin end and peel back. Pinch gently and the tender inner bean will slide right out.

HOW TO USE IT
Peeled favas need to be cooked just until tender, anywhere from a minute for the tiny ones that mostly get tender during the initial blanching process, up to 3 or 4 minutes, depending on size and freshness. You can simmer them in water or warm the favas in a little oil or butter, then add liquid and braise until tender.

Once tender, you can add favas to soups and stews or use in cold or room-temperature salads and antipasti. If you have an abundance, they're delicious puréed to make a dip or bruschetta topping.

PRESERVING OPTIONS
Blanched and peeled favas can be frozen nicely, but be sure they've been blanched for at least 3 minutes to destroy the enzymes that are detrimental to freezing.

RECIPES

Fava Beans with Prosciutto, Mint, and Garlic

SERVES 2

1 tablespoon plus ½ teaspoon coarse salt; more as needed

1½ pounds fresh fava beans in the pod, shelled to yield 1 scant cup)

2 tablespoons extra-virgin olive oil

2 tablespoons minced prosciutto

1 teaspoon minced garlic

½ teaspoon balsamic vinegar

8 large fresh mint leaves, finely chopped (to yield 2 to 3 teaspoons)

Parboil the favas: Fill a 4-quart pot with 2 quarts water and 1 tablespoon of salt and bring to a boil. Fill a large bowl mostly with ice and cover with cold water. Dump the beans into the boiling water and cook for 2 minutes (for small favas) to 3 minutes (for larger favas). Begin timing as soon as the vegetables are in the water; don't wait for it to return to a boil. Use a mesh strainer to transfer the beans to the ice bath as soon as the time's up. Let the beans sit for a minute or two in the ice water to stop the cooking and cool down. Lift the vegetables (use your hands or the strainer) out of the ice bath and let them drain well in one layer on a dishtowel or paper towels.

Slip the beans out of their skins and store them in a shallow container (lined with paper towels to absorb any excess moisture), covered with a slightly damp paper towel or dishtowel. They'll keep in the refrigerator overnight. If you plan to use them right away, make sure they're very dry.

In a medium skillet, heat the oil over medium heat. Add the prosciutto and sauté for 1 minute. Add the garlic and sauté, stirring constantly, until it's very fragrant and just beginning to brown, another 1 to 2 minutes. Add the favas, season with the remaining ½ teaspoon salt, and sauté until the favas are heated and coated well with the pan contents, another 2 minutes. (Some of the beans will begin to turn a lighter color.) Add the balsamic vinegar, turn off the heat, and stir to coat. Add the mint and stir to combine and wilt it. Taste for salt; depending on the saltiness of your prosciutto, add more.

Fava Bean Purée

MAKES ABOUT 1½ CUPS

½ cup extra-virgin olive oil; more for drizzling

2 large cloves garlic, chopped

1 teaspoon finely chopped fresh rosemary or thyme

½ teaspoon kosher salt, plus more to taste

⅛ teaspoon freshly ground black pepper, plus more to taste

3 pounds fava beans, shelled and peeled (to yield 2 cups)

2 tablespoons fresh lemon juice, plus more to taste

Put a 10-inch skillet over medium-high heat. Add ¼ cup of the oil, the garlic, rosemary or thyme, salt, and pepper and cook until you begin to hear a sizzling sound and the aromatics are fragrant, 1 to 2 minutes. Add the fava beans. Stir until the beans are well coated with the oil and aromatics and then add 1 cup water. Bring to a boil, reduce the heat to medium, and cook until the water has nearly evaporated and the fava beans are tender, about 8 minutes. Add more water if the pan looks dry before the favas are done. Remove from the heat.

Transfer the fava mixture to a food processor. Add the remaining ¼ cup olive oil and the lemon juice and purée until smooth, stopping to scrape the bowl as needed. Season to taste with more salt and lemon juice. Drizzle with a little olive oil before serving and serve with pita chips or raw vegetables.

Other recipe ideas

ANTIPASTO WITH SALUMI AND FAVAS Arrange an antipasto platter of boiled favas drizzled with a little olive oil, thin slices of salumi or cured ham, interesting olives, some good cheese (Parmigiano-Reggiano or a first-rate sheep's milk cheese), pieces of preserved lemon, and slices of crusty, chewy bread.

TANGY FAVA BEAN SALAD Create a cold side salad by tossing boiled favas with a sprightly dressing of plain Greek-style yogurt thinned with a little lemon juice and mixed with thinly sliced scallions and lots of chopped chives or dill.

Matteuccia struthiopteris

Fiddleheads

The idea of eating fresh from the forest is romantic—and possible with fiddleheads, tightly spiraled and grass-green emerging fern fronds. Tender fiddleheads are uncultivated and wild and only available for a few weeks in early spring. They are similar to asparagus in flavor and versatility.

PICKING THE BEST

Because fiddleheads are a truly wild food, you'll only find them at farmer's markets or in specialty markets for a short time in the spring, and only in certain regions. They need cold winters and mild summers, so this is a local delicacy for New England, the upper Midwest, and the Pacific Northwest, as well as parts of Canada. Choose fiddleheads that are firm, bright, and tightly curled. Black scale, mold, or mushy spots indicate the vegetables are past their prime.

KEEPING IT FRESH

Fiddleheads are very perishable. Keep them wrapped in a plastic bag in the fridge and use them within 2 days.

PREPARING

Most fiddleheads are covered in a brown papery skin, which should be rubbed or scraped off. Trim the stalks to within an inch of the coiled head. Wash the fiddleheads in several changes of cold water to remove any dirt.

HOW TO USE IT

To avoid any risk of food-borne illness, experts recommend thoroughly cooking fiddleheads, so don't be tempted to eat them raw. Many experts recommend steaming for 15 minutes or boiling for 10 minutes, but most chefs prefer to cook fiddleheads only lightly to preserve their delicate crunch, usually by parboiling and then finishing by sautéing.

PRESERVING OPTIONS

Fiddleheads are wonderful pickled in a slightly sweet brine of cider vinegar, sugar, and mustard. To freeze, blanch in batches for 2 to 3 minutes, plunge in ice water to stop the cooking, drain, and then freeze in airtight containers.

DID YOU KNOW? Some species of ferns are toxic, so it's wise to leave fiddlehead foraging to the experts.

Sautéed Fiddleheads and Morels

SERVES 4

1 pound fiddleheads, washed, trimmed, and any
 papery brown skin rubbed off

2 tablespoons unsalted butter

1 small shallot, minced

¼ pound fresh morels, rinsed and patted dry and
 halved or quartered if large

Salt and freshly ground black pepper

¼ cup crème fraîche

2 teaspoons chopped fresh herbs, such as chervil,
 parsley, or tarragon

Bring a large pot of salted water to a boil and blanch
the fiddleheads for 1 minute. Drain, rinse in cold
water, and pat dry.

 In a large sauté pan, heat the butter over medium-
high heat until foaming, then add the shallot and
cook, stirring, until soft and fragrant, about a minute;
add the morels, season with salt and pepper, and
sauté for another 3 to 4 minutes.

 Add the fiddleheads to the pan and continue
sautéing until tender. Add the crème fraîche and
simmer until it's mostly reduced to a glaze. Fold in
the herbs, taste and correct the seasoning, and serve
right away.

Other recipe ideas

SAUTÉED FIDDLEHEADS WITH PROSCIUTTO RIBBONS
Blanch and sauté fiddleheads until tender, then
toss with thinly sliced prosciutto and a sprinkling of
chopped fresh tarragon and chives.

FIDDLEHEADS WITH SALSA VERDE Simmer
fiddleheads in salted water until tender. Drain and let
cool, then drizzle with fresh herb salsa verde.

CREAMY FIDDLEHEADS WITH GOAT CHEESE Blanch
and then simmer until tender in heavy cream; fold in
some fresh goat cheese just before serving.

Allium sativum cvs.

Garlic and Garlic Scapes

It's hard to imagine a world without garlic. Countless recipes begin by sautéing a little garlic because the cloves of this edible bulb (a member of the lily family) are very flavorful and seem to fit with the flavor palette of cuisines around the globe. Depending on how you cook it, garlic can be a mild, sweet low note in a dish or add an assertive—even spicy—zing.

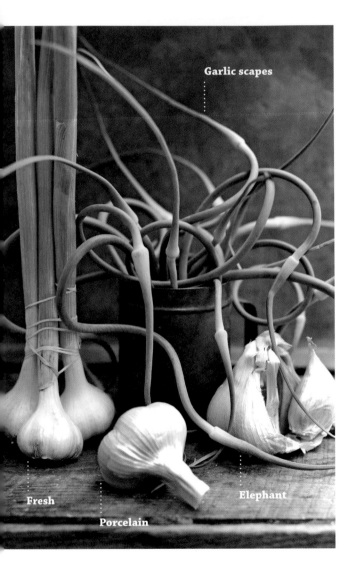

Garlic scapes

Fresh

Porcelain

Elephant

PICKING THE BEST

Garlic farmers cultivate two kinds of garlic:

- **Hardneck:** The bulbs (also called heads) normally have six to eight uniform cloves growing around a hard center shaft, and their size is more regular than the cloves found in many softneck strains. There are three types of hardneck: Rocambole (roh-cam-BOH-lee) garlic, which has tan or white skin around the

bulb and various amounts of purple streaking; porcelain garlic, which has white outer skin with little or no purple coloration; and purple-striped garlic.

- **Softneck:** The bulbs have irregularly shaped cloves. There are two types of softneck: artichoke and silverskin. The bulbs have a covering of thin, pale skin, while the cloves' skin can range in color from rusty red to pale brown. As with hardneck, the flavor of softneck garlic can run from mild to very hot.

- **Elephant garlic:** Not really garlic at all, but a member of the leek family. Mild-flavored with a hint of onion, it's best roasted and makes great soup.

Buy firm, plump, heavy heads with tight, unbroken papery skins. The heavier the garlic, the fresher, juicier, and better tasting it is. Avoid bulbs that are dried out or have soft spots or mold. Green shoots in a bulb are a sign of internal growth in the clove, which is an indication of old garlic. And as with other produce, bigger doesn't necessarily mean better. Varieties vary in size, and many people find that a smaller bulb of garlic has more flavor than a larger one. Resist the convenience of prechopped garlic. It doesn't taste nearly as good as fresh garlic and won't keep as long.

If you grow garlic, or you're browsing the farmer's market in early summer, you might see a curious by-product of garlic—a thick stalk called a scape that forms above the leaves. Many growers believe that removing the scape results in bigger heads of garlic. But another reason people remove scapes is that they make good eating, so pick some up if you get the chance. Look for scapes that are a rich green, smooth, and not limp.

KEEPING IT FRESH

Store garlic in a cool, dry place. For just a few heads, a ventilated ceramic container or garlic keeper is perfect. If you buy a large amount of garlic, hang it in a mesh sack in your basement or garage—as long as it's cool and dry there. Never store garlic in a plastic bag, and keep it out of the fridge, unless you have a low-humidity drawer.

PREPARING

To peel a clove of garlic, first break the skin. Set the clove on a cutting board and cover it with a flat side of a chef's knife. With the heel of your hand, apply light pressure to the knife blade—enough to split the skin, but not so much to crush the clove (unless, of course, you want it smashed). Flick out the germ (the sprout in the center of the clove) with the tip of a knife, especially if it's pronounced and especially for recipes that call for raw or quickly cooked garlic. For quick-cooking, chunky dishes, like pasta sauces and sautéed vegetables, finely mince or thinly slice garlic to get the best release of flavor. For long-cooking braises and stews, roughly chop or thickly slice garlic so it slowly melds with the other ingredients.

HOW TO USE IT

Using garlic raw gives you the most assertive results. Finely chop or mash it to a paste to use in salsas, on bruschetta, in Caesar salad dressing, and in flavored butters for making garlic bread. Cooking mellows garlic's flavor, whether you're sautéing chopped or sliced garlic, letting a smashed clove infuse your oil as you heat it in the sauté pan, or letting whole cloves mellow and soften in a long-cooked braise or soup. Whenever you use garlic with high heat, however, take special care not to let it burn; the acrid flavor of too-dark garlic will ruin your whole dish.

Garlic scapes are easy to cook with, but they're a little fibrous on the outside; the interior is crunchy-tender, with a delicate garlic flavor. Cut them up (straight across, not diagonally, to avoid sharp points) and sauté, roast, or stew. Purée cooked scapes and stir into risotto, rice, or beans. Add raw to stir-fries, potato or pasta salads, omelets, or frittatas. Or purée raw scapes in olive oil and use like pesto as a pasta sauce or as a condiment for grilled chicken and meats.

Rosemary-Garlic Chicken with Apple and Fig Compote

SERVES 4

FOR THE CHICKEN

3 tablespoons fresh rosemary leaves, minced

5 medium cloves garlic, minced

3 teaspoons kosher salt

½ teaspoon freshly ground black pepper, plus more to taste

4 bone-in, skin-on split chicken breasts

1 tablespoon canola oil

FOR THE COMPOTE

1 medium Granny Smith apple, peeled, cored, and cut into ⅓-inch pieces

2 ounces dried figs, cut into small dice (about ⅓ cup; or substitute pitted prunes)

⅓ cup red currant jelly

¼ cup dry white wine, such as Sauvignon Blanc

1 teaspoon dry mustard, preferably Coleman's®

½ teaspoon yellow mustard seeds

Kosher salt and freshly ground black pepper

¼ cup coarsely chopped toasted walnuts

One day ahead, prepare the chicken: In a small bowl, combine the rosemary, garlic, 2 teaspoons salt, and ½ teaspoon pepper. Cut the chicken breasts away from the bones, leaving the skin intact. With a paring knife, cut out the white tendon on the underside of each breast. Rub the rosemary-garlic mixture all over the chicken, including under the skin, taking care to keep the skin attached to the meat. Stack two breasts so that the skin faces outward and each breast's thicker rounded end is on top of the thinner tapered end of the other. Tie the breasts together with kitchen twine, forming a little roast. Repeat with the remaining 2 breasts. Reposition any skin that may have bunched up while tying and season the roasts all over with 1 teaspoon salt and a few grinds of pepper. Put the roasts on a rack over a small baking sheet and refrigerate, uncovered, overnight.

One day ahead, make the compote: Put the apple, figs, jelly, wine, dry mustard, mustard seeds, a generous pinch of salt, and a few grinds of pepper in a small saucepan. Bring just to a boil over medium-high heat and then reduce the heat to a gentle simmer.

Cook, stirring occasionally, until the apples are tender but not mushy, about 10 minutes. Let the mixture cool to room temperature. Store covered in the refrigerator. Bring to room temperature before serving.

Finish the dish: Let the chicken sit at room temperature for 30 minutes. Meanwhile, position a rack in the center of the oven and heat the oven to 450°F.

Heat the oil in a 10-inch skillet over medium-high heat until shimmering hot. Sear the chicken until dark golden brown on all sides, 6 to 8 minutes total. Return the chicken to the rack over the baking sheet, making sure there is space around each bundle. Roast until a thermometer inserted in the center of each bundle reads 165°F, 20 to 30 minutes. Let rest for 15 minutes. Remove the strings from the chicken and carefully slice each bundle on the diagonal into ½-inch-thick medallions. Stir the toasted walnuts into the compote and serve with the chicken.

Linguine with Garlic Scape Pesto

SERVES 4 TO 6
Kosher salt
½ pound garlic scapes
½ cup grated Parmigiano-Reggiano
½ cup blanched almonds
½ to 1 cup extra-virgin olive oil
1 pound dried linguine
Freshly ground black pepper

Put a large pot of salted water on to boil. Chop the garlic scapes into 3-inch pieces. Put the scapes in a food processor and process until finely chopped. Add the Parmigiano-Reggiano, almonds, and ½ teaspoon salt and process until fairly smooth. With the food processor running, slowly drizzle in ½ cup of the olive oil, adding more until the pesto is smooth and creamy. Taste for salt.

Cook the linguine in the boiling water according to the package directions, reserving about ½ cup of the cooking water. Drain well, then toss with the pesto, adding a little pasta water if needed to create a loose and creamy consistency. Season with the pepper and serve right away.

Creamy Roasted Garlic Soup with Sautéed Cauliflower and Fresh Herbs

SERVES 4
FOR THE SOUP
4 heads garlic, loose papery skins removed and ¼ inch of the tops cut off to expose the cloves
3 tablespoons extra-virgin olive oil
½ teaspoon coarse salt, plus more to taste
½ cup chopped onion
1 leek (white and light green parts only), chopped and well rinsed
2 large boiling potatoes, peeled and chopped
1 tablespoon fresh thyme, chopped
½ cup dry white wine
4 cups homemade or reduced-sodium chicken or vegetable broth
Freshly ground black pepper

FOR THE CAULIFLOWER
2 tablespoons olive oil
1 small head cauliflower (2 pounds), cut into small florets (about ½ inch at the widest point)
Kosher salt and freshly ground black pepper
¼ cup chopped fresh sorrel leaves or chives, or a combination, for garnish

Make the soup: Heat the oven to 375°F. Put the garlic heads in a small baking pan. Drizzle on 2 tablespoons of the olive oil and sprinkle on the salt. Add 2 tablespoons water to the pan, cover with foil, and roast until a squeezed clove yields a soft purée, 30 to 45 minutes. When cool, squeeze the pulp from each clove.

In a soup pot over low heat, sweat the onion and leek in the remaining 1 tablespoon olive oil until very soft but not brown, about 10 minutes. Add the potato and thyme and cook for another 1 minute. Turn the heat to medium high, add the wine, and let it reduce to just a few teaspoons, about 4 minutes. Add the broth; bring to a boil. Reduce the heat and simmer for 10 minutes. Add the garlic pulp and simmer until the potatoes are very soft, another 15 to 20 minutes.

Strain the soup, saving both the liquid and solids. In a blender or food processor, purée the solids in batches, using some of the liquid to help it blend. (Be careful to fill the blender no more than one-third full and hold a towel over the lid while you turn it on.) Pour the puréed solids back in the pot. When all the solids are puréed, add as much of the remaining liquid as necessary to get a consistency like heavy cream. Season to taste with salt and pepper.

Sauté the cauliflower: Heat the olive oil in a large sauté pan over medium heat. Add the cauliflower florets and sauté. Once they begin to soften, after about 5 minutes, season with salt and pepper. Continue to sauté until the cauliflower is deep golden brown and tender but still firm, another 7 to 10 minutes.

To serve: Reheat the soup. Ladle it into individual bowls, add the cauliflower, and garnish with the sorrel or chives.

Catalan Mushrooms with Garlic and Parsley

SERVES 6

1 pound medium white mushrooms, stems trimmed to ½ inch and quartered

¼ cup extra-virgin olive oil

¼ cup finely chopped fresh flat-leaf parsley

2 tablespoons finely chopped fresh garlic

1 to 2 teaspoons kosher salt or coarse sea salt

Put the mushrooms in a large bowl of cold water to soak for 10 minutes. Rinse them well and then drain.

Heat a large sauté pan with a tight-fitting lid over medium heat. Add the drained mushrooms to the dry pan, cover immediately, and cook until all the moisture from the mushrooms is leached out, about 20 minutes; to check, lift the lid for a peek and see the once-dry pan filled with liquid.

Remove the lid, raise the heat to medium high, and boil until the liquid evaporates and the mushrooms begin to sizzle in the dry pan but haven't browned; they'll have shrunk considerably and should be firm when poked with a fork. Lower the heat to medium and stir in 1 tablespoon of the olive oil, the parsley, and the garlic. Sauté, stirring frequently, until the garlic softens, another 3 to 4 minutes. Transfer the mushrooms to a serving bowl, stir in the remaining 3 tablespoons olive oil, and season with salt to taste. Serve while hot.

Other recipe ideas

GARLIC-ROASTED CHICKEN Smear mashed roasted garlic under the skin of a chicken, season with salt and pepper, and roast until the chicken is golden brown and cooked through.

ROASTED GARLIC AND WHITE BEAN BRUSCHETTA Mash cooked white beans with some roasted garlic, a little chopped fresh rosemary, and finely grated Pecorino. Spoon onto toasted slices of bread, drizzle with extra-virgin olive oil, and serve as a snack or appetizer.

SPAGHETTI WITH LEEKS AND GARLIC Braise halved garlic cloves and sliced leeks in some white wine and chicken broth until tender, then finish with some cream and herbs and toss with spaghetti.

HERB-GARLIC MARINATED PORK ROAST Make a paste with lots of garlic, rosemary, sage, salt, pepper, and olive oil and rub it on pork tenderloin or pork loin; marinate overnight, then roast or grill.

DID YOU KNOW?

Young garlic that's harvested before the garlic bulb develops underground is called green garlic and is a springtime delicacy. From a distance, green garlic looks just like scallions, but get a little closer and there's no mistaking that familiar garlic scent. The mild flavor means you can put a lot in a dish without fear of overdoing it; green garlic is exceptionally delicious in a puréed soup.

Pisum sativum cvs.

Peas

Quick-cooking green peas come along in the cool days of early spring to brighten up the end of winter. Sweet and tender shelling peas and crispy-crunchy snow and snap peas can go from vine to table in minutes.

PICKING THE BEST

Garden catalogs abound with pea varieties, but they'll generally fall into these three categories:

- **English peas:** Look for gently swelling pods. If the pods are bulging, the peas are likely to be too mature and starchy; if the pods are too flat, the peas within are likely way too small. If the pods look dried or shriveled, you can be sure the peas will have lost their moisture—and their magic.
- **Snow peas:** Pods should be bright green, firm, and flat with tiny peas inside that are barely visible through the pod. Avoid any that are shriveled, wilted, discolored, or slimy.
- **Sugar snap peas:** Pods should be bright green, plump, firm, and crisp; they should snap when you bend them. Some white scarring on the pod is fine. Avoid any that are slimy or wrinkled.

KEEPING IT FRESH

Refrigerated in a tightly sealed plastic bag, peas will last for 4 or 5 days.

PREPARING

- **English peas:** Pop open the pod and remove the peas by sliding them out with your fingertip.
- **Snow peas:** Both sides of the pod can have a tough string. Snap the top and pull down to remove the string on one side. Turn it over, snap the bottom of the pod, and pull down to remove the string from the other side. Use whole, cut into pieces, or sliced into fine julienne strips.
- **Sugar snap peas:** One side of the pod is curved while the other is straight. Snap the top of the pod toward the straight side, then pull down to remove the tough string that runs the length of that side. Use whole or slice diagonally into bits.

HOW TO USE IT

Cook English peas as soon after picking as possible, and as simply as possible—they usually need only about a minute in boiling salted water. If you're adding them to a dish such as a pasta, there's usually no need to precook them. Snow peas and sugar snaps can be eaten fresh, pod and all, as crudités and in salads. You can cook them, too, but keep it quick—just a minute or two in boiling water or a quick sauté in hot oil.

PRESERVING OPTIONS

Peas freeze very well, but like most vegetables, you need to blanch them first to keep the enzymes from breaking them down. Blanch for 1 minute in boiling water, cool immediately, drain, and freeze on a baking sheet until hard. Then pack into zip-top freezer bags.

Fresh Peas with Lemon and Chives

SERVES 3

1 tablespoon plus ¼ teaspoon coarse salt; more as
  needed

8 ounces shelled fresh peas

2 tablespoons unsalted butter

1 large shallot, finely chopped (about 3 tablespoons)

¼ cup heavy cream

2 teaspoons finely chopped fresh chives

¼ teaspoon minced lemon zest

Freshly ground black pepper

Parboil the peas: Fill a medium-large pot (like a
Dutch oven or soup pot—4-quart capacity is fine)
with about 2 quarts water and 1 tablespoon salt and
bring it to a boil. Fill a work bowl mostly with ice and
cover with cold water. Dump your shelled fresh peas
into the boiling water and cook for 2 minutes (for
small peas) to 3 minutes (for older, larger peas). Begin
timing as soon as the peas are in the water; don't
wait for it to return to a boil. Use a mesh strainer to
transfer the peas to the ice bath just as soon as the
time's up. Let the peas sit for a minute or two in the
ice water to stop the cooking and cool down. Lift the
peas out of the ice bath and let them drain well in one
layer on a dishtowel (or paper towels).

Make the sauce: In a medium saucepan, melt the
butter over low heat. Add the chopped shallot and
sauté until softened, 2 to 3 minutes. (Raise the heat
to medium low if necessary, but don't let the shallot
brown.) Add the heavy cream, chives, lemon zest, ¼
teaspoon salt, and a few grinds of pepper. Bring the
mixture to a boil. Boil for 30 seconds, add the peas,
and cook until the cream has thickened enough
to start clinging to the peas (a wooden spoon will
leave a wide path when scraped on the bottom of
the pan) and the peas are well heated, another 1 to 2
minutes. Remove the pan from the heat and taste for
seasoning. Add more salt and pepper if you like and
serve immediately.

Pea, Butter Lettuce, and Herb Salad

SERVES 4

1 cup fresh shelled peas (about 1 pound unshelled)
  or frozen peas

Kosher salt

3 tablespoons extra-virgin olive oil

1 tablespoon fresh lemon juice

1 teaspoon finely grated lemon zest

Freshly ground black pepper

1 small head butter lettuce, washed and dried,
  leaves torn into bite-sized pieces

6 medium radishes, thinly sliced

4 scallions (white and light green parts), thinly
  sliced on the diagonal

¼ cup loosely packed fresh flat-leaf parsley leaves

¼ cup loosely packed fresh chervil leaves

2 tablespoons very coarsely chopped fresh
  tarragon

2 tablespoons thinly sliced fresh chives

3 ounces ricotta salata, shaved thinly with a
  vegetable peeler (optional)

If using fresh peas, sample them. If they are young,
sweet, and tender, keep them raw. If they are older
and a bit tough, blanch them in a small pot of boiling
salted water until just tender, 2 to 4 minutes. Drain
and spread them on a baking sheet in a single layer
to cool. If using frozen peas, thaw them by leaving
them at room temperature or by running them under
warm water.

For the dressing, in a small bowl, whisk the oil,
lemon juice, lemon zest, and salt and pepper to taste.

Just before serving, toss the peas in a small bowl
with 1 tablespoon of the dressing. Toss the lettuce,
radishes, scallions, and herbs in a large bowl with
just enough of the remaining dressing to lightly coat.
Season to taste with salt and pepper.

Arrange the salad on individual serving plates and
top with the peas and the ricotta salata (if using).

DID YOU KNOW? The early leaves and curling tendrils of the pea plant are edible and make a pretty addition to salads and stir-fries. Take a taste to be sure the stems aren't too tough; if so, just use the tender leaves, which have a faint pea flavor.

Stir-Fried Beef with Snow Peas and Shiitakes

SERVES 4

2 teaspoons cornstarch

6 tablespoons homemade or reduced-sodium chicken broth

¼ cup ponzu sauce

1 tablespoon Asian sesame oil

1¼ pounds boneless beef rib-eye steaks, trimmed and thinly sliced across the grain (⅛ to ¼ inch thick)

½ teaspoon kosher salt

Freshly ground black pepper

3 tablespoons neutral oil, such as canola or vegetable

7 to 8 ounces fresh shiitake mushrooms, stems trimmed off and caps thinly sliced

½ pound snow peas, trimmed

3 small or 2 medium scallions (white and green parts), thinly sliced

One 1½-inch piece fresh ginger, peeled and minced (about 3 tablespoons)

2 medium cloves garlic, minced

In a small bowl, stir the cornstarch into 1 tablespoon of the chicken broth until smooth. Stir in the remaining 5 tablespoons broth, along with the ponzu and sesame oil.

Season the sliced beef with the salt and several grinds of pepper. Heat 2 tablespoons of the neutral oil in a large skillet or stir-fry pan over medium-high heat. When the oil is very hot (it should shimmer), add the beef and stir-fry just until it loses its raw color, 2 to 3 minutes. Transfer the beef to a clean bowl. Return the pan to medium-high heat, add the remaining 1 tablespoon oil, and then add the mushrooms and peas. Stir-fry until the mushrooms are tender and the peas are crisp-tender, 4 to 5 minutes. Add the scallion, ginger, and garlic, and stir-fry for 30 seconds. Return the beef to the pan. Give the broth mixture a quick stir to recombine and then pour it into the pan. Cook, stirring, until the sauce thickens, about 1 minute. Serve immediately.

Lightly Spiced Sugar Snap Peas with Mint and Lime

SERVES 2 TO 3

2 tablespoons unsalted butter

¼ teaspoon Thai red curry paste

¾ pound sugar snap peas, trimmed

2 tablespoons thinly sliced fresh mint

2 teaspoons fresh lime juice

Kosher salt

Heat 1 tablespoon of the butter in a medium saucepan over medium heat. As soon as the butter melts, add the curry paste and mash it around with the back of a fork until it's mostly broken up and distributed through the butter. Add the peas and toss with tongs to coat in the butter. Add ⅓ cup water, cover with the lid slightly ajar, raise the heat to medium high, and steam until the peas are almost tender, about 5 minutes. Remove the lid and let any remaining liquid boil off. Stir in the remaining 1 tablespoon butter, the mint, and the lime juice. Season to taste with salt and serve.

Other recipe ideas

THREE-PEA SAUTÉ WITH SESAME Sauté a mix of English peas, snow peas, and snap peas with toasted sesame seeds, slivered scallions, cilantro, and a drizzle of Asian sesame oil.

CRAB AND FRESH PEA SOUP Simmer fresh peas in a reduced-sodium chicken broth, purée, and finish with cream or crème fraîche. Garnish with a mound of fresh crabmeat and a shower of chopped chervil.

SPICY SUGAR SNAP SALAD Toss julienned red bell pepper, coarsely grated carrot, and short pieces of sugar snap peas together in a sweet-spicy vinaigrette for a crunchy salad.

Raphanus sativus and cvs.

Radishes

With their peppery flavor, crunchy texture, bright pink skin, and green leaves, radishes are the epitome of spring. They're simple to prepare and are at their best when used fresh—no cooking required.

Common
Easter Egg

PICKING THE BEST

Radishes taste best when harvested in cool weather, before summer's heat sets in, which makes them bitter. If you can, buy small radishes in bunches with the greens still attached; they will be fresher than those in plastic bags, which may have been sitting around for a while. The tops should look bright green and fresh, and the radishes themselves should be firm and as unblemished as possible.

KEEPING IT FRESH

When you get a bunch home, cut off the greens, wrap the radishes loosely in plastic, and refrigerate for up to a week; bigger specimens, such as watermelon radishes, can be good keepers. If the greens are bright and fresh, keep them refrigerated for 2 to 3 days until ready to use. They're very nutritious and can be cooked as you would chard or mustard greens.

PREPARING

Trim off the stems and roots and wash thoroughly; don't peel. For snacking, you can leave on a few of the pretty greens to use as a "handle."

HOW TO USE IT

Radishes are most often eaten raw, either whole for snacking and dipping, or sliced or grated into salads or slaws. They are a delight when sautéed or braised, however, especially mixed with other young spring vegetables such as baby turnips or peas. Radish tops are delicately peppery and nice when braised, sautéed, or stir-fried.

SURPRISING PAIRINGS

Sweet butter and a sprinkling of sea salt is a classic French counterpoint to peppery radishes. Just dip the radish into soft butter, then into a bowl of crunchy sea salt, or make an open-faced tartine of buttered brown bread topped with thinly sliced radishes.

PRESERVING OPTIONS

Radishes make great refrigerator pickles, especially when mixed with other colorful spring vegetables such as baby carrots and green beans.

RECIPES

Radish and Parsley Salad with Lemon

SERVES 2 TO 3

About 10 medium or 12 small red radishes, scrubbed

3 large ribs celery, ends trimmed and peeled

1 cup tightly packed fresh flat-leaf parsley leaves

1 tablespoon fresh lemon juice, plus more to taste

¼ teaspoon kosher salt, plus more to taste

2 tablespoons extra-virgin olive oil

Freshly ground black pepper

Trim the root and stem end of the radishes. Halve them lengthwise and then slice them ⅛ inch thick; you should have about 1½ cups. Slice the celery crosswise ⅛ inch thick. Combine the sliced radishes, sliced celery, and parsley leaves in a medium bowl. Add the lemon juice, salt, and olive oil; toss well. Add several generous grinds of black pepper, taste and adjust the seasonings, and serve.

Hearts of Palm and Radish Coins with Shrimp

YIELDS 24

3 to 4 hearts of palm (1 to 1½ inches wide), rinsed and cut into ¼-inch-thick coins (you'll need 24)

2 tablespoons plus ¼ teaspoon fresh lime juice

2 tablespoons extra-virgin olive oil

Pinch of sugar

Kosher salt

1 tablespoon mayonnaise, preferably Hellmann's® or Best Foods® brand

¼ teaspoon coriander seeds, toasted and coarsely ground in a mortar

¼ teaspoon freshly grated lime zest

Pinch of cayenne

Freshly ground black pepper

48 small peeled, deveined, and cooked shrimp (71 to 90 per pound or 100 to 150 per pound)

5 to 6 radishes (1 to 1½ inches wide), sliced into ¼-inch-thick coins (you'll need 24)

24 fresh cilantro leaves, for garnish

Lay the palm coins in a single layer in a nonreactive dish. Drizzle with 2 tablespoons of the lime juice, 3 tablespoons water, and the olive oil. Sprinkle with the sugar and a generous pinch of salt. Shake the dish to coat the palm coins, then let sit.

In a medium bowl, mix the remaining ¼ teaspoon lime juice with the mayonnaise, coriander seeds, lime zest, cayenne, a generous pinch of salt, and a pinch of black pepper. Toss the shrimp with the mayonnaise and season to taste with salt and pepper.

Carefully drain the hearts of palm and pat dry with paper towels. Top each radish coin with a palm coin of similar size, 2 shrimp, and a cilantro leaf.

Glazed Radishes

SERVES 3 TO 4

1 pound radishes, scrubbed and trimmed

2 tablespoons unsalted butter

1 teaspoon sugar

¼ teaspoon kosher salt, plus more to taste

½ lemon

Cut any large radishes in half so they're all about the same size. Arrange in a sauté pan just large enough to hold the radishes in a single layer. Add the butter, sugar, and salt. Add enough water to come halfway up the sides of the radishes. Cover the radishes with a pot lid askew, bring the water to a high simmer, then lower the heat and simmer gently.

Start testing after 5 minutes, but it may take up to 10 or 15 minutes; a knife should penetrate easily with just some slight resistance. Add more water if the pan is drying out; if the radishes are tender but there's a lot of liquid left in the pan, turn up the heat and remove the cover to boil away the liquid. When the radishes are done and the water has cooked away, squeeze a little lemon juice into the pan and swirl to coat the radishes. Taste and adjust the salt.

Other recipe ideas

RADISH-MANGO SALSA Toss diced radishes with diced mango, red onion, minced fresh chile, lime juice, and cilantro. Serve with grilled meats and poultry.

ROASTED RADISHES Toss whole radishes with olive oil, fresh thyme, salt, and pepper, then roast in a 400°F oven until tender. Add a squeeze of lemon juice.

Allium Tricoccum

Ramps

If you love onions and garlic, you'll love ramps. Appearing in early spring in woodlands and along stream beds, they look like a flamboyant scallion, with long, flat, graceful leaves and a slender, burgundy-tinged stem leading to a delicate white bulb. Their flavor and scent, too, is over the top—a very pungent, almost spicy, blend of garlic and onions. Fortunately, they mellow a bit with cooking.

PICKING THE BEST
Ramps should have whole, bright green leaves and firm bulbs. Any yellow, withered leaves or slime are signs of age.

KEEPING IT FRESH
Bundle them in damp paper towels, then wrap tightly in plastic and refrigerate for up to a week. Don't trim or wash until you're ready to use them.

PREPARING
Trim the roots, rinse thoroughly, and scrub off any dirt on the bulbs. You can grill and roast them whole, or slice or chop them—greens and all—for sautéing.

HOW TO USE IT
The green tops are milder in flavor than the stem and bulb and are typically used along with them. Sautéing and roasting are classic preparations for ramps, but grilling is also wonderful, as the hint of smoke and char tames their pungency.

SURPRISING PAIRINGS
Ramps can be quite strong so aren't always the best solo players, but they are excellent paired with other spring vegetables, such as morels, asparagus, peas, fava beans, and fiddleheads.

PRESERVING OPTIONS
You can chop and freeze ramps to use in cooked dishes, or bathe them in brine and turn them into refrigerator pickles.

Spring Risotto with Ramps, Peas, and Morels

SERVES 6

2 tablespoons unsalted butter

1 cup trimmed and roughly chopped ramps

2 cups asparagus pieces (1 inch)

7 cups homemade or reduced-sodium chicken broth

¼ cup extra-virgin olive oil

2 cups chopped onion

1 teaspoon kosher salt

½ cup water

2 cups short-grain risotto rice, such as arborio or carnaroli

1 cup dry white wine

1 cup dried morels, soaked in 2 cups hot water for 30 minutes and cut into ¼-inch slices (strain and reserve the soaking liquid)

½ to 1 cup grated Parmigiano-Reggiano, plus more to taste

2 to 3 tablespoons chopped fresh flat-leaf parsley

In a medium sauté pan, heat the butter until foaming, then add the ramps and sauté until softened, about 2 minutes. Add the asparagus and sauté another 1 to 2 minutes. Set aside.

Bring the broth almost to a boil in a large pot. Reduce the heat to very low; the broth should stay hot but not simmer.

Heat the olive oil over medium heat in a heavy 3- to 4-quart straight-sided sauté pan at least 10 inches wide or in a similar-sized Dutch oven. Add the onion and ½ teaspoon salt, and cook slowly, stirring frequently with a wooden spoon until softened, 8 to 10 minutes. Add the water, lower the heat to medium low, and continue cooking until the water is completely gone and the onion is soft and glistening but not browned, another 5 to 10 minutes.

Add the rice to the pan and raise the heat to medium. Cook, stirring constantly, to coat the rice with the oil, about 3 minutes. Toasted rice should still be white and glistening, but you should hear a clicking sound when you stir it.

Pour in the wine and cook, stirring constantly, until it's mostly absorbed, 2 to 3 minutes.

Stir the mushrooms and their soaking liquid into the rice, and cook, stirring, until the liquid is mostly absorbed.

Ladle in 1½ to 2 cups broth to barely cover the rice and stir constantly. Add another ½ teaspoon salt, adjust the heat to maintain a gentle simmer, and keep stirring. When all the liquid has been absorbed and the rice is dry enough that your stirring spoon leaves a trail showing the bottom of the pot, ladle in another cup of broth, again stirring until it's all absorbed. Continue adding broth in 1-cup increments, always stirring, until the rice is nearly but not fully al dente; this is usually 12 to 16 minutes after the first addition of liquid.

When the risotto is a few minutes away from al dente, stir in the sautéed ramps and asparagus.

After you've added 5 cups of liquid, (16 to 20 minutes from the first liquid addition), taste the rice to determine if it's al dente and pleasantly creamy. If it is, remove it immediately from the heat. Otherwise, let it cook a little longer, incorporating more broth. Gently stir in the cheese and parsley and serve immediately.

Other recipe ideas

CHAR-GRILLED RAMPS Wash and trim a bunch of ramps. Brush with olive oil and season well with salt and pepper. Grill over a hot fire until slightly charred and tender. Squeeze some fresh lemon juice over the top and serve alongside grilled steak.

BAKED POTATO WITH RAMPS AND SOUR CREAM Sprinkle some finely chopped ramps onto baked or mashed potatoes, then top with sour cream.

RAMP AND BACON QUICHE Make a quiche filling with crumbled bacon, grated Gruyère, and chopped sautéed ramps. Bake in a crust made from frozen puff pastry.

Rheum rhabarbarum and cvs.

Rhubarb

Rosy red with a unique sweet-tart flavor, rhubarb can give a wonderful seasonal spark to just about any dessert—and some savory dishes, as well; the tricks are knowing how much sugar to add to balance rhubarb's tartness and choosing flavor partners that enhance its elusive sweet edge. When the very first stalks of rhubarb show up at the market in early spring, use them in classic desserts, from pies to crumbles, muffins, and compotes.

PICKING THE BEST

Although rhubarb is usually treated as a fruit and used mainly in desserts, it's technically a vegetable. The edible parts are the fleshy celery-like stalks. If you grow your own, be aware that the green leaves are poisonous if eaten and need to be removed. Look for firm, crisp, unblemished stalks with a bright, intense color. Thinner stalks are the best choice, as larger ones tend to be overly stringy and tough.

KEEPING IT FRESH

Wrap the stalks tightly in plastic and refrigerate them. They should stay crisp for up to 5 days.

PREPARING

Trim off the ends and any leaves still attached. Peel the fibrous exterior only if it's very tough. Cut rhubarb as you would celery, into slices or small dice, depending on the recipe.

HOW TO USE IT

The simplest and most common way to cook rhubarb is to slice it and simmer with some liquid, sugar, and other flavorings. You can also bake with rhubarb by adding it to cake or muffin batters, just as you would blueberries and other fruits.

In sweet preparations, rhubarb needs a good amount of sugar to balance its tartness. Cooking helps offset its natural astringency but also causes it to release a surprising amount of liquid. In compotes or sauces, where a juicy consistency is desirable, this is a boon. But if you're making a filling for a pie or crumble, you need to add a thickener, such as cornstarch or tapioca, to prevent it from being too loose.

For a component in a savory dish, you can accent rhubarb with onion, garlic, and perhaps a touch of balsamic vinegar, but you'll still need some sugar or honey to round off rhubarb's tart edges.

SURPRISING PAIRINGS

The addition of savory ingredients, such as onion, mustard, and cumin, can transform rhubarb into a delicious condiment to serve with pork, poultry, and lamb.

PRESERVING OPTIONS

You can freeze sliced or diced rhubarb in plastic bags for up to 6 months. Frozen rhubarb tends to release more liquid and doesn't hold its shape as well as fresh rhubarb, so use it where texture is not essential. Rhubarb is also excellent in jams, chutneys, and pickles.

Strawberry-Rhubarb Compote with Vanilla and Cardamom

SERVES 4 TO 6

4 cups ½-inch-thick sliced rhubarb (about 1¼ pounds)

½ cup sugar, plus more to taste

6 tablespoons fresh orange juice, plus more to taste

3 tablespoons honey

¼ teaspoon plus ⅛ teaspoon ground cardamom

¼ teaspoon kosher salt

1 small vanilla bean

3 cups hulled and thickly sliced strawberries
    (about 2 pints)

Combine the rhubarb, sugar, orange juice, honey, all the cardamom, and the salt in a heavy 3-quart stainless-steel saucepan. With a paring knife, slit open the vanilla bean lengthwise, scrape out the seeds with the back of the knife, and add the seeds and the scraped pod to the saucepan.

Bring to a simmer over medium-low heat, stirring often. Simmer until the rhubarb releases its juice and becomes tender but still retains its shape, 5 to 6 minutes. Add the strawberries and simmer until they start to soften and the rhubarb breaks down slightly, 1 to 3 minutes.

Pour the mixture into a bowl. Make an ice bath by filling a larger bowl with ice and water. Chill the compote over the ice bath at room temperature, stirring occasionally, until completely cool, 10 to 15 minutes. Discard the vanilla pod. Taste the compote and add more sugar and orange juice, if needed.

DID YOU KNOW? In some regions, rhubarb is known as "pieplant" because it so often ends up in pies.

Cinnamon-Rhubarb Muffins

YIELDS 12 MUFFINS

FOR THE MUFFINS

9 ounces (2 cups) unbleached all-purpose flour

¾ cup sugar

2½ teaspoons baking powder

1 teaspoon ground cinnamon

½ teaspoon baking soda

½ teaspoon kosher salt

1 cup sour cream

4 ounces (8 tablespoons) unsalted butter, melted
    and cooled slightly

2 large eggs

1 teaspoon pure vanilla extract

1½ cups ¼-inch-diced rhubarb (7¼ ounces)

FOR THE TOPPING

3 tablespoons sugar

½ teaspoon ground cinnamon

Position a rack in the center of the oven and heat the oven to 400°F. Line a 12-cup muffin tin with paper or foil baking cups.

Make the muffin batter: In a large bowl, combine the flour, sugar, baking powder, cinnamon, baking soda, and salt and whisk to blend.

In a medium bowl, whisk the sour cream, melted butter, eggs, and vanilla until smooth. Lightly stir the sour cream mixture into the dry ingredients with a spatula until the batter just comes together; don't overmix. Gently stir in the diced rhubarb. The batter will be thick. Portion the batter into the muffin cups, using the back of a spoon or a small spatula to settle the batter into the cups. The batter should mound a bit higher than the tops of the cups.

Make the topping: In a small bowl, combine the sugar and cinnamon and mix well. Sprinkle a generous ½ teaspoon of the cinnamon-sugar mixture over each muffin.

Bake the muffins until they're golden brown and spring back most of the way when gently pressed, and a pick inserted in the center comes out clean, 18 to 22 minutes. Transfer to a rack and let cool in the pan for 5 to 10 minutes. Carefully lift the muffins out of the pan—if necessary, loosen them with the tip of a paring knife—and let them cool slightly. Serve warm.

Rhubarb-Raspberry Galette

YIELDS ONE 12-INCH TART

FOR THE DOUGH

10 ounces (2¼ cups) unbleached all-purpose flour;
   more for rolling

1 teaspoon sugar

¼ teaspoon salt

6 ounces (12 tablespoons) cold unsalted butter, cut
   into small pieces

½ cup ice water

FOR THE FILLING

1½ pounds rhubarb

1 cup fresh raspberries

3 tablespoons unbleached all-purpose flour

1 to 1¼ cups sugar; more for sprinkling

Melted unsalted butter, for brushing

Make the dough: Combine the flour, sugar, and salt;
cut in the butter until the mixture resembles coarse
crumbs. Add the ice water and toss just until the
mixture holds together. Be careful not to overmix.
Press the dough into a ball, cover with plastic wrap,
and refrigerate for at least 30 minutes.

Line a baking sheet with parchment. On a lightly
floured work surface, roll out the chilled dough into a
14-inch round, about ⅛ inch thick. Transfer the dough
to the prepared baking sheet and refrigerate while
preparing the filling.

Make the filling: Trim the ends of the rhubarb
and, if the stalks are more than 1 inch thick, cut them
in half lengthwise. Cut the stalks into 1-inch-long
pieces. In a large bowl, gently toss the rhubarb and
raspberries with the flour and sugar. Let stand until
moist, 5 to 10 minutes.

Assemble the tart: Position a rack in the center
of the oven and heat the oven to 400°F. Remove
the dough from the refrigerator and let sit at room
temperature until it's just pliable, 5 to 10 minutes.
Gently spread the fruit in the center of the dough,
leaving a 2-inch margin around the edge. Carefully
fold the edge of the dough over the fruit, pleating it
as you go. Brush the edge of the dough with melted
butter and sprinkle with sugar. Bake until the pastry
is golden brown and the fruit is soft and bubbling,
45 to 55 minutes. Set on a rack to cool slightly.

Other recipe ideas

GINGER-RHUBARB FOOL Simmer chopped rhubarb
with a bit of sugar and fresh ginger to make a
compote. Let cool and fold into whipped cream. Chill
and serve as a fool.

RHUBARB-APPLE CHUTNEY Simmer chopped
rhubarb and apple with chopped onion, brown sugar,
cider vinegar, mustard seeds, cloves, and other spices
to make a zesty chutney to serve with roast pork or
grilled sausages.

RHUBARB–RED WINE COMPOTE Poach chunks of
rhubarb in red wine with sugar, cinnamon, and a few
cloves. Use as a topping for brown sugar ice cream,
almond pound cake, or angel food cake.

Lactuca sativa cvs.

Salad Greens/Lettuces

Salad greens are a category of produce that's just about perfect: beautiful, easy to grow, easy to prepare, healthful, and often one of the first signs of spring in your garden or at your local market. Salad greens can include anything from the familiar crunchy head of iceberg lettuce to a velvety rosette of mâche—basically anything leafy, relatively tender, and that performs beautifully when lightly dressed and eaten fresh and raw.

PICKING THE BEST

Look for heads or leafy rosettes that are dense and heavy for their size. Leaves should be unblemished. Avoid limp specimens or heads that have brown-edged or brown-spotted leaves or hollow centers—this usually indicates poor handling after harvest. Skip soggy heads that have been spritzed with too much water at the grocery store. For bulk greens, such as arugula or mesclun, be sure to pick through the bin for the best because they can get slimy.

- **Arugula:** Also called rocket, this popular green has elongated oak-leaf shaped leaves that can be baby size (about 3 inches) or full size (up to 7 inches or so). Younger, smaller leaves taste best, with the mature leaves becoming aggressively peppery (though the packaged "baby arugula" is often characterless). You'll sometimes see "wild rocket," a variety that's more spindly than the typical arugula, but that has a lively peppery flavor. Arugula is especially nice with stone fruits.

- **Butterhead, Boston, or bibb lettuce, also called limestone lettuce:** This type grows in softly folding heads and is known for its good flavor and buttery texture. Colors range from pale lime to a more medium green. The succulent leaves surround satiny delicate hearts; some varieties are looser and others tighter.

- **Iceberg or crisphead:** Look for heads with unblemished outer leaves. And check out Batavian varieties whose looser-headed, deeper-colored leaves have the same satisfying crunch. Thick, juicy-sweet crisphead may taste somewhat bland, but its crunchy texture is unparalleled.

- **Leaf or cutting lettuce, such as red leaf, oak leaf, and lolla rossa:** These lettuces have open, loose heads and leaf shapes that range from notched and scalloped to frilly and ruffly. Colors run from bright green to cranberry and burgundy, many with red tips and pale green leaf bases. Individual leaves are generally thinner and more delicate than other varieties, so use them promptly.

- **Mâche:** Also known as cornsalad or lamb's lettuce, this lettuce has oval leaves that grow in small fist-sized rosettes that look like little bouquets. It has a velvety texture and delicate flavor; simple dressings are best.

- **Mesclun:** Often bagged, this type has come to mean a varied mixture of young salad greens. A typical mix could include various baby lettuces, Asian greens, radicchio, young chard or kale, wild greens, or leafy herbs such as chervil. Avoid mixes that are simply chopped-up lettuces.

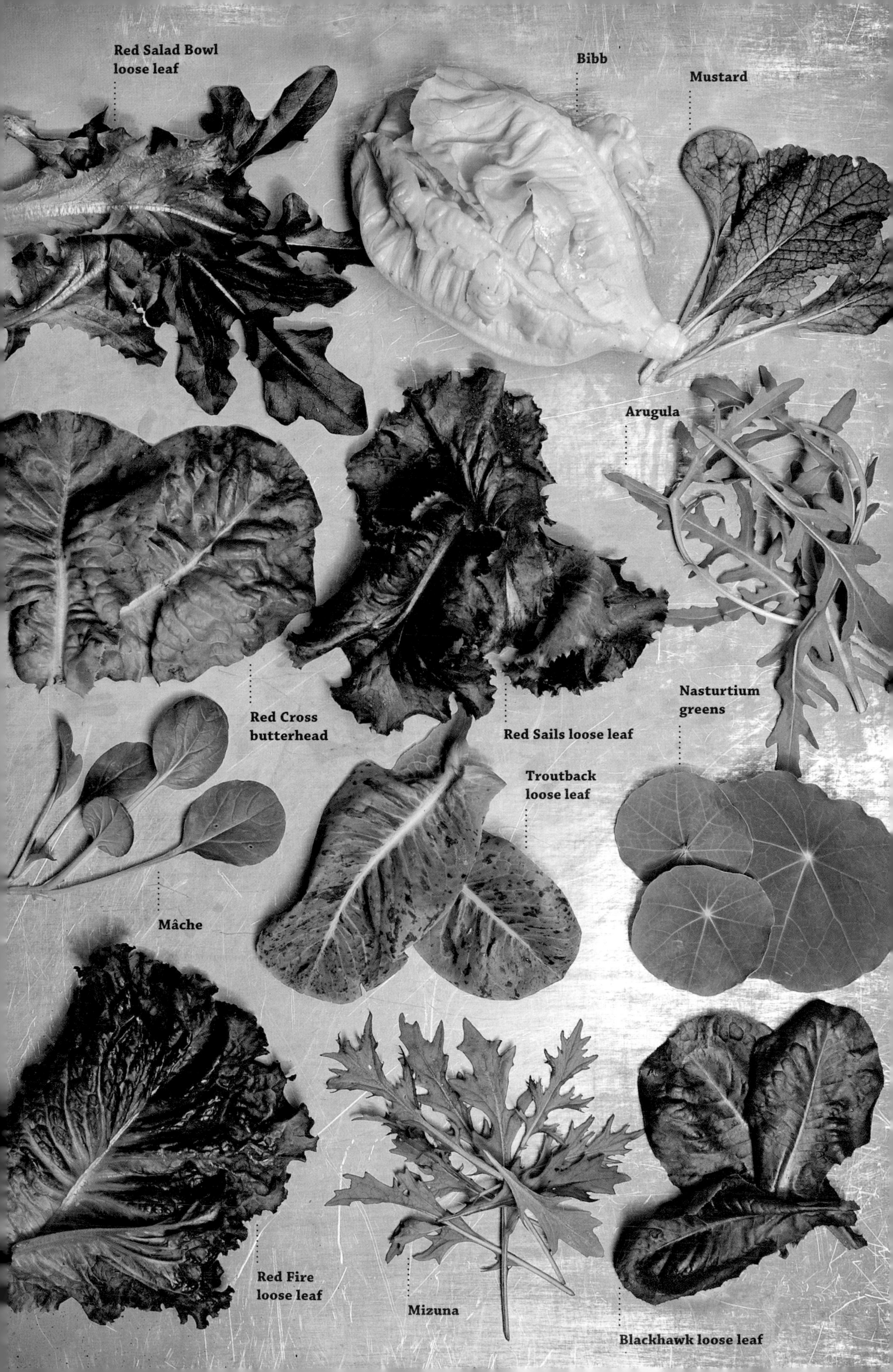

Red Salad Bowl loose leaf

Bibb

Mustard

Arugula

Red Cross butterhead

Red Sails loose leaf

Nasturtium greens

Mâche

Troutback loose leaf

Red Fire loose leaf

Mizuna

Blackhawk loose leaf

• **Romaine:** This lettuce is crunchy, juicy, and sweet with substantial body; you'll find whole heads of romaine (whose outer leaves often need to be discarded) and hearts of romaine, which are the crisp insides of the heads. The leaves stand up well to punchy dressings, and they're a great choice for whole-meal salads with lots of ingredients.

KEEPING IT FRESH

It's best not to wash greens until the day you'll use them, but it's also convenient to have your greens ready to go. If you do prep greens ahead, pack washed and dried leaves loosely in a zip-top bag lined with paper towels, gently squeeze out most of the air, and seal. Try to use salad greens within a few days; they'll lose their texture and body if stored longer than that.

PREPARING

Nothing ruins a salad like gritty greens or bits of decayed leaves, so be sure to wash your greens scrupulously well. Soggy greens are just as bad as gritty greens, so be sure to spin them completely dry. Many bagged greens claim they're already washed; it's up to you to decide whether that's enough for you.

Depending on your salad, tear or slice with a sharp knife large leaves into smaller pieces. If serving a romaine or crisphead lettuce in wedges, trim away the root end but keep the leaves attached and slice into a nice portion.

HOW TO USE IT

The whole point of a salad is to enjoy something fresh and raw, so cooking is not an issue. There are some greens that like a touch of heat, however, such as romaine, which is lovely when you split the head, oil it, and then grill it until just partially softened and browned; dress with good olive oil, lemon juice, and Parmesan or a drizzle of pesto. Members of the chicory family do well with warm dressings, too (see p. 192).

In general, only unite greens and dressing at the last minute, as salad wilts in minutes.

PRESERVING OPTIONS

Salad greens are an ephemeral pleasure, so don't try to freeze or otherwise preserve them.

Forty Shades of Green Salad

SERVES 4

FOR THE VINAIGRETTE

3 tablespoons extra-virgin olive oil

1 tablespoon plus 1 teaspoon fresh lime juice

1 teaspoon honey

Big pinch of kosher salt

1 coarse grind black pepper

FOR THE SALAD

1 large head Boston lettuce, largest outer leaves
   and damaged leaves removed, washed, dried,
   and torn into bite-sized pieces

¾ cup loosely packed fresh flat-leaf parsley leaves

1 large (or 1½ small) Belgian endive, damaged
   leaves removed, halved lengthwise, cored, and
   thinly sliced crosswise (¼ inch)

2 to 3 scallions (white and light green parts), very
   thinly sliced on the diagonal

1 small ripe but firm avocado

Make the vinaigrette: In a small bowl, combine all the vinaigrette ingredients and whisk until thoroughly emulsified (it will look creamy).

Make the salad: In a large bowl, combine the lettuce, parsley, endive, and scallion. Gently toss the greens thoroughly with about 2 tablespoons of the vinaigrette. Mound the greens onto four salad plates (white looks nice), arranging any endive and parsley pieces that have fallen to the bottom of the bowl on top.

Cut the avocado in half and remove the pit. Slide a large spoon between the skin and flesh to peel each half. Slice the avocado halves crosswise into very thin half-moons (⅛ inch thick). For more on pitting and slicing avocados, see p. 295.

With the flat side of a chef's knife, transfer the avocado slices to the bowl, fan them out slightly, drizzle another 1 tablespoon of the vinaigrette over the top, and gently toss just to coat the avocado, keeping the slices somewhat together. Arrange a little pile of avocado slices on each salad, propped up against the mound of leaves. Drizzle the whole salad with a tiny bit more vinaigrette and serve right away.

Bistro Salad with Warm Goat Cheese

SERVES 4

Cooking spray

½ cup toasted hazelnuts (skinned, if you like)

¼-pound log fresh goat cheese

1 tablespoon sherry vinegar

3 tablespoons hazelnut oil

Kosher salt and freshly ground black pepper

4 generous loose handfuls of small lettuce leaves
(or large ones torn up) from a variety (three is
nice) of loose-leaf and butter lettuces (about
6 lightly packed cups), washed and thoroughly dried

Heat the oven to 400°F and lightly coat a baking sheet with cooking spray. Roughly chop half of the hazelnuts and finely chop the other half. Slice the goat cheese into four equal portions (if the slices crumble a bit, simply pat the cheese back together into a sort of patty). Press the finely chopped hazelnuts into the cheese rounds to coat them on all sides. Set the rounds on the baking sheet and bake until heated, about 6 to 8 minutes.

Meanwhile, make the dressing. In a small bowl, whisk the vinegar, oil, a big pinch of salt, and a few grinds of pepper. Taste and adjust the seasonings. When the cheese is ready, toss the lettuce with the dressing in a large bowl until the leaves are evenly coated. Mound the lettuce on individual plates, top with a round of warm goat cheese, and scatter the roughly chopped hazelnuts all over.

Arugula Salad with Blood Oranges, Fennel, and Ricotta Salata

SERVES 6 TO 8

2 teaspoons minced shallot

6 small blood oranges

2½ tablespoons sherry vinegar

¼ teaspoon sea salt or kosher salt, plus more to taste

Freshly ground black pepper

2 tablespoons extra-virgin olive oil

½ pound baby arugula (6 to 7 cups)

1 medium bulb fennel (about ¾ pound)

¼ pound ricotta salata, shaved with a vegetable
peeler to yield about 1 cup

Put the shallot in a small bowl. Squeeze one of the blood oranges to get 2 tablespoons juice. Add the juice and the vinegar to the shallot. Season the mixture with the salt and a few grinds of black pepper. Let sit for 10 minutes and then whisk in the olive oil. Reserve the vinaigrette at room temperature until ready to use (for up to 2 hours) or make up to 1 day in advance and store, tightly covered, in the refrigerator. Bring to room temperature and whisk again before using.

Trim any long stems from the arugula, wash the leaves well, and spin them dry. Put the arugula in a large bowl, cover with a slightly damp towel, and refrigerate until ready to toss.

With a serrated knife, remove the peel and pith from the remaining blood oranges. Cut the oranges in half lengthwise and slice into ¼-inch-thick half-moons. Reserve in a small bowl at room temperature (or refrigerate, tightly wrapped, if working ahead).

Trim the stalks from the fennel bulb. Cut the bulb in half lengthwise through the core. Cut out the core in a wedge. Shave the fennel lengthwise with a vegetable peeler or on a mandoline (see p. 299 for more information). You will have ribbons, not crescents. (If you have crescents, you're slicing crosswise instead of lengthwise.)

Add the fennel to the arugula and toss. Whisk the vinaigrette to recombine. Add the vinaigrette to the arugula and fennel and toss again. Season with salt and pepper. Add the blood oranges and toss gently. Portion onto salad plates and distribute the ricotta salata over each salad.

DID YOU KNOW? While iceberg lettuce delivers a lot of refreshing crunch, that's about all it's got. It has a high water content but very few other nutrients. For more nutrition, choose darker lettuces—the deeper the green, the more phyto-nutrients.

Grilled Hearts of Romaine with Blue Cheese Dressing

SERVES 4

FOR THE DRESSING

1 cup mayonnaise

½ cup sour cream

¼ cup whole milk; more as needed

6 ounces crumbled blue cheese, such as Roquefort or Danish Blue, plus more to taste

1½ tablespoons finely grated shallot

1 clove finely grated garlic

1 tablespoon fresh lemon juice

½ teaspoon kosher salt

⅛ teaspoon freshly ground black pepper, plus more to taste

FOR THE SALAD

2 hearts of romaine lettuce, bases trimmed but left intact, halved lengthwise

Extra-virgin olive oil, for brushing

Kosher salt and freshly ground black pepper

4 slices smoked bacon (preferably applewood-smoked), cooked and crumbled

Make the dressing: In a medium bowl, stir all the ingredients. Cover and refrigerate for at least 3 hours to let the flavors develop. Before using, taste and adjust the seasonings if necessary. The dressing will thicken as it sits and may need to be thinned with more milk.

Prepare the salad: Once the dressing is chilled, heat a gas grill to medium low or prepare a medium-low charcoal fire. (Be sure the grate is hot, too.) Lightly brush olive oil all over the romaine hearts, taking care not to break the leaves. Sprinkle with salt and pepper. Put the lettuce cut side down on the grate, directly over the heat. Grill until the outer leaves are charred and wilted and the lettuce is warm and just barely tender all the way through to the core, 2 to 5 minutes, depending on the heat of your grill. Transfer the lettuce to a clean platter and let rest for 5 minutes.

To serve: Place half a heart of romaine, cut side up, on each plate, top with about 2 tablespoons of the dressing, or more to taste, and sprinkle with the crumbled bacon. Serve immediately.

Other recipe ideas

CHICKEN MILANESE WITH LEMONY SALAD
Toss arugula and other spicy lettuces with some lemon juice, olive oil, and salt and pepper and put a handful on top of a breaded and sautéed chicken cutlet or sliced grilled steak.

ROAST CHICKEN WITH "PAN-DRIPPING" SALAD
Roast a chicken, then use the deglazed pan drippings to make a vinaigrette. Dress a mix of tangy lettuce to serve as a side salad with the chicken and some steamed green beans.

MEDITERRANEAN CHOPPED SALAD Make a crunchy chopped salad by garnishing a bed of chopped, crisp iceberg with chopped ham, salami, tomatoes, cucumbers, peppers, and some finely diced feta cheese; dress with a simple red-wine vinaigrette.

What's in Your Mesclun Mix?

The word mesclun comes from the Latin word *mescluma*, which means mixture. Traditional mesclun (also called misticanza in some regions of Italy) is foraged from the wild and includes tender shoots, leaves, and flowers of edible plants and herbs that grow on the sunny hillsides in the Mediterranean climate. The hallmark of mesclun is a balance of colors, textures, and flavors that range from sweet and tender to bitter and crisp to peppery and pungent.

Supermarket mesclun, which tends to be rather ordinary, is most often a mix of just 10 to 12 varieties. Many farmer's markets and gourmet stores sell distinctive mesclun grown by individual producers. Some of these mixes contain as many as 30 different plants, including flowers and herbs (which are delicate and spoil too rapidly for supermarkets) and things like young dandelion greens, purslane, mizuna, and curly cress, to name a few. These mixes need the simplest dressing to make a great salad.

Four Dressings to Showcase Fresh Lettuces

Spicy Ginger-Lime-Garlic Vinaigrette

MAKES ½ CUP

1 teaspoon finely minced fresh ginger

½ teaspoon finely grated lime zest

½ teaspoon minced garlic

¼ teaspoon Dijon mustard

¼ teaspoon salt

⅛ teaspoon sugar

2 tablespoons plus 2 teaspoons fresh lime juice

1 teaspoon white-wine vinegar

6 drops hot sauce, like Tabasco®, plus more to taste

¼ cup grapeseed oil or other neutral-flavored oil

In a small bowl, whisk the ginger, lime zest, garlic, mustard, salt, sugar, lime juice, vinegar, and hot sauce. Slowly whisk in the oil until the dressing is creamy and blended. Taste and adjust the seasonings. Store in a bottle or jar in the refrigerator for up to 3 days.

Pesto Vinaigrette

MAKES ABOUT 1 CUP

1½ cups lightly packed fresh basil leaves

½ cup extra-virgin olive oil

½ cup fresh, finely grated Parmigiano-Reggiano

3 tablespoons red- or white-wine vinegar

2 tablespoons fresh lemon juice

2 teaspoons finely chopped garlic

½ teaspoon finely grated lemon zest

¾ teaspoon kosher salt

Freshly ground black pepper

Put the basil, olive oil, Parmigiano, vinegar, lemon juice, garlic, and lemon zest in a blender. Blend until smooth. Season with salt and pepper to taste. Store in a bottle or jar in the refrigerator for up to 3 days.

Creamy Herb Dressing

MAKES ABOUT 2 CUPS

¼ small bunch fresh dill, stems removed (about ¼ cup loosely packed leaves)

¼ bunch fresh flat-leaf parsley, stems removed (about ¾ cup loosely packed leaves)

¼ bunch fresh thyme, stems removed (about 2 tablespoons loosely packed leaves)

½ bunch fresh chives, coarsely chopped (⅓ cup)

¾ cup mayonnaise

½ cup buttermilk

2 tablespoons cider vinegar

½ teaspoon kosher salt, plus more to taste

⅛ teaspoon freshly ground black pepper

¾ teaspoon hot sauce

In a food processor, combine the dill, parsley, thyme, and chives with the mayonnaise; process until the herbs are chopped. With the motor running, slowly pour in the buttermilk and then add the vinegar, salt, pepper, and hot sauce. Taste and adjust the seasoning. Pour into a bottle or jar and refrigerate for up to 2 weeks.

Yogurt-Feta Dressing with Fresh Mint

MAKES ABOUT 1 CUP

2 tablespoons fresh lemon juice

1 teaspoon honey

3 tablespoons Greek-style yogurt (like Total) or whole-milk yogurt

5 tablespoons olive oil

¼ cup crumbled feta

2 tablespoons roughly chopped fresh mint

½ teaspoon kosher salt

Freshly ground black pepper

In a medium bowl, whisk the lemon juice and honey. In another bowl, whisk the yogurt and olive oil. Add the yogurt mixture to the lemon juice in a thin stream, whisking constantly. Add the feta, mint, salt, and pepper to taste. Chill, covered, for up to 24 hours.

Rumex acetosa and cvs.

Sorrel

Arrow-shaped sorrel looks delicate, but the spring-green, tender, juicy leaves pack a bright lemony punch that's perfect for salads, sauces, or soups. It's also called garden sorrel or spinach dock.

PICKING THE BEST

For fruitier, less acidic leaves, choose those that are young and small. As the leaves age and grow bigger, they develop a more acidic flavor.

KEEPING IT FRESH

Treat sorrel like you would tender salad greens: Use them fast and keep them away from moisture. Roll them up in paper towels, then tuck into a plastic bag. They should keep for at least 3 days in the fridge.

PREPARING

If the center ribs seem tough, cut them out and tear the leaves into fine or wide ribbons, depending on how you plan to use them.

HOW TO USE IT

Add fresh sorrel to salads and sandwiches, or purée into salad dressing and pasta sauces. When cooked, it loses its bright green color and practically melts away, making it better for puréed soups and sauces.

SURPRISING PAIRINGS

Sorrel's lemony flavor makes it a perfect partner for fish, especially rich salmon.

PRESERVING OPTIONS

Sorrel can be puréed and frozen with a little water in ice cube trays, then popped into soups or sauces. Or turn it into a pesto and freeze. Use within a few months for best flavor.

DID YOU KNOW? There's another plant called sorrel. The Roselle plant, which produces calyxes used to make bright red hibiscus tea and the agua fresca known as agua de Jamaica, is known as sorrel in the Caribbean. However, that plant is unrelated to green, tender common sorrel.

Salmon with Sorrel Sauce and Potato Dumplings

SERVES 6

FOR THE DUMPLINGS

1 pound russet potatoes, preferably Yukon Gold, unpeeled, scrubbed

2 teaspoons salt, plus more to taste

4 ounces sorrel leaves (about 5 cups, lightly packed)

¼ cup olive oil; more as needed, for sautéing

3 egg yolks

⅓ cup semolina

2¼ ounces (½ cup) unbleached all-purpose flour

½ cup fine fresh breadcrumbs

¼ teaspoon fresh grated nutmeg

Freshly ground black pepper

Unsalted butter, for sautéing (optional)

FOR THE SAUCE

3 cups fish stock (or 2 cups bottled clam juice and 1 cup water)

2 tablespoons minced shallot

1 teaspoon minced garlic

6 ounces sorrel leaves (about 7 cups, lightly packed)

½ cup extra-virgin olive oil

Salt and freshly ground black pepper

TO FINISH THE DISH

6 skinless salmon fillets, about 5 ounces each

Salt and freshly ground black pepper

Sorrel leaves (optional)

Make the dumplings: Simmer the whole potatoes in lightly salted water until tender enough to allow a knife point to easily penetrate to the center. Drain and let cool slightly.

Blanch the sorrel in boiling water for a few seconds and refresh in cold water. Drain thoroughly and press out excess moisture. In a food processor or blender, purée the sorrel with the olive oil and egg yolks.

Cut the potatoes into smaller pieces and pass them through a food mill or a ricer (the skins will stay behind) into a mixing bowl. Add the semolina, flour, breadcrumbs, puréed sorrel, nutmeg, 2 teaspoons salt, and pepper to taste. Knead the mixture lightly until it comes together to make an even dough. Cover the bowl with a towel and let rest for 30 minutes.

Lightly flour your hands and the work surface. Portion the dough into a few pieces and roll each piece into a ¾-inch-thick rope. Cut the ropes into 2-inch pieces. Roll the ends of each piece to taper them and make football-shaped dumplings.

Cook the dumplings in a large pot of boiling salted water until they float to the top and feel firm, about 4 minutes. Remove with a slotted spoon, drain, and toss with a little oil to prevent sticking. Use immediately or refrigerate.

Make the sauce: Combine the fish stock, shallot, and garlic in a small, nonreactive saucepan and simmer until reduced to about ⅔ cup. Put the sorrel leaves into the bowl of a food processor, add the hot stock reduction, and process for about 30 seconds. With the motor running, gradually add the olive oil and salt and pepper to taste. Keep warm until ready to serve. The sauce may separate on standing, so whisk it well before serving.

To finish the dish: Run your finger over the salmon fillets to find any pin bones and pull them out with tweezers or by pinching them between your finger and a knife. Season with salt and pepper. Set up a steamer (or a large pot fitted with a rack), bring the water to a boil, put in the fish, cover, and steam until just barely done in the center, 5 to 10 minutes, depending on the shape of the fillets.

Meanwhile, sauté the dumplings in a little oil or butter in a nonstick pan over medium-high heat until they're heated through and slightly browned. Ladle some warm sauce on each plate, and arrange a few dumplings on one side and a salmon fillet on the other. Decorate with more greens, if you like, and serve immediately.

Other recipe ideas

SORREL-CHIVE BUTTER Make a compound butter by mixing equal parts softened butter with chopped sorrel leaves, a small amount of finely chopped chives, and salt to taste. Use it to top grilled fish or chicken or to flavor rice.

SORREL PESTO Experiment with pesto by replacing half or all of the basil in a classic pesto recipe. Toss with fresh linguine and sprinkle with pine nuts.

Spinacia oleracea and cvs.

Spinach

Most of us have heard about the nutritional benefits of spinach, but it's the flavor and versatility that make it a favorite in the kitchen. A bit more muscular and minerally than many greens, raw spinach leaves add a sweet bite to salads, and cooked spinach develops an appealing satiny texture that's great in gratins, soups, and pastas.

Leaf

Baby

PICKING THE BEST

Some spinach leaves are smooth and flat, while others are crinkled or "savoyed." Both kinds are delicious, and both can be young and tender. The savoyed needs extra washing to get rid of the last traces of grit nestled in its crinkles. Because of its crinkles, however, the savoyed type has more body and tends to ship better.

Fresh spinach is sold in bunches or as loose leaves (easiest to find at greenmarkets or farmstands and in bags at some supermarkets). Pick out the large leaves

for cooking and select the smaller, more tender ones for salads. Whether loose or in a bunch, look for fresh-looking, brightly colored leaves; avoid wilted or yellowing leaves. Carefully inspect spinach sold in cellophane bags; check the sell-buy or packing dates, and don't buy any that's slimy or shriveled. For bunched spinach, pay attention to the ratio of stem to leaf, since you'll be trimming away much of the stem. Untie bunched spinach as soon as you get home.

KEEPING IT FRESH
Fresh spinach keeps well for 2 or 3 days sealed in a plastic bag in the fridge.

PREPARING
Unless the leaves are very young, spinach should be stemmed by pulling or cutting the center rib from the leaf. Be sure to remove the tough stems of savoyed spinach. Rinse well by swishing in a large bowl of cool water; lift the leaves from the water rather than pouring through a colander. Very gritty leaves may need a couple of changes of water to be thoroughly cleaned. Even spinach labeled "prewashed" needs at least one rinse to eliminate all grit.

HOW TO USE IT
Spinach is great blanched and creamed, sautéed with brown butter, or wilted and tossed with pasta. It is also a fine salad green or a fresh pizza topping. "Baby" spinach leaves are best eaten raw because they can cook down to a slippery mess. Mature spinach with less tender leaves is the best cooked, where its mineral quality can be tamed with cream, butter, or cheese.

PRESERVING OPTIONS
Blanch well-washed spinach for 3 minutes, cool in an ice bath, drain well, and freeze in airtight plastic bags.

RECIPES

Warm Spinach Salad with Eggs, Bacon, and Croutons

SERVES 6 AS FIRST COURSE

2 large eggs

Kosher salt

4½ tablespoons extra-virgin olive oil

2 cloves garlic, crushed and peeled

3 to 4 ounces rustic, coarse-textured bread, crust removed, cut into ¾-inch cubes (to yield 3 cups)

3 tablespoons sherry vinegar

1 tablespoon Dijon mustard

Freshly ground black pepper

3 slices bacon, cut into ¾-inch squares

1 small shallot, minced (1½ tablespoons)

10 cups loosely packed baby spinach leaves (about 10 ounces), washed and dried

Put the eggs in a small saucepan of water and bring to a boil over medium-high heat. Boil for 4 minutes. Turn off the heat and let cool in the water. When the eggs are cool, crack and peel them. Chop the eggs, season to taste with salt, and set aside.

Position a rack in the center of the oven and heat the oven to 375°F. Heat 1½ tablespoons of the olive oil in a small saucepan over medium-high heat. Add the garlic and cook, stirring occasionally, until it starts to turn golden, about 1 minute. Discard the garlic.

Arrange the bread in a single layer on a baking sheet. Drizzle with the garlic-infused oil, sprinkle with a little salt, and toss. Bake, shaking the bread cubes once, until golden and crisp, 8 to 10 minutes. Remove from the oven and let cool.

In a small bowl, whisk the remaining 3 tablespoons olive oil, the sherry vinegar, and the mustard. Season with salt and pepper to taste.

In a 10-inch skillet, cook the bacon over medium-high heat, stirring frequently, until golden brown and crisp, 3 to 5 minutes. With a slotted spoon, transfer the bacon to a plate lined with paper towels. Add the shallot to the pan and cook, stirring, until softened, about 1 minute. Let the pan cool slightly and add the vinaigrette to the pan, whisking well to blend the ingredients.

Toss the warm vinaigrette with the spinach in a large bowl. Transfer to a platter and garnish with the chopped eggs, bacon, and croutons. Serve.

Spinach Sautéed with Brown Butter and Garlic

SERVES 2

2 tablespoons unsalted butter

2 cloves garlic, gently crushed and peeled

1 large bunch spinach (10 to 12 ounces), thick stems trimmed, leaves washed and dried well

Salt and freshly ground black pepper

1 lemon, halved

In a large sauté pan over medium heat, melt the butter with the garlic until the butter is golden brown and smells nutty; make sure the garlic doesn't burn. Raise the heat to high and add the spinach, in batches if need be, flipping and stirring, until just barely wilted, about 1 minute. Take the pan off the heat; remove the garlic. Season the spinach with salt, pepper, and a squeeze of lemon. Toss and serve immediately.

Other recipe ideas

ASIAN SPINACH SALAD WITH TOASTED CASHEWS Toss spinach with a soy-ginger vinaigrette, shredded cooked chicken, and toasted cashews for a quick Asian salad.

TORTELLINI SOUP WITH SPINACH AND TOMATO Stir a chiffonade of spinach into a soup made from tortellini cooked in chicken broth and canned tomatoes.

GREEK FRITTATA WITH SPINACH AND POTATO Fold chopped cooked spinach into a frittata, along with some crumbled feta, chopped fresh dill, and diced cooked potato.

DID YOU KNOW? Some people report feeling a dry, chalky sensation on the teeth and on the roof of the mouth when eating spinach. Agricultural scientists say that this comes from the leaves' high concentration of oxalic acid.

Urtica dioica

Stinging Nettles

There's something crazy about being able to cook and eat a wild plant that, when raw, causes burning pain with just one touch. It's like being able to eat poison ivy. But there's more than novelty to this nutritious, delicious plant. The leaves are reminiscent of spinach and mustard greens and just as versatile.

PICKING THE BEST

Nettles are covered with tiny stinging hairs that really hurt and can cause redness and itching long after contact, so use gloves when handling them raw; at the farmer's market (which is about the only place you'll find nettles unless you forage them yourself), you'll need to use tongs to put them into your bag. Once cooked, however, the sting is totally gone and nettles behave like any fresh cooking green. Nettles should be bright green and fresh looking. Avoid those that are mushy or have begun to turn brown or yellow.

KEEPING IT FRESH

You can store nettle leaves in a plastic bag in the refrigerator for several days.

PREPARING

Wearing rubber gloves, rinse nettles well, then remove the stems from the leaves. You can leave the leaves whole, chop, or chiffonade; discard the stems.

HOW TO USE IT

Treat nettles like other tender greens such as chard and spinach. You can steam, blanch, or sauté them with a little liquid, then add them to pastas, gratins, risottos, frittatas, and pesto. Or add them directly to soups.

PRESERVING OPTIONS

Nettles can be dried (which destroys the sting) and used as an herbal tea. Or blanch them and use them instead of basil to make pesto, then pack into airtight containers and freeze.

Potato and Nettle Soup

SERVES 4

Kosher salt

1 pound russet potatoes, peeled and cut into
1-inch chunks

½ pound nettles

2 tablespoons unsalted butter

Freshly ground black pepper

1 quart homemade or reduced-sodium chicken broth

½ cup crème fraîche

Simmer the potatoes for about 10 minutes in a large pot of salted water (they will be only partially cooked). Drain and reserve.

Meanwhile, wearing clean rubber gloves, pull the nettle leaves from the stems and rinse well; discard the stems.

Melt the butter in a large soup pot, add the nettles, season with salt and pepper, and sauté for several minutes, tossing until wilted and fragrant.

Add the potatoes and broth; simmer until the potatoes are completely tender, another 10 minutes or so.

Blend in batches until smooth. Put the soup back into the pot, stir in the crème fraîche, and simmer for another couple of minutes. Taste and correct the seasoning as needed.

DID YOU KNOW?

Stinging nettles are incredibly nutritious. They're great sources of iron, vitamins, and calcium and contain more protein than other green vegetables. If you're foraging for your own, gather the spring leaves before they flower, otherwise mineral masses form in the leaves and can cause urinary tract irritation. In fall, nettles are good until they're killed by frost.

Sautéed Nettles with Shallots

SERVES 6

2½ ounces (5 tablespoons) unsalted butter

¼ cup finely chopped shallot

¾ teaspoon ground coriander (preferably from toasted and freshly ground seeds)

Pinch of crushed red pepper flakes

1¼ pounds nettles, tough stems removed and thoroughly washed but not dried (wear rubber gloves when handling)

Kosher salt and freshly ground pepper (preferably white pepper)

Freshly grated nutmeg

Heat the butter in a 12-inch skillet over medium heat. Add the shallot, coriander, and red pepper flakes and cook, stirring occasionally, until the shallot begins to soften but doesn't brown, 2 to 3 minutes. Increase the heat to medium high, and, wearing clean rubber gloves, begin adding the nettles, a large handful at a time, tossing with tongs, until all the leaves are in the skillet. Cook, tossing frequently, until the nettles are wilted and tender, 2 to 4 minutes. If a lot of water remains, cook on high heat until the leaves are coated with butter but not soupy, another 1 to 2 minutes. Season to taste with salt, pepper, and nutmeg.

Other recipe ideas

SPRING GREENS PESTO Make a pesto with spinach, nettles, a couple of ramps if you have them or a couple of scallions, and some fresh parsley or basil. Blanch all the greens briefly before adding to the blender. Use pine nuts or walnuts and a good olive oil.

NETTLE AND LEEK RISOTTO Wilt the nettles in a pan with a little water and a tablespoon of butter until soft, about 4 minutes; drain and chop roughly. Make a risotto using leeks instead of onion in the base. Just as the rice is tender, fold in the nettles; garnish with grated Parmesan.

Everbearing

Alpine

Fragaria ananassa cvs.

Strawberries

Cheerfully red, heart-shaped, and sweet as can be, strawberries are easy to love. They're irresistible when fresh, as their flavor strikes the perfect balance of sweetness and brightness, and they don't have annoying seeds like many other berries. Prep is a breeze—just scoop out the green tops and enjoy.

PICKING THE BEST

Look for berries that are deep red. Varieties that are red all the way through are the sweetest. They should look shiny and taut, not soft or wizened, with fresh-looking green calyxes. Take a big sniff, because fragrance is the best indicator of prime fruit. They should smell like sweet strawberries. Look for locally grown berries at your farmer's market, which are likely to have the best flavor and a more succulent texture than varieties grown for shipping. And if you run across fraises des bois, also called Alpine strawberries, snatch them up and eat them right away; their perfumed flavor is very special.

KEEPING IT FRESH

Don't wash the berries until just before eating. You can leave them out on the counter for just a few hours, covered in a light dishtowel or a moist paper towel. For longer storage, wrap in plastic to keep from drying out, refrigerate, and use within a week. For best flavor, allow to come to room temperature before eating.

PREPARING

Just before using, gently rinse the berries in cool water to wash off any grit; spread out on a clean towel to dry, or pat dry gently. Cut out the green cap with the tip of a small paring knife and serve whole or sliced, depending on your dish.

HOW TO USE IT

Strawberries are the one berry that's rarely cooked; unlike caneberries or blueberries, the flavor doesn't brighten with cooking but rather flattens out a bit, and the texture can become mushy. That being said, strawberries are beautiful when baked with rhubarb into an old-fashioned pie. They're also wonderful when roasted or simmered into a compote or sauce for topping ice cream and other desserts.

SURPRISING PAIRINGS

Balsamic vinegar is an unusual but wonderful partner, as is a splash of rosewater, which brings out the berries' floral notes. Chocolate is a classic pairing, but can be overpowering when not used sparingly.

PRESERVING OPTIONS

Turn strawberries into jams, syrups, and sauces. Freeze the washed, hulled fruit whole on a cookie sheet until hard, then pack into freezer bags, but be aware their color will darken, and they will not be plump and firm when defrosted. To preserve their color and texture during freezing, pack them in sugar: Toss sliced berries with sugar and let sit until the sugar dissolves and the juices become syrupy; whole fruit should be packed with sugar syrup or strawberry juice. You can also freeze the fruit as a purée with a little lemon juice and sugar to preserve the color and flavor.

RECIPES

Chocolate Strawberry Shortcakes

SERVES 9

FOR THE CHOCOLATE BISCUITS

10 ounces (about 2¼ cups) unbleached all-purpose flour

1½ ounces (about ¼ cup plus 3 tablespoons) Dutch-processed cocoa powder, such as Droste®

¼ cup sugar, plus about 3 tablespoons for sprinkling

1½ tablespoons baking powder

¾ teaspoon salt

4½ ounces (9 tablespoons) cold unsalted butter, cut into small pieces

6½ ounces semisweet chocolate, grated or finely chopped (the food processor works well); more for garnish

1¼ cups heavy cream, plus about 3 tablespoons for brushing

1½ teaspoons pure vanilla extract

FOR THE STRAWBERRIES

5 cups ⅛-inch-thick strawberry slices (from about 3 pints); plus 9 to 18 whole hulled strawberries, for garnish

1 to 3 tablespoons sugar, depending on the sweetness of the berries

FOR THE WHIPPED CREAM

1½ cups heavy cream

2 tablespoons sugar

¾ teaspoon pure vanilla extract

Make the biscuits: Line a heavy baking sheet with parchment. Sift the flour, cocoa powder, sugar, baking powder, and salt into a large bowl. Toss with a fork to combine. Cut the butter into the dry ingredients with a pastry cutter or a fork until the largest pieces of butter are the size of peas. Add the grated chocolate and toss to combine. Combine the cream and vanilla in a liquid measure. Make a well in the center of the flour mixture and pour the cream into the well. Mix with a fork until the dough is evenly moistened and just combined; it should look shaggy and still feel a little dry. Gently knead by hand five or six times to pick up any dry ingredients remaining in the bottom of the bowl and to create a loose ball.

Turn the dough out onto a lightly floured work surface and pat it into an 8-inch square, ¾ to 1 inch thick. Transfer the dough to the parchment-lined baking sheet, cover with plastic wrap, and chill for 20 minutes. Meanwhile, position a rack in the center of the oven and heat the oven to 425°F. Remove the dough from the refrigerator and trim about ¼ inch from each side to create a neat, sharp edge (a bench knife or a pastry scraper works well, or use a large chef's knife, being sure to cut straight down). Cut the dough into 9 even squares (about 2½ inches square) and spread them about 2 inches apart on the baking sheet. With a pastry brush or the back of a spoon, brush each biscuit with a thin layer of cream and sprinkle generously with sugar. Bake until the biscuits look a little dry and are mostly firm to the touch (they should spring back slightly when gently pressed), 18 to 20 minutes.

Meanwhile, prepare the berries: Toss the sliced berries with 1 tablespoon sugar and taste. If they're still tart, sprinkle with another 1 to 2 tablespoons sugar. Let sit at room temperature until the sugar dissolves and the berries begin to release their juices, at least 30 minutes but no more than 2 hours.

Whip the cream: Pour the cream into a cold mixing bowl and beat with a hand mixer until it begins to thicken. Add the sugar and vanilla extract and, using a whisk, continue to beat by hand until the cream is softly whipped or until the whisk leaves distinct marks in the cream; it should be soft and billowy but still hold its shape.

Assemble the shortcakes: While the biscuits are still warm, split them in half horizontally with a serrated knife. For each serving, set the bottom half of a biscuit on a plate. Scoop about ½ cup of the berries and their juices over the biscuit. Add a generous dollop of whipped cream and cover with the top half of the biscuit. Top with a small dollop of cream, a sprinkling of grated chocolate, and 1 or 2 whole, hulled strawberries.

Balsamic-Macerated Strawberries with Basil

SERVES 4 AS A DESSERT; 6 TO 8 AS A FILLING OR TOPPING

2 pounds fresh strawberries, rinsed, hulled, and
   sliced ⅛ to ¼ inch thick (about 4 cups)
1 tablespoon sugar
2 teaspoons balsamic vinegar
8 to 10 medium fresh basil leaves

In a large bowl, gently toss the strawberries with the sugar and vinegar. Let sit at room temperature until the strawberries have released their juices but are not yet mushy, about 30 minutes. (Don't let the berries sit for more than 90 minutes or they'll start to collapse.)

Just before serving, stack the basil leaves on a cutting board and roll them vertically into a loose cigar shape. Using a sharp chef's knife, very thinly slice across the roll to make a fine chiffonade of basil.

Portion the strawberries and their juices among four small bowls and scatter with the basil to garnish, or choose one of the serving suggestions below.

- Serve the strawberries over grilled or toasted pound cake. Garnish with a dollop of crème fraîche.
- Put the berries on split biscuits for shortcakes; top with whipped cream and scatter with the basil.
- Mash the berries slightly and fold into whipped cream for a quick fool. Garnish with the basil.

Strawberry Crisp

SERVES 8

3 pints small ripe fresh strawberries, hulled and halved
2½ cups coarse fresh white breadcrumbs
½ cup confectioners' sugar
½ teaspoon finely grated lemon zest
¼ teaspoon salt
½ cup coarsely chopped hazelnuts
2 ounces (4 tablespoons) unsalted butter, melted
3 tablespoons granulated sugar
Heavy cream or vanilla ice cream, for serving
   (optional)

Position a rack in the center of the oven and heat the oven to 375°F.

In a bowl, toss the strawberries, 1 cup of the breadcrumbs, the confectioners' sugar, lemon zest, and salt; scrape into an 8-inch-square Pyrex® baking dish. In another bowl, toss the remaining 1½ cups breadcrumbs with the hazelnuts, melted butter, and granulated sugar; sprinkle evenly over the berries. Bake until the berries are bubbling, about 40 minutes. Let cool on a rack for about 10 minutes.

Spoon the warm crisp into bowls and top with a drizzle of heavy cream or a scoop of ice cream, if you like.

Other recipe ideas

STRAWBERRY-MINT LEMONADE Flavor homemade or store-bought lemonade by muddling some fresh strawberries and mint leaves in each glass.

SPRING BERRY SALAD Accent a salad of peppery arugula, goat cheese crumbles, and hazelnuts with sliced fresh strawberries.

ROASTED STRAWBERRY DESSERT TOPPING Roast whole strawberries with a little butter and brown sugar and use as a topping for ice cream, angel food cake, or rice pudding.

Early Summer

- Apricots
- Artichokes
- Blueberries
- Broccoli
- Cauliflower
- Cherries
- Cucumbers
- Edamame
- Fennel
- Herbs
- Leeks
- Nopales/Prickly Pears
- Okra
- Onions
- Scallions
- Shallots
- String Beans

Prunus armeniaca cvs.

Apricots

The first stone fruit of summer, apricots arrive as the perfect harbinger of warm, golden days to come. Their fragrant, velvety-soft skin is kissed with a modest blush, while the sweet flesh offers richness and complexity even when cooked. Apricots are related to peaches, plums, and other "drupes," or stone fruits.

KEEPING IT FRESH

Keep apricots cool so they don't overripen by storing them in the refrigerator for up to a week. To encourage harder apricots to ripen, leave them in a paper bag at room temperature for a day or two.

PREPARING

The skin on an apricot is thin and tender, so there's no need to remove it (cut out deep blemishes with a paring knife). Gently rinse the fruit, then cut around it vertically along the seam. Twist the halves gently to pry them apart. Nudge the pit from the center with the tip of a knife, then leave the fruit in halves or cut into the size you need.

HOW TO USE IT

An apricot's rich flavor doesn't need much to show it off. Eating out of hand is the perfect way to enjoy an apricot, but this delicate fruit takes well to baking, too, from galettes and tarts to moist muffins, quick breads, and cakes. Apricots are also delicious poached, stewed, or roasted into compotes and chutneys.

SURPRISING PAIRINGS

Pair apricots with herbs such as lavender and rosemary or spices like cinnamon, ginger, and cardamom.

PICKING THE BEST

Ripeness cues can vary slightly between varieties, but you'll know a ripe, juicy apricot by its fruity fragrance and deep, uniform golden color, especially right around the stem, the portion that's the last to ripen. The rosy blush isn't necessarily an indication of ripeness— it's just the side of the fruit that faced the sun while hanging on the tree. A ripe, juicy apricot will be firm and give slightly when pressed. Really ripe fruit with a lot of sugar will even wrinkle a bit.

Some varieties, such as Blenheims, may freckle as they ripen, but that's purely cosmetic and doesn't affect flavor or texture.

PRESERVING OPTIONS

To freeze apricots, halve and pit the fruit, toss with citrus juice, spread on a baking sheet, and freeze until hard; pack in a plastic freezer bag. Food dehydrators are the fastest way to dry apricots, but you can also try oven-drying (130°F for 24 to 36 hours) or sun-drying (you'll need two to four 100°F days). To keep the fruit from turning brown, cut it into $1/4$-inch-thick slices and toss it in citrus juice. Apricots are properly dried when the texture is pliable but not moist.

RECIPES

Quick Apricot Jam

YIELDS 3 CUPS

2 pounds ripe apricots, rinsed, quartered, pitted, and
    unpeeled (about 16)
1 cup plus 3 tablespoons sugar
½ teaspoon fresh lemon juice

In a wide, shallow pan, stir the apricots and the sugar.
Set the pan over medium-high heat and bring to a
simmer, stirring often so the preserves don't stick or
burn. Simmer the jam until it's thick but some chunks
of fruit remain, 10 to 15 minutes. Stir in the lemon
juice and remove the pan from the heat. Let cool,
transfer to a plastic container with a tight-fitting lid,
and refrigerate.

Apricot-Raspberry Buckle

SERVES 8 TO 10

FOR THE STREUSEL

1½ ounces (⅓ cup minus 1 tablespoon) unbleached
    all-purpose flour
¼ cup sugar
1 teaspoon ground cinnamon
Pinch of salt
2 ounces (4 tablespoons) cold unsalted butter, cut
    into small pieces; more for the dish

FOR THE CAKE

6 ounces (1⅓ cups) unbleached all-purpose flour
1½ teaspoons baking powder
½ teaspoon salt
6 ounces (12 tablespoons) unsalted butter, softened
    at room temperature
1 cup sugar
1½ teaspoons pure vanilla extract
¼ teaspoon pure almond extract
3 large eggs
¾ pound firm, ripe apricots (about 4 large), halved,
    pitted, and cut into ¾-inch pieces
    (to yield 2 cups)
2 cups (about 8 ounces) fresh raspberries

Position a rack in the lower third of the oven and heat
the oven to 375°F. Butter a 9-inch-square baking pan.

Make the streusel: In a medium bowl, combine
the flour, sugar, cinnamon, and salt. Add the cold
butter and cut it in with a pastry blender or two table
knives until the butter pieces resemble small peas.
Refrigerate until needed.

Make the cake: Sift the flour, baking powder, and
salt into a bowl and set aside. With an electric stand
mixer (a hand mixer is fine, too), beat the butter
with the paddle attachment on medium speed until
smooth, about 1 minute. Add ¼ cup of the sugar and
the vanilla and almond extracts. Beat 1 minute on
medium speed. Gradually add the remaining ¾ cup
sugar while beating on medium speed. Turn off the
mixer and use a rubber spatula to scrape the bowl
and beater. Beat on medium-high speed until pale
and slightly fluffy (the sugar will not be dissolved),
about 3 minutes. Reduce the speed to medium and
add the eggs, one at a time, mixing until the batter
is smooth each time. Stop and scrape the bottom
and sides of the bowl and beater. On low speed, add
the flour mixture and beat only until incorporated.
Remove the bowl from the mixer and scrape the
beater. The batter will be thick.

Add half of the apricots and half of the raspberries
to the batter and fold them in gently with a large
rubber spatula. Some of the raspberries will break,
giving the batter a pinkish cast; when baked, the pink
will disappear. Spread the batter into the prepared
pan and distribute the remaining fruit evenly on top.

Sprinkle the streusel over the fruit. Bake until the
cake springs back in the center when lightly pressed
and a toothpick comes out clean, 45 to 50 minutes.
Let the cake cool in its pan on a rack, then serve.

Other recipe ideas

ROAST CHICKEN WITH APRICOT PAN SAUCE Make a
sauce for roast chicken by deglazing the roasting pan
with chopped apricots and a splash of water or broth,
seasoning with some curry spices, and finishing with
a squeeze of lemon and a handful of fresh cilantro.

BACON-WRAPPED APRICOTS Stuff a pitted apricot
with a sliver of aged Gouda or manchego cheese and
an almond, then wrap the apricot in bacon. Secure
with a toothpick and grill until the bacon is crisp.

Artichokes

Few vegetables offer such a tactile, hands-on experience as artichokes, which is the immature flower bud of a plant in the thistle family. They're a succulent treat when eaten slowly, leaf by sweet, nutty leaf, until—jackpot!—you reach the meaty heart.

more immature the bud, the better the quality and flavor, so look for those with leaves tightly closed and deep in color. Cold weather, which usually occurs in artichoke's second season (in the fall), can cause brown blistery spots on the outer leaves, but many growers say chill improves flavor and call these artichokes "frost-kissed."

KEEPING IT FRESH

Store in a loose, unsealed plastic bag in the vegetable crisper and use within a day or two. They'll be fine for several days, but the leaves tend to darken and the texture gets spongy.

HOW TO USE IT

The terms artichoke bottom and artichoke heart are often used interchangeably, but there is a difference: The bottom is the base of the artichoke without any leaves. The heart is the part of the base that is still attached to the tender inner leaves. (See p. 294 for how to trim.)

- **Steam:** Depending on their size, steam, stems up, for 30 to 50 minutes or until a leaf in the center pulls out easily.
- **Braise:** Use artichoke bottoms and trimmed baby artichokes. Submerge in a flavorful liquid and simmer until tender.
- **Grill:** Steam trimmed artichokes until tender. Cut in half, brush with olive oil, and grill, turning frequently, until grill marks appear.
- **Marinate the hearts or bottoms:** Cover cooked artichoke hearts, bottoms, or trimmed baby artichokes with a mixture of 8 parts oil to 1 part vinegar or lemon juice. Add herbs and flavorings to taste. Refrigerate for up to 1 week.

PICKING THE BEST

The most prominent perennial cultivar, the Green Globe, tends to be a bit more rounded if it matures in spring and fall, when days are shorter. Green Globes that mature in summer, when days are longer, become more conical. Newer to markets are annual varieties that tend to be large and rounded, like a peony about to open. They're gorgeous, but not as tasty as the Globe, and unlike the Globe, they tend to get tighter as they get older.

Choose specimens that are firm and heavy for their size, which indicates they're moist and meaty. The

Steamed Artichokes with Tarragon-Mustard Vinaigrette

SERVES 4

FOR THE VINAIGRETTE

1 small shallot, minced

1 tablespoon red-wine vinegar

Sea salt

1 teaspoon Dijon mustard

1 teaspoon whole-grain mustard

½ cup extra-virgin olive oil

2 tablespoons chopped fresh tarragon

1 tablespoon chopped fresh flat-leaf parsley

FOR THE ARTICHOKES

Six 1x3-inch strips lemon zest, white pith removed

1 tablespoon black peppercorns

2 dried bay leaves

2 sprigs fresh thyme

Two 3- to 4-inch sprigs fresh tarragon

2 teaspoons kosher salt

4 large artichokes, trimmed

Make the vinaigrette: Mix the shallot with the vinegar and 2 pinches of sea salt and let sit for 5 minutes to mellow the flavors. Whisk in the two mustards and then slowly whisk in the olive oil in a slow, steady stream. When the oil has been incorporated, add the tarragon and parsley.

Prepare the artichokes: In a 6- to 8-quart stockpot, combine 2 cups water with the lemon zest, peppercorns, bay leaves, thyme, tarragon, and 1 teaspoon salt and bring to a boil over high heat. Put a steamer basket in the pot and arrange the artichokes bottom side down in the basket. Sprinkle the artichokes with the remaining teaspoon salt. Cover, reduce the heat to a simmer, and steam until completely tender and the leaves pull away easily, 30 to 45 minutes. Serve the artichokes hot or at room temperature with individual dipping bowls of the vinaigrette.

Slow-Sautéed Artichokes with Lemon Juice and Thyme

SERVES 4

Bottoms from 4 large globe artichokes

3 tablespoons olive oil, preferably fruity and full flavored; more as needed

Salt and freshly ground black pepper

1½ to 2 tablespoons fresh lemon juice

1½ teaspoons very lightly chopped fresh thyme leaves

Cut the artichoke bottoms into quarters (or halves, if small) and put them in a large bowl. Drizzle all over with the olive oil and season with salt and pepper. Set a heavy 8-inch skillet over low heat, and when hot, add the artichokes (they should just cover the bottom of the skillet), scraping out all the oil from the bowl into the skillet with a rubber spatula. Cover the skillet and cook, stirring once or twice, until they're a little less than halfway done, 10 to 15 minutes.

Remove the cover and continue cooking at a low sizzle, turning occasionally, until they're lightly browned and tender-firm when pierced with a skewer, another 8 to 15 minutes. Add the lemon juice and thyme and toss together until the pan juices have thickened to coat the artichokes nicely. Taste and season with more salt, pepper, and olive oil, if you like.

Other recipe ideas

RISOTTO WITH SUCCULENT ARTICHOKE CHUNKS Add meaty sweetness to risotto by folding in cooked quartered artichoke bottoms a few minutes before the rice is done.

BABY ARTICHOKE AND FENNEL RAGOÛT Make a ragoût by braising trimmed baby artichokes with chopped shallot and sliced fennel to serve as a side dish or vegetarian main dish.

ARTICHOKE FRITTATA Enrich a frittata with chunks of cooked artichoke bottoms or quartered hearts. Mix in some feta, lemon zest, sliced basil, and a few chopped sun-dried tomatoes.

Vaccinium corymbosum cvs.

Blueberries

Juicy and sweet—and with a color all their own in the food world—blueberries are a hallmark of summer. Less fragile than some berries, they're cooperative in the kitchen, too, as they're delicious both raw and cooked. And their deep color means they're full of antioxidants, making them an excellent snack for children.

PICKING THE BEST

You can judge some fruit with your nose, but not blueberries, so use your eyes first: Blueberries should have a lovely silvery-white bloom over the dark blue. Look for pints free of small, purplish or greenish immature berries, a sign that they were picked before their peak. Then use the heft test: Berries should be plump and heavy. The surefire way of judging blueberries is to taste a few, because sweetness is variable even within the same pint.

Wild blueberries—much harder to find outside of the Northeast, though they're widely available frozen—are intensely flavored and should be tiny and almost black. Huckleberries are a related wild berry, of which there are many varieties; if you're lucky enough to find them at a market, snap them up and use them right away—they're a fragile and fleeting pleasure.

KEEPING IT FRESH

Before storing your berries, pick through them, discarding any squishy berries that may turn moldy and infect their healthy neighbors. Store the berries in the coldest part of the refrigerator, but not in a drawer, where it's too humid, and don't wash them until you're ready to use them. Freshly picked, they can last for up to 2 weeks in an airtight container, although they can lose moisture during the second week and shrink slightly. For baking, this can work in your favor, however, because the flavor becomes concentrated.

PREPARING

Pick the berries over and discard any immature berries or those past their prime. Remove any stems and rinse the berries briefly in a colander, then shake dry or dry on paper towels. For most recipes, frozen blueberries should not be thawed before adding to a batter. Mix blueberries into batters gently and quickly, using as few strokes as possible to avoid crushing the fruit and turning the batter an unfortunate lavender.

HOW TO USE IT

A bowl of blueberries dusted with confectioners' sugar or glossed with heavy cream is a perfect summer dessert, but blueberries also love to be baked—into pies, cobblers, muffins, pound cake, and pancakes.

Blueberries are rich in pectin; with a bit of gentle cooking, they'll thicken into a delicious compote to drizzle over ice cream.

SURPRISING PAIRINGS

Blueberries have two curious flavor allies: cinnamon and lemon. Just a tiny amount—a squeeze of lemon or a pinch of cinnamon—enhances the berries' own fruity flavor, much the same way vanilla extract complements chocolate. Such a small amount of cinnamon or lemon won't be detectable in the finished dessert, but it will add perceptible depth and complexity.

PRESERVING OPTIONS

To freeze blueberries, rinse them in a colander, dry thoroughly on paper towels, and then spread them on rimmed baking sheets in a single layer until frozen solid. Once frozen, they should go into plastic storage bags.

RECIPES

Blueberry Muffins with Cinnamon Crumble

MAKES 12 REGULAR-SIZE OR 6 LARGE MUFFINS

FOR THE CINNAMON CRUMBLE

2¼ ounces (½ cup) unbleached all-purpose flour
¼ cup packed brown sugar
Scant ½ teaspoon ground cinnamon
2 ounces (4 tablespoons) cold unsalted butter, cut into small pieces

FOR THE MUFFINS

Butter and flour for the muffin tins, or paper muffin liners
6¾ ounces (1½ cups) unbleached all-purpose flour
2 ounces (½ cup) cake flour
1 teaspoon baking soda
½ teaspoon baking powder
½ teaspoon salt
¾ teaspoon ground cinnamon
½ teaspoon grated or ground nutmeg
4 ounces (8 tablespoons) unsalted butter, at room temperature
1 cup sugar
2 large eggs
1½ teaspoons pure vanilla extract
1 cup buttermilk
1 cup fresh blueberries, picked over, or frozen blueberries

Position a rack in the center of the oven and heat the oven to 350°F.

Make the crumble: In a medium bowl, combine the flour, brown sugar, and cinnamon. Add the butter and work it in with your fingertips until you have a uniform, moist crumble. Cover with plastic wrap.

Make the muffins: Butter and flour 12 regular (½-cup) or 6 large (1-cup) muffin tins or line them with paper liners. In a small bowl, sift together both flours, the baking soda, baking powder, salt, cinnamon, and nutmeg. Using a hand mixer or stand mixer fitted with the paddle attachment, cream the butter and sugar in a large bowl until light and fluffy, about 3 minutes. Add the eggs, one at a time, beating well after each addition. Scrape the sides of the bowl and beat in the vanilla. On low speed, add the flour mixture in three additions, alternating with the buttermilk in two additions, ending with the flour. Gently fold in the berries by hand. Spoon the batter into the muffin cups to almost full. Scatter a generous amount of the crumble over the batter in each muffin cup (there may be some left over).

Bake until the tops are golden and spring back when touched lightly and a wooden skewer inserted in the center comes out clean, 20 to 25 minutes for regular muffins, 30 to 35 minutes for large. Let cool in the pan for 5 minutes and then turn out onto a rack. Serve warm (slathered with butter, if you like) or at room temperature.

Blueberry Ice Cream

SERVES 4 TO 6

FOR THE BLUEBERRY SYRUP

2 cups (1 pint) fresh blueberries

¼ cup light corn syrup

½ teaspoon fresh lemon juice

⅛ teaspoon ground cinnamon

1 large egg white

FOR THE ICE CREAM CUSTARD

2 cups half-and-half

5 large egg yolks

½ cup sugar

¾ cup whipping cream

1 teaspoon pure vanilla extract

Make the syrup: In a heavy 2-quart saucepan, combine the berries, corn syrup, lemon juice, and cinnamon. Set the pan over low heat and mash the berries roughly with a potato masher or the back of a large fork. Increase the heat to medium low and bring the mixture to a simmer. Simmer for 5 minutes, stirring occasionally, and then let cool for 5 to 10 minutes.

Put the berries in a fine sieve set over a bowl. Press on the berries to extract all the liquid; discard the solids. You'll have about 1 cup liquid.

In a separate bowl, beat the egg white just enough to loosen and break it up, but try to incorporate as little air as possible. Stir the beaten white into the blueberry syrup just until well combined, cover with plastic wrap, and refrigerate until thoroughly chilled. You can make the syrup up to 3 days ahead of making the ice cream.

Make the custard: In a 1- to 2-quart heavy-based saucepan, heat the half-and-half over medium heat. Bring just to a boil, watching so it doesn't boil over, and then remove it from the heat.

Meanwhile, in a medium bowl, lightly beat the yolks to break them up. Whisk in the sugar just until incorporated. Don't overwhisk; you don't want a very thick, pale mixture. Set the bowl on a damp towel to hold it steady and very slowly pour the hot half-and-half into the egg mixture, whisking constantly so the yolks don't curdle. Rinse the saucepan but don't dry the inside; a film of water helps prevent the custard from sticking to the pot. Have ready a fine sieve set over a bowl. Return the custard to the saucepan and set it over medium-low heat. Stirring constantly with a wooden spoon, cook the custard until it thickens enough to coat the back of the spoon, 7 to 10 minutes; a finger drawn across the back of the spoon should leave a clean trail. Immediately pour the custard through the sieve. Stir in the cream and the vanilla extract and press a piece of plastic onto the surface of the warm custard to keep a skin from forming. Poke a few slits in the plastic with the tip of a paring knife to let the steam escape. Let cool slightly and then refrigerate until well chilled, at least 4 hours but ideally 8 hours or overnight.

Make the ice cream: Stir the blueberry syrup into the chilled custard; mix thoroughly. Pour the mixture into an ice-cream maker and freeze following the manufacturer's instructions. For the most intense flavor, serve right away. Otherwise, store in an airtight container for up to a week; let the ice cream soften in the refrigerator for 10 minutes before serving to coax out more flavor.

Blueberry-Lemon Cornmeal Cake

SERVES 8 TO 10

FOR THE CAKE

6 ounces (1⅓ cups) unbleached all-purpose flour;
more for the pan

¼ cup (1½ ounces) finely ground yellow cornmeal

1 teaspoon baking powder

¼ teaspoon baking soda

¼ teaspoon salt

3 ounces (6 tablespoons) unsalted butter, at room
temperature; more for the pan

1 cup sugar

1 teaspoon finely grated lemon zest

2 large eggs

1 tablespoon fresh lemon juice

½ cup buttermilk

FOR THE TOPPING

1 cup (½ pint) fresh blueberries, rinsed and well dried

1 tablespoon sugar

1 tablespoon unbleached all-purpose flour

Position a rack in the center of the oven and heat the
oven to 350°F. Lightly butter a 9x2-inch round cake
pan. Line the bottom with a parchment round cut
to fit the pan, lightly flour the sides, and tap out the
excess.

In a medium bowl, whisk the flour, cornmeal,
baking powder, baking soda, and salt until well
blended. In a stand mixer fitted with the paddle
attachment (or in a large bowl with a hand mixer),
beat the butter, sugar, and lemon zest on medium
high until well blended and fluffy, about 3 minutes.
Add the eggs, one at a time, beating on medium
speed until just blended and adding the lemon juice
with the second egg (the batter will appear curdled;
don't worry). Using a wide rubber spatula, fold in half
the dry ingredients, then the buttermilk, and then the
remaining dry ingredients. Scrape the batter into the
prepared pan and spread evenly. Bake for 15 minutes.

Meanwhile, make the topping: Combine the
blueberries, sugar, and flour in a small bowl. Using a
table fork, mix the ingredients, lightly crushing the
blueberries and evenly coating them with the flour
and sugar. After the cake has baked for 15 minutes,
slide the oven rack out and quickly scatter the
blueberries evenly over the top of the cake (discard
any flour and sugar that doesn't adhere to the

berries). Continue baking until a toothpick inserted in
the center of the cake comes out clean, another 23 to
25 minutes.

Let the cake cool on a rack for 15 minutes. Run a
knife around the inside edge of the pan. Using a dry
dishtowel to protect your hands, lay a rack on top of
the cake pan and, holding onto both rack and pan,
invert the cake. Lift the pan from the cake. Peel away
the parchment. Lay a flat serving plate on the bottom
of the cake and flip the cake one more time so that
the blueberries are on top. Serve warm or at room
temperature.

Other recipe ideas

BLUEBERRY FOOL Cook blueberries with a hint of
sugar and a pinch of cinnamon to make a compote.
Let cool completely, then fold together with softly
whipped cream to make a fool. Pile into pretty
glasses and serve with a butter cookie.

BLUEBERRY-CASSIS SAUCE Simmer blueberries with
sugar, lemon zest, and a splash of cassis liqueur until
saucy. Serve with pancakes, as an ice cream topping,
or on angel food cake.

PEACH-BERRY COBBLER Mix chunks of fresh peaches
with blueberries, blackberries, and a touch of fresh
ginger. Bake with a biscuit topping until the filling is
bubbly and the biscuits are golden brown. Serve with
ginger ice cream.

Broccoli

Broccoli raab

Broccolini

Brassica oleracea cvs.

Broccoli

Broccoli is a grocery store staple, fairly inexpensive, and almost always in good condition. Its nutty-sweet flavor with only mild hints of cabbage is adaptable enough to go from mac and cheese for kids to a spicy Chinese stir-fry. Like all its cruciferous cousins, such as kohlrabi and cabbage, broccoli also packs a nutritional punch of calcium and antioxidants such as vitamins A, C, and E.

PICKING THE BEST

Look for compact, tightly closed florets and thin-skinned stems. Heads should be deep green. Any yellowing or open flowers is a sign of old age. Avoid broccoli that's dried or cracked on the cut end or that has obviously woody stems. And take a whiff—it should smell fresh, not strong and cabbagey.

At farmer's markets and grocery stores, you'll find some delicious broccoli relatives and lookalikes.

- **Gai lan:** Also called Chinese broccoli, it's flavorful and leafy with thick stems.
- **Broccolini:** A thin-stemmed cross between conventional and Chinese broccoli, it has a flavor reminiscent of both.
- **Broccoli raab:** Also called broccoli rabe or rapini, it's more closely related to turnips, but it looks and tastes similar to broccoli, though it's pleasantly bitter. Broccoli raab can be tough and stringy, so it's best when thoroughly cooked and chopped before serving.

KEEPING IT FRESH

You can store broccoli in a loose plastic bag in the refrigerator crisper drawer for a few days. Keep in mind the stems get tougher and it loses nutrients the longer it's stored.

PREPARING

Cut off any leaves and trim the end of the main stem. Turn the head upside down so you can cut off the florets where they join the main stem. Cut the florets in half or in pieces to make them uniform in size. Peel the main stem, then slice it into sticks or coins.

HOW TO USE IT

If you want to keep the broccoli crisp-tender, steaming is a good choice. The vegetable won't absorb as much water as it does when boiled, and it will retain more nutrients. Be sure to drain it well, patting the florets dry, so they don't become soggy. For more even cooking, slit the stems so they cook at the same rate as the more delicate florets.

Broccoli is also delicious when cooked until completely tender, developing a deeper, fuller taste. Try a long, slow sauté, or braise the broccoli in a little chicken broth.

PRESERVING OPTIONS

Blanch broccoli florets and stems for 3 minutes before freezing in zip-top bags for up to several months.

Roasted Broccoli with Lemon and Pecorino

SERVES 4

1½ pounds broccoli

¼ cup plus 2 tablespoons extra-virgin olive oil

1 teaspoon kosher salt

2 tablespoons fresh lemon juice, plus more to taste

⅓ cup freshly grated Pecorino Romano

Position a rack in the center of the oven and heat the oven to 450°F.

Tear off any broccoli leaves and trim the bottoms of the stems. Cut the florets just above where they join the large stem, and then cut each floret through its stem (but not the buds) so that each piece is about ¼ inch thick at the stem end. Using a vegetable peeler or paring knife, peel the tough outer skin from the large stem, removing as little flesh as possible. Cut the stem into baton-shaped pieces about ¼ inch wide and 2 inches long.

Put the florets and stem pieces on a rimmed baking sheet, drizzle with the olive oil, sprinkle with the salt, and toss well to combine. Spread the broccoli into an even layer and roast until tender and golden brown, 15 to 20 minutes. Transfer the broccoli to a serving platter and toss with the lemon juice to taste and the grated Pecorino.

Crisp Asian Broccoli

Serves 4

1 tablespoon soy sauce

1 teaspoon rice vinegar

1 teaspoon Asian sesame oil

3 tablespoons peanut or canola oil

1 tablespoon fermented black beans, rinsed, dried, and coarsely chopped (optional)

Pinch of crushed red pepper flakes

¾ pound broccoli crowns, cut into medium florets

¼ red bell pepper, finely diced

2 cloves garlic, smashed and peeled

One 1-inch piece fresh ginger, peeled and quartered

Kosher salt

¼ cup water; more if needed

Combine the soy sauce, vinegar, sesame oil, and 1 tablespoon of the peanut or canola oil in a small bowl; set aside.

Turn on the exhaust fan and heat a heavy 12-inch skillet or large wok over high heat for 2 minutes. When the pan is hot, pour in the remaining 2 tablespoons peanut or canola oil; a couple of seconds later, add the black beans (if using), the red pepper flakes, broccoli, red pepper, garlic, and ginger. Season the mixture well with salt and cook, tossing or stirring often, until the broccoli deepens to a dark green and browns in places, 3 to 4 minutes. Reduce the heat to medium low, carefully add the water (it will steam), and cover the pan with the lid ajar. Cook until the broccoli softens but still has some crunch, about 4 minutes. (If the water evaporates before the broccoli is done, add more, 1 tablespoon at a time.)

Stir the soy sauce mixture well and drizzle it over the broccoli, toss well, and serve immediately.

Broccolini with Olives and Capers

SERVES 8

Kosher salt

4 medium bunches broccolini (2 to 2½ pounds)

6 tablespoons extra-virgin olive oil

2 teaspoons minced garlic

2 tablespoons chopped, pitted Kalamata olives

2 tablespoons chopped capers (rinse only if salt-packed)

Freshly ground black pepper

Bring a large pot of salted water to a boil over high heat. Add the broccolini and stir to separate the stems. When the water returns to a boil, adjust the heat to a simmer and cook until crisp-tender, 4 to 5 minutes. Drain well. (The broccolini may be prepared to this point up to 1 day ahead and refrigerated.)

Heat the oil in a large skillet over medium heat. Add the garlic and cook until softened, about 1 minute, taking care not to let it get any color. Add the olives and capers and cook for 1 minute more. Add the broccolini and toss to coat. If the broccolini was cooked ahead, keep tossing until heated through. Season to taste with salt and pepper, and serve.

Campanelle with Broccoli Raab, Sausage, and Olives

SERVES 3 TO 4

Kosher salt

1 pound broccoli raab, thick stems trimmed off, leaves and florets rinsed well

6 ounces dried campanelle pasta (2 cups)

3 tablespoons extra-virgin olive oil

¾ pound sweet Italian sausage (bulk sausage or links removed from casing)

3 cloves garlic, minced

¼ teaspoon crushed red pepper flakes

¾ cup homemade or reduced-sodium chicken broth

½ cup pitted Kalamata olives, quartered

2 teaspoons finely grated lightly packed lemon zest

⅓ cup freshly grated Pecorino Romano

Bring a large pot of well-salted water to a boil over high heat. Have a bowl of ice water ready. Add the broccoli raab and cook until bright green and tender, 2 minutes (the water doesn't have to come back to a full boil once the broccoli raab has been added). With tongs or a slotted spoon, transfer the broccoli raab to the bowl of ice water to stop the cooking. Drain well and gently squeeze the broccoli raab to remove excess water.

Return the pot of water to a boil, add the pasta, cook according to the package directions, and drain.

While the campanelle cooks, heat the oil in a 12-inch skillet over medium-high heat. Add the sausage and cook, stirring and breaking it into smaller pieces with a wooden spoon until it's browned and almost cooked through, 4 to 6 minutes. Add the garlic and red pepper flakes and cook until the garlic is lightly golden, about 1 minute. Pour in the broth and bring to a boil; cook, scraping the pan with a wooden spoon occasionally, until the broth is reduced by about half, 3 to 4 minutes. Add the broccoli raab, olives, and lemon zest, and cook, stirring, until hot, 1 to 2 minutes. Add the pasta and Pecorino to the skillet and toss well. Season to taste with salt and serve immediately.

Other recipe ideas

BROCCOLI BAGNA CAUDA Steam broccoli until just crisp-tender, cool it, and then dip into warm anchovy- and garlic-laced bagna cauda.

PASTA WITH GARLICKY BROCCOLI RAAB Steam broccoli or broccoli raab until just tender, then sauté in olive oil with lots of garlic and some crushed red pepper flakes; chop finely. Boil some pasta and toss with the chopped broccoli mixture, a little pasta water, lemon zest, and lots of Parmesan.

DID YOU KNOW? Broccoli stems can be the best part (even though some stores sell only the florets at a premium price). They're sweet and crunchy when raw, like a young radish, and pleasantly sweet and mild when cooked. Pare the stems deeply with a knife to remove the tough outer layer, then slice them into sticks or across into medallions.

Brassica oleracea cvs.

Cauliflower

Cauliflower, like broccoli and cabbage, is a member of the healthful cruciferous vegetable family. It has often played the role of the wan "crudité" waiting to be dipped into ranch dressing, but when treated with some respect and creativity, cauliflower rewards with sweet, mellow flavors and a texture that can go from creamy to crunchy, depending on how you cook it.

PICKING THE BEST

Usually white to pale yellow in color, cauliflower is composed of florets in stalks that come together to form a rounded head shape. You can also find cauliflower that's purple or deep golden (sometimes called "cheddar" cauliflower). The exotic lime-green Romanesco has conical, spiral florets that look like seashells. Despite their different appearances, all types of cauliflower have a similar sweet, slightly nutty flavor.

Look for compact heads of this cool-weather-loving vegetable that are firm and not limp and that feel heavy for their size. The leaves should be green and look fresh and crisp. Yellow spots on the florets are fine; they only mean that the vegetable got a little "sunburn"—the cauliflower's leaves didn't fully wrap themselves over the florets during growth. Small brown or grayish spots, which are actually a bit of mold, are okay, too; just cut them away during prep.

KEEPING IT FRESH

Keep cauliflower in the crisper drawer of the refrigerator where it should last at least 3 days and up to 5 days if well wrapped.

PREPARING

Always start by trimming away the leaves and the base of the stem. For whole florets, simply cut the florets away from the central stem with a knife. You can also halve or quarter florets for quicker cooking. Slicing them lengthwise about ¼ inch thick gives you the most surface area for browning and is also a good idea for gratins and for deep-frying.

HOW TO USE IT

At it simplest, cauliflower can be steamed until tender and paired with a bright vinaigrette or cloaked in Cheddar cheese sauce. You can simmer it in a light chicken broth and purée into a creamy soup, to serve cold or hot. Cauliflower has a high water content, so high-heat methods, such as roasting or sautéing, are best at concentrating the flavors, bringing out the intensely sweet and nutty character.

PRESERVING OPTIONS

Cauliflower takes well to pickling and is an important part of Italian giardiniera.

White

Purple

Romanesco

Cauliflower Soup with Marcona Almond and Piquillo Pepper Relish

SERVES 8

1 teaspoon kosher salt, plus more to taste

1¾ pounds (6 to 7 cups) cauliflower florets (from 1 medium head)

2 ounces (4 tablespoons) unsalted butter

¼ cup Marcona or regular almonds (roasted and salted), finely chopped

¼ cup jarred piquillo peppers or roasted red peppers, rinsed, seeded, and finely diced

2 tablespoons extra-virgin olive oil

1 tablespoon thinly sliced fresh mint

1 medium clove garlic, minced

½ teaspoon crushed red pepper flakes

Freshly ground black pepper

Bring 6 cups water to a boil in a 4-quart pot over high heat. Add 1 teaspoon salt, then add the cauliflower and boil until very tender, 10 to 12 minutes. Drain the cauliflower in a colander set over a large bowl to catch the cooking liquid and let the cauliflower cool slightly.

Working in two batches, purée each batch of cauliflower with 2 cups of the cooking liquid and 2 tablespoons of the butter in a blender until very smooth. (Be careful to fill the blender no more than one-third full, and hold a towel over the lid while you turn it on.) Season to taste with salt. (The soup can be made up to 4 hours ahead.)

In a small bowl combine the almonds, peppers, oil, mint, garlic, and pepper flakes. Season to taste with salt and pepper. (The relish can be made up to 1 hour ahead.)

When ready to serve, gently reheat the soup over medium-low heat. Garnish each serving with a spoonful of the relish.

Roasted Cauliflower

Cut a small head of cauliflower into florets that are about the same size and toss with 2 tablespoons olive oil, salt, and freshly ground black pepper. Spread on a rimmed baking sheet. Roast in a 400°F oven on the lowest rack, turning every 10 minutes, until golden brown and crisp-tender, 25 to 35 minutes.

Toss basic roasted cauliflower with any of the following:

• fresh lemon juice, minced fresh rosemary, and chopped capers

• orange zest, minced fresh parsley, and sun-dried tomatoes

• pitted and chopped Kalamata olives, crushed red pepper flakes, and bitter greens, such as endive or radicchio, cut into bite-sized pieces; toss with the roasted cauliflower in the pan while still hot

• mustard vinaigrette and minced fresh thyme

Cauliflower with Honey-Lemon Glaze

SERVES 4

¼ cup extra-virgin olive oil

1 medium head cauliflower (1¼ pounds), cored and cut into 1-inch florets (about 7 cups)

½ teaspoon kosher salt

1 medium red onion, finely diced

2 tablespoons honey

1 teaspoon ground coriander

½ teaspoon sweet smoked paprika (pimentón)

¼ teaspoon crushed red pepper flakes

2 tablespoons fresh lemon juice

½ teaspoon finely grated lemon zest

1 tablespoon chopped fresh cilantro, for garnish

Heat 3 tablespoons of the oil in a heavy 12-inch skillet (preferably cast iron) over medium-high heat. Add the cauliflower and the salt and stir to coat. Cook, without stirring, until the cauliflower is browned on one side, about 4 minutes. Turn each piece over and cook, without stirring, until evenly browned on the second side, about 4 minutes more. Reduce the heat to medium and continue cooking, stirring often, until browned all over, about another 4 minutes.

Meanwhile, in a small bowl, stir 2 tablespoons water and the remaining 1 tablespoon oil with the onion, honey, coriander, paprika, and red pepper flakes.

Add the onion mixture to the skillet and cook, stirring occasionally, until the onion is softened, about 1 minute. Continue cooking, stirring constantly, until most of the liquid has evaporated and the cauliflower is glazed, about 4 minutes. Transfer to a serving bowl, stir in the lemon juice and zest, and garnish with the cilantro. Serve immediately.

Cauliflower with Brown Butter, Pears, Sage, and Hazelnuts

SERVES 8 TO 10

3 ounces (6 tablespoons) unsalted butter

1 medium head cauliflower, cut into small florets about ¾ inch wide

½ cup toasted, skinned, and chopped hazelnuts (see p. 300)

8 fresh sage leaves, thinly sliced crosswise

1 teaspoon kosher salt, plus more to taste

½ teaspoon freshly ground black pepper

2 large ripe pears, cored and thinly sliced

2 tablespoons chopped fresh flat-leaf parsley

In a 12-inch skillet over medium-high heat, melt the butter until light brown and bubbly. Add the cauliflower, hazelnuts, and sage. Cook for 2 minutes, stirring occasionally. Season with the salt and pepper and continue cooking, stirring occasionally, until the cauliflower is browned and crisp-tender, another 6 to 7 minutes.

Remove the pan from the heat. Add the pear slices and parsley. Gently toss to combine and warm the pears. Season to taste with more salt. Serve hot or at room temperature.

Other recipe ideas

PENNE WITH CAULIFLOWER Make a pasta sauce from leftover cauliflower. Toss cooked penne with chopped cooked cauliflower and minced garlic, crushed red pepper flakes, and mashed anchovy fillets that have been sautéed in olive oil. Season with salt and freshly ground black pepper, and then stir in a bit of pasta cooking water to get the consistency right.

PURÉED CAULIFLOWER WITH NUTMEG Serve puréed cauliflower instead of mashed potatoes. Boil or steam cauliflower and then purée in a blender or food processor. Add cream or butter and season with salt, freshly ground black pepper, and nutmeg.

BAKED CAULIFLOWER AND CHEESE Substitute cauliflower for macaroni. Steam a head of cauliflower, broken into florets, until just tender; drain well. Arrange in a baking dish, cover with Cheddar cheese sauce, top with fresh rye breadcrumbs tossed in butter, and bake until bubbling and browned.

DID YOU KNOW? Preserve the snow-white appearance of a head of cauliflower as it grows by protecting it from light. When the head reaches the size of a small fist, gather the leaves of the plant up and around the head and secure in place with a soft cord, rubber band, or strips of nylon stockings.

Sour

Bing

Prunus avium cvs. (sweet), Prunus cerasus cvs. (sour)

Cherries

Cherries possess a depth of flavor that sets them apart from so many other sweet-tart fruits. Their taut skin and dense flesh delivers big complex taste, and their colors, of course, are seductive, ranging from ivory with a blush of coral to almost mahogany. And they really are a fleeting pleasure—cherries are one of the few fruits that are still truly seasonal, with a short window of availability in midsummer, usually mid-June through mid-August. We often get a crop of cherries in December, coming from the southern hemisphere, but the quality is rarely as good as the local crops.

PICKING THE BEST

Look for cherries with taut, shiny skin and rich color; ideally, the stems will still be green and flexible. Farmer's markets will feature lots of regional varieties, but most fall into the following categories.

- **Bing:** The most widely available cherry, Bings are large, deep crimson, and plump with almost a snap to the flesh.
- **Rainier and Queen Anne:** Two similar varieties with a yellow and pink blush, these have slightly softer flesh and more delicate flavor.
- **Sour cherries:** A harder-to-find treat, sour cherries are mostly grown for processing rather than sold fresh. Montmorency is the most common sour variety. They're smaller than a Bing, are fire-engine red, and have tart, juicy flesh that is perfect for pies, jams, and other desserts.

KEEPING IT FRESH

Keep cherries in the refrigerator uncovered for up to 5 days, taking them out about an hour before serving for the best flavor. Sour cherries are extremely fragile and prone to bruising, so use them as soon as you can.

PREPARING

To eat out of hand, simply rinse and pull off the stem; be sure to have a bowl for the pits handy. For cooking, remove the pits with a cherry pitter or other gadget— you can poke the looped end of a bobby pin in the stem end and pull the pit out, or push the pit out with a metal pastry tip fitted on the end of your finger.

HOW TO USE IT

Cherries are mostly enjoyed raw, but when cooked, their flavor deepens and the flesh softens and becomes even juicier. They make an excellent compote or chutney, and sour cherries are delicious in pies and tarts.

SURPRISING PAIRINGS

Cherries' deep flavor makes a stunning counterpoint to rich meats such as lamb, pork, duck, and foie gras.

PRESERVING OPTIONS

Cook cherries into jams, jellies, chutneys, or pickles, or put them in a jar with a flavorful alcohol like brandy. If your aim is to keep them as close to their natural state as possible, just freeze them on a cookie sheet until hard, then pack in freezer bags.

······································ RECIPES ··

Cherry, Mango, Kiwi, and Mint Salad

SERVES 6

1 pound fresh sweet cherries, rinsed and pitted

2 large, ripe mangos, cut into 3/4- to 1-inch chunks

2 kiwis, peeled, each cut into 8 lengthwise wedges, and wedges cut in half crosswise

12 large mint leaves, cut in a chiffonade (stacked, rolled, and thinly sliced crosswise)

1/2 cup dessert wine, such as Muscat de Beaumes de Venise

2 tablespoons light brown sugar

1 teaspoon grated orange zest

Pinch of salt

Toss all the ingredients together and refrigerate for at least 2 hours and for as long as 6 hours.

Fresh Cherry Clafoutis

SERVES 6 TO 8

Softened unsalted butter, for the pan

1 cup milk

1/4 cup heavy cream

1/4 cup granulated sugar

3 large eggs

1 tablespoon pure vanilla extract

Pinch of salt

2/3 cup unbleached all-purpose flour, sifted

4 cups pitted fresh cherries (use a sour cherry like Montmorency if possible, but Bing is delicious too)

Confectioners' sugar, for sprinkling

Heat the oven to 350°F. Butter a shallow baking dish (such as a 10-inch quiche mold or pie plate). Combine the milk, cream, sugar, eggs, vanilla extract, salt, and flour in a mixing bowl and beat with an electric mixer on medium speed until frothy, about 5 minutes.

Pour enough batter into the prepared baking dish to make about a 1/4-inch layer; reserve the rest. Bake the thin layer just until it forms a skin, about 5 minutes. Remove the dish and arrange the cherries in a single layer over the surface. Pour the remaining batter over them. Return the clafoutis to the oven and bake until it's puffed and brown and a knife inserted in the center comes out clean, about

35 minutes. Let cool slightly or to room temperature, as you like, and sprinkle with confectioners' sugar before serving.

Poached Cherries

MAKES 2½ CUPS

2/3 cup sugar

3 strips lemon zest, 1x3 inches each

3 strips orange zest, 1x3 inches each

1/4 vanilla bean, split but not scraped

15 peppercorns

1 pound fresh sweet cherries, rinsed and pitted

In a saucepan, bring 1 3/4 cups water, the sugar, citrus zest, vanilla bean, and peppercorns to a boil, stirring to dissolve the sugar. Add the cherries and simmer until they're soft but not falling apart, about 10 minutes. Skim any foam from the surface. Let cool and then refrigerate. Strain the poaching liquid before serving.

Cherry Mousse

SERVES 6

1 pound fresh sweet cherries, rinsed

3 tablespoons confectioners' sugar

2 cups heavy or whipping cream, preferably not ultra-pasteurized

Set aside 6 whole cherries (with stems if they're still attached) and pit the rest. Combine the pitted cherries and 1 tablespoon of the confectioners' sugar in a food processor and purée; they will be slightly chunky.

Whip the cream with the remaining 2 tablespoons confectioners' sugar until medium peaks form. Fold in the cherry purée and portion the mousse into six parfait or serving glasses. Top with the reserved cherries and serve.

Cherry Custard Tart with Sliced Almonds

SERVES 8; MAKES ENOUGH DOUGH FOR TWO 9½-INCH TARTS

FOR THE TART DOUGH

6 ounces (12 tablespoons) unsalted butter, at room
    temperature

4½ ounces (1 cup) confectioners' sugar

1¾ ounces almonds, finely ground in a food
    processor to yield just under ½ cup

1 large egg, at room temperature

½ teaspoon pure vanilla extract

9 ounces (2 cups) unbleached all-purpose flour

¼ teaspoon salt

FOR THE CHERRY CUSTARD FILLING

1 pound fresh sweet cherries, rinsed and pitted

⅔ cup heavy or whipping cream

⅓ cup sugar

2 large eggs

⅓ cup sliced almonds, toasted

Make the dough: Beat the butter and confectioners'
sugar in a heavy-duty mixer with the paddle
attachment until mixed together. Add the ground
almonds, egg, and vanilla, and then the flour and
salt. Mix until just combined. Transfer the dough to
a lightly floured surface, shape into two disks, and
wrap both in plastic. Refrigerate one disk for at least
1 hour and up to 3 days; freeze the other for future use.

Assemble and bake the tart: Position a rack in
the center of the oven and heat the oven to 400°F.
Remove the dough from the refrigerator. On a lightly
floured work surface, roll it into a round ⅛ inch thick.
(If the dough crumbles, it's too cold; gather it into a
ball, knead a few turns, and roll again.)

Transfer the dough by rolling it onto the rolling pin
and then unrolling it over a 9- or 9½-inch fluted tart
pan that's 1 inch deep and has a removable bottom.
Gently ease the dough into the bottom and up the
sides of the pan. To remove excess dough, run the
rolling pin over the top of the edges. Put the pan on a
baking sheet, line the dough with parchment, and fill
it with pie weights, dried beans, or rice. Bake until the
sides are set, 10 to 15 minutes. Carefully remove the
weights and parchment, return the shell to the oven,
and bake until the bottom is set and the crust is light
brown, another 7 minutes.

Spread the cherries in the bottom of the tart crust
in one layer (you can do this while the tart is still

hot). Whisk together the cream, sugar, and eggs and
carefully pour the mixture over the cherries until
the custard comes just to the top of the pan; you
may have a tablespoon or so of custard remaining.
Sprinkle the almonds on top. Return the tart to the
oven and bake until the top is brown and the cherries
are bubbling, about 40 minutes. Let the tart cool
until you can remove it from the pan.

Other recipe ideas

**DUCK BREASTS WITH CHERRY-ROSEMARY PAN
SAUCE** Sauté duck breasts and make a pan sauce
by deglazing with some balsamic vinegar, then
simmering some chicken broth, chopped fresh
cherries, and a sprig of rosemary.

SPICED CHERRY COMPOTE Make a cherry compote
by simmering pitted sweet and tart cherries with
some sugar, a little water, half a vanilla bean, a
cinnamon stick, and half a star anise. Serve over ice
cream or pound cake.

FRESH CHERRY FOCACCIA Press whole pitted
cherries into the dough when making focaccia;
sprinkle the top of the bread with coarse sugar
before baking.

DID YOU KNOW? Cherries can make a real mess! Ripe
cherries are juicy, and the juice stains,
so you'll want to avoid spattering
when pitting them. Try using the
cherry pitter inside of a plastic bag—
your hands will still be pink, but the
rest of your kitchen won't.

Cucumis sativus cvs.

Cucumbers

Cool and refreshing, mild-mannered cucumbers are great supporting players. They add crunch and moisture to salads and sandwiches without imposing a strong flavor. And they're good vehicles—firm, mild, and just the right size to be used as a chip or cracker.

English

Garden

Pickling, or gherkin

PICKING THE BEST

Firmness is your best clue to freshness. Avoid any that are limp, shriveled, or have soft spots. Slender specimens are younger, so they'll likely have undeveloped or fewer seeds.

- **Slicers:** The most common variety, slicers are about 8 inches long with smooth to slightly knobby dark-green skin. They're often waxed to extend their shelf life, so scrub well or peel before using.
- **English:** Also known as greenhouse, European, or seedless, these cukes are longer, very slender, and usually sold in plastic sleeves. They are ideal for slicing into salads and garnishing appetizers.

- **Kerby:** In high summer, these short, bumpy cukes hit local markets. Their firm texture and small seeds make them perfect for pickling, but you can use them raw as well.
- **Asian:** Since they're small, super-crisp, and sweet, Asian cukes are great for snacking out of hand.
- **Lemon cucumbers:** Yellow and roly-poly, these sweet and fragrant cukes look almost like tiny melons. They are delicious with just a bit of salt and olive oil.

KEEPING IT FRESH

Store cucumbers in the crisper drawer, loose or in an open plastic bag, and use within 3 or 4 days.

PREPARING

If the seeds are tiny, you can leave them unless their moisture might dilute your dish. Mature seeds can be intrusive. To remove, halve the cucumber lengthwise and scoop out seeds with a spoon or a melon baller.

Most cucumbers have thick, tough skins, so peel them if cutting them into big chunks. If slicing thinly, leave skins on and enjoy the contrast in color. Some cukes, such as the English variety, have naturally tender skins that don't need peeling. Cucumbers will release water when tossed in sauce. To reduce this, put them in a colander, toss with salt, let sit for 30 minutes, and then rinse, drain, and squeeze.

HOW TO USE IT

Cucumbers are best raw. Use them in a salad, fruity salsas, or creamy raita. Though not common, cucumbers can be baked or sautéed for a mild side dish.

PRESERVING OPTIONS

Cucumbers come into their glory when pickled, either fermented, such as you'd find at a Jewish deli, or quick pickled preserved in vinegar. Make them tangy and dilly or sweet and sour, or Asian style with hot chiles and fish sauce.

Cucumber-Tomato Salad

SERVES 6

2 cucumbers, peeled, halved lengthwise, and seeded

2 ripe red tomatoes, cored

1 shallot, thinly sliced

2 tablespoons good-quality extra-virgin olive oil

2 teaspoons red-wine vinegar

1 tablespoon chopped fresh mint, plus more to taste

1 tablespoon chopped fresh cilantro, plus more to taste

1 tablespoon chopped fresh flat-leaf parsley, plus more to taste

Coarse salt and freshly ground black pepper

Cut the cucumbers in half again lengthwise and then slice them crosswise 1/8 inch thick. Chop the tomatoes into bite-sized pieces. Put the cucumber, tomato, shallot, olive oil, vinegar, mint, cilantro, and parsley in a bowl and toss briefly. Adjust the seasonings and serve.

Greek Salad Skewers

SERVES 4 TO 6

1/4 English cucumber

1/4 teaspoon kosher salt

1/4 teaspoon freshly ground black pepper; more as needed

4 ounces feta cheese, cut into 16 small cubes

8 pitted Kalamata olives, halved

8 ripe grape or cherry tomatoes, halved

2 tablespoons extra-virgin olive oil

Cut four 1/2-inch-thick diagonal slices from the cucumber and then quarter each slice. Set the cucumber pieces on a large serving platter and season with the salt and pepper. Top each with a piece of feta and then an olive half. Stab a toothpick through a tomato half and then thread through one of the cucumber stacks, pushing the toothpick down to secure it. Drizzle with the olive oil, sprinkle with some black pepper, and serve.

Cucumber-Yogurt Soup with Avocado

SERVES 4

1 large sweet white onion, quartered

1 pound cucumbers, peeled, seeded, and cut into big chunks

1 medium ripe avocado

1 1/2 cups plain yogurt (preferably whole milk)

3 tablespoons extra-virgin olive oil

1 to 2 cloves garlic, minced

3/4 teaspoon ground cumin (preferably toasted and freshly ground)

1 teaspoon kosher salt, plus more to taste

1/3 cup loosely packed fresh basil leaves

2 tablespoons fresh mint leaves

2 to 3 tablespoons fresh lemon juice, plus more to taste

Freshly ground black pepper

Put the onion in a food processor; pulse to chop finely. Scoop into a sieve, rinse under cold water, and set aside to drain. Put the cucumber in the food processor; pulse to chop finely. Add the drained onion and pulse to combine. Set aside 3/4 cup of the cucumber-onion mix. Cut the avocado in half and remove the pit. Scoop out the flesh and drop it into the food processor with the remaining cucumber-onion mixture. Add the yogurt, olive oil, garlic, cumin, and salt. Purée until fairly smooth. Using a sharp knife, slice the basil and mint leaves into shreds and stir into the soup along with the lemon juice, 1 cup cold water, and the reserved cucumber-onion mixture. Season to taste with salt and pepper. Cover and chill for several hours. Before serving, check for consistency, adding more water to thin the soup if necessary. Add more lemon juice and salt if needed and serve.

Other recipe ideas

CUCUMBER SALSA Toss diced cucumbers with diced avocado, finely diced onion, lime juice, cilantro, and a pinch each of cumin, salt, and pepper.

COUSCOUS WITH CUCUMBER AND FETA Toss cooked couscous or orzo with diced cucumber, diced feta, torn mint leaves, lemon juice, and olive oil.

Glycine max

Edamame

You've probably been introduced to edamame at a Japanese restaurant, where they're served as a nutty, salty appetizer. But edamame, also called green or fresh soybeans, can be used the way you might use any other fresh bean or even a fava bean—the beautiful color makes them a great addition to salads and side dishes, and edamame are an excellent source of balanced protein, too.

PICKING THE BEST

Fresh edamame are mostly only available at specialty stores or farmer's markets. Try to buy them still attached to the plant, and only buy edamame that are all green; yellowing pods mean beans will be too old. It's more common to find frozen edamame, either shelled or still in the pod. Some markets also carry fully cooked shelled edamame in the produce section.

KEEPING IT FRESH

Keep fresh edamame well wrapped in the crisper drawer for up to a week. Once cooked, they'll be good in the fridge for another 2 to 3 days.

PREPARING

To cook fresh edamame, just boil them in generously salted water until tender, about 5 minutes. Drain well, then dust with sea salt. Frozen edamame are usually parcooked and require just a quick warm-up to be ready to eat. To prepare edamame for snacking out of hand, cook the frozen pods in boiling water until hot or in a dry skillet over high heat until thawed and slightly charred. Sprinkle the pods with kosher or sea salt.

HOW TO USE IT

Edamame are mostly eaten warm or room temperature as an out-of-hand snack, but you can also treat them as you would fava beans—purée them for a dip or spread similar to hummus, sauté them in olive oil and season with herbs, or toss them into a soup or stew during the final minutes of cooking.

DID YOU KNOW?

Edamame are a great source of high-quality protein, with an amino acid balance approaching that of meat—important to vegetarians seeking a balanced diet. A half-cup serving of edamame contains 11 grams of protein.

RECIPES

Red Country-Style Curry with Beef, Shiitakes, and Edamame

SERVES 4

1 pound flank steak

5 ounces fresh shiitake mushrooms

2 tablespoons vegetable oil

3 tablespoons red curry paste

2¾ cups reduced-sodium chicken broth

5 wild lime leaves, torn or cut into quarters (optional)

1½ cups frozen shelled edamame, thawed

3 tablespoons fish sauce

1 tablespoon palm sugar or light brown sugar

¼ teaspoon kosher salt, plus more to taste

Handful of fresh Thai or Italian basil leaves

Hot cooked rice or rice noodles, for serving

1 long, slender fresh red chile (such as red jalapeño or serrano), thinly sliced on the diagonal (optional)

Slice the beef across the grain ¼ inch thick and then cut the slices into 1½- to 2-inch-long pieces.

Trim and discard the stems from the shiitakes; slice the caps ¼ inch thick (you should have 1½ to 2 cups).

Heat the oil in a 2- to 3-quart saucepan over medium heat until a bit of curry paste just sizzles when added to the pan. Add all the curry paste and cook, pressing and stirring with a wooden spoon or heatproof spatula to soften the paste and mix it in with the oil, until fragrant, about 2 minutes.

Increase the heat to medium high and add the beef. Spread in an even layer and cook undisturbed until it just begins to lose its pink color, about 1 minute. Turn the beef and continue cooking, stirring occasionally to coat it with the curry paste, until most of the beef no longer looks raw, 1 to 2 minutes.

Stir the shiitakes into the beef. Add the chicken broth and stir again. Add half the lime leaves (if using) and bring to a simmer. Simmer gently, stirring occasionally, until the shiitakes are tender and the beef is cooked through, about 5 minutes.

Add the edamame, stir well, and cook for a minute, just to blanch them. Add the fish sauce, sugar, and salt, stirring to combine. Remove from the heat. Tear the basil leaves in half (or quarters if large), and stir them into the curry, along with the remaining lime leaves (if using). Let rest for 5 minutes so the flavors

can develop. Season to taste with salt. Serve with rice or noodles, garnished with the chile slices (if using).

Toasted Corn, Cherry Tomato, and Edamame Salad

SERVES 4 TO 6

1 cup frozen shelled edamame

5 tablespoons extra-virgin olive oil

2¼ cups fresh corn kernels (from about 3 medium ears)

2 tablespoons plain low-fat yogurt

2 tablespoons fresh lemon juice

1 teaspoon clover honey

½ teaspoon minced garlic

¼ teaspoon kosher salt, plus more to taste

Freshly ground black pepper

1 heaping cup quartered cherry tomatoes (about 15)

¼ cup very thinly sliced fresh mint

¼ cup very thinly sliced fresh basil

Cook the edamame according to package directions. Drain and set aside to cool completely.

Heat 1 tablespoon of the oil in a large skillet over medium heat. Add the corn and cook, stirring occasionally, until the kernels are golden brown in patches, about 9 minutes. Transfer to a bowl to cool.

In a small bowl or liquid measuring cup, whisk the yogurt, lemon juice, honey, garlic, and salt. Slowly pour in the remaining 4 tablespoons oil, whisking constantly until blended. Season to taste with salt and pepper.

In a medium bowl, combine the cooled edamame and corn, tomatoes, and herbs. Gently toss. Add half of the vinaigrette and toss. Add more vinaigrette and salt and pepper to taste. Serve at room temperature.

Other recipe ideas

GARLICKY EDAMAME Toss cooked edamame with oil, garlic, and parsley and serve as a side dish.

VEGETABLE STIR-FRY Stir-fry strips of red and yellow bell pepper, sliced red onion, fresh corn kernels, and edamame for a colorful and nutritious stir-fry.

Foeniculum vulgare and cvs.

Fennel

Many cooks are bewildered by fennel, with its "bagpipe" stalks and frilly green fronds. But once you learn to focus on the bulb, using the tops for flavoring other dishes, you will reap a crisp reward with a pleasantly sweet anise or licorice-like flavor. And fennel has two distinct personalities: fresh and crunchy raw, or sweet and silky cooked.

PICKING THE BEST

Choose clean, firm bulbs with no sign of browning. Any attached fronds should look fresh and bright green in color.

KEEPING IT FRESH

You can refrigerate fennel tightly wrapped in a plastic bag for up to 5 days. It's easier to fit it in the fridge if you cut off the stalks first; just wrap the bulb and stalks separately. Fennel will dry a bit after cutting, so if slicing it ahead, keep the slices wrapped in damp paper towels.

PREPARING

Fennel can seem unwieldy to work with at first, but once you cut off the stalks (slice them close to the bulb), you'll find you have a more manageable vegetable. Peel the stringy fibers off the outer layer of the bulb with a peeler or sharp paring knife. Then cut the bulb into wedges and braise or roast them, or cut it into slices for sautéing or tossing with pasta. The core is edible, but it can be a bit tough. It's best to remove most or all of it when eating fennel raw; when cooked, the core will become soft. For more cutting instructions, see p. 299.

Add fennel stalks to a vegetable broth—they add quite a bit of anise flavor. The stalks also freeze well in plastic bags. Use the mildly anise-flavored fronds as you would a fresh herb.

HOW TO USE IT

Fennel lends itself to almost any cooking method. The fronds can be minced and added to soups and stews as you would an herb. The stalks make a great bed for roasting fish. The bulbs are delicious when roasted at high temperatures or slowly sautéed in a bit of olive oil. Braising yields luxuriously creamy fennel. No matter what cooking method you use, fennel that's thoroughly cooked (be sure to use plenty of moisture or fat) becomes almost creamy, losing the crunch it has when raw but gaining sweetness. Even the core becomes tender and mild, so don't remove it when cooking fennel; it helps hold the wedges together.

PRESERVING OPTIONS

You can freeze fennel, but only if you plan to use it in cooked dishes, as the texture will be soft when thawed. Cut into thick slices or chunks, blanch for 3 minutes, drain, and chill, then pack into airtight freezer bags.

Braised Fennel with Tomato, Green Olives, and Capers

SERVES 4

1 large bulb fennel, trimmed (¾ to 1 pound after trimming)

8 large green Sicilian or Cerignola olives

¼ cup extra-virgin olive oil

1 large yellow onion, thinly sliced

1½ teaspoons kosher salt

1½ cups peeled, seeded, and diced fresh tomato (2 or 3 small tomatoes), or a 28-ounce can whole tomatoes (preferably San Marzano), drained, seeded, and diced

3 tablespoons capers, drained and rinsed

1½ tablespoons chopped fresh flat-leaf parsley

Cut the fennel bulb in half lengthwise and then cut each half lengthwise into four 1½-inch-thick wedges. Trim a little of the core but leave enough to hold the layers together.

With a paring knife, slice the olive flesh off the pits lengthwise.

In a 12-inch skillet, heat the olive oil over medium-high heat. Add the fennel, one cut side down, and reduce the heat to medium. Cook, turning once with tongs, until the wedges are lightly browned on both cut sides, 2 to 3 minutes per side. Add the onion and salt. Cook, stirring occasionally and gently so as not to break up the fennel wedges, until the onion is slightly softened and browned, about 5 minutes.

Add the tomatoes, capers, and olives to the pan along with 1 cup water. Bring to a simmer, cover, and reduce the heat to medium low or low, to maintain a steady simmer. Cook until the fennel wedges are fork-tender, 20 to 25 minutes. Uncover, raise the heat to high, and simmer briskly until most of the liquid evaporates, leaving a thick sauce, 3 to 5 minutes. Gently stir in the parsley. Let rest for 15 minutes before serving.

Arugula and Fennel Salad with Orange and Fennel Seed Dressing and Toasted Hazelnuts

SERVES 4

½ teaspoon fennel seeds

¼ cup fresh orange juice

1 tablespoon fresh lemon juice

1 tablespoon minced shallot

2 teaspoons finely grated orange zest

Scant ¼ teaspoon minced garlic

¼ teaspoon Dijon mustard

1½ tablespoons extra-virgin olive oil

1½ tablespoons hazelnut oil

Kosher salt and freshly ground black pepper

1 small bulb fennel

5 ounces arugula, trimmed, washed, and dried (about 5 cups)

¼ cup hazelnuts, toasted and coarsely chopped

Toast the fennel seeds in a small dry skillet over medium heat for about 2 minutes. Transfer to a cutting board and let cool. Chop them coarsely.

Combine the orange juice, lemon juice, shallot, orange zest, and garlic in a small bowl. Let sit for 20 minutes and then stir in the fennel seeds and Dijon mustard. Whisk in the olive oil and hazelnut oil and season to taste with salt and pepper.

Cut off the top and bottom of the fennel bulb. Cut it in half lengthwise. Lay one half flat on its cut surface and slice crosswise as thinly as possible. Stop slicing when you hit the core (a little core is all right, but you don't want wide areas of core in your slices). Repeat with the second half. You should have about 1½ cups sliced fennel.

Put the fennel in a large bowl with the arugula and toasted hazelnuts. Toss with enough dressing to lightly coat the leaves (you may not need all of the dressing). Season with salt and pepper and serve.

Other recipe ideas

SAFFRON-FENNEL SEAFOOD SOUP Make a savory tomato and fennel broth, then poach chunks of halibut and shrimp in it; garnish with a saffron-scented red pepper mayonnaise.

Rosemary

Oregano

Spearmint

Sage

Purple basil

Lemon
thyme

Basil

Italian parsley

Tarragon

Herbs

From the piny accent of rosemary in a long-simmered braise to the bright top notes of fresh chives sprinkled on potato salad, herbs lift the flavor and appeal of everything from soup to dessert. The world of herbs is vast, and each variety brings a distinct character to your dish. And herbs are easy to grow, so you can always have a pot in a sunny window for an instant accent to whatever you're cooking.

PICKING THE BEST

Herbs are generally sold in bunches or in plastic containers. Look for herbs that are bright, crisp, and aromatic, and avoid those that are wilted or yellowing. Give them a sniff—there should be no moldy odor. If you're buying a bunch that's been spritzed by the grocery store produce mister, be sure to shake off excess water before you put it in your bag.

KEEPING IT FRESH

A little time spent when you get home from the store can add days to the life span of your herbs. First, take the herbs out of the plastic and shake off any excess water. Remove wire twists or rubber bands and pull off wilted or slimy leaves. Dampen a length of paper towel, wring it out well, and loosely wrap up the herbs. Put the wrapped herbs in a plastic bag, press out any air, and close tightly, or put the wrapped herbs in a plastic food storage box. Change the paper towels every few days. Try to store herbs in a warmer part of the fridge, as very cold temperatures can blacken them. Most fresh herbs will last up to a week, with the exception of chervil, which will last only a few days. Bay, thyme, and rosemary can last 10 days or more.

Roots draw off moisture from the leaves, so if your herbs still have roots attached (you often see cilantro this way) cut off the roots and lower stems to prevent the top leaves from wilting. If the roots are large, save them to use in stocks and soups; they freeze well.

PREPARING

When ready to use, fill a bowl with cool water and gently swish the herbs to rinse off any grit. Lift them out and dry thoroughly in a salad spinner or blot gently between dishtowels. Rosemary and thyme usually just need a quick wipe rather than an actual washing. Wash, dry, and chop herbs just before use; they'll stay fresher and more potent that way. And always use a sharp chef's knife so you don't bruise the leaves as you chop.

HOW TO USE IT

The amount of herbs to use depends on quality and your own taste, but don't be shy about quantities, especially when infusing whole sprigs in a stew or soup. You don't want an herb to overwhelm a dish, but you do want it to add to its character. Taste often and adjust amounts as you cook.

Botany aside, in the kitchen, herbs can be grouped into two categories: hardy, which are tougher with assertive and often resinous flavors, and tender, which are generally lighter and have more delicate leaves. Hardy herbs include bay, marjoram, oregano, sage, savory, rosemary, and thyme. Tender herbs include basil, chervil, chives, cilantro, dill, mint, parsley, and tarragon.

As a rule, the hardy herbs are best when they have time to cook. Add whole fresh sprigs of herbs, such as rosemary and thyme, early in cooking for soups, stews, and braises to add a bass note of herbal flavor; remove them before serving. For easy retrieval, tie the sprigs with kitchen twine and tie the end of the twine to the pot handle.

Most tender herbs should be added toward the end of cooking, and very delicate herbs, such as cilantro and chervil, are better added off the heat so their flavors don't dissipate. The stems of cilantro and parsley, however, release wonderful flavors during simmering in a stock, sauce, or stew. When you don't have the fresh herbs called for in a recipe, use basil, parsley, or thyme. These versatile herbs complement a wide range of foods.

SURPRISING PAIRINGS

While herbs are most often paired with savory food, a few are wonderful with sweets. Pair basil with stone fruits, such as peaches, or berries, especially strawberries. Rosemary is a nice accent to lemon or grapefruit desserts; it's even delicious with chocolate.

PRESERVING OPTIONS

Bay, marjoram, mint, oregano, rosemary, sage, and thyme retain much of their aromatic quality when dried. You can dry your own store-bought or garden-grown herbs in a dry, well-ventilated space away from direct sunlight or a heat source. The best method is to dry the leaves on a screen, but herb bundles can also be wrapped in a paper bag and hung until brittle in a warm, airy place. This will take 3 to 5 days (or longer), depending on the weather. Stem the dried leaves and store them, in covered glass jars, for up to 1 year.

More tender herbs, including basil, chives, cilantro, dill, parsley, and tarragon, are best preserved by freezing. Some, like basil, will turn black, and all will lose their texture, but frozen herbs keep their fresh flavor for using in cooked dishes. They will last for up to 6 months when frozen using any of these three techniques:

- **Whole herbs:** Pack sprigs of clean, dry herbs in airtight containers or food storage bags and freeze.
- **Chopped herbs:** Roughly chop the herbs, pack them into ice-cube trays, fill the trays with water, and freeze.
- **Herb purée:** Purée herbs in a blender or food processor with just enough vegetable or olive oil to make a thick paste. Freeze in ice-cube trays or in small portions in food storage bags.

RECIPES

Sautéed Chicken Paillards with Herb Salad and White Balsamic Vinaigrette

SERVES 4

1 tablespoon white balsamic vinegar
1½ teaspoons white-wine or cider vinegar
½ small shallot, finely chopped
¼ teaspoon Dijon mustard
1¼ teaspoons kosher salt
¾ teaspoon freshly ground black pepper
3 tablespoons plus 2 teaspoons olive oil; more as needed
8 boneless, skinless, thin-cut (¼- to ½-inch-thick) chicken breast cutlets (1½ to 1¾ pounds)
5 cups mixed baby greens
3 cups mixed fresh, tender herb leaves, such as flat-leaf parsley, mint, chives, tarragon, basil, and chervil, roughly torn if large

In a small bowl, mix both vinegars with the shallot, mustard, and ¼ teaspoon each salt and pepper. Slowly whisk in 3 tablespoons of the oil.

Season the chicken on both sides with 1 teaspoon salt and ½ teaspoon pepper. Heat the remaining 2 teaspoons oil in a 12-inch skillet over medium-high heat until hot. Working in two to three batches to avoid crowding, cook the chicken until lightly browned on both sides and just cooked through, 1 to 3 minutes per side. Transfer each batch to a platter, cover loosely with foil, and keep warm. If the pan seems dry at any point, add another 2 teaspoons oil.

Combine the greens and herbs in a large bowl. Add about three-quarters of the vinaigrette and toss well. To serve, arrange two cutlets on each serving plate and drizzle the remaining dressing over the chicken. Divide the herb salad among the four plates, piling it attractively onto the chicken.

Basil Pesto

MAKES 1½ CUPS

1 tablespoon plus 1 teaspoon kosher salt

3 cups packed basil leaves

¼ cup ice water

1 to 2 cloves garlic, smashed and peeled

½ cup pine nuts

¼ cup grated Parmigiano-Reggiano

1 teaspoon freshly ground black pepper

½ cup extra-virgin olive oil, preferably a fruity one

Bring 2 quarts water seasoned with 1 tablespoon of the salt to a rolling boil. Meanwhile, set up an ice bath by combining ice and water in a medium bowl.

Put the basil in the boiling water, pressing it gently under the water, and cook for just 2 or 3 seconds. Quickly remove the basil from the water (a Chinese strainer works great here) and plunge it immediately into the ice bath to stop the cooking process. Let cool completely for 2 minutes.

Remove the basil from the ice bath and squeeze it lightly with your hands or in a clean dishtowel to remove most of the excess water.

Chop the basil coarsely with a sharp knife and then put it in a blender. Add the ¼ cup ice water, garlic, pine nuts, cheese, the remaining 1 teaspoon salt, and the pepper. Blend until the basil is coarsely puréed, scraping down the sides and adding more water to facilitate blending only if needed. Be patient; don't add more water if it isn't necessary. With the blender running, add the oil in a steady stream until the pesto looks creamy and emulsified. Cover and store in the refrigerator for a few days or in the freezer for up to a few months.

Mustard and Rosemary Roasted Potatoes

SERVES 4 TO 6

⅓ cup plus 1 tablespoon Dijon mustard

¼ cup olive oil

1 tablespoon dry vermouth or other dry white wine

2 cloves garlic, minced

1 tablespoon chopped fresh rosemary

1 teaspoon kosher salt

Freshly ground black pepper

2 pounds red-skinned potatoes, cut into ¾- to 1-inch dice

Heat the oven to 400°F. In a large bowl, whisk the mustard, olive oil, vermouth, garlic, rosemary, salt, and pepper to taste. Add the potatoes and toss to coat. Dump the potatoes onto a large rimmed baking sheet and spread them in a single layer. Roast, tossing with a spatula a few times, until the potatoes are crusty on the outside and tender throughout, 50 to 55 minutes. Serve hot.

Minty Quinoa Tabbouleh

SERVES 6 TO 8

1½ cups quinoa

1½ teaspoons kosher salt, plus more to taste

1½ cups seeded and finely diced tomato (about 1 large tomato)

1 cup finely chopped fresh flat-leaf parsley (about 2 bunches)

1 cup peeled, seeded, finely diced cucumber (about ¾ of a large cucumber)

½ cup thinly sliced scallion greens

½ cup extra-virgin olive oil, plus more to taste

6 tablespoons fresh lemon juice, plus more to taste

¼ teaspoon ground cumin

⅛ teaspoon ground cinnamon

½ cup finely chopped fresh mint

Rinse the quinoa well in a bowl of cool water and drain. Bring the quinoa, ½ teaspoon salt, and 3 cups water to a boil in a medium saucepan over high heat. Cover, reduce the heat to medium low, and simmer until the water is absorbed and the quinoa is translucent and tender, 10 to 15 minutes. (The outer germ rings of the grain will remain chewy and white. Some germ rings may separate from the grains and will look like white squiggles.) Immediately fluff the quinoa with a fork and turn out onto a baking sheet to cool.

When cool, fluff the quinoa again and transfer to a large bowl. Add the tomato, parsley, cucumber, scallion, oil, lemon juice, cumin, cinnamon, and 1 teaspoon salt. Toss well. Cover and refrigerate to let the flavors mingle, at least 2 hours or overnight.

Before serving, let sit at room temperature for 20 to 30 minutes. Stir in the mint. Taste and add more oil and lemon juice (you'll probably need at least 1 tablespoon of each) and more salt as needed.

Beef Tenderloin Medallions with a Rosemary and Thyme Crust

SERVES 4

½ cup loosely packed medium-finely chopped fresh
    flat-leaf parsley

2 tablespoons medium-finely chopped fresh
    rosemary

1½ tablespoons lightly chopped fresh thyme

1½ teaspoons kosher salt

Coarsely ground black pepper

8 beef tenderloin medallions (2¼ pounds total),
    ¾ inch thick

¼ cup olive oil; more as needed

Using your fingers, thoroughly mix the parsley, rosemary, thyme, salt, and several grinds of pepper in a shallow baking dish or pie plate. Gently flatten the medallions between your hands to about ½ inch thick. Coat the medallions with the herb mixture by pressing them gently into the herb mixture on one side, then on the other.

Heat the olive oil in a 12-inch skillet over high heat. When the first wisp of smoke rises from the oil, use tongs to set four medallions in the pan in a single layer. Cook until the herbs on the bottom turn very deep brown, 2 to 3 minutes. Turn the medallions over and cook the other side to the same deep brown, about 2 minutes; this should give you medium-rare medallions. Scrape out any stuck-on bits, add a bit more oil to the pan, let it get hot, and cook the other four medallions. To test for doneness, cut a small slit into a medallion and peek inside; remember that the meat continues to cook as it rests. Transfer the medallions to a warm platter and let them rest in a warm place, such as the back of the stove, for 5 minutes before serving.

Mixed Herb Salad with Honey-Lime Dressing

SERVES 8

FOR THE SALAD

4 cups mixed mesclun greens

2 cups coarsely chopped bibb lettuce

1 cup very thinly sliced green cabbage

1 cup fresh basil leaves, preferably Thai basil, large
    leaves coarsely torn

1 cup fresh mint leaves

1 cup fresh cilantro leaves, coarsely chopped

4 small scallions (white and green parts), sliced into
    1-inch lengths

1 cup cherry or grape tomatoes, halved

½ cup very thinly sliced red onion

½ cup very thinly sliced red bell pepper

FOR THE DRESSING

2½ tablespoons fresh lime juice

2½ tablespoons honey

2 teaspoons fish sauce

⅛ teaspoon minced garlic

2 tablespoons thinly sliced fresh red or green chile or
    both (optional)

Kosher salt and freshly ground black pepper

Make the salad: In a large bowl, combine all the ingredients.

Make the dressing: In a small bowl, whisk the lime juice, honey, fish sauce, garlic, and chile, if using. Season to taste with salt and pepper.

Just before serving, toss the salad with just enough of the dressing to coat it lightly—you may not need all of the dressing.

Roast Rack of Lamb
with Lemon-Mint Salsa Verde

SERVES 8

2 medium lemons

1 cup packed fresh spearmint or grapefruit mint
   leaves (1 ounce)

2 tablespoons chopped garlic

2 teaspoons kosher salt

1 teaspoon freshly ground black pepper

½ cup extra-virgin olive oil

3 frenched racks of lamb (8 ribs, and 1 to
   1½ pounds each)

Finely grate 1 tablespoon zest from the lemons and
then squeeze them to yield 3 tablespoons juice.
Combine the zest and juice with the mint, garlic, salt,
and pepper in a food processor. Pulse a few times and
then with the motor running, add the oil. Reserve
¼ cup of the salsa verde and refrigerate.

Trim the fat on the lamb racks to a ¼-inch-thick
layer. Poke holes all over the lamb with a fork to help
the marinade penetrate. Lightly score the fat layer
about 1/16 inch deep in a ½-inch diamond pattern.
Arrange the racks, fat side up, in a 9x13-inch baking
dish, overlapping the bones if necessary to fit the
racks in the dish. Brush the remaining salsa verde all
over the racks. Cover and refrigerate for at least
8 hours and up to 24 hours.

Heat the oven to 425°F. Take the lamb out of the
fridge and arrange the racks, fat side up, in a large
roasting pan (or rimmed baking sheet)—they should
fit in one layer. Brush the top and sides of each rack
with 1 tablespoon of the reserved salsa verde. Roast
for 15 minutes. Brush with 1 tablespoon more of
the salsa verde and continue to roast to an internal
temperature of 130° to 135°F for medium rare, another
15 to 20 minutes. Let the meat rest for 5 minutes
before carving into chops. Drizzle the remaining salsa
verde over each serving.

Rice Pudding with Bay Leaves

SERVES 4 TO 6

Softened unsalted butter, for the dish

⅓ cup arborio rice

3½ cups milk

1 fresh bay leaf or 2 dried

Pinch of salt

⅓ cup granulated sugar

1 vanilla bean, split, seeds scraped and reserved
   (or 1 teaspoon pure vanilla extract)

½ cup heavy cream

¼ cup golden raisins

¼ cup currants

Heat the oven to 350°F and butter a shallow
1½-quart baking dish. In a medium saucepan,
combine the rice, milk, bay leaf, salt, and sugar.
Bring the milk almost to a boil and then reduce the
heat and cook at a vigorous simmer, stirring from
time to time, until the rice begins to soften but isn't
completely tender to the tooth, 10 to 12 minutes.
Discard the bay leaf.

Combine the vanilla seeds and pod (if using) and
the cream in a small pan. Scald the cream; set aside
to cool. (If you're using vanilla extract, add it now.)
Discard the vanilla bean pod. Add the raisins and
currants to the rice and pour the mixture into the
baking dish.

Bake uncovered until a golden skin forms on the
top, 20 to 25 minutes. The pudding will be a little
soupy the first day and will thicken and improve by
the second and third days.

Other Recipe Ideas with Herbs

Basil

- Make a salsa cruda with diced ripe yellow and red tomato, red onion, fresh or smoked mozzarella, shredded basil leaves, and fruity olive oil to serve over capellini.
- Chop citrus fruits, shallots, and basil leaves for a relish to serve on grilled fish, such as tuna and mahi-mahi.
- Make a basil butter and smear it under the husk before grilling or roasting sweet corn.

Bay leaves

Choose Mediterranean over California bay; remove bay leaves from the dish before serving.

- Add bay leaves to slow-cooked sauces, stocks, seafood poaching liquid, or cream- and cheese-based sauces.
- Thread fresh bay leaves (soak them in cold water to soften) on beef, chicken, or tuna brochettes before grilling.
- Poach pears in red- or white-wine syrup flavored with bay leaves and a strip of orange zest or lemon zest.

Chervil

- Try chervil with its relative, the carrot, in a cream of carrot soup or with sautéed carrots and shallots.
- Make a sauce for red snapper with chopped tomato, shallot, olive oil, and chervil.

Cilantro

- Add chopped cilantro to tomato-, chile-, and fruit-based salsas, to accompany grilled meat, fish, or poultry.
- Make curried chicken salad with apples, celery, and chopped cilantro leaves.
- Stir-fry vegetables and beef and make a sauce with soy sauce, Asian sesame oil, fresh ginger, and cilantro leaves.

Dill

- Make a sauce of mustard, oil, sugar, salt, dill, and a dash of cider vinegar to serve with gravlax or cold shrimp.
- Add chopped dill to mayonnaise-based salads like potato salad, egg salad, or salade russe (cooked vegetables dressed first in vinaigrette, drained, and tossed with dill mayonnaise).

Epazote

- Add to a Mexican bean dish to lend complexity and cut the heaviness with its slight turpentine flavor.

Lemon thyme

- Simmer a generous sprig in a seafood stew with chunks of cod, shrimp, and clams and a touch of saffron.
- Make a marinade for chicken with chopped lemon thyme, shallot, olive oil, and lemon juice.

Lemon verbena

- Make a lemon verbena butter to top broiled shrimp, scallops, or mild-tasting white fish, such as red snapper or halibut.
- Flavor iced tea with lemon verbena and thyme.
- Crush a few leaves of lemon verbena and put them in a steamer basket when you steam chicken or fish for a lightly perfumed dish.

Lovage

- Add chopped lovage to a garlic and white-wine sauce for steamed clams or a shallot and white-wine sauce for mussels.
- Add lovage leaves to tomato sauce to use in a baked eggplant-filled cannelloni.

Marjoram

- Toss steamed green beans with gently heated crème fraîche, lemon zest, and marjoram.
- Use marjoram in mustard sauces or tomato sauces for stewed rabbit dishes or to season chicken or pork sausages.

Mint

- Make a Lebanese salad with toasted pita, chopped tomato, diced cucumber, and chopped mint.
- Add lots of fresh mint—spearmint is nice—to tea generously sweetened with sugar, as the Moroccans do.
- Combine mint (peppermint, if you can find it) with chocolate for a cool note in desserts like mint chocolate chip ice cream, flourless chocolate cake with mint-infused custard sauce (crush the mint leaves and steep in the hot milk before making the custard), or mint-frosted brownies.

Oregano

- Make a vinaigrette of olive oil, red-wine vinegar, lemon juice, and chopped oregano; toss with greens, feta, tomato, Kalamata olives, and egg wedges for a classic Greek salad.
- Cook ground lamb with tomato, red wine, and oregano; top with a creamy custard sauce, and then bake for Greek moussaka.

Parsley

- Make a chicken salad with lemon zest, toasted pine nuts, currants, chopped parsley, and mayonnaise.
- Make gremolata—a mixture of finely chopped flat-leaf parsley, garlic, lemon zest, and orange zest—and serve over braised veal shanks or clams steamed in white wine.
- Make a persillade, a mixture of finely chopped parsley and garlic, and toss with pan-fried potatoes to accompany a grilled steak.

Rosemary

- Brush toasted bread with olive oil and finely chopped rosemary before topping with fresh goat cheese, white bean spread, or eggplant caponata.
- Rub chopped rosemary on aged beef or game birds before grilling or roasting.
- Stuff a chicken with a few rosemary sprigs, a quartered lemon, and a handful of peeled garlic cloves; roast, then squeeze the lemon over the chicken before serving.

Sage

- For a fettuccine sauce, combine and gently heat heavy cream, peas, sage, nutmeg, grated Parmesan, and thin strips of prosciutto.
- Rub a mixture of chopped sage leaves, crushed black peppercorns, olive oil, and sea salt on pork or veal before roasting or grilling.

Summer savory

- Make a gratin of flageolet beans, sautéed onion or shallot, carrots, sprigs of summer savory, and chicken stock. Top with breadcrumbs and more summer savory and bake in a slow oven.

Tarragon

- Make a julienne of carrot salad and dress with tarragon leaves, fresh lemon juice, Dijon mustard, chopped shallot, and a light-tasting olive oil.
- Toss tarragon leaves with fresh sliced white mushrooms, snipped chives, sherry vinegar, and a mild oil such as canola.
- Flavor hollandaise sauce with a reduction of wine vinegar, tarragon, and shallot (basically a béarnaise), and serve with pan-seared steak.

Thyme

- Mash chopped thyme with Roquefort cheese and chopped walnuts and serve with grilled steak.
- Cook sprigs of thyme with French green lentils and use as a bed for sautéed or grilled salmon.

Wild lime leaves

- Add several fresh leaves to white rice at the start of cooking for a perfumed pilaf.
- Infuse into chicken broth along with a few slices of fresh ginger for a Thai-inspired soup base.

Allium porrum cvs.

Leeks

The flavor of a leek is like an onion but more herbaceous, though not like any herb in particular. While onions add a single-edged sweetness, leeks add both sweetness and vegetable flavor. This is why they offer such depth and complexity and why, as a stand-alone vegetable, they're especially interesting and flavorful.

PREPARING

Leeks are grown with soil piled all around them, so dirt and grit settles between their onion-like layers. The easiest way to clean a leek is to trim the root end and the dark green tops and cut it in half lengthwise (or, if you want to retain the appearance of whole leeks in your dish, just cut about two-thirds of the way through the stalk). Hold the leek root end up under cold running water and ruffle the layers as if they were a deck of cards. Do this on both sides a couple of times until all the dirt has been washed out. (See p. 301 for more information on cleaning leeks.)

HOW TO USE IT

Leeks are useful in so many dishes, and they make a great base for stuffings, stews, soups, and sautés. A leek's herbal-sweet flavors and silky texture can take center stage, too. Though garlic, scallions, and onions can be tossed into a dish raw, leeks must always be cooked, and when grilled, they first need a short parcooking. And while some vegetables benefit from al dente cooking, leeks definitely don't. They needn't be cooked to death, but in order to get tender, velvety leeks, you must cook them until they're soft or you'll get a fibrous, indigestible result.

PICKING THE BEST

When buying leeks, look for firm, undamaged stalks and fresh-looking, brightly colored tops. The darker the tops, the older and tougher the leeks. Because the edible parts of leeks are the white and light green portions (the tough, dark green tops are usually cut off and discarded or used to flavor broths), you want leeks with as much white stalk as possible.

SURPRISING PAIRINGS

A garnish of fried leeks can add a wonderful texture and savory flavor to almost anything. Simply slice thin and fry in olive oil until golden and crisp, then use them to top creamy soups, casseroles, and even pasta.

KEEPING IT FRESH

Wrapped in a damp paper towel and stored in a plastic bag in the refrigerator, leeks will last for at least a week.

PRESERVING OPTIONS

Slice the white part of the leek, blanch for 2 to 3 minutes, drain, and chill well. Spread onto a sheet pan and freeze until hard, about 30 minutes, then pack into airtight freezer bags.

Salmon Fillets with Herbed Leeks

SERVES 4

FOR THE FISH

4 salmon fillets (6 ounces each)
Salt and freshly ground black pepper
Extra-virgin olive oil
4 leaves fresh sage
4 sprigs fresh thyme
Grated zest of ½ lemon

FOR THE LEEKS

1 tablespoon unsalted butter
2 tablespoons olive oil
3 large or 4 medium leeks (white and light green
    parts), washed, dried, and diced (to yield 3 cups)
½ teaspoon salt, plus more to taste
4 cloves garlic, minced
1 tablespoon minced fresh sage
1 tablespoon minced fresh thyme
Freshly ground black pepper

Season the fish fillets with salt and pepper. Drizzle them lightly with olive oil, rub them with the sage and thyme, and spread with the lemon zest. Lay a sage leaf and a sprig of thyme on each fillet. Cover with plastic wrap and refrigerate for up to an hour.

Position a rack in the center of the oven and heat the oven to 400°F. In a wide, heavy sauté pan, heat the butter and olive oil until very hot. Add the diced leeks, stir to coat well, and reduce the heat to medium low. Salt them lightly, stir again, and continue to cook slowly until the leeks are soft, about 15 minutes, stirring occasionally and adding a few tablespoons of water if the pan gets too dry or the leeks are browning too much. Add the garlic, minced herbs, salt, and pepper and cook for a few minutes until the garlic is soft and fragrant. Spread the leeks in the bottom of a 2 ½-quart ovenproof baking dish. Lay the fish fillets on top and bake until a paring knife inserted in the fish feels warm when touched to your lip, about 20 minutes. To serve, spoon the herbed leeks over each fillet.

Creamy Baked Leeks with Garlic, Thyme, and Parmigiano

SERVES 8

1 teaspoon unsalted butter, for the dish
½ teaspoon kosher salt, plus more to taste
8 large leeks (ideally with several inches of white)
2 teaspoons lightly chopped fresh thyme
1 cup heavy cream
2 large cloves garlic, smashed and peeled
⅓ cup finely grated Parmigiano-Reggiano

Heat the oven to 350°F. Rub the bottom of a shallow 10x15-inch rectangular baking dish with the butter. Sprinkle ¼ teaspoon salt over the bottom of the pan.

Cut the dark green and all but about 1 inch of the light green parts off the top of the leeks. Peel away any tough or damaged outer leaves. Cut the roots but leave a bit of the base intact to hold the leek together. Cut each leek in half lengthwise. Gently wash under running water, fanning the layers to rinse thoroughly. Pat the leeks dry and then arrange cut side down, in the baking dish. They should fit snugly, but if they are crowded, turn a few on their sides. Sprinkle with the thyme and ¼ teaspoon salt.

Heat the cream and garlic in a small saucepan over high heat. As soon as the cream comes to a rolling boil (watch carefully and don't let it boil over), remove the pan from the heat and let sit for 5 minutes. Pour the cream and garlic evenly over the leeks.

Cover the leeks with a piece of parchment cut to fit inside the pan. Bake until the thickest ends are tender all the way through when pierced with a knife and the cream is almost entirely reduced, about 35 minutes. Sprinkle with the Parmigiano and salt to taste. Bake just until the cheese melts, another 1 to 2 minutes. Transfer the leeks to a warm serving platter.

Other recipe ideas

CREAMY LEEK AND PROSCIUTTO PASTA Toss cooked fettuccine with sautéed leeks, sliced prosciutto, cream, and lemon zest.

ALSATIAN LEEK TART Make a quiche or tart with a filling of sautéed leeks, crumbled bacon, and Gruyère cheese.

Opuntia ficus-indica

Nopales/Prickly Pears

For many of us, the sight of flat green paddles stacked high on market shelves is unexpected, especially if the thorns have not been removed. Like nettles, nopales offer a tiny thrill—eating a dangerous plant! But the true appeal of nopales, which are the leaves of the prickly pear cactus plant, is their fresh flavor: slightly sour and reminiscent of a green bean crossed with asparagus. The crisp-juicy texture is delicious in salads and tacos.

PICKING THE BEST

Select pads that are a rich, even green and are supple, with no shriveling.

KEEPING IT FRESH

Keep nopales tightly wrapped in plastic and refrigerated for up to 2 weeks.

PREPARING

Most nopales will already be scraped to remove the thorns, but if not, use a vegetable peeler or paring knife and very carefully—wear heavy gloves—cut away the thorns. Scrub the pads to remove any nodes (where thorns are developing). Wash the pads well with cool water and cut away any blemished areas. Cut the pads into long slices or leave whole, depending on your recipe.

HOW TO USE IT

Nopales are most often grilled or boiled. Take care not to overcook them, which brings out a slightly slimy texture, much like okra. You can also cut nopales into small strips to toss into a salad, stew, or taco filling. For a change, next time you make salsa verde, add chopped, cooked nopales for a more substantial texture and flavor. Or give them the chiles rellenos treatment and stuff with cheese, dip in batter, and fry.

DID YOU KNOW? The mucilaginous juice of nopales is high in soluble and insoluble fiber, as well as essential amino acids, helping to control blood sugar. Studies are even underway to determine how nopales can be used to treat diabetes. Historically, the indigenous people of the Americas considered nopales medicinal, something that hasn't changed much even today; you can find nopale juice or powder in homeopathic remedies.

Scrambled Eggs and Nopales with Cilantro

SERVES 2

1 tablespoon olive oil

2 tablespoons finely chopped onion

2 teaspoons chopped fresh hot chile, such as jalapeño

3 tablespoons diced nopales

4 eggs, beaten

Kosher salt and freshly ground black pepper

1 tablespoon chopped fresh cilantro

In a heavy pan over medium heat, heat the oil, then add the onion and chile and sauté until soft and fragrant, about 2 minutes. Add the nopales and sauté until heated through, another minute.

Pour in the eggs and scramble. Season with salt and pepper to taste, then fold in the cilantro and serve right away.

Other recipe ideas

MEXICAN SALAD Mix boiled and diced nopales with chunks of tomato, diced onion, and fresh cilantro. Toss with fresh lime juice and olive oil, then pile onto lettuce leaves. Top with crumbled queso fresco or mild feta cheese.

FRIED NOPALE STRIPS Cut nopales into strips, dredge in flour, then dip in egg and roll in breadcrumbs, cornmeal, or flour. Fry until the coating is browned and crisp and the nopales are tender. Serve with dried chile salsa.

MELTED-CHEESE NOPALES Boil whole paddles until tender, about 15 minutes, then butterfly, leaving one edge attached. Stuff with cheese, then batter and fry until golden and the cheese is melted.

GRILLED SHRIMP AND NOPALES Make a salad of grilled shrimp, grilled and sliced nopales, and chunks of tomato, seasoned with garlic, jalapeño, cilantro, lime, and olive oil.

Hibiscus esculentus cvs.

Okra

No single vegetable can conjure up an entire cuisine as instantly as okra. Say the word and you'll be instantly transported to the South, where myriad complex, gutsy dishes using this vegetable abound. Okra is a love-it or hate-it vegetable because of its texture, which can be a bit slimy if it's not prepared correctly. These recipes will change all that.

PICKING THE BEST

Choose young tender pods that are firm, velvety green, and have a crisp texture that snaps easily. Avoid any limp or shriveled pods. The best pods are usually between 2 and 4 inches.

KEEPING IT FRESH

Store fresh okra in the refrigerator and use within a day or two. Beyond that, it begins to lose its freshness, flavor, and nutrients.

PREPARING

Rinse and dry, then trim the stem ends if they look tough or old. Depending on your recipe, leave whole or cut into chunks or slices. Some people claim an aversion to okra because of its texture, but frying it hot and fast before adding it to gumbo or other stews keeps it from getting slimy.

HOW TO USE

Dredge in cornmeal or dip whole pods in batter and deep-fry as a side dish, or cut into slices and add to soups and stews; okra tends to soften and break down during cooking and its mucilaginous texture will thicken the dish slightly.

PRESERVING OPTIONS

Pickled okra is a Southern favorite, and you can freeze okra easily, too. Blanch whole for 3 to 4 minutes, let cool, spread on trays and freeze until firm, then pile into airtight freezer bags.

Seafood Gumbo

SERVES 6 TO 8

1½ pounds medium shrimp (41 to 50 per pound or
   51 to 60 per pound) or 2 pounds if using head-on
   shrimp

2 cups chopped white onion (about 1 large onion;
   reserve the skin)

1 cup chopped celery (about 2 medium stalks; reserve
   the trimmings)

¼ cup plus 6 tablespoons vegetable oil

1 pound fresh or thawed frozen okra, sliced ¼ inch
   thick (about 4 cups)

½ cup unbleached all-purpose flour

1 cup chopped green bell pepper (about 1 medium
   pepper)

1 cup canned crushed tomatoes

1 tablespoon dried thyme

1 bay leaf

2 teaspoons kosher salt, plus more to taste

1 teaspoon freshly ground black pepper, plus more
   to taste

½ pound fresh or pasteurized lump crabmeat (about
   1½ cups), picked over for shells

1 cup fresh shucked oysters (halved if large)

½ cup thinly sliced scallion (about 8; white and light
   green parts)

Hot sauce

¼ cup hot cooked white rice per serving

Make the shrimp stock: Remove the shrimp heads, if
necessary. Peel and devein the shrimp and refrigerate
the shrimp until needed. Combine the shrimp peels
and heads and the reserved onion skin and celery
trimmings in a 6- to 8-quart pot. Cover with 9 cups
cold water and bring to a boil over high heat. Reduce
the heat to a vigorous simmer and cook, uncovered,
for 10 minutes. Strain and reserve. You should have
about 2 quarts.

Prepare the okra: In a 10-inch straight-sided sauté
pan, heat ¼ cup of the vegetable oil over medium-
high heat until hot. Fry the okra in two batches
until it becomes lightly browned on the edges, 3 to
5 minutes per batch (fry undisturbed for the first
minute or two until browning begins and then stir
once or twice to flip most pieces and brown evenly).

With a slotted spoon, transfer each batch of okra to a
plate or platter lined with paper towels.

Make the roux: Heat the remaining 6 tablespoons
oil over medium-high heat in a 6-quart Dutch oven.
Once it's hot, add the flour and stir constantly with a
wooden spoon or heatproof spatula until the roux is
the color of caramel, about 5 minutes. Add the onion
and stir until the roux deepens to a chocolate brown,
1 to 3 minutes. Add the celery and bell pepper and
cook, stirring frequently, until slightly softened, about
5 minutes. Add the shrimp stock, okra, tomatoes,
thyme, bay leaf, salt, and pepper. Adjust the heat to
medium low or low and simmer uncovered, stirring
occasionally, for 45 minutes.

Serve the gumbo: Five minutes before serving, add
the shrimp, crabmeat, oysters, and scallion. Discard
the bay leaf. Add hot sauce, salt, and pepper to taste.
Serve in large soup bowls over ¼ cup cooked rice per
serving. Pass additional hot sauce at the table.

Other recipe ideas

STEWED TOMATOES AND OKRA Cook some bacon,
then cook some sliced onion in the bacon fat. Add
okra and canned tomatoes and simmer until the okra
is tender and the sauce is thick.

OKRA FRITTERS Make a thick fritter batter and fold
in chopped okra, then fry and serve with a spicy
dipping sauce.

SPICED INDIAN BHINDI Make an Indian-inspired
dish by sautéing sliced onion with cumin, coriander,
turmeric, and a little chile, then add sliced okra, some
canned tomatoes, and a few spoonfuls of yogurt.
Simmer until the okra is tender and the sauce is
concentrated.

Allium cepa cvs.

Onions

Onions are so easy to find, inexpensive, and unobtrusive—waiting patiently in our cupboards—that they're probably taken for granted. But the many members of the allium family bring a range of flavor from spicy-hot to sweet, mellow, and meaty, adding delicious dimension to many dishes.

PICKING THE BEST

The many varieties of onion fall into two basic types: fresh and storage. The type you choose depends on how you plan to use it.

- **Fresh onions:** These arrive in spring and early summer and have thin, shiny skins, a high water content, and scant amounts of the sulfur compounds that make other onions so pungent. They're mild and sweet with a texture that's both juicy and crisp, making them excellent choices for using raw in salads and on sandwiches. Fresh onions include:

- **Spring onions:** Sold in bunches with their tubular stems still attached. The entire onion is edible and they're at their best when raw.

- **Sweet onions:** Often appear as regional varieties, including Vidalia, Maui, Texas Sweet, and Walla Walla. These can look like large yellow onions and usually have a light papery skin, but they are perishable and won't keep long in the cupboard.

- **Scallions and leeks;** see p. 92 and p. 80.

- **Storage onions:** These are picked at the peak of the summer harvest season, then "cured" by a drying process that gives them their familiar dry, papery skin, which protects the onion during shipping and helps prevent decay. Storage onions are firmer and have less water than fresh onions; they also have a much stronger, more pungent flavor. Rather than being labeled by variety, common storage onions

are generally labeled by color: yellow, white, and red. Though you'll often only see white onions labeled as Spanish, this slightly sweeter variety can come in all three colors. Same goes for Bermuda, another mild variety with a flatter shape.

Some distinctive storage onions include:

- **Pearl onions:** Onions whose growth has been stunted in the field. These tiny gems are delicious when peeled and left whole to cook in stews and casseroles. They may be white, red, or tan.

- **Cipollini onions:** Small, flat-shaped spheres that are popular in Italy. They have a well-developed flavor that's a little sweet. Traditionally served whole in Italian sweet-and-sour sauce, they are also good marinated and pickled or roasted whole.

- **Torpedo onions:** Shaped like a slender football or torpedo. Popular in the Mediterranean, these red onions are sweeter than most storage onions.

- **Red onions:** Have a crisp texture, mild flavor, and bold color and are best when eaten raw. Slice them for a sandwich or burger, or chop for a salad or salsa.

- **Shallots;** see p. 94.

Regardless of buying fresh or storage type, choose firm bulbs with no soft spots, bruises, or other signs of damage. The necks should be tightly closed. They should be heavy for their size, with dry, papery skins. Check for moldy spots, especially with fresh onions.

White

Cipollini

Vidalia

Boiling

Pearl

KEEPING IT FRESH

Fresh onions: Use spring onions soon after you buy them; they'll keep in the refrigerator for about 3 days. Sweet onions are full of juice and fragile, with tissue-thin skins, so treat them gently. If you plan to use them within a week or so, you can leave them out on the counter. For longer storage, put them in a cool place, protected from light; an open brown paper bag works well. You can also store them loose in your fridge's crisper drawer, on top of a piece of newspaper to keep them dry. Don't store in a plastic bag, as their juiciness makes them prone to mold.

Storage onions: Keep any storage onions in a cool, dry, well-ventilated spot.

PREPARING

All onions need peeling and some kind of trimming, slicing, or chopping, which, of course, means one thing—tears. Cutting into an onion releases sulfur compounds that irritate your eyes. There are plenty of suggested remedies for this—from wearing goggles to cutting the onion under running water—but the most practical approach is to have good ventilation and use a sharp knife and good technique so you can complete the task as fast as possible. For cutting techniques, see p. 303.

Peeling a large onion isn't difficult, but peeling lots of little pearls or cipollinis can be a challenge, which is made easier by blanching: Bring a small saucepan of water to a boil and fill a medium bowl with ice water. Trim both ends of each onion and put them in the boiling water for about 30 seconds. Transfer the onions to the ice water to stop the cooking. Once cool, use a paring knife to slip off the skins.

HOW TO USE IT

Use sliced or chopped onions as a zesty garnish on soups and stews, salads, and sandwiches. Sauté onions to use as part of a mirepoix to build a foundation for dishes, or cook onions long and slow to caramelize their abundant sugars and create a component to add rich, savory flavor. You can also roast onions, in wedges or whole, until sweet and tender, and onions take well to grilling, though they need moderate temperatures so that they may soften without burning.

All onions oxidize when cut, and the longer cut raw pieces are exposed to air, the more they oxidize and develop off flavors. Slice onions just before you plan to use them. If you're cooking them, get the onions in the hot pan as soon as you've cut them. Onions to be eaten raw can be sliced and kept in ice water for several hours before serving. An ice water bath will also tame their pungency. Marinating red onions briefly in a vinaigrette (or other acidic bath) accentuates their bright purple color.

PRESERVING OPTIONS

Pickled onions are delicious, and you can freeze chopped or sliced onions; unlike many vegetables, there's no need to blanch onions first. Pack into airtight freezer bags.

DID YOU KNOW? The big market for sweet onions in this country got its start when Texas farmers began growing milder Bermuda onions at the turn of the 20th century. They couldn't keep up with demand, so researchers started experimenting and eventually developed a sweet hybrid that would become the parent of Texas Sweet and Vidalia onions.

RECIPES

Fried Onion Rings

SERVES 8

9 ounces (2 cups) unbleached all-purpose flour

¾ teaspoon salt; more for sprinkling

12 ounces flat beer, at room temperature

¼ cup peanut oil; more for frying

4 large, rather flat onions (about ¾ pound each)

2 egg whites

In a large bowl, combine the flour and salt. In a medium bowl, combine the beer and oil and pour into the flour mixture, stirring constantly with a whisk until just combined. Don't beat the batter. Let stand for at least 1 hour.

Peel the onions, cut them into ½-inch slices, and carefully separate them into rings. Heat at least 2 inches of oil in a large pot over high heat. While the oil is heating, beat the egg whites until they hold stiff peaks. Gently fold the whites into the batter. When the oil reaches 365°F (test with an instant-read thermometer or, if you don't have one, drop a small amount of batter into the oil; if it sizzles immediately, the oil is ready), dip the rings into the batter and then drop them into the oil in batches; don't crowd the pot. Fry until golden brown, 2 to 3 minutes on each side. Remove the rings with a wire-mesh strainer and let excess oil drip back into the pot. Drain on a rack set over a baking sheet and serve when you have a plateful. Wait for the oil to return to 365°F before adding the next batch, and try to maintain that temperature as you fry. Have guests salt their onion rings at the table.

Roasted Onions Stuffed with Prosciutto and Parmesan

SERVES 4

4 medium yellow onions or small sweet onions

2 tablespoons olive oil

1½ cups dry white wine

Kosher salt and freshly ground black pepper

2 sprigs fresh thyme, plus 1½ teaspoons chopped

⅔ cup dry breadcrumbs

½ cup grated Parmigiano-Reggiano

¼ pound prosciutto, coarsely chopped

2 tablespoons heavy cream

1 tablespoon chopped fresh flat-leaf parsley

Heat the oven to 425°F. Slice off the top quarter of the onions. Peel them and trim the bottoms just enough to make them sit flat.

Heat the oil in a heavy-based ovenproof skillet until hot. Put the onions, cut side down, into the pan and cook just until the cut side is well browned, about 5 minutes. Take the pan off the heat. Turn the onions cut side up and pour the wine over them. Sprinkle them with salt and pepper. Add the thyme sprigs to the pan and bake the onions until just tender when poked with a knife, about 1 hour.

Remove the onions from the skillet (reserving the liquid in the pan) and let them cool slightly. With a spoon, scoop out the inside of each onion, leaving a rim ¼ to ½ inch thick (about two layers of onion). Chop enough of the scooped-out onion to make about ⅓ cup.

In a medium bowl, mix the chopped onion with the breadcrumbs, Parmigiano, prosciutto, cream, chopped thyme, and parsley. Season with salt and pepper. Divide the filling among the hollowed onions, return the onions to the skillet with the liquid, and put the skillet back in the oven. Bake until the onions are very tender and the filling is hot, about 20 minutes. Serve with some of the pan juices spooned over the onions.

French Onion Soup

SERVES 6

2 ounces (4 tablespoons) unsalted butter

6 large yellow onions (about 3¼ pounds total), sliced about ⅛ inch thick

Salt and freshly ground black pepper

2 teaspoons unbleached all-purpose flour

1 cup dry white wine (not oaky), such as Sauvignon Blanc or Pinot Grigio

8 cups homemade chicken or beef broth, or reduced-sodium chicken broth

1 sprig fresh flat-leaf parsley, 1 sprig fresh thyme, and 1 bay leaf, tied together with kitchen twine

1 baguette, cut into as many ³∕₈-inch slices as needed to cover six soup crocks

1½ cups (about 6 ounces) grated Gruyère cheese

In a large, wide soup pot (at least 4½ quarts), melt the butter over medium heat. Add the onions and season lightly with salt and pepper. (It might seem like you have far too many onions, but they'll cook down to about one-quarter of their original volume.) Cook the onions gently, stirring frequently, until they're very soft and have begun to turn a dark straw color, 35 to 45 minutes.

When the onions are ready, stir in the flour and cook for 3 to 4 minutes, stirring frequently. Pour in the wine and increase the heat to medium high, stirring and scraping to loosen any caramelized juices, until the liquid is mostly reduced, 5 to 8 minutes. Add the broth, toss in the tied herbs, and bring to a simmer. Season to taste with salt and pepper and simmer for 20 to 30 minutes to infuse the broth with onion flavor; the onions should be soft but not falling apart. Remove the herb bundle and taste the soup for seasoning. The soup can be made ahead to this point and then cooled and refrigerated for a few days.

To serve, heat the oven to 350°F, put the baguette slices on a rack, and toast lightly (7 to 10 minutes); set aside. Increase the oven temperature to 450°F. Bring the soup back to a simmer. Set six ovenproof soup crocks on a heavy baking sheet and ladle the soup into the crocks. Float a few toasted baguette slices on top, enough to cover the soup surface without too much overlap. Top the bread with a handful (about ¼ cup) of the grated Gruyère. Slide the baking sheet into the oven and bake until the cheese is melted

and just browning in spots, 10 to 12 minutes. Serve the soup right away, while the crock is hot and the cheese is still gooey.

Braised Asparagus and Cipollini Onions with Pancetta and Balsamic Butter Glaze

SERVES 3 TO 4

1 pound medium or thick asparagus

2 teaspoons balsamic vinegar

2 teaspoons fresh lemon juice

1 teaspoon Dijon mustard

1 teaspoon honey

2 tablespoons extra-virgin olive oil

1½ ounces thinly sliced pancetta, cut into slivers (about ⅓ cup)

1 tablespoon plus 1 teaspoon unsalted butter

5 ounces small cipollini onions (about 6) or large shallots (about 6), halved and peeled (quartered if very large)

¼ teaspoon kosher salt; more as needed

⅓ cup homemade or reduced-sodium chicken broth

Cut off the tough ends of the asparagus so that all the spears are about 6 to 7 inches long; you should have about 10 ounces of trimmed asparagus. Combine the balsamic vinegar, lemon juice, mustard, and honey in a small bowl; set aside. Heat 1 tablespoon of the oil in a 10-inch straight-sided sauté pan over medium-high heat. Add the pancetta strips and cook, stirring frequently, until browned and crisp, 2 to 3 minutes (don't let them burn). Take the pan off the heat and transfer the pancetta to a plate, leaving behind as much fat as possible.

Return the pan to medium-high heat, add 1 tablespoon of the butter to the fat in the pan, and swirl to melt (there will be browned bits on the bottom of the pan). Add the onions and a pinch of salt and sauté until nicely browned on all sides and beginning to soften, 2 to 3 minutes. Take the pan off the heat and transfer the onions to another plate.

Return the pan to medium-high heat and add the remaining 1 tablespoon oil, the asparagus, and ¼ teaspoon salt. Toss well. Cook without stirring until the bottoms of the spears are nicely browned, 3 to 4 minutes. Toss and turn over, and cook for another 1 to 2 minutes to lightly brown the other side. Return the onions to the pan, stir, and pour the chicken broth over the top. Cover the pan and simmer until the liquid is almost completely reduced, about 3 minutes.

Uncover, add the balsamic and Dijon mixture, stir to coat thoroughly, and cook for a few seconds until it has a glazey consistency. Add the remaining 1 teaspoon butter and toss to melt and combine, scraping up any browned bits in the pan with a heatproof spatula or a wooden spoon. Toss in the crisped pancetta. Serve right away as individual servings or pour and scrape the contents of the pan onto a small platter and serve family style.

Marinated Tomatoes with Pickled Red Onions and Gorgonzola

SERVES 8

1½ cups red-wine vinegar

1½ teaspoons kosher salt, plus more to taste

1 small red onion (about 6 ounces), peeled, halved, and very thinly sliced crosswise

¼ cup thinly sliced fresh chives

2 tablespoons extra-virgin olive oil

2 teaspoons balsamic vinegar

Freshly ground black pepper

2 pounds ripe tomatoes, preferably heirlooms of various colors (3 or 4 medium large)

3 ounces Gorgonzola dolce or other blue cheese, crumbled (¾ cup)

In a medium bowl, stir the red-wine vinegar with 1¹/₂ teaspoons salt until it has dissolved. Add the onion. If the vinegar doesn't cover the onion, add water to cover. Let sit for 15 minutes.

Meanwhile, in a small bowl, whisk the chives, olive oil, and balsamic vinegar. Season to taste with salt and pepper. Core and cut the tomatoes in half lengthwise and then cut each half lengthwise into ¼-inch-thick slices. Put the tomatoes in a wide serving bowl. Pour the vinaigrette over the tomatoes and marinate them for 15 minutes.

Drain the onion, pressing lightly to squeeze out any vinegar. Rinse the onion and then squeeze again. Add the onion to the tomatoes and toss. Season with salt and pepper, top with the cheese, and serve.

Balsamic-Glazed Grilled Sweet Onions

SERVES 4

2 pounds sweet onions (such as Vidalia, Walla Walla, Maui, or Texas Sweet)

Olive oil, for grilling

1 cup balsamic vinegar

1 tablespoon chopped fresh thyme leaves

½ teaspoon crushed pink peppercorns (optional)

½ teaspoon kosher salt, plus more to taste

Peel and trim the onions. Cut them crosswise into ½-inch-thick slices. Insert a toothpick horizontally halfway into each slice to hold the onion rings together.

Prepare a medium-low charcoal fire or heat a gas grill on medium low for 10 minutes. Brush the grill grate clean and wipe it with a paper towel dipped in oil. Brush both sides of the onion slices with olive oil and grill, covered, turning every 10 minutes, until soft and well browned on the outside, 35 to 40 minutes total. (A little blackening is fine, but try not to char the onions.) Stack the onions on a large sheet of foil and wrap loosely. Set aside while you make the glaze.

Pour the balsamic vinegar into a small saucepan and add the thyme leaves, pink peppercorns (if using), and salt. Boil, uncovered, over medium-high heat until the vinegar has reduced to about ¼ cup and has a syrupy texture, 8 to 10 minutes. Let cool briefly and season to taste with salt, if necessary.

Transfer the onions to a dish. Remove the toothpicks and any extremely charred layers, if necessary. If the balsamic glaze has thickened, reheat it gently until pourable. Pour the glaze over the onions and brush to distribute it evenly. Serve warm or at room temperature.

Other recipe ideas

CHERRY-STUDDED RICE PILAF WITH CARAMELIZED ONIONS Caramelize two sliced onions and season with allspice, cinnamon, and cloves. Make a rice pilaf with basmati rice and fold in the onions, some dried sour cherries, and shelled pistachios.

Allium fistulosum and cvs.

Scallions

This slender member of the onion family is often thought of as just a garnish, but the sweet, mild flavor of scallions means they have amazing versatility. Sure, you can sprinkle thin scallion slices on soups, salads, or pastas just before serving for an extra hit of flavor and color, but when grilled, braised, or roasted, scallions are delicious all on their own.

KEEPING IT FRESH

If you want to store scallions for more than a day or so, trim away the last few inches of the green tops, which get slimy fast; otherwise leave whole. Wrap scallions in a paper towel and put them in a zip-top bag in the refrigerator. They will keep for up to a week.

PREPARING

Remove a couple of inches from the green tops, which often have a scraggly texture. Rinse scallions under cold running water and pull off any bruised or slimy outer leaves, then trim off the hairy roots.

HOW TO USE IT

Both the white and green parts of the scallion are used in cooking. The dark green ends have a delicate sharpness reminiscent of chives and a light, crisp texture, but they wilt and discolor when cooked too long, so are often added to a dish just before serving. The white parts have an oniony punch, and because their texture is more substantial, they withstand longer cooking times.

PRESERVING OPTIONS

Scallions can be chopped and frozen, tightly sealed in a freezer bag, but since they'll lose their crisp texture, they're best used in cooked dishes and not as a garnish.

PICKING THE BEST

Choose scallions, sometimes called green onions, with full white bulbs and firm green tops. Avoid scallions with soggy or browned green parts—they're past their prime.

SURPRISING PAIRINGS

Few of us would want to eat raw onions as a crudité, but raw scallions are much milder, needing just a creamy dip to balance their bite. Grilling also mellows them out, so you can serve them on their own with a vinaigrette, garlicky aïoli, or spicy romesco sauce.

Summer Corn Chowder with Scallions, Bacon, and Potatoes

SERVES 6

5 ears fresh sweet corn
7 ounces scallions (about 20 medium)
3 slices bacon, cut into ½-inch pieces
1 tablespoon unsalted butter
1 jalapeño, cored, seeded, and finely diced
1 teaspoon kosher salt, plus more to taste
Freshly ground black pepper
3½ cups reduced-sodium chicken broth
1 large Yukon Gold potato (8 to 9 ounces), peeled
    and cut into ½-inch dice (about 1½ cups)
1½ teaspoons chopped fresh thyme
2 tablespoons heavy cream

Husk the corn and cut off the kernels. Reserve two of the corn cobs and discard the others. Trim and thinly slice the scallions, keeping the dark green parts separate from the white and light green parts.

Cook the bacon in a 3- or 4-quart saucepan over medium heat until browned and crisp, about 5 minutes. With a slotted spoon, transfer the bacon to a paper-towel-lined plate. Pour off and discard all but about 1 tablespoon of the bacon fat. Return the pan to medium heat and add the butter. When the butter is melted, add the white and light green scallions and the jalapeño, salt, and a few grinds of black pepper. Cook, stirring, until the scallions are very soft, about 3 minutes.

Add the broth, corn, corn cobs, potato, and thyme and bring to a boil over medium-high heat. Reduce the heat to medium low and simmer until the potato is completely tender, about 15 minutes. Discard the corn cobs.

Transfer 1 cup of the broth and vegetables to a blender and purée. (Hold a towel over the lid while you turn it on.) Return the purée to the pot and stir in the cream and all but ⅓ cup of the scallion greens. Simmer, stirring occasionally, for a couple of minutes to wilt the scallions and blend the flavors. Season to taste with salt and pepper and serve sprinkled with the bacon and reserved scallions.

Steamed Black Cod with Scallions

SERVES 4

One 2-inch piece fresh ginger, peeled
1 teaspoon reduced-sodium soy sauce
1 teaspoon sugar
4 skinless black cod fillets (about 4 ounces each)
12 scallions (dark green parts only), cut into 2-inch
    pieces on the diagonal
2 tablespoons canola oil
¼ cup Shaoxing (Chinese rice wine)
1 cup long-grain white rice, preferably jasmine,
    cooked according to package directions

With a rasp-style grater, grate the ginger into a fine sieve set over a large bowl. Use the back of a spoon to press down on the pulp to release the juice; discard the pulp. Stir in the soy sauce and sugar. Add the fish, turn to coat, cover, and marinate for 20 minutes at room temperature.

Set a steamer (western style or Asian bamboo) over a pot with at least 1 inch of simmering water. On a plate that can fit in the steamer, arrange the fish so the fillets fit without touching (discard the remaining marinade). Distribute the scallions around the fish and put the plate in the steamer. Cover and steam the fish until just cooked through, 4 to 5 minutes.

Heat the oil in a small pan over medium heat and add the Shaoxing. Allow it to sizzle for just a few seconds and remove from the heat.

Portion the rice among four dinner plates. Top the rice with the fish and scallions (transfer directly from the steamer without attempting to remove the plate). Spoon the Shaoxing sauce over all and serve.

Other recipe ideas

CREAMY SCALLION PASTA SAUCE Make a simple pasta sauce by sautéing scallions and mixing them with cream, Parmigiano, and plenty of black pepper.

STIR-FRIED EGGPLANT AND SCALLIONS Try a stir-fry with scallions, thinly sliced zucchini, small chunks of Japanese eggplant, and sliced shiitake or cremini mushrooms. Season with ginger, garlic, and a touch of Asian sesame oil to finish.

Allium cepa var. aggregatum

Shallots

Shallots seem to be the "sophisticated" members of the onion family, perhaps because they're called for in so many French recipes. Crisp, with a refined, delicate flavor, shallots add character to dishes without the aggressive bite of raw onion. Some people think shallots have a slight garlicky flavor, combining the best of both of its allium cousins.

PICKING THE BEST
Buy firm shallots with no soft spots, bruises, or other signs of damage. They should be heavy for their size, with dry, papery skins.

KEEPING IT FRESH
Store shallots in a cool, dry, well-ventilated spot for up to a month.

PREPARING
Shallots sometimes have more than one lobe; just break the lobes apart and treat them as individual shallots. Peel shallots before using, then slice or dice as you would an onion.

HOW TO USE IT
Use minced shallot to add some backbone to a beurre blanc or vinaigrette. Whole or halved shallots are wonderful alone or as part of a roasted vegetable dish. Caramelized shallots make a savory condiment to serve with beef.

SURPRISING PAIRINGS
Caramelized shallots are just as delicious, if not more so, than caramelized onions. Combined with a little sugar and balsamic vinegar, or even robust fruits like blackberries or pears, you can turn caramelized shallots into a versatile jam to serve with cheese, pâté, roasted meats, or sandwiches.

PRESERVING OPTIONS
Shallots can be pickled, just like regular onions. You can also freeze shallots, in chunks, sliced, or chopped. Unlike most vegetables, you don't need to blanch shallots before freezing them; simply store in an airtight freezer bag.

DID YOU KNOW?

The French often use a variety of shallots that we rarely find on our shores: gray shallots, so named for their grayish skin and white flesh. They don't store well and they're harder to peel, but their flavor is more complex.

Glazed Carrots and Shallots with Thyme

SERVES 4

1½ pounds carrots (about 8), peeled and trimmed

8 ounces shallots (about 5 or 6 medium), ends
   trimmed, peeled, and cut in half or in quarters
   if large

About 1 cup homemade or reduced-sodium chicken
   broth

2 tablespoons unsalted butter

2 teaspoons kosher salt; more as needed

1 teaspoon sugar

1 teaspoon chopped fresh thyme

Cut the carrots in half lengthwise. Holding your
knife at a sharp angle, cut each half into ¼-inch-
thick slices to make half-moons. Put the carrots and
shallots in a 10- to 12-inch sauté pan and add enough
broth to come halfway up the sides of the vegetables.
Add the butter, salt, and sugar and bring to a boil
over high heat. Cover the pan with the lid slightly
askew, reduce the heat to medium high, and cook at
a steady boil, shaking the pan occasionally, until the
carrots are tender but not soft (a paring knife should
enter a carrot with just a little resistance), 8 to
10 minutes. Uncover, add the thyme, and continue to
boil until the liquid evaporates. Continue to cook the
carrots and shallots over medium-high heat, stirring
occasionally, until they begin to caramelize and turn
golden brown, 3 to 4 minutes. Taste and add a pinch
more salt, if necessary, and serve.

Roasted Rosemary Butternut Squash and Shallots

SERVES 4

3 cups ¾-inch-diced, peeled butternut squash
   (from about a 2-pound squash)

4 medium shallots

2 tablespoons extra-virgin olive oil

1 teaspoon chopped fresh rosemary

1 teaspoon kosher salt; more as needed

½ teaspoon sugar

½ teaspoon freshly ground black pepper

Position a rack in the center of the oven and heat the
oven to 450°F.

Put the squash on a heavy-duty rimmed baking
sheet. Peel and quarter each shallot and add them
to the squash. Drizzle the oil over the vegetables;
toss to coat. Sprinkle the rosemary, salt, sugar, and
pepper over the squash; toss to coat. Distribute the
vegetables evenly on the baking sheet. Roast for
20 minutes. Stir, then continue roasting until the
vegetables are tender and lightly browned, another
10 to 15 minutes. Before serving, taste and season
with more salt if needed.

Other recipe ideas

CRISP SHALLOT GARNISH Fry thinly sliced shallots in
hot oil until they're about the color of a brown paper
bag. Drain on paper towels, season with salt, and use
as a crunchy garnish for fish, steak, or salads.

MAPLE-PECAN-SHALLOT BUTTER Make a compound
butter to serve on sweet potatoes, winter squash,
or pork tenderloin by working minced shallot, fresh
thyme leaves, finely chopped pecans, some pure
maple syrup, and a touch of cayenne into softened
butter.

**WHOLE-GRAIN MUSTARD AND SHALLOT PAN
SAUCE** Make a sauce for steak by sautéing chopped
shallots and minced garlic, then adding some red
wine and beef or chicken broth and reducing to a
glaze. Whisk in whole-grain mustard and finish
with some butter.

Phaseolus vulgaris cvs.

String Beans

String beans have a compelling, pick-me-up-with-your-fingers character, which may be why even kids love them. Their flavor can range from nutty to grassy, but always with a sweet meatiness that's a versatile partner to other flavors.

PICKING THE BEST

Any variety of string bean should feel heavy and plump, and break with a good, clean snap when bent. While the most common type of bean is green and moderately sized (such as Blue Lake and Kentucky Wonder), you'll also find tiny, fine haricots verts, yellow "wax" beans, purple varieties (though their color will fade to dark green as you cook them), and flatter Romano beans, which need long cooking but are deeply flavorful and meaty.

KEEPING IT FRESH

Store beans in a plastic bag in the refrigerator for no more than a couple of days; they shrivel quickly.

PREPARING

Most modern varieties of string bean—also called green beans—don't have much of a string, but to check, snap off the stem end. If you find only a small string attached, don't bother pulling it; just go ahead and work in bunches, cutting off the tops, and the tails if you like, though many cooks like to leave that little curlicue end. If the string is long and tough, work individually, snapping off both ends of each bean and pulling the string down from top to tail. If the string is tender, gather a small bunch and cut off the stem ends. The thin, pointy end that looks like a tail can also be trimmed, though it's not necessary unless it's especially tough.

If you're serving the beans for a party, cutting them into halves or thirds makes eating them a little easier. Slice them on a diagonal for more visual interest.

HOW TO USE IT

String beans are highly adaptable and do well with many cooking methods, each one bringing out a different aspect of the bean's personality. Sautéing the beans helps to create layers of flavor; parboiling the beans before sautéing helps to keep the bright color and control texture. Boiling string beans gives you consistently tender texture throughout—toothsome but not crunchy or fibrous. Braising beans makes them tender and allows them to absorb the flavors of the other ingredients in the recipe. Roasting beans caramelizes the outside and creates a fullness of flavor that's delicious.

PRESERVING OPTIONS

String beans are perfect for pickling, as they hold their texture well, and are the perfect shape to pick up and munch as a tangy snack or hors d'oeuvre.

Chinese long

Yellow wax

Haricots verts

Purple wax

Green Beans with Meyer Lemon Vinaigrette and Parmesan Breadcrumbs

SERVES 8 TO 10

½ cup fresh breadcrumbs

½ cup plus 2 tablespoons extra-virgin olive oil

½ teaspoon kosher salt; more as needed

¼ teaspoon freshly ground black pepper, plus more to taste

½ cup freshly grated Parmigiano-Reggiano

Finely grated zest of 1 Meyer lemon

¼ cup fresh Meyer lemon juice

¼ cup heavy cream

2 pounds fresh green beans, trimmed

Heat the oven to 350°F. In a small bowl, toss the breadcrumbs with 2 tablespoons of the oil, a generous pinch of salt, and a few grinds of pepper. Arrange in a single layer on a rimmed baking sheet and toast until golden brown, about 10 minutes. Let cool and then transfer to a bowl and mix in the cheese.

In a medium bowl, whisk the lemon zest and juice, cream, ½ teaspoon salt, and pepper. Slowly whisk in the remaining ½ cup oil.

Bring a large pot of salted water to a boil over high heat. Cook the green beans in the boiling water until tender, 4 to 6 minutes; drain well. Toss the beans with the vinaigrette. Taste and adjust the seasoning if necessary. Transfer the beans to a serving platter and sprinkle with the breadcrumbs.

Chinese Restaurant-Style Sautéed Green Beans

SERVES 2 TO 3

1 tablespoon reduced-sodium soy sauce

1 tablespoon honey

1 tablespoon unsalted butter

2 tablespoons extra-virgin olive oil

12 ounces fresh green beans, trimmed

Kosher salt

1 tablespoon minced garlic

Combine the soy sauce, honey, and 1 tablespoon water in a small dish and set near the stove. Set a shallow serving dish near the stove, too.

In a 10-inch straight-sided sauté pan, heat the butter with the olive oil over medium-high heat. When the butter is melted, add the green beans and ½ teaspoon salt and toss with tongs to coat well. Cook, turning the beans occasionally, until most are well browned, shrunken, and tender, 7 to 8 minutes. (The butter in the pan will have turned dark brown.)

Reduce the heat to low, add the garlic, and cook, stirring constantly with a heatproof rubber spatula, until the garlic is softened and fragrant, 15 to 20 seconds. Carefully add the soy mixture (you'll need to scrape the honey into the pan). Cook, stirring, until the liquid reduces to a glazey consistency that coats the beans, 30 to 45 seconds.

Immediately transfer the beans to a serving dish, scraping the pan with the spatula to get all of the garlicky sauce. Let sit for a few minutes and then serve warm.

Spiced Green Beans Braised with Tomatoes and Onions

SERVES 4 TO 6

¼ cup extra-virgin olive oil

1 medium onion (about 8 ounces), halved lengthwise, trimmed, and thinly sliced lengthwise (about 2 cups)

1 pound fresh green beans, stem ends trimmed

½ teaspoon kosher salt; more as needed

¼ teaspoon freshly ground black pepper; more as needed

2 cups canned diced tomatoes (from a 28-ounce can), drained

4 large cloves garlic, thinly sliced

1 teaspoon sugar

¾ teaspoon ground allspice

½ teaspoon ground cinnamon

In a 12-inch skillet with a lid, heat the olive oil over medium heat. Add the onion and cook, stirring occasionally, until soft and lightly golden, 4 to 5 minutes. Add the green beans, salt, and pepper, and stir well. Reduce the heat to medium low and cook, stirring occasionally, until the onions are caramelized and the beans start to soften and brown lightly, about 10 minutes.

Add the tomatoes, garlic, sugar, allspice, and cinnamon. Stir well, reduce the heat to low, cover, and cook, stirring occasionally, until the beans are very tender throughout, 15 to 20 minutes, or longer if a softer texture is desired. Season to taste with salt and pepper. Serve warm or at room temperature.

Garlic-Roasted Green Beans and Shallots with Hazelnuts

SERVES 4

6 medium shallots

1 pound fresh green beans, trimmed

5 medium cloves garlic, coarsely chopped

3 tablespoons extra-virgin olive oil

1 teaspoon kosher salt

½ teaspoon freshly ground black pepper

¼ cup finely chopped fresh flat-leaf parsley

¼ cup coarsely chopped toasted hazelnuts

1 teaspoon finely grated lemon zest

Position a rack in the center of the oven and heat the oven to 450°F.

Slice each shallot lengthwise into ¼-inch slices. Put the shallots, green beans, and garlic in a large bowl; toss with the oil. Sprinkle the salt and pepper over the vegetables and toss again. Transfer to a 10x15-inch Pyrex dish and roast until the vegetables are tender and very lightly browned, stirring once, 18 to 20 minutes.

Meanwhile, combine the parsley, hazelnuts, and lemon zest in a small bowl. Sprinkle the parsley mixture over the roasted vegetables and toss to coat. Serve immediately.

Other recipe ideas

FRENCH POTATO SALAD WITH GREEN BEANS Add green beans to a warm potato salad made with small red-skinned potatoes. Toss with chopped shallots and a creamy mustard vinaigrette.

SAUTÉED BEANS AND MUSHROOMS Stir up a flavorful sauté of green beans, slivered onion, sliced mushrooms, chopped garlic, olive oil, salt, and pepper. Add a dash of balsamic vinegar at the end.

SWEET-AND-SOUR BEAN SALAD Mix a colorful bean salad of cooked green and yellow string beans with chickpeas and diced raw onion, celery, and bell pepper. Marinate in a sweet-sour vinaigrette. Just before serving, toss with chopped fresh chervil or mint.

Late Summer

- Blackberries
- Chiles
- Corn
- Eggplant
- Figs
- Grapes
- Melons
- Olives
- Peaches and Nectarines
- Plums
- Raspberries
- Shell Beans
- Summer Squash
- Sweet Peppers
- Tomatillos
- Tomatoes

Rubus fruticosus and cvs.

Blackberries

Blackberries are less available than strawberries or raspberries and more indicative of the season. When you find a batch of berries that are perfect—sweet and perfumed with just a touch of winyness—snap them up. Eat them out of hand and also use them in pies, cobblers, and more.

PICKING THE BEST

Blackberries are drupes, meaning each berry is formed of lots of tiny fruits, called drupelets. When blackberries are ripe, their skin is delicate, shiny, and black (if they're reddish, they aren't ripe yet). Unlike raspberries, which are hollow in the center, blackberries have a tiny white core. At the market, look for berries without stems; stems indicate that they were picked before ripening, and they don't get any sweeter once they're off the bush. Carefully look into the basket to check for mold or crushed berries, which you want to avoid. And take a sniff—ripe blackberries will be perfumed.

Blackberries have some hybrid cousins that are similar but with their own character. Marionberries are a blackberry cultivar grown in the Pacific Northwest; boysenberries, loganberries, and tayberries are blackberry-raspberry hybrids, though they look and taste more like a lighter, reddish blackberry.

KEEPING IT FRESH

Blackberries aren't as fragile as some berries, but they are still quite perishable. Pick out any soft or moldy berries; don't wash your berries until you're ready to use them. Store them on the counter if using within a few hours; otherwise keep refrigerated for 3 or 4 days. To keep them from getting crushed, tip them onto a paper-towel-lined plate or tray so they're in a single layer.

PREPARING

Blackberries generally don't have stems or leaves attached, so all you need to do is rinse, gently dry, and either eat out of hand or use in a recipe.

HOW TO USE IT

A bowl of ripe blackberries as a snack is a privilege of summer, but blackberries take nicely to cooking, too. A blackberry pie, cobbler, or crisp is an ideal way to showcase the sweet-tart berry, and blackberries and their cousins make delicious compotes and jams.

PRESERVING OPTIONS

Blackberries and their cousins freeze well. Just rinse, dry gently, and spread onto a tray. Freeze until the berries are hard, then pile into an airtight freezer bag. If you're freezing with plans to make jam later, portion your berries into amounts that correspond to your recipes.

RECIPES

Blackberry Grunt

SERVES 6

FOR THE BERRIES

6 cups (3 pints) blackberries

¾ cup sugar

1 tablespoon grated lemon zest

FOR THE DUMPLING DOUGH

4½ ounces (1 cup) unbleached all-purpose flour

2 tablespoons sugar

1 teaspoon baking powder

½ teaspoon baking soda

⅛ teaspoon salt

1 ounce (2 tablespoons) unsalted butter, melted

½ cup buttermilk; more as needed

1 tablespoon sugar mixed with ½ teaspoon ground
cinnamon

Vanilla ice cream, for garnish (optional)

Prepare the berries: In a deep 10-inch skillet that has
a tight-fitting lid, combine the berries, sugar, zest, and
⅓ cup of water.

Make the dough: In a bowl, stir the flour, sugar,
baking powder, baking soda, and salt. Stir in the
melted butter. Add enough of the buttermilk to form
a soft, sticky dough that's slightly wetter than a
biscuit dough.

Meanwhile, bring the berry mixture to a boil over
high heat, stirring once or twice. Reduce to a simmer
and, using a soupspoon, spoon the dough over the
fruit, creating about 8 small dumplings. Sprinkle the
dumplings with the cinnamon-sugar mixture. Cover
the skillet tightly with the lid or foil and steam over
medium-low heat, uncovered, until the dumplings
are set and the surface is dry when touched with
a fingertip, about 15 minutes. (If you're not sure if
the dumplings are done, you can gently break one
open with a fork.) Try not to remove the lid (which
would let steam escape) before 15 minutes, and if the
dumplings need further cooking, quickly return the
lid. Serve immediately, spooning the warm grunt (it
will be fairly liquidy) into small bowls. Garnish with
vanilla ice cream, if you like.

Three-Berry Fool

SERVES 4

1⅓ cups (a generous ½ pint) blackberries

½ cup sugar; more as needed

2 tablespoons Grand Marnier® or other orange
liqueur; more as needed

1 teaspoon grated lemon zest; more as needed

½ cup raspberries

6 large, plump strawberries, hulled, quartered, and
smashed with a fork (to yield ½ cup pulp)

1¼ cups cold ultra-pasteurized heavy cream

In a small saucepan, mix the blackberries, sugar,
Grand Marnier, and lemon zest. Simmer over medium
heat until the juices are released and the sugar is
dissolved, stirring frequently, about 5 minutes. Strain,
pressing with the back of a spoon to force the pulp
through the strainer. Discard the seeds. Add the
raspberries and the smashed strawberries to the
hot mixture, pressing gently on the raspberries to
crush them slightly. You'll have about 1⅓ cups of
berry mixture. Chill until very cold, about 3 hours.
Taste and add more sugar, liqueur, or zest if needed,
remembering that the flavors will be muted when
you fold the purée into the cream.

In a chilled bowl, whip the cream to firm but not
stiff peaks. With a rubber spatula, gently fold 1 cup of
the chilled berry mixture into the whipped cream just
until incorporated. Serve immediately or refrigerate
for up to 24 hours. Just before serving, drizzle the
remaining berry mixture over the fool.

Other recipe ideas

BALSAMIC BERRY SALAD Top arugula and sliced
Belgian endive with a few chunks of ripe peaches, a
handful of blackberries or boysenberries, and a few
dollops of goat cheese and dress with a balsamic
vinaigrette.

HERB AND BERRY CHICKEN SALAD Fold blackberries
into a chicken salad made with shredded rotisserie
chicken, tarragon mayonnaise, and some crunchy
chopped celery. Top with toasted slivered almonds.

Capsicum annuum cvs.

Chiles

One reason to love chiles is their beauty. With their glossy-smooth skins, sensuous shapes, and colors from deep green to crimson, chiles look stunning just in a heap on your counter. But their range of flavor is what endears them to the cook—their heat, of course, but other flavors from mild and grassy to fruity and pungent. The best chiles have a balance of both heat and complex flavor.

PICKING THE BEST

There are hundreds of varieties of chiles, and in a typical supermarket or farmer's market you can find at least a half-dozen. No matter which variety you choose, look for shiny, firm pods with strong, uniform color. They should feel dense and heavy for their size, even the little ones. Avoid chiles that are flaccid, wrinkled, blemished, or discolored. All chiles mature from green to their final color; while their flavor intensifies as they ripen, even the green ones can be very hot.

- **Jalapeño:** Hot, with thick-walled crunchy flesh. They're usually sold medium to dark green or maturing to red. They're a good all-purpose chile for many recipes. Dried and smoked jalapeños are called chipotles.
- **Anaheim:** Mild and meaty with thick succulent flesh. They're also called New Mexico chiles, long green, Hatch, and Chimayo. Use stuffed for chiles rellenos or to add flavor without much heat.
- **Serrano:** Quite hot, small, and slender, with medium-thick walls. Great for piquant salsas or casseroles or pickled in escabeche.
- **Thai and other Asian varieties:** Slender and thin-walled with a very hot, nutty flavor. They're sometimes available green but usually are lipstick red. Perfect for all kinds of stir-frying or to flavor vinegar and other condiments.

- **Habanero:** Extremely hot, with a marvelous fruity quality. The name refers to a specific pod from the Yucatan Peninsula, but there are a similar-looking group of chiles from the Caribbean called Scotch Bonnets. Habanero chiles are a brilliant orange at maturity, but there's also a red cultivar. Habaneros are a classic ingredient in Caribbean and South American barbecue marinades and pastes, and they're the principal ingredient in fiery table sauces from those areas.
- **Pasilla:** Mild, with glossy, forest-green flesh, turning red-brown at maturity. Their flavor is mild and raisin-like, with smoky overtones. Chopped pasillas can be added to braised vegetables, soups, or stews.
- **Poblano:** Mild to medium. Fat, wide, and dark green, the poblano is rich in flavor with succulent flesh. Poblanos are one of the most commonly used chiles in Central Mexican cooking, both fresh and dried (ripened, dried poblanos are called ancho chiles). Poblanos and pasillas are similar and often confused.

KEEPING IT FRESH

Store in a plastic bag in the fridge for up to 3 days; for longer storage, wrap in a dry dishtowel tucked inside a paper bag in the fridge for up to 2 weeks.

Poblano

Jalapeño

Habanero

Dried chipotle

Cubanelle

Dried green

Anaheim

Serrano

PREPARING

It may sound crazy, but it really is a good idea to wear rubber gloves when handling fresh chiles. Their oils can get onto your skin and be very irritating, and you can unwittingly transfer the heat to your eyes or lips.

To chop, carefully cut away the stem and cluster of seeds, then cut the chile in half lengthwise. With the tip of the knife, scrape away the white ribs and seeds—the ribs are where the heat-producing capsaicin is concentrated (if you're looking for lots of heat, leave the ribs and seeds intact). Slice into strips and chop or mince according to the recipe. Wash your hands, the knife, and the cutting board well with soap and water after handling fresh chiles.

HOW TO USE IT

Chiles are excellent raw, either sliced or minced and added to salsas and salads, but their flavor mellows and develops with heat, as well—simmered in soups and stews or roasted and peeled before adding to anything from an enchilada to macaroni and cheese. They are also excellent grilled or battered and fried.

PRESERVING OPTIONS

There are many ways to preserve chiles, from dehydrating to crushing into powders to making oils and vinegars. For the home cook, pickling chiles is a good method. It's easy and it also displays the chiles' beauty and preserves their fleshy-crunchy textures.

DID YOU KNOW?

Chiles' heat comes from capsaicin, an alkaloid found only in chiles. The compound is contained in the sacs along the fruits' inner walls, so when you cut into a chile, the capsaicin mingles with the seeds and the skin. Levels vary depending on the chile variety and are further modified by climate and growing conditions. One plant can produce chiles that range dramatically in heat level. The level of heat is measured in Scoville units, with a typical jalapeño measuring around 5,000 units while a Tabasco chile might clock in at 50,000 units.

Poblanos Stuffed with Cheddar and Chicken

SERVES 4

4 large poblano chiles
2 medium tomatoes, chopped
½ medium white onion, chopped
1 large clove garlic, chopped
1 teaspoon dried oregano, crumbled
1 teaspoon ground cumin
Generous pinch of ground cinnamon
½ teaspoon kosher salt, plus more to taste
1 tablespoon olive oil
2 cups shredded cooked chicken, preferably dark meat
1½ cups cooked brown or white rice
2 cups grated sharp or extra-sharp white Cheddar (about 7 ounces)
¼ cup chopped fresh cilantro (including some tender stems)
1 tablespoon fresh lime juice

Position a rack about 4 inches from the broiler and heat the broiler on high. Line a large rimmed baking sheet with foil.

Slit the chiles from stem to tip and set on the baking sheet. Broil, turning every few minutes, until blackened all over, 5 to 8 minutes. Let cool slightly, peel off the skins, and cut out the seed cores, leaving the stems on. Turn the chiles inside out, flick out any remaining seeds, and turn right side out. Return the poblanos to the baking sheet.

Purée the tomato, onion, garlic, oregano, cumin, cinnamon, and salt in a food processor. Heat the oil in a 12-inch skillet over medium heat. Add the purée and cook, stirring frequently, until the liquid has evaporated and the mixture looks thick and pulpy, 8 to 11 minutes. Remove the pan from the heat. Stir in the chicken and rice, and then 1 cup of the cheese, the cilantro, and the lime juice. Season to taste with salt. Divide the filling among the peppers, wrapping the sides of the peppers up and around the filling, some of which will still be exposed.

Broil the peppers until the cheese is melting and the top is beginning to brown, about 4 minutes. Top with the remaining 1 cup cheese and broil until the cheese is completely melted, about 2 minutes.

Green Chile Sauce

MAKES ABOUT 4 CUPS

7 to 8 ounces tomatillos (about 5 medium)

1 quart homemade or reduced-sodium chicken broth

1 ¼ to 1 ½ pounds fresh Anaheim chiles (6- to 8-inch
chiles), roasted, peeled, seeded, and coarsely
chopped

2 teaspoons minced yellow onion

1 teaspoon dried oregano, or 2 teaspoons chopped
fresh oregano

1 clove garlic, minced

½ teaspoon kosher salt, plus more to taste

¼ teaspoon ground white pepper

2 tablespoons cornstarch, dissolved in 2 tablespoons
water

Hot sauce (optional)

Put a medium saucepan of water on to boil and
remove the papery outer skin from the tomatillos.
Boil the tomatillos until soft, 5 to 10 minutes. Drain
and purée in a blender or food processor. Return the
tomatillos to the saucepan along with the broth,
chiles, onion, oregano, garlic, salt, and pepper. Bring
to a boil over medium-high heat and then reduce the
heat and simmer for 10 minutes. Add the cornstarch
slurry; stir well. Simmer, stirring occasionally, until
the sauce is thickened slightly and reduced to 4 to
4½ cups, another 5 to 15 minutes. Adjust the seasonings if needed, including adding hot sauce if the
sauce isn't spicy enough.

Pickled Chile Peppers

MAKES 1 PINT

2 cups whole fresh chiles, not more than 4 inches long

1½ teaspoons mixed pickling spices

1 teaspoon salt

½ cup distilled white vinegar

Cut a small slit in each chile to allow the pickling
brine to penetrate. In a clean, hot, 1-pint jar, put the
pickling spices and salt. Tightly pack in the chiles,
arranging them stem up. In a small stainless-steel
saucepan, bring the vinegar to a boil and pour it over
the chiles. Follow with boiling water, leaving ½ inch
headspace. Let cool and store in the refrigerator for up
to 1 month or process for 10 minutes using the boiling-
water method (see the sidebar at right).

The Boiling-Water Method for Canning Chiles

1. Wash the jars and screw bands with
hot, soapy water and rinse them well.
Follow the manufacturer's directions for
preparing the lids. The jars must be hot
when you pack them; otherwise, the hot
brine may cause them to shatter.

2. Pack the jars tightly, and then pour
in the hot brine to cover the vegetables,
allowing the specified amount of
headspace (the space between the rim of
the jar and its contents).

3. Remove air bubbles by slowly raising
and lowering a chopstick or a plastic
blade around the inside of the jars. This
is crucial: A trapped air bubble may
shatter a jar as it heats. Add more brine
to cover the vegetables, if necessary.

4. Wipe the jars' rims with a damp
cloth; put on the lids. Twist the screw
bands into place.

5. Set the jars on a rack in a canner or
pot that's half-filled with very hot water
(but not boiling, which may cause the
jars to break). Add hot water to cover
the jars by 2 inches of water. Cover the
pot, turn the heat on high, and bring
the water to a boil. When it starts to boil
(you'll have to peek), begin timing—see
your recipe for processing time.

6. Remove the jars immediately when
the time is up. Cool undisturbed for at
least 12 hours. Never tighten the bands
after the jars have been processed, as
this could break the seal.

7. Test the seals. After the jars have
cooled, remove the screw bands and lift
the jar by its lid. (Do this over a towel to
catch the jar if it hasn't sealed properly.)

**8. Store sealed jars in a cool, dry
place.** Unsealed jars should be stored in
the refrigerator and used quickly.

Spicy Asian Roasted Broccoli and Snap Peas

SERVES 4

5 cups broccoli florets (from about 2 broccoli crowns)

3 cups (about 12 ounces) fresh sugar snap peas

6 to 8 red or orange fresh Thai chiles, stems trimmed

3 tablespoons extra-virgin olive oil

2 tablespoons plus 1 teaspoon Asian sesame oil

1 teaspoon kosher salt

2 tablespoons fresh cilantro leaves, chopped

1½ tablespoons light-colored (white or yellow) miso

1 tablespoon honey

2 teaspoons sambal oelek (Asian chile paste)

1 teaspoon finely grated orange zest

1 teaspoon grated fresh ginger

1 clove garlic, minced

Position a rack in the center of the oven and heat the oven to 450°F.

Put the broccoli, peas, and chiles in a large bowl; toss with 2 tablespoons of the olive oil and 2 tablespoons of the sesame oil. Sprinkle with salt and toss again. Transfer the vegetables to a 10x15-inch Pyrex dish and roast, stirring once, until the peas are lightly browned and the broccoli tops are quite dark in spots, about 22 minutes.

Meanwhile, in a small bowl, whisk the remaining 1 tablespoon olive oil, 1 teaspoon sesame oil, cilantro, miso, honey, sambal oelek, orange zest, ginger, and garlic. Pour the mixture over the roasted vegetables and toss to coat. Remove the chiles (or leave them in for color but warn diners not to eat them). Serve immediately.

Quesadillas with Roasted Poblanos and Onions (Rajas)

SERVES 4

2 small fresh poblano chiles

1 tablespoon plus 2 teaspoons vegetable oil

½ large white onion, thinly sliced lengthwise (about 1½ cups)

Kosher salt and freshly ground black pepper

Four 8-inch flour tortillas

2 cups grated Monterey Jack cheese (about 8 ounces)

½ cup loosely packed fresh cilantro

½ cup sour cream

Roast the peppers: Turn a gas burner to high and char the poblanos over the flame, turning with tongs as soon as each side becomes fully blackened, about 6 to 8 minutes per pepper. (If you don't have a gas stove, you can char poblanos similarly over a hot grill fire or lay them on a foil-lined baking sheet and char them under a hot broiler, turning them with tongs.)

Immediately after roasting, put the poblanos in a bowl, cover, and set aside to steam and loosen the skins. When they're cool enough to handle, peel the charred skin off with your hands or a small paring knife. Pull out and discard the stems and seed clusters. Slice the peppers into ¼-inch-wide strips and put them in a small bowl.

Put a baking sheet in the oven and heat the oven to 150°F (or its lowest setting).

Make the rajas: Heat 1 tablespoon of the oil in a 10- or 12-inch nonstick skillet over medium-high heat. Add the onion and cook, stirring frequently, until soft and lightly browned, 3 to 5 minutes. Add the poblano strips, season with a generous pinch of salt and a few grinds of pepper, and cook, stirring occasionally, until the peppers are heated through, another 1 to 2 minutes. Transfer to a plate and wipe the skillet clean.

Make the quesadillas: Heat ½ teaspoon of the oil in the skillet over medium-high heat until hot. Add 1 tortilla and scatter over it a quarter of the cheese, a quarter of the poblano mixture, and a quarter of the cilantro. When the tortilla smells toasty and the bottom is browned in spots, in 1 or 2 minutes, fold it in half, pressing it with a spatula to flatten it. Transfer to the baking sheet in the oven to keep warm. Repeat with the remaining ingredients to make three more quesadillas. Cut each quesadilla into wedges and serve with the sour cream on the side.

Shredded Carrots with Jalapeño, Lime, and Cilantro

SERVES 6

8 medium carrots (about 1½ pounds)

¼ cup extra-virgin olive oil

3 tablespoons fresh lime juice

1 medium jalapeño, cored, seeded, and minced

Kosher salt and freshly ground black pepper

½ cup coarsely chopped fresh cilantro, plus whole
   cilantro leaves for garnish (optional)

Peel and grate the carrots using either the large
holes on a box grater or a food processor fitted with
a medium grating attachment. Put the grated carrots
in a large bowl.

In a small bowl, whisk the oil and lime juice.
Add the jalapeño and season to taste with salt and
pepper.

Add the dressing and chopped cilantro to the
carrots and toss. Season to taste with salt and
pepper, garnish with the cilantro leaves (if using), and
serve.

Other recipe ideas

HOT-CHILE CORNBREAD Add some finely chopped
jalapeños to your favorite cornbread recipe before
baking. A little chopped fresh oregano or thyme
would be good as well.

MAPLE-CHILE GLAZED PORK Mix chopped poblanos
with chopped garlic, maple syrup, and a pinch of salt.
Roast a pork tenderloin and about 5 minutes before
cooking is done, spread the glaze over the meat and
finish cooking.

SCALLOPED SWEET POTATOES AND CHILES Gently
fold slices of sweet potato and regular potato with
roasted, chopped poblanos or Anaheim chiles, and
some shredded Gruyère or Monterey Jack cheese.
Arrange in a baking dish, top with cream, and bake
until bubbly and browned.

Know Your Ground Chiles

Most fresh chiles have a dried chile
counterpart, either whole or ground as
chile powder. While the dried version
will still be spicy, it will display a whole
new set of slightly smoky, fruity flavors.
Here are a few key dried chiles that are
often available ground.

PASILLA (dried pasilla)
Heat level: moderate
Flavor: sweet berry-like
Use in: mole sauce, chili, beef stews,
braised pork

NEW MEXICO (dried Anaheim)
Heat level: moderate
Flavor: earthy fruit
Use in: enchilada sauces, ground-beef
taco filling

CHIPOTLE (dried and smoked jalapeño)
Heat level: hot
Flavor: smoky sweet
Use in: barbecue sauce, spice rubs for
grilling, mayonnaise

ANCHO (dried poblano)
Heat level: moderate
Flavor: fruity-sweet
Use in: black beans, mole sauce, spice
rub for grilled shrimp or pork

Zea mays cvs.

Corn

Corn's sweet, nutty flavor appeals to everyone, and the "delivery method"—the cob—makes eating corn just plain fun. The mellow character of corn makes it a perfect complement to many other summer vegetables, such as chiles, sweet peppers, squash, and tomatoes, so it's easy to incorporate into meals. Corn is one thing that should never be eaten out of season.

PICKING THE BEST

There are four types of sweet corn: standard sweet, sugar-enhanced, supersweet, and synergistic. These names explain the differences among them in terms of sweetness, tenderness, and how well they store.

If you really want to know what type of corn you're buying, ask the farmer or your produce monger, but be prepared to try something new each time. The corn variety you saw on your last visit to the market is probably not the same one you're going to find on your next. In general, the more sugary varieties of corn take longer to grow and appear later at the market.

- **Standard sweet:** Common varieties include the white and yellow Butter and Sugar and Silver Queen, with white kernels. This type of corn has a traditional corn flavor and texture, although sweetness varies among varieties. Its sugars are quicker to convert to starch, so it doesn't keep long after harvest.
- **Sugar-enhanced:** Delectable, Kandy Korn, and Seneca Dancer are three popular varieties. Known for having a more tender texture than the standard type, sugar-enhanced corn is widely popular. Its degree of sweetness changes with the variety, but the conversion of sugar to starch is slower than that of standard sweet corn, so it holds up better.
- **Supersweet:** Varieties include Sun & Stars and Xtra-Sweet. The most sugary of all, this type of corn has less true corn flavor and a firmer, almost crunchy texture, because the skin on the kernels is tougher. It holds its sweetness longer than any other type of corn, which is why you'll often see it in supermarkets, where the corn isn't typically freshly picked.
- **Synergistic:** A popular variety is Serendipity. This type has both the tenderness of sugar-enhanced corn and the more pronounced sweetness of supersweet. It requires more time to mature than sugar-enhanced corn and can be watery if harvested too soon.

Look for plump, green ears that have fresh-looking cuts at their stems and slightly sticky brown silk at the top. If the supermarket is your only option, you'll have to adopt a more hands-on approach: feel the ears to suss out how plump they are and whether the rows of kernels are fully formed. Gently part the ends of the husks at the ear tip and take a peek at what's inside.

The kernels should be firm and shiny. When buying corn, there's only one absolute rule: never buy shucked corn. This trick hides the evidence of old corn: dried cuts on the stems, lackluster husks, and wilting silk.

KEEPING IT FRESH

Don't shuck the corn until you're ready to use it. If you're not going to cook it the day you buy it, stow the ears in the refrigerator, loosely wrapped In a dry plastic bag, but don't wait more than a day because corn's sugars will turn to starch over time.

PREPARING

Pull off the husks and as many of the fine silks as you can, then wipe off remaining silks with a damp cloth.

HOW TO USE IT

If corn is truly fresh and sweet, you can eat the kernels raw. Or cook the ears quickly to soften and develop flavors. The simplest method for cooking corn is to plunge it in rapidly boiling water for 2 minutes. The water should be unsalted; salted water tends to make the kernels tough. You can also steam the ears. Grilling corn adds a smokiness that enhances its flavor. Some cooks peel off the outer layers of husk, leaving a few inner layers, and grill the corn for 10 to 15 minutes; it steams a bit but still picks up the flavor of the grill. Other cooks like to peel off all the husks and silks, rub the corn with oil and seasonings, and grill directly over a medium fire for 10 minutes, turning frequently.

Cut kernels off the cob and add them to quick breads, pancakes, pastas, puddings, salsa, salads, and soufflés. (See p. 297 for more on cutting corn off the cob.)

SURPRISING PAIRINGS

Corn and chile go well together. The Mexican snack called *elote* bring these two together in a way that becomes addictive. Steam or grill an ear of corn, slather with butter then mayonnaise, then sprinkle generously with grated cotija cheese and cayenne pepper, and squeeze fresh lime juice over top.

PRESERVING OPTIONS

Cut the kernels off the cobs and blanch them in boiling water for 1 or 2 minutes. Drain, let cool, then spread in a single layer on a baking sheet and freeze until hard. Store in an airtight container for up to 3 months.

See p. 297

.... RECIPES ....

Fresh Corn Pancakes with Maple Syrup

MAKES ABOUT 16 FOUR-INCH PANCAKES
Kernels from 1 ear sweet corn (1 cup)
2 cups buttermilk
2 large eggs
3 ounces (6 tablespoons) unsalted butter, melted; more for serving
4½ ounces (1 cup) unbleached all-purpose flour
½ cup yellow cornmeal
2 teaspoons sugar
½ teaspoon baking soda, sifted to remove lumps
1 teaspoon kosher salt
Pure maple syrup, for serving

Bring a small pot of water to a boil. Add the corn kernels and blanch for 1 minute. Drain and set aside.

In a small bowl, whisk the buttermilk, eggs, and butter. In a larger bowl, whisk the flour, cornmeal, sugar, baking soda, and salt to blend. Add the wet ingredients to the dry and stir until just combined— there will still be lumps. Gently fold in the corn.

Lightly oil a griddle or cast-iron skillet and heat until it's medium hot; a few droplets of water will dance on the surface for a few seconds before disappearing. For each pancake, pour about ¼ cup batter onto the griddle and spread into a circle. When a few bubbles break on the top and the bottom is lightly golden, gently flip each pancake and cook until golden on the bottom, 1 to 3 minutes per side. Cook the remaining batter in batches, as necessary. Serve right away with butter and maple syrup.

Other recipe ideas

CORN AND VEGETABLE TART Fill a partially baked tart shell with raw corn, sautéed diced bell pepper and onion, sautéed sliced mushrooms, and chopped blanched spinach, all bound with beaten eggs and a spoonful of creamy ricotta or goat cheese. Bake until just set, then serve warm with a green salad on top.

TANGY CORN SAUTÉ Sauté freshly cut corn kernels in olive oil and butter until just browned and getting a touch sticky. Season with fresh lime juice, hot sauce, and finish with finely sliced fresh basil.

Western, or globe

Graffiti

Italian

Solanum melongena cvs.

Eggplant

Eggplant may be one of the more mysterious elements in the produce aisle, not just because of its unusual range of vibrant colors and sensuous shapes, but also because it undergoes one of the more dramatic transformations during cooking. Raw, it's unpalatable—just spongy and dry. But cooked, it becomes creamy and silky with a mellow nuttiness. Eggplant also is greedy for other flavors, soaking up whatever it's cooked with, thereby extending the flavors in your dish.

PICKING THE BEST

The big, dark purple globe eggplant is ubiquitous, but fortunately many other more intriguing varieties have made their way into our markets recently.

- **Western or globe eggplant:** The most common and versatile variety, its larger size enables you to get slices and chunks. It varies in size from ¾ pound to 1¼ pounds, with dark purple skin.
- **Italian eggplant:** Smaller than the globe variety, Italian eggplant is lobed, with dark purple skin and green leaves.
- **Chinese eggplant:** Elongated and slender with light purple skin, Chinese eggplant is quick-cooking, which makes it a good candidate for stir-frying.
- **Japanese eggplant:** Like Chinese eggplant, Japanese eggplant is elongated, slender, and quick-cooking. This variety has dark purple skin. Its brownish leaves distinguish it from the Italian eggplant.
- **White eggplant:** Oval, with a beautiful eggshell-white hue, the flesh of white eggplant is especially creamy and less bitter than darker eggplant.
- **Southeast Asian eggplant:** The size of a cherry tomato, and green-striped, white, orange-red, or purple, these varieties can be quite bitter and are best for pickling.

No matter which variety you choose, look for eggplant with smooth, shiny skin that's unwrinkled. The fruit should feel firm and spring back slightly when you touch it. Try to find an eggplant with a stem that looks moist, as if recently cut.

KEEPING IT FRESH

It's best to use eggplant when it's very fresh, but it will keep for 2 or 3 days in the crisper drawer of the refrigerator. Eggplant can also be frozen (see preserving options on p. 114).

PREPARING

In smaller eggplant, seeds aren't a problem, but a mature globe eggplant can contain many small seeds, which can darken and become bitter as the eggplant matures. Eggplant with parts of dark, hardened pulp with lots of dark seeds will be a disappointment—these parts must be removed; otherwise, the flavor and the texture of the finished dish will suffer.

The larger varieties of eggplant benefit from peeling, because the peel can be slightly tough, but most of the smaller types need only their stem ends trimmed.

Globe eggplant are spongy and can soak up oil, so salting is a good idea. According to food scientist

113

Harold McGee, salting draws out water and helps collapse the air pockets in globe eggplant's spongy flesh,
which makes the eggplant much less able to soak up
lots of oil during cooking.

HOW TO USE IT

Eggplant is one vegetable for which slight under-
cooking will not work. It must be completely cooked
through until it's soft, smooth, and creamy. The best
cooking methods include high heat and some fat,
both of which transform the flesh from vegetal to rich.
Frying, stir-frying, grilling, or roasting are perfect for
slices or chunks, and char-roasting a whole eggplant
over a grill produces a deep smoky flavor. The charred
skin peels off easily.

PRESERVING OPTIONS

Eggplant freezes well but should be frozen within a
few days after harvesting in order to preserve its firm
texture. Blanching is required to deactivate surface
enzymes that contribute to a change in color and flavor. The eggplant should be sliced thinly, dropped in a
boiling water-lemon juice mixture, and blanched for
4 minutes. Once cooled completely in an ice water
bath then drained, the eggplant slices can be stored
in zip-top freezer bags. Frozen eggplant will keep for
up to a year.

Grilled Eggplant
with Toasted Breadcrumb Salsa Verde

SERVES 4 TO 6 AS A SIDE DISH

FOR THE SALSA VERDE

½ cup fine fresh breadcrumbs, preferably from a
   rustic French or Italian loaf

¼ cup plus ½ tablespoon extra-virgin olive oil; more
   as needed

1 small shallot, very finely diced

2½ teaspoons red-wine vinegar, plus more to taste

Kosher salt

¼ cup chopped fresh flat-leaf parsley

1 tablespoon chopped fresh basil

1 tablespoon chopped fresh mint

½ tablespoon chopped fresh marjoram or oregano

½ tablespoon capers, rinsed well and coarsely
   chopped

1 anchovy fillet (preferably salt-packed), rinsed and
   finely chopped

FOR THE EGGPLANT

1 large globe eggplant (about 1 pound), trimmed and
   cut into ½-inch-thick rounds

3 tablespoons extra-virgin olive oil; more as needed

Kosher salt

Make the salsa verde: Heat the oven to 375°F. Put
the breadcrumbs in a pie plate or on a small rimmed
baking sheet, drizzle ½ tablespoon of the olive oil
on top, and mix well to evenly coat the crumbs.
Spread out the crumbs and toast in the oven, stirring
occasionally, until very crisp and golden brown, about
12 minutes. Let cool.

Combine the shallot, vinegar, and a pinch of salt in
a small bowl. Let sit for at least 10 minutes and up to
2 hours.

Combine the remaining ¼ cup oil with the herbs,
capers, and anchovy in a medium bowl. Set aside
until ready to serve.

Grill the eggplant: Prepare a medium-high charcoal or gas grill fire. Brush both sides of the eggplant slices with olive oil and season with salt. Grill
(covered on a gas grill; uncovered on a charcoal grill)
until golden-brown grill marks form, 3 to 4 minutes.
Turn the eggplant and grill until tender and well
marked on the second side, 3 to 4 minutes more. The

interior should be grayish and soft rather than white and hard.

To serve: Combine the shallot mixture and the toasted breadcrumbs with the herb mixture. If the salsa verde seems too dry, add a bit more olive oil. Season to taste with more salt or vinegar, if necessary—it should have a nice acidic kick. Spoon the salsa verde on top of grilled eggplant slices or serve on the side.

Make Ahead: You can grill the eggplant in advance and serve it at room temperature, but wait until just before serving to combine the shallot mixture with the toasted breadcrumbs, so the breadcrumbs stay crunchy.

Eggplant and Tomato Gratin with Mint, Feta, and Kalamata Olives

SERVES 6 TO 8 AS A SIDE DISH; 4 AS A MAIN DISH

FOR THE EGGPLANT

2 pounds eggplant

½ tablespoons olive oil

½ teaspoon kosher salt

FOR THE ONIONS

2 tablespoons olive oil, plus more for the baking dish

2 medium onions (14 ounces total), thinly sliced

2 cloves garlic, minced

TO ASSEMBLE THE GRATIN

1¼ pounds ripe red tomatoes, cored and cut into ¼-inch slices

¼ cup plus 1 tablespoon chopped fresh mint

6 ounces (1 cup) crumbled feta

⅓ cup pitted and quartered Kalamata olives

Kosher salt and freshly ground black pepper

⅓ cup fresh breadcrumbs

1½ tablespoons plus 1 teaspoon olive oil

⅓ cup toasted chopped pine nuts

Cut and cook the eggplant: Trim the ends from the eggplant and, using a vegetable peeler, peel off ½-inch strips of skin along the length of the eggplant every ½ inch or so. (Or leave the eggplant unpeeled, if you like.) Cut the eggplant crosswise into ⅜-inch slices and cut the widest slices in half.

Heat the oven to 450°F. Cover two baking sheets with parchment, lightly brushed with olive oil. Arrange the eggplant slices in one layer on the parchment, brush with the remaining oil, and season with the salt. Roast until lightly browned and somewhat shrunken, about 25 minutes, rotating the pans after 12 minutes. Let cool. Reduce the oven temperature to 375°F.

Cook the onions: In a medium skillet, heat the olive oil over medium heat. Add the onion and sauté, stirring frequently, until limp and golden brown, about 20 minutes. Reduce the heat to medium low if they're browning too quickly. Add the garlic and sauté until soft and fragrant, 1 to 2 minutes. Spread the onions and garlic evenly in an oiled 2-quart shallow gratin dish (preferably oval). Let cool.

Assemble the gratin: Put the tomato slices on a shallow plate to drain for a few minutes; discard the collected juices. Sprinkle 1 tablespoon of the mint over the onion in the gratin dish. Starting at one end, lay a row of slightly overlapping tomato slices across the width of the dish; sprinkle with some mint and feta. Next, lay a row of eggplant slices against the tomatoes (overlapping the first row by two-thirds). Sprinkle again with mint and feta. Repeat with alternating rows of tomato and eggplant slices, seasoning each as you go, and occasionally pushing the rows back. Tuck the quartered olives randomly between the tomato and eggplant slices.

In a small bowl, mix the breadcrumbs, 1½ tablespoons of the olive oil, and pine nuts. When the gratin is full, sprinkle the vegetables with about ½ teaspoon salt and any remaining mint and feta. Season lightly with pepper, drizzle with the remaining 1 teaspoon olive oil, and cover with the breadcrumb and pine nut mixture. Cook until well browned all over and the juices have bubbled for a while and reduced considerably, 65 to 70 minutes. Let cool for at least 15 minutes before serving.

Other recipe ideas

FRESH MOZZARELLA AND EGGPLANT PASTA Toss sautéed chunks of eggplant with diced tomato, fresh basil, and tiny mozzarella balls with pasta cooked al dente; add grated Parmigiano-Reggiano on top.

CREAMY GRILLED EGGPLANT BRUSCHETTA Make a bruschetta topping by grilling eggplant and onion slices, then coarsely chopping them. Mix with a little reduced heavy cream, minced garlic, and fresh thyme. Spoon onto broiled baguette slices and serve warm.

Ficus carica and cvs.

Figs

Silky and oozing with sweetness, fresh figs announce that summer is in full tilt. Once you're lucky enough to eat a tree-ripened fig with its warm, syrupy juices beading on the surface, you'll get hooked on this sensuous and ancient fruit.

Brown Turkey   **Mission**

PICKING THE BEST

The many varieties of fig can be used interchangeably in cooking. Here are some varieties you're likely to find:

- **Mission:** Dark purple skin and reddish brown flesh. Missions are intense and favorites for cooking.
- **Brown Turkey:** A large southern fig, with brownish skin and pink flesh.
- **Royal Mediterranean:** Green-skinned with a purple tinge; the flesh is a whitish pink.
- **Calimyrna:** Green skins and ivory-colored flesh; used for drying and eating out of hand.

- **Kadota, White King, Everbearing, and Strawberry:** Other varieties that you may find at the market to cook and to eat out of hand.

Ripe figs are fragile and soft with thin skin that's moist, fragrant, and sweet. An unripe fig, on the other hand, is firm with a white layer between the skin and the dry, undeveloped center. Avoid figs that are resting on flattened sides or are slumped in their containers; they're likely to be overripe and soured.

KEEPING IT FRESH

When you find ripe figs, use them fast or stash in the refrigerator. Most will hold for a few days, but ripe figs can spoil, even in the fridge. Coax slightly underripe figs to ripeness by leaving them on the counter for a day or two. Store in a single layer rather than on top of one another—they're less likely to spoil that way.

PREPARING

A fig's skin is tender and edible so it doesn't need peeling except for any rough patches or when the skin is still on the thick side. It's a good idea, though, to rinse off any dust. If the stem is long or tough, trim it off.

HOW TO USE IT

Beyond the simple pleasure of eating a ripe fig out of hand, there are lots of ways to use figs in the kitchen. Splitting and stuffing with a salty cheese, incorporating into a pan sauce for rich meat or poultry, adding to salads, roasting with butter and sugar, baking into tarts and cakes, even using in ice cream are all ways to enjoy the luscious flavor and texture of figs.

PRESERVING OPTIONS

Only freeze figs in peak condition. Trim off stems and either halve or slice. Spread on a tray and freeze until firm, then pile into airtight freezer bags.

Grilled Figs with Goat Cheese and Mint

SERVES 4

½ cup (3½ to 4 ounces) soft fresh goat cheese

2 tablespoons fresh breadcrumbs

About 6 fresh mint leaves, stacked, rolled into a
    cylinder, and cut into thin strips

1 tablespoon finely chopped fresh flat-leaf parsley

Kosher salt and freshly ground black pepper

12 fresh Mission figs

12 very thin slices pancetta (¹⁄₁₆ inch or less)

1 tablespoon honey

½ teaspoon very finely chopped fresh thyme
    (optional)

In a small bowl, combine the goat cheese, breadcrumbs, mint, and parsley; season with salt and
pepper. Cut the figs nearly in half lengthwise, keeping
them attached at the broad end. Hollow the center
slightly with your thumb. Stuff each fig with about
1 teaspoon of the goat cheese mixture and squeeze
very gently to close.

Wrap a slice of pancetta around each fig, overlapping with each revolution. Don't wrap the
pancetta too tightly or you'll force the filling out
or cause the figs to split. Cover the figs with plastic
wrap and refrigerate (up to 1 day ahead) until ready
to grill.

Grill the figs over a moderately hot fire to crisp
the pancetta and to warm the figs and cheese, 8 to
10 minutes. Transfer the figs to a serving dish.
Combine the honey and thyme, if using, and drizzle
over the figs. Serve with good crusty bread.

Fig and Anise Ice Cream

MAKES 6 CUPS

1½ pounds ripe figs, stems removed and unpeeled

⅓ cup plus 2 tablespoons sugar

2 cups cream or half-and-half

⅓ cup honey

1 teaspoon anise seeds

3 large eggs, separated

1 cup crème fraîche

Purée the figs in a food processor or blender. Transfer
the purée to a 10-inch skillet with ⅓ cup of the sugar.
Cook over medium heat, stirring often to prevent
sticking, until the figs have thickened into a jam,
about 30 minutes.

In a saucepan, heat the cream, honey, and anise
seeds over medium heat. Bring to a boil, stirring to
dissolve the honey. Whisk a little of the hot cream
into the egg yolks, and then whisk them back into the
pan. Cook over low heat, stirring constantly, until the
mixture thickens and coats the spoon. Immediately
transfer to a bowl. Stir in the fig purée and crème
fraîche and chill thoroughly.

When the fig mixture is cool, whisk the egg whites
until foamy; add the remaining 2 tablespoons sugar
and continue beating until soft peaks form. Fold the
egg whites into the cooled fig purée, and then freeze
in an ice-cream maker, following the manufacturer's
instructions.

Other recipe ideas

HONEY-WALNUT BITES Make a deep crosscut
in a fig, spoon some soft cheese, such as ricotta,
mascarpone, or farmer's cheese, into the center,
drizzle with warm honey, and serve with walnuts.

CARAMEL-ROASTED FIGS Caramelize some sugar,
pour it over whole figs arranged in a baking dish,
and roast the figs in the caramel until tender and
collapsed. Cool the figs, then serve over ice cream or
fresh ricotta, with the caramel drizzled over the top.

Vitis vinifera cvs.

Grapes

Grapes are one of those fruits we've gotten used to seeing in grocery stores all year long, often looking a bit bland and lifeless. A grape at its prime is plump, fragrant, and juicy, bursting with flavor. And a cluster of grapes is visually stunning, available in colors ranging from jade green to lustrous blue-black. Grapes are very obliging to the cook as well, offering an instant snack or a sweet addition to both sweet and savory dishes with minimal prep.

PICKING THE BEST

Fall is also the time of year when you'll come across the widest variety of grapes.

- **Autumn Royal grapes** have large, oval-shaped, black berries. Sweet, with a classic grape flavor, these seedless grapes pair well with salty foods like prosciutto and salted nuts.
- **Champagne grapes** have delicate, sweet, pea-size berries that need gentle handling. These seedless grapes are not used in sparkling wine but are so named because they're thought to resemble tiny bubbles.
- **Concord grapes,** available for only a brief time in the fall, have thick skins, juicy flesh, large seeds, and a strong strawberry-like flavor. They come in purple and white varieties and are ideal for juices and jellies.
- **Green Thompson grapes** are the top seller at the supermarket. Large and seedless, they have firm skins that make them very durable. Their mild flavor pairs well with citrus.
- **Muscat grapes** usually have seeds and come in black and white varieties. Prized for their honey-floral flavor and perfume, they're used for both eating (they're delicious with cheese) and making wine.
- **Red Flame grapes** are sweet in flavor with a crunchy texture. They're ideal for both eating out of hand and cooking, as they keep their shape well and acquire a deeper flavor when heated.

No matter what variety of grape, choose clusters that are plump and firm with no bruising, soft spots, or broken skins. Avoid bunches with stems that are toughened or browned with age. The stem end of the grape bunch should be green and very pliable.

KEEPING IT FRESH

Store grapes loosely covered in plastic wrap (a paper bag will also work) in the refrigerator without washing them. They should last about a week. When ready to eat or use in a dish, let them warm up a bit for the best flavor.

PREPARING

Many grape varieties have a white powdery coating called "bloom." This delicate natural protection helps keep the grapes from losing moisture, so wait to wash them until just before serving. Grapes should be rinsed in a colander under running water. If you're using grapes in a recipe and they contain seeds, you can halve the grapes and flick out the seeds with the tip of a sharp paring knife.

HOW TO USE IT

Grapes are, of course, perfect for eating out of hand, but they also can be used in fruit salads, cold soups, relishes, sautéed to accompany rich meat and poultry, baked into a focaccia or tart, and frozen to make granitas.

PRESERVING OPTIONS

Quickly freeze grapes on a baking sheet in a single layer and then seal them in airtight freezer bags. Because of their high sugar content, grapes won't freeze solid, but will have the consistency of ice pops—a delicious low-calorie frozen treat.

Grapes are fun to pickle in a vinegar-and-sugar brine and some spices such as mustard seed or cinnamon. Serve them alongside sliced prosciutto or salami. And of course, dried grapes become raisins.

White

Red

Purple

Bulgur and Grape Salad with Walnuts and Currants

SERVES 6

1 cup medium-grind bulgur wheat

1 cup seedless red grapes, cut in halves or quarters, depending on size, or Champagne grapes

1 cup small-diced celery (about 3 ribs)

⅓ cup chopped toasted walnuts

½ cup packed coarsely chopped fresh flat-leaf parsley

3 tablespoons dried currants

3 tablespoons walnut oil, preferably roasted

3 tablespoons white balsamic vinegar

2 tablespoons minced shallot

½ teaspoon kosher salt

Freshly ground black pepper

In a small saucepan, bring 1 cup water to a boil over high heat. Stir in the bulgur, remove from the heat, cover, and let sit until the water is completely absorbed and the bulgur is tender and cooled to room temperature, about 1 hour. Transfer to a large bowl. Add the grapes, celery, walnuts, parsley, currants, walnut oil, vinegar, shallot, and salt; toss well. Season to taste with more salt and pepper.

Sautéed Sausages with Grapes and Balsamic-Glazed Onions

SERVES 4

3 tablespoons olive oil

8 links sweet Italian sausage (about 1¾ pounds), pricked with a fork

1 large yellow onion, thinly sliced (about 2 cups)

½ teaspoon kosher salt

2 tablespoons balsamic vinegar

½ cup reduced-sodium chicken broth

20 seedless red grapes, halved

2 tablespoons chopped fresh oregano

Heat 1 tablespoon of the oil in a large (12-inch) sauté pan over medium heat until it's shimmering. Add the sausages and cook, turning every couple minutes, until they're browned all over, about 8 minutes. Transfer to a large plate.

Add the remaining 2 tablespoons oil and the onion to the pan, sprinkle with the salt, and cook, stirring occasionally, until the onion softens completely and starts to turn light brown, about 7 minutes. Add the balsamic vinegar and chicken broth and scrape the bottom of the pot with a wooden spoon to incorporate any browned bits.

Reduce to a gentle simmer (medium low or low, depending on your stovetop). Add the sausages and grapes, cover the pot with the lid ajar, and cook, stirring occasionally, until the sausages are cooked through (slice into one to check), about 25 minutes. Serve immediately, sprinkled with the oregano.

Braised Chicken with Gewürztraminer and Grapes

SERVES 6

1 tablespoon olive oil

12 bone-in, skin-on chicken thighs, trimmed (about 3½ pounds total)

Kosher salt

1½ cups red or green seedless grapes or Muscat grapes

2 cups finely chopped yellow onion

2 medium cloves garlic, chopped

One 750-ml bottle medium-dry Gewürztraminer

2 cups homemade or reduced-sodium chicken broth

1 tablespoon chopped fresh thyme or 1 teaspoon dried, crumbled

½ cup heavy cream

2 teaspoons cornstarch

Freshly ground black pepper

Heat the oil in a 7- to 8-quart enameled Dutch oven over medium-high heat. Season the chicken generously with salt. Working in batches so as not to crowd the pan, sear the chicken, turning once, until golden brown, 10 to 12 minutes per batch. Transfer the chicken to a large bowl.

When all the chicken is browned, pour off all but 2 tablespoons of fat. Add the grapes and cook until just tender, about 3 minutes. With a slotted spoon, transfer the grapes to a small bowl. Reduce the heat to medium and add the onion and a pinch of salt to the pan. Cook, stirring frequently, until tender, about 7 minutes. Add the garlic and cook, stirring, to soften, 1 to 2 minutes. Pour in the wine and simmer, stirring up the browned bits on the bottom of the pan, until the wine reduces by almost half, about 5 minutes.

Return the chicken to the pan, along with any accumulated juices. Add the broth and sprinkle with the thyme. Bring to a simmer, reduce the heat to medium low, cover, and cook until the chicken is very tender, about 25 minutes. Transfer the chicken to a bowl.

Raise the heat to medium high and boil the liquid until reduced to about 2½ cups, about 12 minutes. In a small bowl, whisk the cream with the cornstarch, then whisk the cream mixture into the sauce. Cook, whisking constantly, until the sauce simmers and thickens to the consistency of heavy cream, 1 to 2 minutes. Season to taste with salt and pepper. Return the chicken to the pan. Simmer gently over medium-low heat until the chicken is heated through. Stir in the reserved grapes. The chicken skin will be soft—remove it prior to serving, if desired.

Other recipe ideas

GREEN GRAPE SALSA Roughly chop green grapes and toss with finely chopped poblano or green bell pepper, some minced jalapeño, chopped scallions, lime juice, a touch of vegetable oil, and lots of fresh mint. Serve with grilled pork chops.

HONEY-POACHED GRAPE TART Gently simmer seedless red grapes in a mixture of honey and white wine for 3 to 4 minutes; take out the grapes and cook the liquid to a nice syrup. Top a custard tart with the grapes and drizzle with the syrup.

REFRESHING SUMMER WINE COCKTAIL Infuse Sauvignon Blanc with some rosemary, mint, and lemon zest. Freeze seedless grapes, then put a few in each glass and top with infused wine.

Honeydew

Piel de Sapo
(frog skin)

Sugar Baby
watermelon

Cantaloupe

Cucumis spp. and cvs.

Melons

Like sweet corn and beefsteak tomatoes, richly perfumed melons are a focal point of summer eating. The season's long days and warm nights are just the conditions needed for these luscious fruits to mature and ripen. Melons are just as delicious as a first course for a summer dinner as they are a sweet ending to one, and a slice of cool melon in the morning is a perfect way to start a lazy summer day.

PICKING THE BEST

There are countless varieties to choose from; new types of melons appear all the time, but here are some of the most popular:

- **Cantaloupes:** The most popular domestic melons, cantaloupes have a sweet, nutty taste. An Eastern-style cantaloupe is larger, with soft, thick, juicy flesh; at farmer's markets, you may see it labeled as a muskmelon, a more traditional term. All cantaloupes are ripe when the skin under the netting is a golden sandy color rather than green or bright orange. Western Shipper type cantaloupes, which are smaller and less aromatic than Eastern-style melons, have crunchy-firm flesh and tight, small netting.
- **Casabas:** Casabas deliver an extraordinary melon flavor. With a hard rind to protect its soft ivory flesh, this melon keeps well into winter.
- **Charentais:** A renowned French variety, these plump 2-pound fruits have either smooth or slightly ribbed and sutured gray-green rinds and bright-orange flesh. When ripe, Charentais have a complex, sweet flavor with a luscious flowery aroma and a smooth and creamy texture.
- **Christmas or Santa Claus melons:** These have holiday names because they keep in storage for up to several months and are perfect to buy in late fall for

holiday meals. These football-shaped fruits weigh 5 to 7 pounds and have rinds that are a mottled dark green streaked with gray-yellow markings. The flesh is juicy with a mellow, refreshing taste that's not quite as sweet as a honeydew, reminiscent of a complex Riesling wine.

- **Crenshaws:** Also known as Cranshaws and weighing 8 to 10 pounds, the rinds of these melons are yellow with some green streaks or blotches. The thick, peach-colored flesh tastes like a cross between cantaloupe and honeydew and is meltingly tender. When ripe, Crenshaw melons yield slightly to the touch and feel very heavy for their size.
- **Galias:** Originally developed by breeders in Israel, these were the first hybrid of intensely perfumed Middle Eastern melons. They have a rich green and gold close-netted rind and dense, pale green flesh; they weigh 2 to 3 pounds. Highly aromatic, Galias have intense spicy-sweet flesh and are prized as luscious dessert melons.
- **Honeydews:** Reliably sweet and juicy, they keep quite well for thin-skinned melons. They can withstand being picked slightly underripe and shipped without damaging their taste and texture.
- **Orange-fleshed honeydews:** These combine cantaloupe flavor with the flowery overtones of honeydew taste; fruits average 2 to 5 pounds.

- **Seedless watermelons:** Among the most recently developed melons, they can be round or oval and weigh 10 to 20 pounds. These juicy, easy-to-eat watermelons may have some edible white seedlike structures, but no true hard seeds.
- **Yellow seedless watermelons:** With brittle, pastel yellow flesh that's just as fragrant, juicy, and sweet as their red cousins, these melons have a sherbet-like flavor.

Look for unblemished melons that are firm, with absolutely no soft or bruised spots. Both netted and smooth-skinned varieties should be without wrinkles or bumps on their rinds. Fully ripe fruit should feel quite heavy for its size. Pick up a few and choose the heaviest melon you can find. Ripe melons make a hollow sound when you tap them, rather than just a dull thud. Give it a thump with your knuckles and listen. The melon should smell sweet and flowerlike or richly perfumed, never unpleasantly musky or slightly fermented. The stem end is the best place to smell for ripeness, although some very aromatic thin-skinned varieties are fragrant all over. If a melon has absolutely no smell, it may be underripe, so choose another.

KEEPING IT FRESH

Once you get your ripe melons home, store them in the refrigerator. If you suspect your melon is underripe and hard, you can help it get softer and slightly juicier by putting it in a paper bag on the counter for a day or so, but melons don't actually ripen once picked, so the flavor won't improve. Plan to use melons within a few days. One exception is Christmas melons, a class of Spanish melons that can be kept for up to 6 weeks longer than others.

Take melons out of the refrigerator about half an hour before you plan to eat them because most of these fruits have a perfumed fragrance and sweetness that's dampened by the chill of the refrigerator. Plan to serve them when they're still slightly cool to enjoy their natural aroma and sweetness.

PREPARING

The first step for a melon is to cut it in half and scoop out the seeds. Next is peeling, unless you want to serve a wedge or a half a small melon and just scoop out the flesh as you eat. You can also cut the flesh from the skin and score it into chunks so it's easier to eat at the table. For other uses, such as slicing for appetizers or cutting into cubes for a fruit salad, you need to peel away the hard skin. Whether serving peeled or whole, always wash the outside of a melon in water before peeling: Bacteria sometimes like to hang out on melon skin and can be dragged into the melon flesh by your utensils.

HOW TO USE IT

Many people eat melons only for breakfast or occasionally add them to fruit salads, but melons are really quite versatile. They can be part of a main course, savory salad, and of course dessert. One caveat for using melons in a recipe is to be sure the other ingredients enhance rather than overpower the melon's true flavor.

SURPRISING PAIRINGS

Melons of all kinds, from crisp Asian types to honeyed casabas, have an affinity to salty as well as spicy flavors such as chiles and black pepper. Freshly ground dried chiles, like pasilla or ancho, or chopped fresh green chiles, like jalapeños, enhance the sweetness of melon.

PRESERVING OPTIONS

Melons aren't the best choice for freezing, since the texture will become watery and mushy and they're generally served raw, not cooked. However, you can make frozen treats from melons and extend their fresh taste this way.

RECIPES

Melon, Mint, and Watercress Salad with Salt-Cooked Snapper

SERVES 4 AS A FIRST COURSE

1 cup loosely packed fresh mint leaves

2 cups loosely packed watercress leaves

1½ cups diced cantaloupe or other mixed melons

1 teaspoon kosher salt

½ pound red snapper fillet, cut into four pieces

⅓ cup plus 1 tablespoon fresh lemon juice

½ teaspoon sugar

Portion the mint, watercress, and melon onto four salad plates, reserving some watercress for a garnish.

In a frying pan, sprinkle the salt evenly over the surface and heat over high heat until very hot. Add the snapper and cook for 1 minute. Turn the snapper over, add 3 tablespoons of the lemon juice, and cover the pan. Reduce the heat to low and cook until the fish is lightly browned, about another 2 minutes.

Dissolve the sugar in the remaining lemon juice. Portion the fish and pan juices among the plates and drizzle with the sweetened lemon juice. Garnish with the reserved watercress and serve.

Prosciutto with Marinated Melon

SERVES 8 TO 10

1 medium (4-pound) ripe honeydew melon (or any kind of melon except watermelon)

Juice of ½ lime

½ teaspoon crushed red pepper flakes

¼ teaspoon kosher salt

4 fresh mint leaves, torn into small pieces

6 ounces paper-thin slices prosciutto di Parma or prosciutto San Daniele

1 tablespoon extra-virgin olive oil

Cut off the stem and blossom ends of the melon. Stand the melon on one cut end and slice off the remaining rind. Cut the melon in half lengthwise from stem to blossom end and scoop out the seeds. Halve each melon half, so that you have four long wedges. Slice the wedges crosswise about ¼ inch thick. Gently toss the melon in a bowl with the lime juice, red pepper flakes, salt, and half of the mint.

Arrange on a platter, drape the prosciutto on top, and drizzle with the olive oil. Sprinkle with the remaining mint and serve immediately.

Melons with Ginger Syrup

SERVES 6

¼ cup sugar

One 3½-inch piece fresh ginger, peeled and very thinly sliced

8 cups mixed ¾-inch melon cubes (from 5 to 8 pounds melon)

Leaves from 5 sprigs mint (small leaves left whole; larger leaves sliced into thin strips)

Combine the sugar with ¼ cup water in a small saucepan. Bring to a simmer over medium heat, stirring occasionally until the sugar dissolves. Add the ginger and reduce the heat to low. Cook for 7 minutes to let the ginger infuse. Strain through a fine sieve, let cool, and refrigerate until completely chilled.

Just before serving, mix the melon cubes in a large serving bowl and pour on just enough of the ginger syrup to lightly coat the melon, about ¼ cup. Toss with the mint leaves.

Other recipe ideas

AGRODOLCE FRUIT SALAD Scoop the seeds out of a small melon and fill the cavity with strawberries that have been soaked in balsamic vinegar.

CANTALOUPE COCKTAIL Purée cantaloupe with a few cubes of crushed ice and add a splash of rum. Sweeten to taste with some honey to make a refreshing summer cooler.

SPICED MELON DRESSING Toast some pink peppercorns and crush them lightly. Purée a few slices of very ripe, fragrant melon, such as Galia. Season with lime juice, salt, a pinch of chile powder, and the peppercorns, then enrich with some olive oil to make a tangy-sweet dressing for more chunks of melon served on spicy greens, such as arugula or watercress.

Olea europaea and cvs.

Olives

Olives are one of life's perfect foods: salty, tangy, bitter, and sweet all in one. They're both simple and sophisticated, delectable eaten on their own as well as tossed into stews and salads or puréed to make a luscious spread. They're also relatively low in calories and high in healthful monounsaturated fats.

PICKING THE BEST

One of the best features of many modern grocery stores is the olive bar: an array of olives, from tiny Niçoise to walnut-size Cerignolas, ready to be scooped into plastic tubs and taken home to serve with cocktails. All olives ripen from green to black, through intermediary stages of reddish, brown, and purple.

- **Castelvetrano:** Round and shockingly green, these Sicilian olives are fleshy and buttery with only a very mild tang.
- **Cerignola:** From southern Italy along the Adriatic coast, these bright green giants have mild, sweet, dense flesh that clings to the pit. Cerignolas' color makes them a standout for snacking or serving with drinks. They're a good choice for those who don't like strong-flavored olives. Black, ripened Cerignola olives are even milder than green ones.
- **Cracked Provençal olives:** Brine-cured and then cracked, packed, and marinated with herbes de Provence and olive oil, these olives are great for hors d'oeuvres. Cracked Provençals have firm flesh and a deliciously mild, herbal flavor.
- **Kalamata:** Named for the region in Greece where they are produced, Kalamatas are great for eating and cooking. They are medium-sized with thick flesh and a not overly strong flavor. Picked ripe, Kalamatas are slit, brine-cured, and then packed in vinegar. Easy to pit, they're delicious in Greek

salads with feta, fresh tomatoes, and cucumbers.
- **Lucques:** French table olives with an elegant oval shape and tender flesh, Lucques are mild and buttery; they're particularly good served with apéritifs and a dish of salted nuts.
- **Manzanilla:** These pale green to green-brown olives from Spain are the classic accompaniment to a glass of dry sherry, as is the custom in southern Spain. Manzanillas have crisp flesh with an oily texture and slightly smoky, rich flavor.
- **Niçoise:** This French favorite is produced in the region around the Riviera. These olives have a sharp, somewhat sour taste and often come packed with herbs. A classic component of *salade niçoise*, the pitted olives also make a fine, full-flavored tapenade.
- **Oil-cured or salt-cured olives:** Mostly produced in Greece and northern Africa, especially Morocco, these olives have a meaty texture and a slightly bitter, smoky flavor. Oil-cured olives are easy to pit because of their pliable, leathery flesh. Greek oil-cured olives tend to be milder, while French oil-cured olives have an almost whiskey-like flavor.
- **Picholine:** These small brine-cured French olives have crunchy flesh and a salty-sweet flavor; they're delicious with before-dinner drinks.
- **Sicilian:** Large, brownish-green and brine-cured, these olives have soft-textured and somewhat tart but mild flesh. Sicilian-style olives are produced in

French Picholine

Oil-cured

Niçoise

Kalamata

Italian Cerignola

Sicilian

Greek Gaeta

Greek black

California and are often offered cracked or occasionally packed with chile peppers and olive oil in their finished brine.

KEEPING IT FRESH

Always keep olives moist, either in brine or sprinkled with olive oil. Store olives in the refrigerator, but be sure to let them come to room temperature before serving. Drain brine-packed olives before serving, reserving the brine for storage. Rinse the portion you're going to use before eating or cooking with them. If you need to make extra brine, dissolve 1 tablespoon kosher salt in a pint of water. If the olives you're serving will be sitting out for awhile, dress them with a little olive oil to keep them from drying out.

Though olives are preserved, they don't last forever. If you see tiny white spots on them, it's time to toss them. But don't be fooled by tiny droplets of olive oil that may solidify on the olives in the chill of the fridge; those will melt away after a few minutes at room temperature.

PREPARING

Olives with pits tend to have more flavor than those already pitted. If you don't have an olive- or cherry-pitter, crush the olive with the broad side of a chef's knife, cracking the flesh and making the pit easy to pick out. Crushed olives are also easier to chop.

HOW TO USE IT

Olives don't need cooking, so they can be added to dishes at any stage. Add them directly to salads or a finished dish as a garnish. Or allow them to simmer along with stews and braises.

PRESERVING OPTIONS

Unless you have access to raw olives, the olives you encounter will already be preserved in brine or cured in oil. If you're lucky enough to have a glut of olives, you can pit and purée them to create a simple tapenade and then freeze that.

DID YOU KNOW? Olives are inedible straight from the tree. They contain a very bitter compound—oleurpein—so they need to be cured before eating. The curing process preserves them, making them available year-round, though they're harvested in the fall.

RECIPES

Niçoise Olive Vinaigrette

MAKES ¾ CUP

2 tablespoons minced pitted Niçoise or other black olives

2 anchovy fillets, rinsed and minced

1 tablespoon finely chopped capers

½ teaspoon finely minced garlic

½ teaspoon finely chopped shallots

3 to 4 tablespoons sherry vinegar

6 tablespoons extra-virgin olive oil

In a shallow bowl, combine the minced olives, anchovies, capers, garlic, shallots, and 3 tablespoons of the vinegar. Whisk in the oil until well combined. Add more vinegar to taste.

Grilled Chicken Breasts with Green Olive Relish

SERVES 4

4 boneless, skinless chicken breast halves

About ¾ cup extra-virgin olive oil

Kosher salt and freshly ground black pepper

½ pound whole green olives (about 1½ cups), such as Lucques or Picholine, rinsed, pitted, and coarsely chopped

¼ cup blanched almonds, lightly toasted and roughly chopped

2 tablespoons capers, rinsed and coarsely chopped

2 tablespoons roughly chopped fresh flat-leaf parsley

2½ teaspoons finely grated lemon zest

1½ teaspoons chopped fresh thyme

1 small clove garlic, pounded to a paste with a pinch of kosher salt

Prepare a hot grill fire.

Put one chicken breast on one side of a large piece of plastic wrap. Drizzle about 1 teaspoon oil on the breast and loosely fold half of the plastic wrap over the chicken. (There should be enough room to allow the chicken to expand when you pound it.) Using a meat mallet or a heavy sauté pan, pound the chicken so that it's about ½ inch thick. Discard the plastic wrap and repeat the process with the remaining breasts. Season the chicken with salt and pepper on both sides and coat with 2 tablespoons of the oil. Let sit at room temperature while you prepare the other ingredients.

In a medium bowl, combine the olives, almonds, capers, parsley, zest, thyme, garlic, and ½ cup oil.

Lay the chicken on the grill and cook, undisturbed, until it has grill marks, 2 to 3 minutes. Flip the chicken and continue to grill until it's cooked through, about 2 to 3 minutes more. Transfer to a clean cutting board. Let rest for 2 to 3 minutes. Holding your knife at an angle, cut the chicken into ½-inch-thick slices and arrange them on a platter or on four dinner plates. Spoon the relish on top or to the side of the chicken and serve immediately.

Pasta with Tuna, Tomatoes, and Green Olives

SERVES 3 TO 4

Kosher salt

4 tablespoons extra-virgin olive oil

2 to 3 large cloves garlic, minced

Generous pinch of crushed red pepper flakes

3 tablespoons finely minced fresh flat-leaf parsley

2 cups very finely chopped canned tomatoes with
    their juices

1 teaspoon fennel seeds, crushed in a mortar or spice
    grinder

1 can (6 to 7 ounces) imported tuna packed in olive
    oil, well drained and very finely minced

⅓ cup pitted and quartered green olives

¾ pound dried penne, rigatoni, spaghetti, or perciatelli

Bring a large pot of salted water to a boil over high heat. Heat 3 tablespoons of the olive oil in a 12-inch skillet over moderate heat. Add the garlic, red pepper flakes, and 2 tablespoons of the parsley, and sauté briefly to release the fragrance of the seasonings. Add the tomatoes and fennel seeds. Bring to a simmer, adjust the heat to maintain the simmer, and cook, stirring occasionally, until the sauce is thick and well blended, about 10 minutes.

Stir in the minced tuna and olives. Season with salt and remove from the heat while you cook the pasta.

Cook the pasta in rapidly boiling water. When the pasta is a few minutes away from being finished, return the tomato sauce to moderate heat and add enough of the hot pasta water—about ⅔ cup—to thin the sauce to a nice consistency. Keep the sauce warm over low heat.

When the pasta is about 1 minute shy of al dente, scoop out and set aside ½ cup of the pasta cooking water and then drain the pasta. Return the pasta to the hot pot and stir in the sauce. Cook together over moderately low heat for about 1 minute, stirring and adding some of the reserved pasta water if needed to thin the sauce. Stir the remaining 1 tablespoon olive oil into the pasta and sauce. Serve the pasta immediately in warm bowls, garnishing each portion with a little of the remaining parsley.

Sun-Ripened Tomato and Black Olive Salad

SERVES 6

1 cup pitted Niçoise or Kalamata olives

2 pounds heirloom tomatoes (about 6), assorted
    colors and sizes

1 medium shallot, minced

Sea salt and freshly ground black pepper

1 tablespoon sherry vinegar

1 tablespoon coarsely chopped fresh flat-leaf parsley

3 tablespoons extra-virgin olive oil

Slice the olives into quarters. Core the tomatoes and slice them into large bite-sized wedges or large cubes. Put the olives, tomatoes, and shallot in a large bowl and season with salt and pepper to taste. Add the sherry vinegar and parsley. Season again with salt and pepper to taste; then add the olive oil and toss. (The salad may be prepared up to 2 hours ahead, covered, and left at room temperature. Toss again before serving.)

Other recipe ideas

OLIVE-STUDDED FOCACCIA Stud focaccia dough with pitted green and black olives and brush with rosemary-infused olive oil.

ZESTY OLIVE APPETIZER Season a blend of olives with some olive oil mixed with minced garlic, chopped sun-dried tomatoes, crushed red pepper flakes, and a pinch of smoked paprika.

ORANGE AND OLIVE SALAD Combine orange slices, sliced red onion, and pitted, oil-cured black olives that have been plumped in sherry vinegar and olive oil. Sprinkle with cilantro and mint.

Nectarine

Saturn, or "donut"

White flesh

Yellow flesh

Prunus persica cvs., prunus persica var. nectarina cvs.

Peaches and Nectarines

A juicy, ripe peach is rarely found at the supermarket, because much of what makes it to the store is bred for shipping rather than flavor. The real prizes are found at local farmstands and markets, so grab them while you can. Nectarines are related to peaches and share their sweet-tart, satiny-textured flesh but not the fuzz. And while nectarines tend to be smaller and perhaps not so lush, they're nonetheless a delicious taste of summer.

PICKING THE BEST

A perfectly ripe peach should be firm. The only soft places will be the bruises left by other people pinching the peach before you got there. A ripe peach feels heavy in the palm of your hand, but it will give a little. Look for the golden or creamy background color of the skin at the stem end of the peach. Don't be duped by a provocative blush color (varieties are being developed that are nearly 90% blush). The background color of the skin is all-important.

Size is crucial, too. Bigger is better when it comes to peaches. Bigger peaches seem to be sweeter, more fully developed in flavor. Sniff the peach you're considering: You can smell the nectar in a riper peach.

Nectarines, also sweet and juicy when ripe, are closely related to peaches. When ripe, nectarines are golden yellow with blushes of red. Choose fruit that is rosy, fragrant, and gives slightly to the touch. Avoid bruised or blemished nectarines, as well as those that are hard or very green, which might spoil before they fully ripen.

KEEPING IT FRESH

Supermarket peaches often fail us because they're smaller, picked greener, and stored longer. But if imperfect peaches are all that's available, you can ripen them in a brown paper bag or a ripening bowl.

If you've picked firm, ripe fruit with good background color at the stem end, the peaches will soften in 3 or 4 days, and a lovely fragrance will beckon you. They'll keep in the refrigerator for a couple of days longer. Don't wash peaches until you're ready to use them or they're likely to develop mold.

Underripe nectarines will in ripen in a few days at room temperature—you can speed up this process in the same way as for peaches, by storing them loosely in a paper bag. Ripe nectarines will keep in the refrigerator for about a week.

PREPARING

For eating out of hand, all that's needed for a peach or nectarine is a quick rinse. For cooking, whether you peel your peaches is up to you, and nectarine skin is tender enough to leave on.

When peeling a peach, the trick is to remove the skin while keeping as much flesh as you can on the peach. The best way to do this is to quickly blanch the peaches before you peel them. See more on p. 305.

To slice a peach, run a small knife from stem to tip, cutting right through to the pit. Turn the peach in your hand, making one cut after another and letting the slices fall into a bowl. Most peaches we buy are freestone, so their pits can be coaxed out with the tip of a knife; if a nectarine is ripe, its pit will come away come away easily. Once exposed to the air, peach flesh tends to turn brown quickly. To keep the color bright, sprinkle the slices with a bit of lemon juice.

HOW TO USE IT

Peaches and nectarines are most often eaten out of hand or used in desserts. Their tender juicy flesh and perfumed flavor can get lost when paired with more robust ingredients, though assertive accents such as chiles can be a nice surprise. Traditional desserts such as cobblers and pies are perfect destinations for these tender stone fruits.

SURPRISING PAIRINGS

Peaches and nectarines are soft and subtle but the perfumed sweetness of the ripe fruit has enough character to stand up to the zing of hot chile. In fact the earthiness and heat of a chile—fresh or dried—can make the fruit even more luscious tasting. Try the combination in fresh salsa, with diced fruit, minced jalapeño, diced red onion, and some lime juice, or try sprinkling some smoky ancho chile powder over grilled peach halves as a side dish for grilled pork.

PRESERVING OPTIONS

Peaches and nectarines make beautiful preserves, and they also freeze well. Cut ripe fruit into chunks or slices (peel peaches first). Spread the chunks on trays and freeze until firm, then pile into airtight freezer bags.

···· RECIPES ····

Bellini Pops

MAKES 10 POPS

16 to 18 ounces ripe peaches (about 4 medium), peeled, pitted, and chopped
¾ cup sugar
2¼ teaspoons fresh lemon juice
1½ cups Prosecco

Stir the peaches, sugar, and lemon juice in a medium saucepan. Bring to a boil over high heat, reduce the heat to medium, and simmer, stirring frequently, until the mixture is thick and syrupy, 10 to 15 minutes. Most of the peaches will have broken down, with some softened chunks remaining.

Transfer the mixture to a blender and blend until smooth. Add the Prosecco and blend briefly to incorporate it. Let the mixture cool to room temperature and then refrigerate until cold.

Divide the mixture among ten 3-ounce pop molds or wax-lined paper cups and freeze until just barely set, about 1½ hours. Insert craft sticks and freeze until firm, at least 6 hours more. When ready to serve, unmold or peel off the paper cups. The pops can be frozen for up to 3 days.

Peaches and Nectarines with Rosemary and Honey Syrup

SERVES 6

¼ cup honey
¼ cup sugar
1 sprig (4½ inches long) fresh rosemary; more for garnish
4 medium white or yellow peaches (or 2 of each)
4 medium white or yellow nectarines (or 2 of each)

Combine the honey, sugar, and ½ cup water in a small saucepan. Bring to a simmer over medium heat, stirring occasionally, until the sugar dissolves. Add the rosemary and reduce the heat to low. Cook for 7 minutes to let the rosemary infuse. Strain through a fine sieve, let cool, and refrigerate to chill completely.

Just before serving, halve and pit the peaches and nectarines. Cut the fruit into ¼-inch slices and put them in a large serving bowl. Pour on just enough of the rosemary syrup to lightly coat the fruit, about 6 tablespoons. Garnish with fresh sprigs of rosemary, if you like.

Duck Breasts with Peaches and Tarragon

SERVES 4

Two 1-pound boneless duck breasts
¾ teaspoon kosher salt
¾ teaspoon freshly ground black pepper
1 tablespoon unsalted butter
2 medium shallots, thinly sliced (½ cup)
6 tablespoons dry white wine or dry vermouth
6 tablespoons reduced-sodium chicken broth
3 medium peaches (or 4 medium nectarines), pitted
    and sliced ½ inch thick
1 tablespoon chopped fresh tarragon leaves
2 teaspoons mild honey, such as clover honey

Position a rack in the center of the oven and heat the oven to 425°F. Score the skin and fat on each breast without cutting into the meat. Season with ½ teaspoon salt and ¼ teaspoon pepper.

Heat a 12-inch ovenproof skillet over medium heat. Add the breasts, skin side down, and cook until the skin is browned and crisp, about 6 minutes. Flip and put the skillet in the oven. Roast until an instant-read thermometer inserted in the center registers 130° to 135°F for medium rare, 8 to 9 minutes.

Transfer the duck to a cutting board. Discard all but 1 tablespoon fat from the skillet. Swirl in the butter and return the skillet to medium heat. Add the shallot and cook, stirring often, until softened, about 2 minutes. Add the wine and simmer until reduced by half, about 2 minutes. Add the broth and simmer until reduced by half, another 2 minutes. Add the peaches, tarragon, honey, ¼ teaspoon salt, and ½ teaspoon pepper. Stir until the sauce is bubbling, 1 minute. Slice the duck and serve with the fruit sauce.

Pork Tenderloin with Tequila–Hot Pepper Glaze and Grilled Peaches

SERVES 4 TO 6

3 tablespoons hot pepper jelly
2 tablespoons silver or gold tequila
2 tablespoons orange or pineapple juice
1 teaspoon finely grated orange zest
2 pork tenderloins (1 to 1¼ pounds each), trimmed of
    excess fat and silverskin and patted dry
Kosher salt and freshly ground black pepper
2 to 3 medium firm-ripe peaches or nectarines,
    halved and pitted
2 tablespoons extra-virgin olive oil

Prepare a medium-hot grill. In a small bowl, whisk the jelly, tequila, orange or pineapple juice, and orange zest. Generously season the pork with salt and pepper. Coat the pork and the peaches with a thin film of the olive oil.

If using charcoal, bank the coals so that one side of the grill is cooler. Grill the pork over the hotter side of the grill, turning it until all sides develop grill marks, about 2½ minutes per side. Move the pork to the cooler side of the grill (on a gas grill, lower the heat to medium or medium low) and brush the pork all over with the glaze. Cover the grill or set a disposable aluminum pan over the pork. Grill for 5 minutes and then turn once and brush again with the glaze. Cover and continue grilling until the pork's internal temperature reaches 145°F, about another 5 minutes. Brush the pork with the glaze again, transfer it to a clean cutting board, and cover it loosely with foil to rest for about 5 minutes.

Meanwhile, grill the peaches, cut side down, over the hotter part of the grill (on a gas grill, raise the heat to medium high) until grill marks appear, 3 to 4 minutes. Turn the peaches over and brush with the glaze. Continue grilling until warmed through, another 3 to 4 minutes.

Carve the pork into 1- to 2-inch slices and arrange on a platter with the peaches. Sprinkle lightly with salt, drizzle with any leftover glaze and juices from the pork, and serve.

Peach and Blueberry Galette

SERVES 8 TO 10

FOR THE CRUST

6³/₄ ounces (1¹/₂ cups) unbleached all-purpose flour; more for rolling

1 tablespoon sugar

¹/₂ teaspoon salt

5¹/₂ ounces (¹/₂ cup plus 3 tablespoons) unsalted butter, chilled and cut into ¹/₂-inch dice

1 large egg yolk

3 tablespoons whole milk

FOR THE FILLING

1 pound peaches, peeled and cut into ¹/₂-inch slices (about 2 cups)

³/₄ pound blueberries, rinsed and picked through (about 2 cups) (1 pint)

¹/₄ cup light muscovado sugar or light brown sugar

2 tablespoons unbleached all-purpose flour

¹/₄ teaspoon ground cinnamon

Pinch of salt

1 large egg, beaten

2 tablespoons demerara sugar

Make the dough: Combine the flour, sugar, and salt in a stand mixer fitted with a paddle attachment at low speed. Add the butter to the flour. Mix until the flour is no longer white and holds together when you clump it with your fingers, 1 to 2 minutes. If there are still lumps of butter larger than the size of peas, break them up with your fingers.

In a small bowl, beat the egg yolk and milk, and add to the flour mixture. Mix on low speed just until the dough comes together, about 15 seconds; the dough will be somewhat soft. Turn the dough out onto a sheet of plastic wrap, press it into a flat disk, wrap it in the plastic, and let rest in the refrigerator for 15 to 20 minutes before rolling out. Meanwhile, position a rack in the center of the oven and heat the oven to 350°F. Line a large rimmed baking sheet with parchment paper.

Make the filling and roll out the dough: In a medium bowl, toss the peaches and blueberries with the muscovado sugar, flour, cinnamon, and salt.

Lightly flour a large work surface and roll out the dough to a 12- to 13-inch round. Transfer to the prepared baking sheet. Arrange the fruit in the center

of the dough, leaving about 1¹/₂ inches of space around the perimeter of the dough empty. Fold the outside edge of the dough over the fruit, making occasional pleats. Brush the crust with the egg. Sprinkle the demerara sugar evenly over the dough and fruit.

Bake the galette until the crust turns a light brown and the filling bubbles, about 50 minutes. Let cool for 10 minutes, then cut into wedges and serve warm.

Peach or Nectarine Cobbler with Star Anise

SERVES 8

FOR THE FILLING

¹/₂ cup packed light brown sugar

1 tablespoon cornstarch

Scant ¹/₄ teaspoon freshly ground star anise

Pinch of salt

3 pounds firm-ripe peaches or nectarines (about 6 large or 8 medium), pitted

1 teaspoon pure vanilla extract

FOR THE COBBLER TOPPING

4¹/₂ ounces (1 cup) unbleached all-purpose flour; more for rolling

¹/₃ cup fine cornmeal

¹/₃ cup packed light brown sugar

1¹/₂ teaspoons baking powder

¹/₄ teaspoon salt

Pinch of freshly ground star anise

2 ounces (4 tablespoons) cold unsalted butter, cut into ³/₄-inch pieces; more for the baking dish

6 tablespoons heavy cream

Lightly sweetened whipped cream, for garnish

Position a rack in the center of the oven; heat the oven to 375°F. Lightly butter a 10-cup baking dish (10x2-inch round or 9-inch square).

Make the filling: In a large bowl, mix the brown sugar, cornstarch, ground star anise, and salt until combined; break up any lumps.

Cut the fruit into 1-inch-wide wedges and cut each wedge in half crosswise. Add the fruit and vanilla to the dry ingredients and toss to coat evenly. Pour the fruit and its juices into the buttered baking dish, scraping the bowl of any sugar. Spread the fruit evenly.

Make the topping: In a food processor, combine
the flour, cornmeal, brown sugar, baking powder, salt,
and ground star anise. Pulse briefly to blend. Add the
cold butter pieces and pulse until they're the size of
small peas. Pour the cream over the dough and pulse
just until moist crumbs form. Dump the dough onto
a lightly floured work surface. Gather the dough and
press it to form a square that's 1 inch thick. Lightly
flour the dough. Roll it out, flouring as needed, to a
½-inch-thick rectangle; it should measure about
5x9 inches. Cut the rectangle in half lengthwise,
and cut each half into four pieces, each about
2½ x 2¼ inches.

Arrange the dough squares on top of the fruit,
leaving space around each one. Bake until the filling
is bubbling and the topping is nicely browned, about
40 minutes. The cobbler is best when served warm
on the same day it's baked, preferably with a little
lightly sweetened whipped cream on the side.

Individual Nectarine Tarts

MAKES 8 TARTS

2 sheets (each about 9½x10 inches) prepared puff
    pastry (Pepperidge Farm® works fine), thawed
2 pounds ripe nectarines, pitted and cut into
    ⅛-inch slices
¼ cup sugar
2 ounces (4 tablespoons) unsalted butter, cut into
    small bits

Cut each pastry sheet in half lengthwise and then
crosswise into quarters. Line two baking sheets with
parchment and heat the oven to 425°F.

Roll out each pastry rectangle until it's about
7½x5 inches; don't worry about keeping it a perfect
rectangle. Arrange the pastry on the baking sheets,
and fold up the two long edges of each to make
about a ½-inch border. Arrange the sliced fruit down
the center of each rectangle, sprinkle with sugar, and
dot with butter. Bake in the hot oven until the pastry
is deep golden brown on the bottom and the fruit
looks slightly browned around the edges, 20 to
30 minutes. Serve warm.

Peach-Champagne Granita

MAKES ABOUT 6 CUPS

3 pounds ripe peaches (about 10), with skins
Pinch of salt
1 tablespoon fresh lemon juice
3 tablespoons Champagne
1 cup simple syrup

Wash and pit the peaches. Put them in a nonreactive
pot with the salt, lemon juice, and Champagne. Cook
until soft, stirring often, so the peaches don't scorch.
Cool and then purée in a food processor until smooth.
Combine with the simple syrup and freeze in a plastic
container with a tight-fitting lid for at least 24 hours.
When ready to serve, let the container sit on the
counter for about 20 minutes. Then, using an ice
cream scoop or larger spoon, scrape the ice. Transfer
to chilled serving dishes and serve. Keep any leftover
granita in the freezer for 6 weeks.

Other recipe ideas

**BAKED PEACHES WITH AMARETTI AND BLACKBERRY
SAUCE** Fill the cavities of halved peaches with
a mixture of butter, sugar, crushed amaretti
cookies, and chopped toasted almonds.
Bake the fruit with a splash of sweet white
wine until tender and juicy and serve with a
blackberry coulis.

**GRILLED PEACHES AND POUND CAKE WITH GINGER
WHIPPED CREAM** Brush peach or nectarine
halves and thick slices of pound cake with
melted butter. Grill on a very clean grill until
golden brown and the fruit is soft. Slice
the fruit, pile it onto the cake, and top with
sweetened whipped cream that's folded with
chopped candied ginger.

NECTARINE-CHILE SALSA Dice ripe nectarines
and toss with minced fresh chile (such as
habanero), lime juice, diced red onion, sliced
basil, and a touch of olive oil. Serve with grilled
pork tenderloin or grilled halibut.

Prunus domestica cvs.

Plums

When summer's in full swing, one of the most seductive sights at farmer's markets and produce stands is plums. From celadon green to flame red to ruby and deep purple, these taut-skinned, glossy beauties are irresistible. And plums are sassy—bursting with juice but not too sweet—so they make a great snack and are terrific for cooking and baking.

PICKING THE BEST

Once harvested, plums don't store well and must be shipped and sold within 10 days, so growers produce several varieties (there are more than 200 varieties of plums!) that ripen on a staggered schedule from mid-May through October to ensure constant supply. What this means is that the red or purple plums you saw on your last market visit are probably not the same varieties you'll find on your next.

- **Black Amber and Laroda:** These black plums have a scarlet cast. Their flavor is relatively mild, but their dark skin adds depth of color to a compote.
- **Ebony:** A black plum with yellow flesh, Ebony slices tossed with sugar are delicious with homemade biscuits and softly whipped cream.
- **Frontier:** Another black plum with sweet pink flesh, Frontier can be very sweet when picked ripe and is good for eating out of hand.
- **Greengage:** This old-fashioned, flavorful plum is called Reine Claude in France and is similar to the Wickson, another green plum with lovely yellow flesh and an elegant teardrop shape.
- **Italian prune:** This small European plum (*Prunus domestica*) is usually dried or stewed, but it's excellent in rustic tarts and galettes because it doesn't give off so much juice that the crust gets soggy.
- **Mariposa and Elephant Heart:** These red-skinned plums have watermelon-red flesh that's looks beautiful in tarts and compotes. Their sour skin adds zing.
- **Santa Rosa:** With its rosy-orange flesh and tart, wine-red skin, Santa Rosa is wonderful in sorbets and ice cream.
- **Shiro:** The skin of this yellow plum is thin, almost translucent, allowing the golden flesh to shine through. Lower in acid than other varieties, Shiro is delicious in compotes and sorbets.

For baking: Go for firm-ripe plums. The ideal fruit for baking is neither supersoft nor rock hard but somewhere in between. Take a plum and squeeze it gently in the palm of your hand. It should smell fragrant and feel firm yet springy. These plums are easy to slice, and during baking they become tender without losing their shape or releasing too much juice. If you can find only very firm plums, let them ripen in a paper bag at room temperature for a couple of days.

For eating: Choose firm plums that give slightly to light pressure. Avoid fruit with cracks, blemishes, or soft spots. Don't be put off by the silvery-gray film that coats plums—it's natural.

KEEPING IT FRESH

Underripe plums should be stored at room temperature until they soften slightly. Otherwise, refrigerate ripe plums in a plastic bag for up to 4 days.

Flavorosa

Santa Rosa

Pluot

PREPARING

Plums are pretty simple to prepare, though their small pits can sometimes be stubborn. Rinse and dry your plum, then cut around the fruit from "pole to pole," and twist to separate the halves. Flick or pry out the pit with the tip of a paring knife. Depending on your recipe, use the halves as is or cut into slices or chunks.

If you're using plum slices or halves in a tart or pie, leave the skins on for the color they bring. But if you're going to purée your plums, skin them first, even if they're to be strained (the skins can make a purée unpleasantly acidic). If the plums are ripe, the skins should easily pull away. If they're firm, slice a small x in the skin and pour boiling water over them. Drain them after just a minute or two, and the skins will be loosened enough to peel right off.

HOW TO USE IT

Plums are wonderful in the kitchen because they respond well to heat, becoming succulent and sweet yet holding their shape fairly well. Tart varieties usually need more sugar—often more than the recipe calls for. The sweeter varieties may want a little lemon juice or orange juice to give them some zing.

SURPRISING PAIRINGS

Plums and cardamom are an exquisite duo— probably not a surprise to any northern European bakers, who undoubtedly have encountered the combination in German plum cake (*Pflaumenkuchen*). The highly fragrant spice seems to enhance the spiciness of the fruit, whether in baked goods, compotes, sorbet, or jams. Just be careful not to overdo the cardamom, which gets medicinal when too strong.

PRESERVING OPTIONS

While Damson plum preserves and Satsuma plum jam are justly famous, any type of plum makes a wonderful jam. And you can freeze plum halves or wedges to use in desserts later; freeze the fruit on trays and then pile into airtight freezer bags, or submerge the fruit in a light sugar syrup or in peach, white grape, or apple juice and then freeze in the liquid. The syrup or juice helps prevent oxidation as well as freezer burn.

.... RECIPES ....

Plum Coffee Cake with Brown Sugar and Cardamom Streusel

SERVES 8

FOR THE STREUSEL

2¼ ounces (½ cup) unbleached all-purpose flour

¼ cup packed dark brown sugar

⅛ teaspoon kosher salt

Pinch (about ¹⁄₁₆ teaspoon) of ground cardamom

1½ ounces (3 tablespoons) unsalted butter, melted; more as needed

FOR THE CAKE

2 large eggs

½ cup granulated sugar

¼ cup packed dark or light brown sugar

¼ cup whole milk

1½ teaspoons pure vanilla extract

6¾ ounces (1½ cups) unbleached all-purpose flour; more for the pan

1½ teaspoons baking powder

½ teaspoon salt

½ teaspoon ground cardamom

4 ounces (8 tablespoons) cold unsalted butter, cut into small pieces; more softened for the pan

3 medium firm-ripe plums, pitted and quartered

Make the streusel: Put the flour, brown sugar, salt, and cardamom in a small bowl and stir with a fork until thoroughly combined. Drizzle the melted butter over the mixture and stir with the fork until the mixture resembles a clumpy dough. Using your fingers, break the mixture into pistachio-sized clumps and large crumbs. (If the streusel is sandy and won't clump, add a little more melted butter, 1 teaspoon at a time.) Refrigerate the streusel while you prepare the cake batter.

Make the cake: Position a rack in the center of the oven and heat the oven to 375°F. Lightly butter and flour an 8x8x2-inch straight-sided cake pan.

Beat the eggs lightly in a small mixing bowl. Whisk in the granulated sugar, brown sugar, milk, and vanilla until well blended. Set aside.

In a large bowl, whisk the flour, baking powder, salt, and cardamom until well blended. Add the butter pieces to the bowl and cut them into the flour with a pastry blender until the mixture resembles a very coarse meal strewn with pieces of butter the size of small peas and oat flakes.

Add the egg mixture to the flour mixture. With a wooden spoon, fold and stir until you have a thick batter that's speckled with visible lumps of butter, 45 seconds to 1 minute.

Scrape the batter into the prepared pan and spread it evenly. Break up the streusel mixture with your fingers and sprinkle half of it evenly over the batter. Arrange the plum quarters skin side down on the batter, with each piece at a 45-degree angle to the sides of the pan. Sprinkle the remaining streusel evenly over the cake.

Bake the cake for 20 minutes and then rotate the pan. Continue baking until the top of the cake is golden brown and a toothpick inserted in the center comes out with a few moist crumbs clinging to it, another 15 to 20 minutes.

Let the cake cool in its pan on a rack for at least an hour before cutting. Serve warm or at room temperature.

Pan-Seared Salmon with Plum-Cucumber Salad

SERVES 4

4 small ripe plums (12 ounces), pitted and thinly sliced
½ cup seeded, small-diced English cucumber
¼ cup small-diced red onion
¼ cup small-diced orange bell pepper
Scant ¼ cup small fresh cilantro leaves
4 teaspoons canola oil
2 teaspoons seasoned rice vinegar
¾ teaspoon kosher salt
¼ teaspoon freshly ground black pepper
Four 6-ounce skin-on salmon fillets (preferably scaled, each about 1 inch thick)

Stir the plums, cucumber, red onion, bell pepper, cilantro, 2 teaspoons of the canola oil, the vinegar, ¼ teaspoon salt, and ⅛ teaspoon pepper in a medium bowl. Set the salad aside at room temperature.

Season both sides of the salmon with ½ teaspoon salt and ⅛ teaspoon pepper. Heat the remaining 2 teaspoons canola oil in a 12-inch skillet over

high heat. Swirl to coat the pan. When the oil is shimmering hot, add the fillets skin side down and cook without moving for 30 seconds. Reduce the heat to medium high and continue to cook until the skin is well browned and the sides of the fillets are opaque about halfway up, 2 to 4 minutes. Turn the salmon and cook, without moving, until the fillets are slightly firm to the touch, another 3 to 4 minutes. Serve skin side up with the salad.

Vanilla and Ginger Roasted Plum Compote

SERVES 6

6 firm-ripe black or red plums, halved and pitted
Unsalted butter, for the baking dish
3 to 4 tablespoons sugar
1 teaspoon grated lemon zest
1 tablespoon fresh lemon juice
1 tablespoon rum, preferably dark
1½ teaspoons pure vanilla extract
½ teaspoon grated fresh ginger
Pinch of salt
Vanilla ice cream, for serving

Position a rack in the center of the oven and heat the oven to 425°F. Slice the halved plums into four wedges each. Generously butter an 8x11-inch baking dish (or one just large enough to hold the plums).

In a mixing bowl, toss the plums with 3 tablespoons of the sugar, the lemon zest, lemon juice, rum, vanilla, ginger, and salt. Toss well. Taste one of the plum wedges; if it's still tart, sprinkle in the remaining 1 tablespoon sugar. Pour into the baking dish and roast, gently stirring occasionally, until the plums are tender and juicy, 10 to 20 minutes. Don't overcook them or they'll fall apart.

Let the plums cool for at least 5 minutes or up to an hour before serving. Serve the plums hot or warm with vanilla ice cream and spoon the juices over the top.

Plum Grunt with Swirled Biscuit Topping

SERVES 10 TO 12

FOR THE PLUM FILLING

1 cup sugar

1 tablespoon cornstarch

½ teaspoon freshly grated nutmeg

⅛ teaspoon ground cloves

2 tablespoons unsalted butter

¼ cup molasses

2 teaspoons pure vanilla extract

3 pounds plums (about 40), halved and pitted (Italian prune plums are good but any variety will do)

FOR THE BISCUIT DOUGH

5¾ ounces (1¼ cups) unbleached all-purpose flour; more for rolling

1¾ ounces (⅓ cup) yellow cornmeal

2 tablespoons sugar

2 teaspoons baking powder

¼ teaspoon baking soda

¼ teaspoon salt

2 ounces (4 tablespoons) cold unsalted butter, cut into tablespoon-sized pieces

½ cup sour cream

FOR THE BISCUIT SWIRL FILLING

2 tablespoons unsalted butter, melted

2 tablespoons sugar

1 teaspoon ground cinnamon

Make the plum filling: In a small bowl, combine the sugar, cornstarch, nutmeg, and cloves. Melt the butter in a heavy 4-quart saucepan over medium heat. Stir in the molasses, vanilla, and sugar mixture. Cook, stirring with a wooden spoon, until the sugar is dissolved, about 2 minutes. Add the plums and stir to combine well. Raise the heat to high and bring the mixture to a boil. Cover the pan, reduce the heat to medium, and cook for 3 minutes, stirring occasionally, just to partially cook the plums. Remove the pan from the heat and set aside, uncovered, until needed.

Position racks in the lower third and bottom of the oven and heat the oven to 425°F.

Make the biscuits: In a large bowl, whisk the flour, cornmeal, sugar, baking powder, baking soda, and salt to blend. Add the butter pieces and cut them in with a pastry blender or two table knives until the butter pieces resemble small peas. Add the sour cream and work it into the flour mixture with a rubber spatula

until you have several large lumps of dough that appear quite dry. Turn the shaggy-looking mixture out onto an unfloured work surface and use both hands to quickly knead the clumps of dough just until they gather into one mass. The dough will be stiff and only slightly sticky. Shape the dough into a 4x6-inch rectangle. Lightly flour your work surface. With a long side of the dough nearest you, roll the dough into an 8x12-inch rectangle. Turn the dough over from time to time during the rolling and dust it lightly with flour if it's sticky. Square the edges of the dough with your fingertips to keep it in a rectangle.

Add the swirl filling: Brush the dough with the melted butter. Combine the sugar and cinnamon in a small bowl and sprinkle it evenly over the dough, leaving a 1-inch margin at the dough's farthest edge uncovered. Roll up the dough like a jelly roll, starting with the long edge nearest you. Pinch the seam's edges to seal. With the seam side facing down, cut the roll with a sharp knife into twelve 1-inch slices.

Assemble and bake: Pour the plum mixture (which may be warm or hot) into a wide baking dish (about 8x12 inches, or 2½ quarts, so the biscuits will fit in a single layer). Arrange the biscuits, cut side up, over the fruit mixture, leaving an inch or so of space between the biscuits. Put the pan in the lower third of the oven and set a baking sheet lined with aluminum foil on the rack below to catch any juices that might bubble over. Bake until the biscuits are well browned and the juices are very bubbly, 25 to 30 minutes. Put the pan on a rack to let cool. Serve warm or at room temperature.

Other recipe ideas

HERB-ROASTED PLUMS Roast halved plums with sprigs of rosemary and thyme, olive oil, sliced shallot, and a generous grind of black pepper and serve as a side dish to roast pork.

PLUM-ALMOND COBBLER Toss sliced plums with sugar, cinnamon, nutmeg, and a tiny bit of almond extract. Top with a biscuity dough and bake, sprinkling with sliced almonds and turbinado sugar about 15 minutes before the end of cooking.

PLUM-PEPPER SALSA Toss diced plums with diced red onion, diced sweet red pepper, and cilantro, and dress in an orange-balsamic dressing for a salsa.

All about Pluots

Take a closer look next time you're shopping for plums, and you'll see that they're sharing shelf space with a new hybrid—the pluot, also called an aprium. A cross between plum and apricot, pluots come in several varieties, such as Flavor King, Flavor Rich, and Dapple Dandy, or Dinosaur Egg.

They look like large speckled plums with unusual colors. Depending on the variety, the skin can be purplish black, reddish pink, or gold, and the flesh can range from red to yellow. Pluots usually taste more like a plum with a hint of apricot, but each variety exhibits a different combination of these flavors. Pluots are ripe when they're fragrant and yield to gentle pressure. They bruise easily and should be handled with care. Eat them alone or use in any recipe calling for plums.

Pluot-Raspberry Sorbet

MAKES 6 CUPS

1¾ cups sugar

1 cup fresh raspberries (or frozen, thawed)

6 very ripe pluots or plums, pitted and quartered

2 tablespoons vodka

1 tablespoon fresh lemon juice

In a saucepan, combine the sugar and 1¾ cups water over high heat. Stir occasionally until the sugar is completely dissolved and the syrup is simmering, about 5 minutes. Remove from the heat. You should have a little more than 2½ cups syrup.

In a medium saucepan, combine the raspberries and pluots with 1 cup of the warm syrup. Poach the fruit over medium-low heat until it's very soft, 5 to 10 minutes. Allow the fruit and syrup to cool briefly and then purée the mixture in a food processor or blender. Strain the purée through a fine sieve into a medium bowl.

Combine the purée with 1½ cups of the syrup, the vodka, and the lemon juice. Let the mixture cool to room temperature. For faster freezing, transfer the cooled mixture to the refrigerator to chill there first. Freeze the mixture in an ice-cream maker, following the manufacturer's instructions.

Summer-
bearing red

Everbearing
gold

Everbearing red

Rubus idaeus and cvs.

Raspberries

Raspberries are the gems of summer—small, intense, and exquisite. They're fantastic as is, needing very little dolling up to shine and sparkle—a dusting of confectioners' sugar or a slick of heavy cream. But they also shine in salads and desserts of all kinds.

PICKING THE BEST

The most common raspberries are red, but you'll find black, golden, and even pink raspberries at farmer's markets and specialty stores. The differences in flavor are subtle, but a mix is beautiful.

Look for plump, fragrant berries. When shopping, examine the box to check for freshness. If you see juice stains, it's probably a sign of moldy berries inside. Hold the closed raspberry container upside down. If berries stick to the bottom inside liner, they're crushed and it's likely some are moldy, so choose another box. Even in the height of summer, berries are a bit of an investment, so befriend your produce merchant and request a taste before you buy.

KEEPING IT FRESH

Raspberries are very perishable, so don't count on keeping them for more than a day or two; if you're not using them within a few hours, keep them in the refrigerator. Tip them onto a paper-towel-lined plate so the berries are in a single layer and won't crush each other.

PREPARING

Despite that big explosion of fresh berry flavor, raspberries are extremely fragile. Washing berries isn't ideal, but if you want to be safe, wash them right be-fore using them. Fill a bowl with cold water, gently add the berries, and then lift them out with your hands—again, gently. Let the berries dry in a single layer on a baking sheet lined with paper towels.

If you're baking with raspberries, be sure to taste your berries before starting the recipe. If the berries are very sweet, you may want to reduce the sugar a little. On the other hand, if they seem a bit lackluster, a bit more sugar, some lemon juice, and even a pinch of salt will do wonders to amp up their flavor.

HOW TO USE IT

Pour a drizzle of rich cream over a bowl of perfectly ripe raspberries and revel in summer. To use the berries in cooking, add them to any recipe that calls for berries, but know that the fragile texture of raspberries means they don't keep their shape well, and their flavor can flatten out a bit.

PRESERVING OPTIONS

Raspberry jam is a glorious way to preserve the sweet flavor of raspberries. If you have more berries than you know what to do with, freeze them in a single layer until firm, and then transfer them to airtight freezer bags. While the texture of the thawed berries will be mushy, the flavor will still be bright so the fruit can be used in baking or for jam.

.... **RECIPES** ....

Chocolate-Raspberry Tart with a Gingersnap Crust

SERVES 8 TO 10

Vegetable oil for the pan

About 40 gingersnap wafers (to yield 1½ cups finely ground)

2 ounces (4 tablespoons) unsalted butter, melted

Scant 2 pints (3½ cups) fresh raspberries

8 ounces semisweet or bittersweet chocolate, finely chopped

1¼ cups heavy cream

Small pinch of salt

Position a rack in the center of the oven and heat the oven to 325°F. Oil the sides and bottom of a 9½-inch fluted tart pan with a removable bottom. In a food processor, grind the gingersnaps until they're the texture of sand. Transfer to a bowl, add the melted butter, and work it in by squishing the mixture together with your hands. Press into the sides and bottom of the oiled tart pan. Set the pan on a baking sheet and refrigerate for 20 minutes to firm. Bake the tart crust on the baking sheet until fragrant, about 15 minutes, checking and rotating if needed to make the sure the crust doesn't get too dark. Set on a rack to cool.

Meanwhile, pass 1 cup of the berries through a food mill fitted with a fine disk or force them through a fine sieve, mashing with a wooden spoon, into a medium bowl. You'll have about ½ cup purée; set it aside and discard the contents of the strainer. Put the chopped chocolate in a medium bowl. Heat the cream just until boiling. Pour the hot cream over the chopped chocolate; whisk to blend. Stir in the raspberry purée and the salt. Pour the mixture (called a ganache) into the cooled tart shell. Refrigerate until the ganache is fairly firm, about 1 hour. Arrange the remaining raspberries on top of the ganache; they should completely cover the surface. Chill until the ganache is completely firm, about 30 minutes, and serve.

Raspberry Buttermilk Cake with Vanilla-Scented Crème Fraîche

SERVES 12 TO 16

FOR THE CRUMB TOPPING

2¼ ounces (½ cup) unbleached all-purpose flour

⅓ cup firmly packed light brown sugar

¼ teaspoon kosher salt

2 ounces (4 tablespoons) unsalted butter, chilled

FOR THE CAKE

1 pint (2 cups) fresh raspberries

13½ ounces (3 cups) unbleached all-purpose flour; more for the pan and the berries

4 teaspoons baking powder

1 teaspoon baking soda

¾ teaspoon kosher salt

6 ounces (12 tablespoons) unsalted butter, softened at room temperature; more for the pan

1½ cups sugar

3 large eggs

2 teaspoons pure vanilla extract

1½ cups buttermilk

FOR THE VANILLA CRÈME FRAÎCHE

1 pound (2 cups) crème fraîche

1 teaspoon pure vanilla extract

1 tablespoon sugar

Make the crumb topping: Mix the flour, brown sugar, and salt in a medium bowl. Cut the butter into chunks and add to the dry mixture. Rub the flour and butter between your fingers until the mixture just comes together and has a nice crumbly texture. (This topping can be made ahead and stored, tightly covered, in the refrigerator for up to a week.)

Make the cake: Rinse the raspberries well in a colander under running water and spread on paper towels. Let the berries air-dry for at least 15 minutes. Meanwhile, position a rack in the center of the oven and heat the oven to 350°F. Generously butter and flour a 12-cup Bundt pan. In a medium bowl, mix the flour, baking powder, baking soda, and salt.

In the bowl of a stand mixer fitted with a paddle attachment or with a hand-held electric mixer, whip the butter and sugar on medium-high speed until light and fluffy, about 3 minutes. Add the eggs one at a time, beating well for 15 seconds after each addition. Scrape the bowl, add the vanilla, and continue whipping until the mixture is light and fluffy, 1 to 2 minutes. On low speed, add the dry ingredients one-third at a time, alternating with the buttermilk ½ cup at a time. After the last addition of buttermilk, scrape the bowl, increase the speed to medium and beat for about 15 seconds to mix the batter fully.

Transfer the berries to a medium bowl and toss gently with 2 teaspoons flour. Gently fold the berries into the cake batter with a rubber spatula to avoid crushing the berries too much. Scrape the batter into the prepared pan with the spatula, level the batter, and sprinkle with the crumb topping.

Bake until a toothpick or wooden skewer comes out clean when inserted into the middle of the cake, 45 to 55 minutes. Let the cake rest for 10 minutes before turning it out onto a rack. Flip the cake back over so that the crumb topping is on top. Let cool completely and wrap tightly. Store at room temperature overnight before slicing.

Make the vanilla crème fraîche: In the bowl of a stand mixer fitted with a whisk attachment or with a hand-held electric mixer, whip the crème fraîche, vanilla extract, and sugar until soft peaks form, about 2 minutes. Cover and refrigerate until ready to use.

To serve: Slice the cake and serve each slice with a dollop of the crème fraîche.

Arugula Salad with Nectarines and Fresh Raspberry Vinaigrette

SERVES 6

1 small shallot, minced

3 tablespoons raspberry vinegar

½ teaspoon grated orange zest

1 tablespoon fresh orange juice

Kosher salt

2 ripe nectarines, halved and pitted

6 tablespoons extra-virgin olive oil

Freshly ground black pepper

⅔ cup fresh raspberries

½ pound baby arugula or 1 pound arugula (about
    4 small bunches), stems trimmed, thoroughly
    washed, dried, and torn into bite-sized pieces
    (about 8 loosely packed cups)

Combine the shallot with the raspberry vinegar, orange zest, half of the orange juice, and a pinch of salt. Set aside.

Slice the nectarines into ¼-inch wedges; toss with the remaining orange juice and set aside.

Gradually whisk the olive oil into the shallot and vinegar mixture and add a few grinds of pepper. In a small bowl, very lightly mash the raspberries, allowing them to keep some of the original shape, and then stir them gently into the vinaigrette. Just before serving, put the arugula in a large bowl and toss with half the dressing to coat the leaves lightly. Toss the nectarines with 1 tablespoon of the vinaigrette. Arrange the arugula on a platter or individual serving dishes, topping the greens with the nectarine slices. Drizzle with a bit more dressing and serve.

Other recipe ideas

RASPBERRY AND CHAMPAGNE ICE CREAM FLOATS
Put a few raspberries in tall glasses. Top with a small scoop of vanilla ice cream. Drizzle with framboise or other raspberry eau de vie into each glass, then top with another few raspberries and another small scoop of ice cream. Pour ½ cup Champagne into each glass. Serve immediately with a straw and a long-handled spoon.

SPARKLING RASPBERRY-MINT PUNCH Make a lightly sweetened mint tea and mix it with a fresh raspberry purée from which you've strained the seeds. Muddle some fresh mint in the bottom of a tall glass, add some ice, the berry tea mix, and top with a splash of sparkling water.

RHUBARB-RASPBERRY GALETTE Make a buttery pastry dough and roll into a round. Toss chopped rhubarb and raspberries with some sugar and a little flour and pile in the center of the dough; fold up the edges and bake until the crust is golden brown and flaky and the fruit is juicy and bubbling. Serve with whipped cream sweetened with brown sugar and a touch of balsamic vinegar.

Phaseolus vulgaris cvs.

Shell Beans

There are thousands of varieties of shell beans, in many beautiful colors and patterns. They're creamy and flavorful when cooked and nutritional powerhouses as well. Fresh shell beans aren't always easy to find—look at farmer's markets or grow them in your own garden.

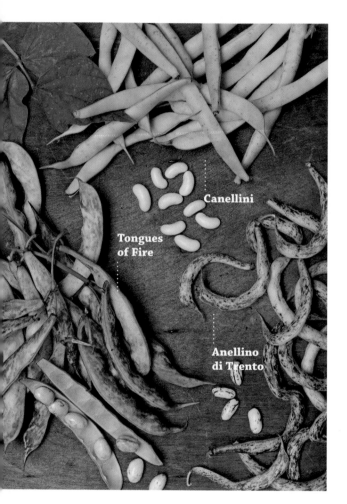

Canellini

Tongues of Fire

Anellino di Trento

- **Flageolet:** A delicate kidney-shaped pale green bean that's beautiful with lamb.
- **Jacob's Cattle:** A kidney-shaped bean with vivid burgundy spots. It holds its shape well during cooking and has a rich but slightly green-bean flavor.
- **Tarbais:** A white bean from the French Pyrenees region, often used in cassoulet.
- **Tongues of Fire:** A red-speckled bean that's part of a larger category of red-striped shell beans called French horticultural beans.

KEEPING IT FRESH

Keep shell beans at room temperature for a few days or up to a week in the refrigerator in a paper bag to allow for a little air circulation.

PREPARING

To prepare shell beans, break open the pods along the seams and use your thumb to coax out the beans.

HOW TO USE IT

To cook shell beans, simmer until tender in lightly salted water or reduced-sodium broth with some onion and a bundle of bay leaves, fresh thyme, and parsley stems. Once shell beans are tender—between 20 and 30 minutes, depending on variety and maturity—they're ready to be marinated for a salad, tossed with pasta, combined with a mirepoix of sautéed vegetables, or puréed with olive oil for a delicious spread. The vivid markings on the raw beans fade with cooking.

PICKING THE BEST

Shell beans are best when pods are full and slightly soft, indicating the beans are mature but not dry. Avoid pods that are withered or have watery or brown spots. Many heirlooms are showing up at farmer's markets.

Fava beans, also called broad beans, are a type of shell bean;. learn about fava beans on pp. 8–9 and 298.

- **Cannellini:** The classic Italian shell beans. Cooked cannellini are good for minestrones and salads because they hold their shape and have a creamy texture.
- **Cranberry:** Plump with beautiful deep pink mottling and a creamy finished texture.

PRESERVING OPTIONS

If you grow shell beans, dry them by leaving the pods on the plant and letting them dry naturally, until you hear the beans rattle inside. Split the pods, remove the beans, and store in jars or bags. Cook as you would any dried bean.

Gratin of Shell Beans and Sausage

SERVES 6

FOR THE BEANS

1 pound fresh Tarbais or flageolet beans

1 large onion, quartered

1 head garlic, cloves separated but not peeled

1 bay leaf

1 sprig fresh sage

1 sprig fresh thyme

2 teaspoons salt

FOR THE GRATIN

6 tablespoons olive oil or rendered duck fat, or a
   combination

2 large onions, finely diced

¼ teaspoon salt, plus more to taste

¼ teaspoon freshly ground black pepper, plus more
   to taste

1 tablespoon finely chopped fresh thyme

1 tablespoon finely chopped fresh sage

6 to 8 cloves garlic, minced

1 pound French-style garlic sausage or sweet Italian
   sausage

Homemade or reduced-sodium chicken broth, if
   needed

2 cups homemade breadcrumbs

Prepare the beans: In a large heavy-based pot, cover the beans with 8 cups cold water. Add the onion, garlic, bay leaf, sage, thyme, and salt; bring to a boil over high heat. Reduce the heat to a bare simmer, skimming any foam that rises to the surface. Simmer gently until the beans have softened, 30 to 45 minutes, or longer depending on the beans. Allow the beans to cool in the broth. Refrigerate overnight to let the flavors meld.

Make the gratin: Heat the oven to 450°F. Drain the beans, reserving the cooking liquid. Discard the garlic and any stems from the herbs.

In a frying pan, heat 4 tablespoons of the olive oil over medium heat. Add the onion, ¼ teaspoon salt, and ¼ teaspoon pepper; cook until the onion is soft and lightly browned, about 10 minutes. Add the thyme, sage, and garlic; cook for another 1 minute.

In a large bowl, combine the beans with the onion mixture. Taste for seasoning and add more salt and pepper if needed. The mixture should be highly seasoned. Transfer the beans to a shallow 2½-quart casserole.

In a hot frying pan, brown the sausages well on all sides. Let the sausages cool before cutting them into 1 ½-inch-thick slices. Arrange the sliced sausages over the beans, then push them down beneath the surface of the beans with a wooden spoon.

Bring the reserved cooking liquid to a boil and pour enough of it into the casserole to barely cover the beans (add chicken broth if there isn't enough). Sprinkle the breadcrumbs over the top and, with a wooden spoon, push them down a bit to absorb some of the liquid. Drizzle the remaining 2 tablespoons olive oil over the top. Cover with aluminum foil, set the pan on a baking sheet to catch any drips, and bake for 30 minutes. Reduce the heat to 325°F and continue cooking for 45 minutes. Remove the foil and cook until the surface is golden brown and the juices are bubbling, about another 15 minutes.

Other recipe ideas

SUMMER MINESTRONE Simmer fresh shell beans in chicken or vegetable broth along with diced onion, minced garlic, and a sprig of rosemary and thyme. Add diced tomatoes and summer squash for the last 10 or 15 minutes of cooking. Finish with a handful of fresh basil leaves and a shower of grated Parmesan.

CROSTINI OF SHELL BEANS AND TUNA CONFIT Simmer shell beans with garlic and herbs until tender, then purée with olive oil to make a spread. Top crostini with the beans and a few flakes of tuna cooked in olive oil.

ORECHIETTE, BROCCOLI RAAB, AND WHITE BEANS Blanch the broccoli raab in the pasta cooking water, then sauté with some olive oil, red pepper flakes, and garlic until tender. Toss the raab and some cooked white beans with the cooked pasta, add a handful of grated Parmesan, and moisten with pasta cooking water.

Globe, or Eight Ball

Squash blossom

Heirloom scallopini

Gold Bar, or
yellow zucchini

Globe

Zucchini

Tatuma
(Mexican Gray)

Cucurbita pepo cvs.

Summer Squash

Summer squash ripening in gardens and piled high on the stands at farmer's markets is one of the happiest sights of summer. The diverse shapes and vibrant colors are a pleasure for the eyes, but the real reward comes from coaxing them to their succulent best in the kitchen. When cooked to perfection, all squash are nutty, sweet, and delicious, whether steamed, sautéed, poached, baked, or grilled.

PICKING THE BEST

When squash is allowed to grow too big, it gets watery, tough, and tasteless, so always opt for younger and smaller, which are more tender because the skin is still thin and the seeds are unformed. Look for squash that's brightly colored, firm, and plump, with a filled-out look and no blemishes. The skin should have a smooth, glossy sheen (though there are some heirloom varieties that have naturally bumpy skins). Stay away from bruised, dull-looking, or flaccid squash, which will be bland and watery.

You can discover new varieties at every farmstand, but in general, summer squash fall into these categories:

• **Green zucchini:** usually medium or dark green with tiny golden flecks; its skin is smooth or lightly ridged. Zucchini-type squash is best when no more than 6 inches long. Lebanese zucchini (also called Middle Eastern) is shorter and plumper than its darker relatives, with a blunt, rounded bottom end. This celadon-colored squash has thin, tender skin and meltingly creamy flesh.

• **Golden zucchini:** Sunny yellow and shaped just like its green cousin; Gold Rush is a good choice.

• **Pattypans:** Generally denser and meatier than other summer squash. You'll find green and gold pattypans, such as Sunburst. Thanks to the scalloped edges, pattypans slice up into beguiling shapes, or they can be hollowed out and stuffed. The best specimens are between 2 and 4 inches in diameter.

• **Round:** Tender and rich-tasting, such as Ronde de Nice or Eight Ball. Handle this easy-bruising squash gently and use it promptly for the freshest taste and texture. Steam or sauté small ones whole or halve and stuff larger ones.

• **Yellow straightneck:** Mild and tender, but with a tendency toward blandness. A good variety is Butter Stick.

• **Yellow crooknecks:** Buttery flavor and creamy texture. Choose small ones that are no more than 4 or 5 inches long. Varieties with full S-shaped necks have the best flavor.

KEEPING IT FRESH

Store summer squash in a plastic bag in the fridge for 3 to 4 days, taking care not to let other objects bruise their skin.

PREPARING

Scrub gently under the faucet, taking care not to abrade the skin. There's no need to peel summer squash; besides contributing color and nutrients, the skin helps the vegetable hold together when cooked.

HOW TO USE IT

Summer squash are mild and therefore quite versatile, but they do benefit from deft seasoning so "mild" doesn't mean "bland." Mediterranean flavors such as garlic, basil, and olive oil are nice partners, as are ginger, soy, and other Asian seasonings. Summer squash are watery, so they do best with high-heat cooking, which will cook off the water and concentrate their flavors; sautéing and grilling are great for squash, as is layering into a gratin, perhaps with some cheese for depth of flavor.

Try cutting zucchini into different shapes, depending on how you're using it. A medium dice (⅓ to ½ inch) is perfect for sautés, but for a more refined look, or to add to a dish during just the last few minutes of cooking, cut the squash into small (¼-inch) dice. Round or half-moon slices are good for soups and gratins. Julienne squash is perfect for stir-fries and slaws. For layering in a lasagna and for frying, cut whole squash into thin, lengthwise slices. And with a V-slicer, you can make long zucchini strings, which are great to toss into soups or cook lightly and coat with a dressing to serve as a side dish.

PRESERVING OPTIONS

You can deal with the dubious benefit of having an overproductive squash plant by making zucchini marmalade, or you can freeze any type of summer squash to use in cooked dishes later. Cut into thick slices, blanch for 2 to 3 minutes, cool, and drain well, then seal in airtight freezer bags. To use in baked goods like zucchini bread, you can grate the squash first, then blanch it by steaming in small quantities for 1 to 2 minutes until translucent. Pack in measured amounts into containers or freezer bags, then cool before freezing.

RECIPES

Pan-Seared Summer Squash with Crisp Rosemary

SERVES 3 TO 4

3 tablespoons extra-virgin olive oil

14 ounces small zucchini and yellow squash (about 1 each), cut into ½-inch rounds

½ teaspoon kosher salt

Freshly ground black pepper

1 tablespoon whole fresh rosemary leaves

Heat the oil in an 11- to 12-inch skillet (preferably cast iron) over high heat until shimmering hot. Arrange the squash in the skillet, cut side down and in a single layer. Season with ¼ teaspoon of the salt and a few grinds of pepper. Sprinkle the rosemary over the squash and sear the squash undisturbed until deep golden brown, 3 to 5 minutes. Using tongs, turn the squash onto the other cut side. Sprinkle with another ¼ teaspoon salt and cook until tender and nicely browned on the second side, about 2 minutes more. Transfer the squash and crisp rosemary to plates or a serving bowl.

Zucchini and Summer Squash Gratin with Parmesan and Fresh Thyme

SERVES 6 TO 8

FOR THE ONIONS

2 tablespoons olive oil

2 medium onions (14 ounces total), thinly sliced

2 cloves garlic, minced

TO ASSEMBLE THE GRATIN

1¼ pounds ripe red tomatoes, cored and cut into ¼-inch slices

¾ pound zucchini or other green summer squash (about 2 small), cut into ¼-inch slices on the diagonal

¾ pound yellow summer squash or golden zucchini (about 2 small), cut into ¼-inch slices on the diagonal

3 tablespoons olive oil

¼ cup fresh thyme leaves

1 teaspoon coarse salt

1¼ cups freshly grated Parmigiano-Reggiano

Freshly ground black pepper

Cook the onions: In a medium skillet, heat the olive oil over medium heat. Add the onion and sauté, stirring frequently, until limp and golden brown, about 20 minutes. Reduce the heat to medium low if it's browning too quickly. Add the garlic and sauté until soft and fragrant, 1 to 2 minutes. Spread the onion and garlic evenly in the bottom of an oiled 2-quart shallow gratin dish (preferably oval). Let cool.

Assemble the gratin: Heat the oven to 375°F. Put the tomato slices on a shallow plate to drain for a few minutes and then discard the collected juices. In a medium bowl, toss the squash and zucchini slices with 1 ½ tablespoons of the olive oil, 2 tablespoons of the thyme, and ½ teaspoon of the salt. Reserve half of the cheese for the top of the gratin. Sprinkle 1 tablespoon of the thyme over the onions in the gratin. Starting at one end of the baking dish, lay a row of slightly overlapping tomato slices across the width of the dish and sprinkle with a little of the cheese. Next, lay a row of zucchini, overlapping the tomatoes by two-thirds, and sprinkle with cheese. Repeat with a row of squash, and then repeat rows, sprinkling each with cheese, until the gratin is full.

Season lightly with pepper and the remaining ½ teaspoon salt. Drizzle the remaining 1½ tablespoons olive oil over all. Combine the reserved cheese with the remaining 1 tablespoon thyme and sprinkle this over the whole gratin. Cook until well browned all over and the juices have bubbled for a while and reduced considerably, 65 to 70 minutes. Let cool for at least 15 minutes before serving.

Sautéed Zucchini with Sun-Dried Tomatoes and Basil

SERVES 4

3 small or 2 medium zucchini (about 1 pound)

½ teaspoon kosher salt, plus more to taste

3 tablespoons extra-virgin olive oil

2 cloves garlic, smashed and peeled

2 oil-packed sun-dried tomatoes, drained and finely diced

6 fresh basil leaves, torn into large pieces

Freshly ground black pepper

1 teaspoon fresh lemon juice

Wash the zucchini well to remove any grit and dry them with paper towels. Trim off the ends and

quarter the zucchini lengthwise. Slice off the top ¼ to ½ inch of the soft seed core by running a sharp knife down the length of each quarter; it's all right if some of the seeds remain. Arrange the zucchini, cut side up, on a baking sheet lined with paper towels. Sprinkle with the salt and set aside for 10 minutes. Blot the quarters dry with the paper towels. Cut each quarter on the diagonal into ¾-inch-thick diamonds.

Heat a 12-inch skillet over medium-high heat for 1 minute. Pour in 2 tablespoons of the oil. When the oil is hot, add the zucchini and garlic and sauté, stirring occasionally, until the zucchini browns and softens enough that you can cut through it with the side of a fork, about 5 minutes. Take the pan off the heat, toss in the sun-dried tomatoes and basil, and season generously with salt and pepper. Drizzle with the lemon juice and the remaining 1 tablespoon oil and serve immediately.

Zucchini and Yellow Squash Ribbons with Daikon, Oregano, and Basil

SERVES 8

3 small zucchini (about 1 pound)

3 small yellow summer squash (about 1 pound)

1 large daikon radish (about ½ pound)

20 medium basil leaves, very thinly sliced

2 teaspoons chopped fresh oregano

6 tablespoons extra-virgin olive oil

2 tablespoons fresh lemon juice

1 teaspoon finely grated lemon zest

Kosher salt and freshly ground black pepper

Small basil leaves, for garnish (optional)

Trim the ends of the zucchini and yellow squash. With a vegetable peeler, shave the zucchini lengthwise into long, wide strips about 1/16 inch thick. When you get to the center of the zucchini, where the seeds are, turn it over and slice from the other side until you get to the center again. Discard the center. Put the zucchini ribbons in a large bowl. Slice the yellow squash using the same technique and add them to the zucchini. Peel off and discard the rough exterior peel of the daikon and then shave the daikon as you did the squash. Add the strips to the bowl with the squash, along with the basil and oregano.

In a small bowl, whisk the olive oil, lemon juice, and lemon zest. Season to taste with salt and pepper.

Toss the vegetables with enough of the vinaigrette to lightly coat them (you may not need all of the vinaigrette) and season to taste with salt and pepper. Serve immediately, garnished with the small basil leaves (if using).

Puréed Summer Squash Soup with Raita

SERVES 4

FOR THE RAITA

½ cup whole-milk yogurt

¼ teaspoon kosher salt, plus more to taste

1 teaspoon vegetable oil

½ teaspoon brown mustard seeds

¼ teaspoon cumin seeds

½ teaspoon onion seeds (optional)

FOR THE SOUP

12 sprigs fresh cilantro with roots, if possible
    (1 packed cup); more leaves for garnish

1 small head garlic, cut across the equator, plus
    1 tablespoon minced garlic

3 tablespoons unsalted butter

1 large onion, sliced (to yield 1½ cups)

2 teaspoons kosher salt, plus more to taste

1 tablespoon minced fresh ginger

2 tablespoons minced jalapeño

½ teaspoon cumin seeds

½ teaspoon coriander seeds

⅛ teaspoon cardamom seeds or 1 green cardamom
    pod (optional)

1 pound zucchini or other summer squash, sliced
    ½ inch thick

¼ teaspoon fresh lime juice

Make the raita: In a bowl, combine the yogurt and salt. Heat the oil in a small pan over medium heat until it shimmers. Add the mustard seeds, cumin seeds, and onion seeds, if using. When they start to pop, add the oil and seeds to the yogurt. Stir, taste, and add salt, if needed.

Make the soup: Put the cilantro, halved garlic head, and 5 cups water in a large saucepan or a stockpot. Bring to a boil, reduce to a simmer, and cook uncovered for 15 minutes. Strain the broth.

Melt the butter in a large heavy saucepan over medium heat. Add the onion, 2 teaspoons salt, ginger, jalapeño, cumin seeds, coriander seeds, and cardamom, if using. Cover and cook, stirring

occasionally, until the onion is translucent, about 10 minutes; don't let it brown. Stir in the 1 tablespoon minced garlic and the zucchini, cover, and cook, stirring occasionally, until the squash is softened, about 5 minutes. Add 4 cups of the broth, bring to a simmer, and cook until the zucchini is tender, about another 3 minutes.

Purée the mixture in a blender (be careful to fill the blender no more than one-third full, and hold a towel over the lid while you turn it on). Strain the mixture and add the lime juice; taste and add salt if needed. Serve warm, garnished with 1 to 2 tablespoons raita and the cilantro leaves.

Summer Squash Salad
with Lemon, Capers, and Parmigiano

SERVES 6 TO 8

1 clove garlic

Kosher salt

¼ cup fresh lemon juice

½ cup extra-virgin olive oil

1 pound summer squash (yellow squash, zucchini, or
    a mix)

Freshly ground black pepper

4 cups loosely packed baby arugula

½ cup fresh flat-leaf parsley leaves

½ cup chopped fresh chives, cut into ½-inch lengths

2 tablespoons capers, rinsed well

1 ounce (¼ cup) finely grated Parmigiano-Reggiano;
    plus a chunk to shave, for garnish

In a mortar or using the flat side of a chef's knife, mash the garlic to a paste with a pinch of salt. Put the paste in a small bowl (or keep it in the mortar) and whisk in the lemon juice. Let sit for 5 to 10 minutes and then whisk in the olive oil.

Using a mandoline or a sharp chef's knife, cut the squash diagonally into very thin (¹⁄₁₆- to ⅛-inch) ovals. Put the squash in a medium bowl, season with salt and pepper, and gently toss with about two-thirds of the vinaigrette.

Combine the arugula, parsley, chives, and capers in a separate bowl, season with salt and pepper, and toss with just enough vinaigrette to lightly coat. Taste both the squash and herbs and adjust the seasoning with salt or pepper if necessary. Layer about a third of the squash in a shallow bowl or platter, scatter about a third of the arugula mixture on top, and sprinkle with a third of the grated Parmigiano. Repeat the process with the remaining squash and arugula mixture, sprinkling each layer with grated Parmigiano. For garnish, use a vegetable peeler to shave long strips from the chunk of Parmigiano onto the salad. Serve immediately.

Other recipe ideas

PATTYPAN GRATIN WITH CRUNCHY CRUMB TOPPING For a quick gratin, layer thin slices of yellow and green pattypan squash and tomato in an oiled shallow baking dish. Season well with salt, pepper, and minced fresh herbs like basil, oregano, marjoram, and summer savory. Sprinkle with breadcrumbs and grated Parmesan, drizzle with olive oil, and bake until golden.

SOUTHWESTERN SQUASH AND VEGETABLE STEW Simmer a summer stew of zucchini, tomatoes, sweet onions, bell peppers, and corn or hominy. Season with cumin, fresh oregano, and chopped or puréed roasted mild chiles like poblanos. Garnish with sour cream and chopped fresh cilantro.

SQUASH AND PEPPER SLAW Make a colorful slaw by tossing blanched julienned squash, red and yellow bell peppers, and carrots with blanched baby green beans. Dress with a vinaigrette of olive oil, red-wine vinegar, and Dijon mustard.

SQUASH AND LEMONGRASS SOUP Make an Asian-inspired soup by simmering chicken broth with a piece of lemongrass, a pinch of crushed red pepper flakes, and thinly sliced shiitake mushrooms. A few minutes before serving, add long strings of summer squash. Garnish with sliced scallions, cilantro, and lime juice.

ZUCCHINI LASAGNA Lighten a traditional lasagna by nestling lengthwise slices of blanched zucchini on top of meat sauce, or use the slices as a layer with béchamel and cheese in a vegetarian lasagna.

Prepping and Cooking Squash Blossoms

If you grow summer squash yourself, or if you're lucky enough to be near a farmer's market, you can enjoy the delicious bonus that summer squash has to offer—the blossoms. Squash plants produce separate male and female flowers. The male blossoms stand atop tall, thin stems; the female flowers are borne close to the plant, and often have baby fruits already formed below them. Either can be harvested, but if you pick female blossoms, you'll sacrifice potential squash.

Harvest squash blossoms early in the day, dip them in a bowl of cool water to rinse away dust, and then shake gently to dry. Pinch off the stamen in the center of each flower. Cut the yellow flowers crosswise into a chiffonade and use as a garnish or fry them whole, filled or not (goat cheese seasoned with fresh herbs is a classic filling). Twist the petal tips to close them, dip in an egg beaten with a little milk, roll in cornmeal, and fry until golden. Drain briefly on paper towels, then serve right away.

Capsicum annuum cvs.

Sweet Peppers

The flavor of sweet peppers balances a vegetal huskiness with sugary sweetness, and the texture is either a pleasing crunch when raw or a silky tenderness when cooked.

PICKING THE BEST

Bell peppers are the most available pepper, but most stores offer at least a few more options, and in late summer, farmer's markets are a rich source. Plus these are all fairly easy to grow in your own backyard, provided you've got lots of sun. Here are some favorites:

• **American bell peppers:** Blocky and uniform in shape with three or four lobes and thick, crunchy walls, these come in a wide range of colors: green, cream, yellow, orange, red, and even chocolate brown. Green peppers, which are the least ripe and can be harsh, do have their place in some dishes, but ripe bell peppers have a gentler flavor. The most commonly available sweet pepper, American bells, are a delicious multipurpose pepper: great for frying, roasting, grilling, stuffing, pickling, or eating out of hand.

• **Cubanelles:** A specialty of the Caribbean and Cuba, Cubanelles are about 4 to 6 inches long. They're mild and delicious fried up for a po' boy, Philly cheesesteak, or traditional Cuban sandwich filled with onions and slow-roasted pork. You can also pickle them or slice them for crispy baked or fried rings.

• **Holland peppers:** Also called Lamuyotype peppers, Holland peppers are similar to American bells, but they're more elongated and somewhat irregular in shape. Like standard American peppers, you'll see them in a range of colors. Once shipped in from the Netherlands, they're now easier to find here.

• **Italian bull's horn or Italian frying peppers:** The

Godzillas of the pepper world, they can grow as long as 12 inches. Green early in the season but deep yellow or red when fully ripe, they have crisp, very sweet flesh that's perfect for slow sautéing in fruity olive oil with a little garlic and fresh herbs.

• **Pimientos:** These classic thick-walled peppers are heart-shaped or look like ribbed, flattened globes. They're bright crimson or yellow and have thick, sweet, crunchy flesh. Pimientos can be eaten like an apple.

• **Pimientos de padrón:** A tiny pepper that's becoming more available now that Spanish food is popular, you fry these in olive oil and sprinkle with salt to eat as a tapa. Most *padróns* are very mild, but one or two in each batch will be super hot—it's a game to see who gets the hot one at a tapas bar.

• **Round cherry peppers:** Both sweet and hot varieties are available. Stuff sweet ones with feta or mozzarella. Pickle them with chunks of other vegetables such as carrots, cauliflower, and cucumbers for a beautiful way to preserve the tastes of summer.

• **Sweet banana wax peppers:** Mild tasting and crisp, with thinner walls than American bell peppers, banana peppers can also be quite pungent. Mild varieties come early in the season and are good for pickling, for salads, or sautéed with pork or chicken.

• **Sweet Hungarian peppers:** These can be pointy, blunt, or lobed but are generally smaller than American bells. They range in color from chartreuse to pale yel-

Banana wax chile

Bell pepper

Mini sweet pepper

Mini sweet pepper

Yellow chile

Cherry bell chile

Hungarian wax chile

low to soft orange and bright red, and from sweet to hot. With their mild but full flavor, they're great in stews, soups, stir-fries, or stuffed and baked.

When you're choosing any type of sweet pepper, freshness is critical for good quality and flavor. Select bright, firm peppers with no soft spots or blemishes. Skins should be glossy and smooth with a visible sheen. Look for strong, clear color, whether it's ivory, yellow, gold, orange, crimson, or chocolate. Fully colored peppers have more sugars, better flavor, and are higher in beta-carotene and vitamin C. Stay away from rubbery, bruised, or dull-skinned peppers.

KEEPING IT FRESH

Store peppers in the fridge in plastic bags and bring them to room temperature before using. You'll get the best texture and flavor this way. Peppers will last up to about a week; after that, they tend to mold. Sometimes the mold is only apparent once you cut into the pepper, so be sure to check the interior.

PREPARING

For most preparations, you'll need to remove the stem, seeds, and interior ribs and then slice or dice. See how on p. 307. Peppers are especially delicious broiled or grilled until their skins blacken. Once cool, the charred skin peels easily away from the flesh, which has become soft and tender from the heat.

HOW TO USE IT

Most pepper varieties are multipurpose. They're good for frying, roasting, grilling, pickling, or just eating fresh. That said, some are more suited than others to certain kinds of cooking. Thin-walled peppers like Cubanelles are often called frying peppers because they fry up more easily than thick-walled peppers do, while fleshy peppers like regular American bells and old-fashioned pimientos are better for stuffing and roasting. Little round cherry peppers are easiest to pickle whole.

PRESERVING OPTIONS

Having frozen pepper strips can make stir-fries and fajitas a quick dinner option. Fleshy peppers freeze best. Core, seed, and cut into strips. Lay on a tray and freeze until firm, then pile into airtight freezer bags.

Charred Peppers with Garlic and Sherry Vinegar

SERVES 6

6 medium red bell peppers
3 tablespoons extra-virgin olive oil
½ teaspoon kosher salt, plus more to taste
4 medium cloves garlic, very thinly sliced (about 1 tablespoon)
3 tablespoons sherry vinegar
Freshly ground black pepper

Prepare a charcoal grill fire or heat a gas grill to medium. Rub the peppers with 1 tablespoon of the oil, set them on the grill, and char on all sides, 8 to 12 minutes total. If the peppers still feel a bit firm, put them in a bowl and cover with plastic—the residual heat will finish cooking them. Or, if the peppers are tender, let them cool at room temperature.

When the peppers are cool enough to handle, skin, core, and seed them. Cut or tear the peppers into strips about ½ inch wide and put them in a medium bowl. Season with ½ teaspoon salt.

Put the remaining 2 tablespoons oil and the garlic in a small skillet and cook over medium heat until the garlic begins to sizzle and turn golden brown, 1 to 2 minutes. Remove the pan from the heat and carefully add the vinegar. Pour the garlic mixture over the peppers and let cool at room temperature. Season to taste with salt and pepper.

DID YOU KNOW? All sweet peppers start green and then ripen to the color that they're bred to be (and purple peppers turn green when you cook them, so if you like the color, use them raw). At the green stages, peppers are less sweet and can be harder to digest.

Grilled Southwestern Potato and Pepper Salad

SERVES 10 TO 12

2 large red onions, cut into ½-inch disks and threaded onto metal skewers

4 red bell peppers, halved, cored, and seeded

¾ cup extra-virgin olive oil

2 tablespoons plus 2 teaspoons kosher salt; more as needed

1 teaspoon freshly ground black pepper; more as needed

1½ cups cooked fresh corn kernels (from 2 ears)

½ pound bacon (8 to 9 slices), cooked until crisp, drained, and crumbled

¾ cup chopped fresh cilantro

1 teaspoon chili powder

3 pounds red potatoes, cut into 1½-inch pieces

3 tablespoons cider vinegar; more as needed

Heat a gas grill to medium or prepare a charcoal fire with medium- and low-heat areas. Put the onions and peppers on a rimmed baking sheet and sprinkle with 2 tablespoons of the oil, 2 teaspoons of the salt, and the pepper. Turn and rub the vegetables to coat all over with the oil and seasonings.

Grill the vegetables, covered, until they have good grill marks, about 5 minutes. Flip, cover, and continue to grill until the peppers are softened and nicely browned, about another 5 minutes. As they finish cooking, transfer the peppers to the baking sheet. Reduce the heat to medium low or transfer the onions to the cooler part of the fire and continue cooking until they are just tender and browned (it's fine if they're charred in places), about another 8 minutes. Move to a cutting board and let cool. Scrape the skins off the peppers if you like. Coarsely chop the peppers and onions and toss in a large serving bowl with the corn, bacon, cilantro, and chili powder.

Put the potatoes in a large pot, cover with cold water by a couple of inches, stir in the remaining 2 tablespoons salt, and bring to a boil. Reduce to a simmer, cover, and cook until the potatoes are just tender, 12 to 15 minutes. Drain and toss with the grilled vegetables, the remaining ½ cup plus 2 tablespoons oil, and the vinegar. Season with salt, pepper, and more vinegar to taste. Let sit for at least 30 minutes and up to 2 hours at room temperature before serving.

Chilled Oven-Roasted Yellow Pepper Soup

SERVES 6

8 yellow bell peppers

⅓ cup extra-virgin olive oil; more for drizzling

1 large yellow onion, coarsely chopped

1 jalapeño, cored and seeded

1 tablespoon chopped fresh rosemary

2 cups homemade or reduced-sodium chicken broth

Generous pinch of sugar

1½ teaspoons kosher salt or fine sea salt, plus more to taste

¼ teaspoon freshly ground pepper, plus more to taste

¼ cup sliced fresh chives (¼ inch long)

Position a rack in the center of the oven and heat the oven to 400°F. Put the bell peppers on a rimmed baking sheet and roast in the oven, turning every 15 minutes, until browned and wrinkled all over, 45 to 60 minutes. Remove the peppers from the oven, cover with a dishtowel, and set aside to cool. Seed, peel, and cut the peppers into quarters.

Heat the oil in a 4-quart saucepan over medium heat. Add the onion, jalapeño, and rosemary and cook, stirring occasionally, until the onion starts to brown, 8 to 10 minutes. Stir in the bell pepper and any accumulated juices, broth, sugar, salt, black pepper, and 1½ cups water. Bring to a simmer over medium-high heat, cover, reduce the heat to low, and simmer for 5 minutes to blend the flavors. Remove from the heat and let cool slightly.

Purée the soup in batches in a blender or food processor. (Be care to fill the blender no more than one-third full and hold a towel over the lid while you turn it on.) Strain the purée through a fine sieve into a bowl, using a ladle to push as many of the solids through as possible. Discard the solids in the sieve and refrigerate the soup for at least 3 hours or overnight.

Once chilled, season the soup to taste with salt and pepper. Serve in chilled bowls, sprinkled with the chives. Finish each serving with a drizzle of olive oil.

Peperonata on Baguette Toasts

SERVES 6 TO 8

1 baguette, cut on the diagonal into ⅓-inch slices

½ cup extra-virgin olive oil; more for the toasts and
seasoning (about 7 tablespoons)

2 pounds (about 7) assorted mild to medium-hot
fresh peppers, cored, seeded, and cut into
½-inch dice

½ pound chanterelle, white button, or cremini
mushrooms, cleaned, stems trimmed, and roughly
chopped (to yield about 2½ cups)

½ large yellow onion, roughly chopped (to yield 1 cup)

1 tablespoon minced garlic

¼ cup pitted and chopped Kalamata olives

¼ cup pitted and chopped green olives, such as
Picholine or Lucques

¼ cup finely chopped fresh flat-leaf parsley

3 tablespoons capers, drained and chopped

2 tablespoons red-wine vinegar; more for seasoning

1½ teaspoons anchovy paste

Kosher salt and freshly ground black pepper

Make the baguette toasts: Heat the oven broiler. Put
the baguette slices on a rimmed baking sheet and
brush on both sides with olive oil. Put the slices under
the broiler, turning once, until golden and toasted.

Make the peperonata: Heat ½ cup of the olive
oil in a 12-inch sauté pan or skillet over high heat.
Add the diced pepper, mushrooms, and onion and
sauté, stirring frequently, until the liquid released
by the vegetables evaporates and the vegetables
start to brown, 10 to 12 minutes. Reduce the heat to
medium. If the pan seems too dry, add a little more
oil. Continue cooking until the onion is translucent
and the peppers and mushrooms are extremely soft,
about another 15 minutes. Add the garlic and sauté
for 1 minute. Remove the pan from the heat and stir
in the olives, parsley, capers, vinegar, and anchovy
paste. Stir in more oil to make the peperonata
moist and oily. Season to taste with salt and black
pepper and add more vinegar if needed. Transfer the
peperonata to a bowl and refrigerate or serve right
away with baguette toasts.

Honey-Balsamic Baked Chicken with Tomatoes, Mushrooms, and Peppers

SERVES 4

1 chicken (3½ to 4 pounds), cut into quarters

1 medium red bell pepper, cored, seeded, and cut into
1-inch pieces

1 medium yellow bell pepper or Italian frying pepper,
cored, seeded, and cut into 1-inch pieces

½ pound mushrooms (button, cremini, or other),
cleaned and cut into quarters

One 14½-ounce can diced tomatoes, drained

3 tablespoons olive oil

2 tablespoons balsamic vinegar

1 tablespoon chopped fresh rosemary

1½ teaspoons coarse salt

Freshly ground black pepper

1½ tablespoons honey

Heat the oven to 425°F. Rinse the chicken and pat it
dry with paper towels. Cut away any excess fat and
tuck the wings behind each breast.

In a large, shallow baking pan (the 10½x15½-inch
Pyrex is ideal), toss the fresh pepper, mushrooms,
and tomatoes. Drizzle the oil and vinegar over
the vegetables and sprinkle with the rosemary,
½ teaspoon salt, and lots of black pepper. Toss until
well coated. Dredge the chicken pieces, skin side
down, in the vegetable mixture so that they get
coated in the oil and vinegar and turn them over.
Sprinkle with the remaining 1 teaspoon salt and more
pepper. Drizzle the skin with the honey. Bake until the
chicken is well browned and cooked through, 50 to
60 minutes.

Grilled Eggplant with Roasted Red Pepper Relish

SERVES 4

FOR THE RELISH

1 tablespoon dried currants

½ tablespoon red-wine vinegar

½ tablespoon balsamic vinegar

1 small clove garlic

Kosher salt

1 large red bell pepper or 2 small pimientos

2 tablespoons pine nuts, lightly toasted and coarsely chopped

1½ tablespoons extra-virgin olive oil

1 tablespoon chopped fresh marjoram

Pinch of cayenne; more to taste

3 tablespoons chopped fresh flat-leaf parsley (optional)

FOR THE EGGPLANT

1 large globe eggplant (about 1 pound), trimmed and cut into ½-inch-thick rounds

3 tablespoons extra-virgin olive oil; more as needed

Kosher salt

Make the relish: Combine the currants and both vinegars in a small bowl.

With a mortar and pestle, pound the garlic and a pinch of salt to a paste, or mince the garlic, sprinkle with salt, and mash into a paste with the side of a chef's knife.

Set the bell pepper directly on a gas burner, under a hot broiler, or on a hot charcoal or gas grill. Keep rotating the pepper until it's evenly charred all over. Transfer to a small bowl, cover tightly with plastic, and let cool.

When cool enough to handle, peel the pepper over the same bowl to catch any juice; discard the skin. Don't rinse the pepper—it's fine if a few charred bits remain. (It's helpful to rinse your fingers occasionally.) Still working over the bowl, split the pepper and remove the stem and as many of the seeds as possible. Set the juice aside. Cut the pepper into very small dice and put in a medium bowl. Strain the pepper juice over the pepper. Add the currants and vinegar, garlic paste, pine nuts, olive oil, marjoram, and cayenne and stir. Season to taste with salt and cayenne.

Grill the eggplant: Prepare a medium-hot charcoal grill fire or heat a gas grill to medium high. Brush both sides of the eggplant slices with olive oil and season with salt. Grill (covered on a gas grill; uncovered on a charcoal grill) until golden-brown grill marks form, 3 to 4 minutes. Turn the eggplant and grill until tender and well marked on the second sides, another 3 to 4 minutes. The interior should be grayish and soft rather than white and hard.

When ready to serve, stir the relish again and spoon it over the grilled eggplant, or serve it on the side. Garnish with parsley, if using.

Other recipe ideas

INVOLTINI OF ROASTED PEPPERS Roast and peel red peppers and cut the flesh into even strips. Lay a small basil leaf, an anchovy fillet, and a stick of provolone cheese in the center and roll up. Secure with a toothpick and drizzle with fruity olive oil.

PIPERADE, POLENTA, AND POACHED EGGS Slowly sauté a mix of sweet peppers, sliced onion, and garlic slivers in lots of olive oil until very soft and starting to caramelize. Season with smoked paprika and a touch of sherry vinegar. Serve over soft polenta with a poached egg on top.

Physalis ixocarpa and cvs.

Tomatillos

Small, round fruits encased in a delicate, papery husk, tomatillos are a distant relative of the tomato and a staple of Mexican cooking; they're also called husk tomatoes. It's hard to resist their tangy, almost citrusy flavor, which turns slightly sweet with cooking and brings a tart, zesty flavor to sauces and salsas.

PICKING THE BEST

Look for firm fruits without blemishes and with their papery husks firmly attached. When fresh, tomatillos are a vibrant green color. Don't buy ones that have turned a yellowish green, as they're past their prime.

KEEPING IT FRESH

Store tomatillos with their husks in a paper bag and refrigerate for up to a week.

PREPARING

To prep tomatillos, peel the husk and rinse off the sticky residue it leaves behind. You don't need to remove the seeds. If eaten raw, tomatillos can be a little acidic and sharp-tasting. When cooked, their flavor tends to mellow, letting their sweeter side shine.

HOW TO USE IT

Toss raw chopped tomatillos in salads, or roast or grill them whole and add them to salsas and dips, either chopped or puréed. You can also cut them into wedges before stirring into stews and braises, or sauté them in small chunks and add them to omelets or scrambled eggs.

PRESERVING OPTIONS

You can freeze tomatillos to use later in puréed salsas and other recipes where a slightly soft texture won't matter. Remove the husks and carefully wash off any sticky residue. Cut large tomatillos in half or leave smaller ones whole. Spread on a tray and freeze until firm, then pile into airtight freezer bags.

DID YOU
KNOW?

Tomatillos have a relative—the ground cherry, also called the cape gooseberry. These are much smaller, usually yellow-gold, and very sweet. Look for the pineapple tomatillo, a ground cherry that is remarkably fruity.

Quick Beef Enchiladas with Salsa Verde

SERVES 4

Kosher salt

1 pound tomatillos (about 15 medium), husks
removed and fruit rinsed

3 jalapeños, cored and halved lengthwise (seeded,
if you like)

1 large yellow onion, half cut into 4 wedges, half
chopped

⅔ cup roughly chopped fresh cilantro

Kosher salt

1½ tablespoons canola oil

1 pound lean ground beef

2 teaspoons ground cumin

¼ teaspoon freshly ground black pepper

Eight 6-inch corn tortillas

1½ cups shredded Monterey Jack cheese

Bring a medium pot of salted water to a boil. Add the
tomatillos, jalapeño, and onion wedges; cover and
simmer until tender, about 10 minutes. Drain well
and transfer to a blender along with ⅓ cup of the
cilantro. Purée until just slightly chunky and season
to taste with salt.

Meanwhile, heat 1 tablespoon of the oil in a large
skillet over medium-high heat. Add the beef, chopped
onion, cumin, 1 teaspoon salt, and the black pepper
and cook, stirring occasionally to break up the meat,
until cooked through, about 5 minutes. Stir ½ cup of
the salsa verde into the beef.

Position a rack about 6 inches from the broiler
and heat the broiler on high. Grease a 9x13-inch
metal or ceramic baking dish with the remaining
½ tablespoon oil.

Wrap the tortillas in a few slightly damp paper
towels and microwave on high until warm, 30 to
45 seconds. Working with one at a time, spoon some
beef mixture down the center of the tortilla and
sprinkle with 1 tablespoon of the cheese. Roll up
snugly and transfer to the baking dish, seam side
down. Repeat with the remaining tortillas and beef
mixture. Pour the remaining salsa verde over the
enchiladas and sprinkle with the remaining cheese.
Broil until golden brown and bubbly, 3 to 5 minutes.
Garnish with the remaining cilantro and serve.

Spice-Rubbed Tilapia with Tomatillo, Black Bean, and Mango Salad

SERVES 4

One 15-ounce can black beans, drained and rinsed

½ pound tomatillos, husks removed, fruit rinsed and
cut into small dice

1 medium ripe mango, peeled, pitted, and cut into
small dice

½ cup small-diced red onion (from ¼ large onion)

⅓ cup fresh lime juice

⅓ cup plus 2 tablespoons vegetable oil

¼ cup chopped fresh cilantro

Freshly ground black pepper

1½ teaspoons chili powder

1 teaspoon ground cumin

1 teaspoon dried oregano

1 teaspoon kosher salt

4 skinless tilapia fillets (about 4 ounces each)

Put a heatproof serving platter on a rack in the center
of the oven and heat the oven to 200°F.

In a medium bowl, combine the beans, tomatillos,
mango, red onion, lime juice, ⅓ cup of the oil, the
cilantro, and a few grinds of black pepper; toss gently.
Let sit at room temperature while you cook the fish.

Mix ¼ teaspoon pepper with the chili powder,
cumin, oregano, and salt. Rub both sides of the tilapia
with the mixture. In a 12-inch nonstick skillet, heat
the remaining oil over medium-high heat until hot.
Cook two of the fillets until lightly browned, opaque,
and cooked through, about 2 minutes on each side.
Transfer the fish to the platter in the oven while you
cook the remaining fillets. Transfer to the platter
and spoon half of the salad on top. Serve with the
remaining salad on the side.

Other recipe ideas

GRILLED STEAK WITH TOMATILLO-AVOCADO SALSA
Marinate a skirt steak in lime juice, garlic, and chile
powder. Grill and top with tomatillo and avocado salsa.

CHILLED TOMATILLO SOUP Simmer tomatillos in
chicken broth, chill, and purée, then fold in chopped
cucumber, avocado, tomato, and bell pepper for a
tomatillo gazpacho.

Lycopersicon esculentum cvs.

Tomatoes

The flavor of a juicy, ripe tomato still warm from the sun is the essence of summer. But tomatoes are also a delight when cooked and play a key role in dishes from summery soups to soul-warming hearty braises.

PICKING THE BEST

Look for tomatoes with intact skins and no bruises, firm but yielding under gentle pressure and with a deep color. Color is an indicator only if you know what the variety should look like when ripe. Heirloom varieties are often misshapen and mottled, so don't be put off by cracked skins, as long as they aren't leaking juice. And check the fragrance: Sniff and pass on any tomato that doesn't transport you toward summer.

Tomatoes generally fall into one of three categories.

- **Beefsteaks:** Big and juicy, often slightly flattened, lumpy and lobed, beefsteaks produce succulent slices for sandwiches and platters of sliced tomatoes. Brandywine is a popular heirloom beefsteak that's meaty, sweet, and a deep mauve; Big Boy is a reliable hybrid beefsteak. A beefsteak has smaller seed cavities and therefore a greater ratio of flesh to juice and seeds than other kinds of tomatoes.
- **Slicers:** More uniform and round, slicers tend toward mid-size, making them versatile for sandwiches, pizzas, and casseroles, as well as sauces and salsas. Early Girl is a popular slicing tomato variety.
- **Cherries:** Ranging from jellybean-size "grape" tomatoes to jawbreaker-size cocktail tomatoes, cherries are versatile enough to go from a snack to a salad to a skewer to be tossed onto a grill. Cherry tomatoes may be round, oval, or even pear-shaped and range in color from white through yellow, orange, red, green, and purple. A standout variety is Sungold.

The term "heirloom" is not a strict definition but rather refers to older, interesting varieties that have been propagated because of their eating qualities rather than other commercial attributes such as ability to ship. Every seed company and dedicated backyard gardener has favorites, and farmer's markets are fertile ground for discovering new varieties. With heirlooms, the color is often an indicator of flavor, be it sweet or tart. Here's a guide by color.

- **Red or pink varieties** offer a balance of acid and sweetness that is closest to what is thought of as the classic tomato flavor. The Brandywine variety is the most common because it's hardy and travels well.
- **Yellow and orange varieties,** such as Lemon Boy, are the lowest in acid, with a sweet flavor.
- **Purple or black heirlooms** usually appear more deep maroon or brown, like Cherokee Purple and Carbon. Most have a smoky-sweet flavor and are more acidic than the yellow or green varieties.
- **White varieties,** like White Beauty, tend to have a yellow tinge and a slightly lower acid content than red heirlooms. Their much higher sugar content makes them the sweetest of the heirlooms.
- **Green varieties,** such as Green Zebra, are lower in acid than red ones, with a flavor both sweet and tart.
- **Roma-shaped varieties,** such as Opalka, are meaty, with few seeds, making them good for sauces.

Cherry

Heirloom

Grape

- **Cherry tomato heirlooms**, such as Sugary, Fond Mini, Red Currant, and Mirabel, are very sweet and juicy.

KEEPING IT FRESH

Leave tomatoes at room temperature until you're ready to use them. Refrigeration causes loss of flavor and a mealy texture. Temperatures colder than 50°F will destroy their flavor and texture.

PREPARING

At a minimum, you'll want to cut out the core of the tomato, which can be hard and unsightly. Certain recipes will call for peeling and seeding as well, in order to use only the flesh; seeds and skins can be texturally annoying in a sauce or soup. But peeling and seeding is time-consuming and fussy, so only do it in dishes where the refinement will be perceptible.

To slice a tomato, use a very sharp knife; serrated knives do a good job, cutting the skin without crushing the tomato. If you need tomato pulp without the skin, try cutting the fruit in half horizontally and grating its flesh on the large holes of a grater. The tomato is quickly reduced to a purée and the skin is left behind.

HOW TO USE IT

While the most sublime use for a tomato might be as a warm-from-the-sun snack, tomatoes are incredibly versatile. They of course feature prominently in salads, but also make beautiful salsas when chopped and spiked with fresh chile and herbs. Tomatoes break down nicely when simmered, so are perfect for soups, stews, and braises. Roasting tomato halves brings out a mellow depth of flavor that's incomparable. See how to roast on p. 167. And if you have garden tomatoes that haven't ripened, green tomatoes are delicious breaded and fried or in gratins, salsas, and pickles.

PRESERVING OPTIONS

Tomatoes can be preserved by drying with a dehydrator, and canning—using the pressure-canner method—keeps garden-fresh tomato flavor available year-round. A simple way to preserve tomatoes is to cut them into chunks, spread the chunks on sheet pans, freeze until hard, and then pile the frozen chunks into airtight zip-top bags.

Unripe green tomatoes are famously good pickled in vinegar seasoned with salt, dill, and garlic, just like dill pickles made from cucumbers.

.... RECIPES ....

Andalusian Gazpacho

SERVES 4

2 cloves garlic, sliced

1 large green bell pepper, cored, seeded, and coarsely chopped (to yield 2 cups)

1½ pounds ripe, very red tomatoes (about 4 large), cut into large pieces

One 3-inch-long piece baguette, sliced and dried overnight or until hard

½ cup good-quality extra-virgin olive oil

2 tablespoons sherry vinegar or red-wine vinegar, plus more to taste

2 teaspoons coarse salt, plus more to taste

Freshly ground black pepper (optional)

1 cup peeled, diced cucumber, for garnish (optional)

1 cup diced onion, for garnish (optional)

Put the garlic, green pepper, tomatoes, bread, olive oil, vinegar, and salt in a food processor. Pulse until the ingredients begin to purée (if the bread is hard, it may bounce about and take a while to break down); continue processing until the mixture is as fine a purée as possible, 3 to 5 minutes.

Pass the soup through a large fine sieve set over a large bowl, pressing until only solids remain in the sieve; discard the solids. Stir in ¼ to ½ cup water, or enough to give the soup the consistency of a thin milkshake. If you want a thicker soup, add less water or none at all. Add more salt and vinegar to taste. Cover and refrigerate until well chilled (or serve it immediately with a few ice cubes in each bowl).

Ladle the gazpacho into chilled bowls or cups. Grind fresh pepper on top, if you want, and pass bowls of diced cucumber and onion, if using, so people can garnish their own.

DID YOU KNOW? The most potent tomato flavor can be captured by making "tomato water"— a clear, thin juice that adds intense raw tomato flavor to soups, salad dressings, and cocktails. Purée some ripe flavorful tomatoes then drain the purée overnight through a sieve lined with cheesecloth set over a bowl (do this in the fridge).

Heirloom Tomato Napoleon with Parmesan Crisps and Herb Salad

SERVES 4

FOR THE PARMESAN CRISPS

2½ cups grated Parmigiano-Reggiano

FOR THE VINAIGRETTE

1 small shallot, minced (about 1½ tablespoons)

4 teaspoons Champagne vinegar

1 teaspoon Dijon mustard

Kosher or sea salt and freshly ground black pepper

2 tablespoons extra-virgin olive oil

2 tablespoons grapeseed oil or canola oil

FOR THE SALAD

1 cup baby arugula leaves

1 cup fresh flat-leaf parsley leaves

1 cup fresh basil leaves, torn into bite-sized pieces
    if large

½ cup fresh tarragon leaves

½ cup 1-inch-long fresh chive pieces

20 small nasturtium leaves (optional)

Kosher salt and freshly ground black pepper

Sixteen ⅓-inch-thick heirloom tomato slices,
    preferably of different colors, sizes, and shapes
    (2 to 3 pounds)

About 20 various heirloom cherry tomatoes, halved
    or quartered

Make the Parmesan crisps: Position a rack in the center of the oven and heat it to 375°F. Line a rimmed baking sheet with a nonstick baking liner or parchment. Spread the grated cheese over the entire surface of the liner. Bake until the cheese is amber brown, about 18 minutes. Remove from the oven and cool. Break into irregular pieces (each about 3 inches across). You'll need 12 pieces for the napoleons, but this batch makes extra to cover the inevitable breaking (and snacking).

Make the vinaigrette: Put the shallot, vinegar, mustard, and a pinch each of salt and pepper in a small bowl or dressing cruet. Allow the shallots to sit in the vinegar for at least 20 minutes and up to 1 hour. Whisk or shake in both oils. Season to taste with more salt and pepper.

To serve: In a large bowl, mix the arugula, parsley, basil, tarragon, chives, and nasturtium leaves (if using). Lightly dress with some of the vinaigrette. Season to taste with salt and pepper.

Portion the salad onto four salad plates. Arrange a large tomato slice on each salad, sprinkle lightly with salt, and top with a piece of Parmesan crisp. Continue to alternate the lightly salted tomatoes and cheese pieces until you have used 3 pieces of the Parmesan crisp in each napoleon. Finish off the top of each napoleon with an unsalted tomato slice. Arrange the cherry tomatoes around the napoleons and drizzle any remaining vinaigrette around the plates. Sprinkle everything with salt and pepper. Serve immediately.

Red Potato and Tomato Gratin with Leeks, Gruyère, and Rosemary

SERVES 6 TO 8

FOR THE LEEKS

1½ tablespoons olive oil; more for the dish

3 cups sliced leeks (about 3 large, white and light
    green parts only), washed thoroughly

FOR THE POTATOES

1¼ pounds red potatoes, unpeeled, cut into ¼-inch
    slices

½ teaspoon kosher salt; more for boiling the
    potatoes

1½ tablespoons olive oil

2 teaspoons chopped fresh rosemary

TO ASSEMBLE THE GRATIN

1 teaspoon chopped fresh rosemary

1¼ pounds ripe tomatoes, cored and cut into
    ¼-inch slices

1¾ cups grated Gruyère cheese

½ teaspoon kosher salt

Freshly ground black pepper

1½ tablespoons olive oil

⅔ cup fresh breadcrumbs mixed with 2 teaspoons
    olive oil

Cook the leeks: Heat the olive oil in a medium skillet (preferably nonstick) over medium heat. Add the leeks and sauté, stirring frequently, until limp and lightly browned, about 15 minutes. Spread the leeks evenly in the bottom of an oiled 2-quart shallow gratin dish (preferably oval). Let cool.

Cook the potatoes: In a medium saucepan, cover the potato slices with well-salted water and bring to a boil. Reduce the heat to a gentle boil and cook for 5 minutes, or until the potatoes are just barely

tender. Drain and rinse under cold water until cool.
Pat dry. Toss the potatoes with the salt, olive oil, and
rosemary.

Assemble the gratin: Heat the oven to 375°F.
Sprinkle ½ teaspoon of the chopped rosemary over
the leeks. Starting at one end of the baking dish, lay
a row of slightly overlapping tomato slices across
the width of the dish. Prop the tomatoes against the
dish at a 60-degree angle. Cover the row of tomatoes
with a generous sprinkling of Gruyère. Next, arrange
a row of potato slices over the tomatoes. Sprinkle
again with Gruyère. Repeat with alternating rows of
tomatoes and potatoes, sprinkling each with cheese,
until the gratin is full.

Sprinkle about ½ teaspoon salt and the remaining
½ teaspoon rosemary over all and season with
pepper. Drizzle with the olive oil. Mix any remaining
Gruyère with the breadcrumb mixture and spread
this over the whole gratin. Cook until the gratin is
well-browned all over and the juices have bubbled for
a while and reduced considerably, 60 to 65 minutes.
Let cool for at least 15 minutes before serving.

Fiery Green Tomato Salsa

MAKES ABOUT 2 CUPS

2 green tomatoes (about ½ pound each), sliced
    ½ inch thick
1 fresh medium jalapeño
2 red ripe tomatoes (about 6 ounces each)
½ small onion, chopped
1 tablespoon olive oil
1 tablespoon fresh lemon juice
1 tablespoon minced fresh oregano or mint leaves
Pinch of sugar
Kosher salt and freshly ground black pepper

Grill the green tomatoes over hot coals or broil
(about 4 minutes per side) until seared but not soft;
chop them coarsely. Broil or grill the jalapeño until
blackened, seal it in a paper bag for 5 minutes, and let
steam. Peel and seed it; mince the flesh. Halve the red
tomatoes, squeeze out the juice, and coarsely chop
them. Combine all the ingredients, mixing well. Taste
and adjust the seasonings.

Fresh Tomato Sauce with Herbs and Olives

MAKES ENOUGH SAUCE FOR 4 TO 5 SERVINGS

3 tablespoons extra-virgin olive oil
3 large cloves garlic, peeled and lightly smashed
3 tablespoons chopped mixed fresh herbs (such as
    equal parts oregano, rosemary, and thyme)
1 cup coarsely chopped pitted Gaeta or Kalamata
    olives
1½ pounds cherry tomatoes, rinsed and halved
½ teaspoon kosher salt, plus more to taste
Freshly ground black pepper
1 pound dried fusilli, gemelli, or other short, sturdy
    pasta
Freshly grated Parmigiano-Reggiano or Pecorino
    Romano (optional)

In a 10- or 11-inch sauté pan, heat the oil and
garlic over medium-low to medium heat, stirring
occasionally, until the garlic infuses the oil but
doesn't brown, 3 to 5 minutes. Using a fork, fish out
and discard the garlic. Sprinkle in the herbs and olives
and raise the heat to medium. Stir to combine and
sauté for about a minute. Add the tomatoes, salt,
and pepper to taste. Simmer, stirring occasionally
and adjusting the heat to maintain a lively but not
too vigorous simmer, until the tomatoes have been
reduced to a thick, pulpy sauce, 15 to 20 minutes.

While the sauce is cooking, bring a large pot
of abundantly salted water to a vigorous boil and
cook the pasta until al dente. Drain it well. Taste the
sauce and adjust the seasonings if needed. Toss the
pasta with three-quarters of the sauce and divide
among individual serving bowls. Spoon a little of the
remaining sauce over each serving and sprinkle on
the cheese, if you like.

Other recipe ideas

TOMATO-CUCUMBER BREAD SALAD Dice an
assortment of heirloom tomatoes and toss with
diced English cucumber, diced red bell pepper, and
cubes of stale country bread. Dress with a vinaigrette
of red-wine vinegar, extra-virgin olive oil, salt, freshly
ground black pepper, and torn fresh basil.

Roasting Tomatoes

For a secret ingredient to make your summer meals more special, try slow-roasting tomatoes. This technique is so easy and yields such delicious results that you'll soon add it to your repertoire once you've tried it. Not only does slow-roasting concentrate and caramelize the flavor of a beefsteak tomato, but it also gives the tomato a meatier, more robust texture.

Roasted tomatoes become versatile ingredients, perfect for tossing into pasta or salads, layering on sandwiches and crostini, or just using as a terrific side dish for grilled or roasted meats. They keep in the refrigerator for at least a week, and they freeze well, too, tucked into an airtight zip-top bag. A bonus is the lovely tomato-infused olive oil left over after roasting; drizzle it over grilled vegetables or on crusty bread, or use it in a vinaigrette.

Slow-Roasted Summer Tomatoes

MAKES 24 TOMATO HALVES

1 cup plus 3 tablespoons extra-virgin olive oil
4½ to 5 pounds medium-large ripe beefsteak
   tomatoes (about 12), stemmed but not cored
Kosher salt
Sugar
Scant 1 tablespoon balsamic vinegar
3 to 4 cloves garlic, very thinly sliced
2 tablespoons fresh thyme leaves

Heat the oven to 350°F. Line a 12x17-inch rimmed baking sheet or two 9x12-inch rimmed baking sheets with foil (use Pyrex baking dishes if you don't have a rimmed sheet because the tomatoes will leak lots of juice). If you have parchment, put a sheet on top of the foil. Coat the pan or pans with 3 tablespoons of the olive oil.

Cut the tomatoes in half through the equator (not through the stem). Arrange the halves, cut side up, on the baking sheet, turning to coat their bottoms with some of the oil. Sprinkle a pinch each of salt and sugar over each half, and drizzle each with a few drops of balsamic vinegar. Arrange the garlic over the halves and top with a generous sprinkling of thyme. Pour the remaining 1 cup olive oil over and around the tomato halves.

Roast in the center of the oven until the tomatoes are concentrated, dark reddish brown (with deep browning around the edges and in places on the pan), and quite collapsed (at least half their original height; they will collapse more as they cool), about 3 hours for very ripe, fleshy tomatoes and about 4 hours for tomatoes that are less ripe or that have a high water content. Let cool for at least 10 to 15 minutes and then serve warm or at room temperature. Be sure to reserve the tomato oil (keep refrigerated for up to a week) to use on its own or in a vinaigrette.

Plum tomato variation: Substitute plum tomatoes, cut in half through the stem end and seeded. The roasting time will be about 2 hours. Roasted plum tomato halves hold together particularly well; layer them in a terrine or roll them up, stuffed with goat cheese and basil, as an appetizer.

Fall

- ⬧ Apples
- ⬧ Beets
- ⬧ Belgian Endive
- ⬧ Brussels Sprouts
- ⬧ Cabbage
- ⬧ Carrots
- ⬧ Celeriac
- ⬧ Chicories
- ⬧ Collard Greens
- ⬧ Cranberries
- ⬧ Jícamas
- ⬧ Kale
- ⬧ Kohlrabi
- ⬧ Mushrooms
- ⬧ Nuts
- ⬧ Parsnips
- ⬧ Pears
- ⬧ Persimmons
- ⬧ Potatoes
- ⬧ Quinces
- ⬧ Rutabagas
- ⬧ Sweet Potatoes
- ⬧ Swiss Chard
- ⬧ Turnips
- ⬧ Winter Squash

Malus cvs.

Apples

An apple is more than just a piece of fruit—it's the embodiment of wholesomeness, hominess, and, well, everything that's as American as apple pie. Apples are obliging, too—easy to find, relatively inexpensive, and easy to store. Plus a crisp sweet-tart apple is a satisfying snack that can be enjoyed at a moment's notice. Apples are also welcome to the cook because just as other fruits of high summer are disappearing, the new crop of apples arrives, promising fresh, ripe fruit for many more weeks.

PICKING THE BEST

Apples range in taste from just plain sweet to spicy-sweet to tart; in texture from downright hard to crisp and juicy to dry to mealy; and in color from blackish red to palest yellow. Some are tender skinned, others have thick, waxy coats, and still others—the russets—have tough, leathery skins. It's hard to think of another fruit that's available in more varieties than apples. With all those choices, picking one can be tricky because each variety has a unique flavor and behaves a little differently when cooked.

Look for hard, fresh-smelling fruit with a full aroma and a smooth, tight skin. Good-tasting apples aren't necessarily pretty—some of the best varieties aren't—but they should be free of bruises and blemishes. If you're buying U.S.-grown apples in the dead of winter, choose carefully, because after months of storage, apples may look great but can be mealy and mushy. Once the domestic apple harvest is over, keep an eye out for imports from Chile, New Zealand, and Australia, which start shipping in February, the beginning of autumn in the southern hemisphere. Look for varieties like Braeburn, Fuji, and Granny Smith.

Farmer's markets will offer heirloom varieties, which are often as appealing for their old-fashioned names—Ashmead's Kernel, Opalescent, Belle de Boskoop, Cox's Orange Pippin—as for their flavors. But grocery stores now carry a wide range of apple varieties.

- **Braeburn:** Can be eaten out of hand or used in cooking. Firm and juicy, it has a pleasant, sweet-tart flavor. It's harvested in late October and, if handled properly, will store well.
- **Cortland:** A good choice for a fresh fruit salad because its very white flesh is slow to turn brown. A good all-purpose apple, it's harvested in September and October.
- **Empire:** A super-crisp eating apple that tastes similar to a McIntosh. Picked starting in September, it's best eaten raw or in salads.
- **Fuji:** A relative newcomer to the apple scene that has skyrocketed in popularity. Sweet and juicy, it's excellent eaten fresh. It's best October through December but stores extremely well if refrigerated.
- **Gala:** A New Zealand native now grown in the U.S., it's a medium-sized apple with a unique yellow-, orange-, and red-striped skin. Outstanding for

Golden Delicious

Idared

Rome

Stayman Winesap

Pink Lady

Cortland

McIntosh

Red Delicious

Mutsu

Jonagold

Lady

Honeycrisp

eating fresh, in salads, or cooked for desserts and applesauce.

- **Golden Delicious:** Ranges from pale green to warm yellow, but the more yellow the fruit, the sweeter and softer it is. Use it in tarts and salads.
- **Granny Smith:** Harvested in October, it stores well, and imports make it available year-round. It's a little tart for some, but it's a good cooking and baking apple. Paler green fruit is usually riper and sweeter.
- **Honeycrisp:** A recent newcomer, a cross between a Macoun and a Honeygold apple. It's extremely crisp and juicy, with a good balance between sweet and tart. Honeycrisps are harvested a bit later in the season and are often quite large. They are good keepers, staying crunchy rather than turning mealy.
- **Macoun:** A relative of the McIntosh but with a deeper carmine skin and more versatile in the kitchen. It's harvested in late September and October.
- **McIntosh:** A favorite variety in the Northeast, where it's eaten fresh and used for applesauce. It doesn't keep well, so enjoy it around harvest time in September.
- **Piñata (also called Pinova):** A cross between a Golden Delicious and two heirlooms—Cox's Orange Pippin and the Duchess of Oldenburg. It's crisp, nicely sweet-tart, and an excellent apple for eating out of hand. Piñatas are harvested in the fall but stored until January because cold storage intensifies their flavor.
- **Pink Lady:** Crisp and crunchy, a fine-grained cross between Golden Delicious and Lady Williams. It doesn't brown as fast as other apples, so it's great for salads. Pink Lady comes to market in October and is available through spring.
- **Red Delicious:** Has brilliant crimson skin and unique five-knob base. This apple is best eaten raw. Harvested in October, it's available year-round, but avoid it in the spring and summer, when it tends to be soft and mealy.
- **Rome:** With its soft, round shape, it is a popular choice for baked apples. It's good for cooking and baking.

KEEPING IT FRESH

Once you get apples home, refrigerate them and keep them away from strong-smelling foods, as apples easily absorb odors. Discard any rotting apples; they emit gases that are damaging to other apples, fruits, and vegetables.

PREPARING

Apple skin adds color, but it can also be slightly tough, so peel or not according to your final dish. Halve the apple then cut out the core with an apple corer or a paring knife, or cut the apple into wedges and then slice off the core.

Many recipes suggest immediately tossing peeled apples in lemon juice to keep them from turning brown, but if you're going to cook the apples you needn't bother. A little surface browning won't affect the apple's flavor.

HOW TO USE IT

We all know the value of eating an apple as a daily snack, but apples also are great partners in the kitchen, especially in rustic dishes such as cabbage and applesauce. Their sweet flesh breaks down with long cooking, so if incorporating them into stews, add them later in the cooking process.

PRESERVING OPTIONS

Apples freeze well for use in baking and other cooked dishes. The simplest way is to peel and core the apples, then cut into wedges or thick slices. Toss the apple with a mixture of ½ teaspoon (1,500 mg) ascorbic acid (also known as Fruit-Fresh®) and 3 tablespoons water; this will help prevent darkening. Spread the slices on trays and freeze until hard, then pile into airtight freezer bags.

Ginger Apple Crumb Pie

SERVES 8 TO 12

FOR THE TOPPING

4½ ounces (1 cup) unbleached all-purpose flour

⅓ cup granulated sugar

2 tablespoons firmly packed light brown sugar

1½ teaspoons ground ginger

⅛ teaspoon salt

¼ pound (8 tablespoons) cold unsalted butter, cut into 8 pieces

FOR THE CRUST

5¾ ounces (1 ¼ cups) unbleached all-purpose flour

¼ teaspoon salt

1½ ounces (3 tablespoons) cold vegetable shortening, cut into ½-inch dice

1½ ounces (3 tablespoons) cold unsalted butter, cut into ½-inch dice

2½ to 3½ tablespoons very cold water

FOR THE FILLING

3 pounds Braeburn or Gala apples (about 6 medium) peeled, cored, and cut into ¼-inch-thick slices

2 teaspoons finely grated fresh ginger

½ cup sugar

3 tablespoons unbleached all-purpose flour

1 ounce (2 tablespoons) unsalted butter, cut into very small pieces

Make the topping: In a medium bowl, combine the flour, granulated sugar, brown sugar, ground ginger, and salt. Whisk to blend. Add the butter and work it in well with your fingers until the mixture holds together in small clumps and there are very few fine grains left in the bowl. Refrigerate until ready to use.

Make the crust: In the bowl of a stand mixer (or a large mixing bowl), whisk the flour and salt to blend. Add the shortening and butter. Starting on low speed and then shifting to medium, beat with the paddle attachment (or cut in by hand) until the largest pieces of fat are about the size of peas, 1 to 2 minutes. With the mixer running on low (or mixing by hand), sprinkle on 2½ tablespoons of the water and blend until the dough just comes together into clumps; if the dough is too dry to do this, add the remaining water ½ tablespoon at a time. With your

hands, shape the dough into a 4-inch-wide disk. Wrap in plastic and refrigerate for at least 30 minutes.

Roll out the dough between two sheets of plastic wrap. (If the dough was chilled for more than 30 minutes, you may need to let it warm up at room temperature to become pliable.) Occasionally loosen and reapply the wrap and continue rolling until you have an 11- to 12-inch round that's about ⅛ inch thick. Remove the top sheet of plastic. Turn a standard 9-inch metal or glass pie plate (1¼ inches deep) upside down over the center of dough. Slip your hand under the plastic and turn the pie plate right side up. Slip the dough into the pan to fit snugly and carefully remove the plastic. Trim the dough overhang to about ¼ inch, fold it under to create a thicker edge, and flute the edge. Cover loosely with plastic and refrigerate for at least 30 minutes or until ready to use.

Position a rack in the lower third of the oven and heat the oven to 425°F.

Make the filling: In a large bowl, toss the apples with the grated ginger, distributing the ginger as evenly as possible. Add the sugar and flour and toss to coat evenly.

Scrape the apple mixture into the pie shell and mound it slightly in the center. Dot with the butter. Top with the crumb topping, keeping it as clumpy (not sandy) as you can. Try to cover all the apples. If any crumbs roll off the pie, gather them up and reapply.

Put the pie on a foil-lined baking sheet. Bake for 20 minutes and then reduce the heat to 375°F. Bake until the apples are tender (a skewer inserted into the center of the pie will meet slight resistance) and the juices are bubbling around the edges, another 30 to 35 minutes; if the top starts to brown too quickly after about 20 minutes, cover the pie loosely with foil. Let cool on a rack for 3 to 4 hours to let the juices set.

Apple and Fennel Slaw

SERVES 8 TO 10

2 tablespoons fresh lemon juice

3 tart apples, like Gravensteins

2 small bulbs fennel, trimmed and cut into matchsticks

1 small red onion, cut in half and very thinly sliced

¼ cup extra-virgin olive oil

2 tablespoons chopped fresh flat-leaf parsley

Salt and freshly ground black pepper

Put the lemon juice in a large bowl. Cut one of the apples in half, core it, and julienne it. Put the cut apple in the bowl and toss it with the lemon juice to keep it from browning. Repeat with the other apples. Toss in all of the remaining ingredients. Let stand for at least 20 minutes at room temperature. Add salt and pepper to taste and serve.

Endive, Apple, and Walnut Salad with Roquefort

SERVES 6

1½ tablespoons sherry vinegar

Scant ½ teaspoon kosher salt

¼ cup walnut oil

1 small handful watercress (1½ ounces) or fresh flat-leaf parsley leaves

1 medium eating apple, such as Braeburn, Red Delicious, or Fuji

4 heads Belgian endive, wiped clean and brown leaves removed

3 ounces (¾ cup) walnuts, lightly toasted and crumbled

¼ pound Roquefort cheese

Freshly ground black pepper

In a small bowl, combine the vinegar and salt; slowly whisk in the walnut oil. Put the watercress in a salad bowl. Quarter and core the apple, slice it ⅛ inch thick, and then cut the slices crosswise. Add the apple to the salad bowl. Slice the endive heads on a sharp diagonal into ¼-inch-wide strips, turning the heads as you slice and whittling down to the core. Add the endive to the salad, along with the walnuts. Toss the salad with the vinaigrette and arrange on plates. Crumble the Roquefort onto each serving, finish with a few grinds of pepper, and serve.

Chopped Shrimp "Waldorf" Salad

SERVES 6 TO 8

1 pound large shrimp (31 to 40 per pound), peeled and deveined

½ cup mayonnaise

⅓ cup buttermilk

1 tablespoon fresh lemon juice, plus more to taste

1 tablespoon roughly chopped fresh tarragon

1 teaspoon Dijon mustard

Kosher salt and freshly ground black pepper

2 cups ¼-inch-diced sweet apples, preferably Fuji (about 1½ medium apples)

2 cups red seedless grapes, halved

1½ cups ¼-inch-diced celery (3 to 4 ribs)

⅓ cup blanched slivered almonds, lightly toasted

1 tablespoon thinly sliced fresh chives (optional)

12 tender butter lettuce leaves

Put the shrimp in a steamer basket over simmering water and steam until just cooked through, about 3 minutes (the center should still be slightly translucent). Let cool.

In a medium bowl, whisk the mayonnaise, buttermilk, lemon juice, tarragon, and mustard. Season with salt and pepper to taste.

Cut the shrimp into ½-inch pieces and mix in a large bowl with the apples, grapes, celery, and almonds. Toss with enough of the dressing to coat the ingredients well (you may not need it all). Taste and add more salt, pepper, or lemon juice as needed. Sprinkle with the chives, if using. Serve the salad on beds of lettuce leaves or put the leaves next to the salad and have guests spoon some of the salad into a leaf and roll it up to eat out of hand.

Honey-Spice Apple Butter

MAKES ABOUT 1½ CUPS

2 pounds McIntosh apples, peeled, cored, and cut into
   1-inch chunks

2 cups apple cider

¼ cup dark brown sugar

¼ cup honey

⅛ teaspoon ground cinnamon

Pinch of ground allspice

Pinch of kosher salt

Combine apples and cider in a heavy-based 3-quart saucepan. Bring to a boil over medium-high heat, then reduce the heat to a simmer. Cook, stirring occasionally, until the apples have broken down, about 30 minutes. Use a rubber spatula to force the mixture through a medium sieve into a bowl. Rinse the saucepan and return the mixture to the pan. Whisk in the brown sugar, honey, cinnamon, allspice, and salt.

Bring back to a simmer over medium heat and adjust the heat to maintain a vigorous simmer. Cook until the mixture reduces and thickens to a spreadable consistency, about 75 minutes. As the mixture cooks, stir occasionally at first and then more frequently as it thickens; keep in mind that the apple butter will thicken a little more as it cools. Scrape the apple butter into a storage container and press a piece of plastic wrap directly on the surface to prevent a skin from forming as it cools. Once completely cool, you can remove the plastic, cover with a lid, and refrigerate for up to 2 weeks.

Other recipe ideas

SAVORY SIDE DISH FOR PORK Sauté sliced onion until soft and caramelized, then sauté apple slices and combine the two with some fresh sage, a squeeze of lemon juice, and plenty of black pepper.

CURRIED APPLE AND LEEK SOUP Sauté leeks and apples with mild curry powder and some fresh ginger, then simmer in chicken broth until tender, and finish with a touch of cream.

FLAT APPLE TART Roll out a sheet of thawed frozen puff pastry, brush with butter, top with an even layer of thinly sliced apples. Fold the edges, brush with butter, sprinkle with sugar, and bake until golden.

Choosing the Right Apple

A common dilemma for the cook is how to know which apple is right for your recipe—in some cases, you need one that will hold its shape, for other recipes, you want it to break down into a purée; these two traits are certainly not interchangeable. Here are some guidelines by variety, as well as flavor you can expect when cooked.

Braeburn: Great texture—soft but still holds its shape. Flavor is on the sweet side. These soften nicely.

Cortland: Good complex flavor with well-rounded sweetness.

Empire: Fairly juicy, tart, and perfumed.

Fuji: When cooked, flavor is flat and texture is like reconstituted dried apple. Avoid for cooking.

Golden Delicious: Holds its shape fairly well but gets a bit mushy. Very juicy but flavor lacks complexity.

Granny Smith: Holds its shape fairly well. Flavor is not as "appley" as others, but is fine when teamed with a softer, more perfumed apple.

Macoun: Not very juicy. Nice pink color and great flavor.

McIntosh: Practically purées itself when cooked. Sweet with a pretty pink hue. Great in applesauce and preserves.

Red Delicious: Flavorless when cooked. Save this one for the lunchbox.

Rome: Softens but holds its shape nicely. Quite juicy, with a complex sweet-tart flavor.

Ruby Queen

Detroit

Beta vulgaris cvs.

Beets

Full of sweetness and saturated color, beets become tender and full-flavored when cooked, making them an ideal ingredient for salads, side dishes, and soups. And although we think of beets mainly as root vegetables, the whole plant is edible. You can use the small, tender leaves raw in salads, and sauté or braise the larger leaves as you would Swiss chard or kale.

PICKING THE BEST

While most of us are familiar with red-purple beets, you can also find golden, striped (known as Chioggia beets), and white varieties. Your best bet for finding such varieties is the farmer's market. Baby beets are those harvested when young.

Look for smooth skins and tap roots that aren't too shaggy. If the greens are attached, that's a good sign of freshness in general, but look specifically for the bunch with the brightest and greenest leaves.

KEEPING IT FRESH

Kept in a cool place, beets will last for weeks. Store beets and leaves separately in loosely closed plastic bags in the crisper drawer of the refrigerator. Use the leaves within 2 days.

PREPARING

Leave beets whole and unpeeled when boiling or steaming to retain their juices. After they're cooked, the skins rub off easily with a paper towel. For roasting, peel and cut them first so they get nice and browned. Consider wearing plastic gloves when handling beets, especially cooked ones, as their juices can stain hands, as well as dishtowels, cutting boards, and counters.

HOW TO USE IT

Beets are almost always used cooked. Steamed or boiled and tossed with a bright dressing, beets make a delicious salad. For a composed salad, cut them into chunks or slices. Grate uncooked beets and toss with a mustardy vinaigrette for the classic French hors d'oeuvre salad. Roasted beets can accompany hearty winter meats or be part of an antipasto course, and while beet soups aren't common, beet-based borscht is one of the most celebrated soups of all.

SURPRISING PAIRINGS

The sweet earthiness of beets pairs deliciously with strong salty cheeses. Try a blue cheese such as Roquefort or Maytag® blue in a beet salad, or pair beets with a tangy feta. Orange is a complement to beets, enhancing the sweetness while playing down the minerality and earthiness. Dressings made with orange juice or orange zest are delicious on beets.

PRESERVING OPTIONS

Pickling is a lovely way to preserve the sweet, dense flesh of beets, and while the color of pickled beets fades a bit, they look like jewels in the jar.

Ruby Salad with Crumbled Feta and Spicy Pepitas

SERVES 8

FOR THE BEETS

1 bunch small beets (4 to 5), trimmed and scrubbed

2 to 3 sprigs fresh thyme or rosemary, or 3 fresh bay leaves

½ teaspoon kosher or sea salt

1 tablespoon olive oil

FOR THE VINAIGRETTE

1 tablespoon Dijon mustard

2 tablespoons sherry vinegar

2 tablespoons fresh lemon juice

¼ teaspoon kosher salt

Freshly ground black pepper

¼ cup extra-virgin olive oil

FOR THE SPICY PEPITAS

6 ounces pepitas (hulled pumpkin seeds, available in natural-foods or specialty stores)

1 teaspoon corn or peanut oil

1 teaspoon pure chile powder (such as New Mexico or ancho)

¾ teaspoon kosher salt

FOR THE SALAD

4 cups very thinly sliced red cabbage (from 1 very small head)

1 medium red onion, very thinly sliced

4 ounces (4 cups) mixed baby greens

6 ounces feta, crumbled (about ½ cup)

Roast the beets: Heat the oven to 400°F. Line a rimmed baking sheet with foil. Put the beets, herbs, salt, and a drizzle of olive oil in the center; toss to coat. Fold the foil into a loose-fitting but tightly sealed packet around the beets. Roast on the baking sheet until the beets are tender, about 1 hour and 20 minutes. Let the beets cool completely in the foil. When cool, use a paring knife to peel and slice the beets into wedges (6 to 8 per beet.) The beets can be roasted up to 2 days ahead and refrigerated.

Make the vinaigrette: In a small bowl, combine the mustard, vinegar, lemon juice, salt, and a few grinds of pepper. Gradually whisk in the oil.

Toast the pepitas: Heat the oven to 375°F. In a small bowl, toss the pepitas with the oil, chile powder, and salt. Spread evenly on a rimmed baking sheet and roast until golden and fragrant, 6 to 8 minutes (you'll hear them popping). Let cool completely on the baking sheet. If making ahead, store in an airtight container.

Make the salad: Combine the cabbage and onion in a medium bowl and set aside. Up to an hour before serving, add the beet wedges to the cabbage and onion; toss gently with half of the vinaigrette.

Just before serving, add the baby greens, half of the feta, and half of the pepitas; toss with the remaining vinaigrette. Arrange on a big serving platter and garnish with the remaining feta and pepitas.

Spiced Pickled Beets

MAKES ABOUT 3 PINTS

8 to 9 medium-small beets (about 2¼ pounds), trimmed and scrubbed

2 tablespoons olive or canola oil

1½ cups red-wine vinegar

½ small red onion, thinly sliced lengthwise

⅓ cup light brown sugar

2 tablespoons kosher salt

1 teaspoon yellow mustard seeds

1 teaspoon fennel seeds

1 teaspoon black peppercorns

½ teaspoon whole allspice

Heat the oven to 400°F. Put the beets in a glass baking dish (8-inch square works well). Drizzle them with the oil and 2 tablespoons water. Seal the pan tightly with aluminum foil and roast the beets until just soft enough to pierce with a fork, 50 to 55 minutes. Transfer the beets to a cutting board. When cool enough to touch, rub off their skins with paper towels and quarter them lengthwise (or cut them into sixths if large).

Put the remaining ingredients and ¾ cup water in a small saucepan. Bring to a boil. Pack the beets in a 2-quart heat-resistant glass bowl or measuring cup. Pour the hot brine over the beets. Let cool to room temperature and then cover and refrigerate for at least 2 and up to 14 days.

Chilled Beet Soup with Horseradish Sour Cream

SERVES 4

1½ pounds small or medium beets
    (about 2 bunches, trimmed), well scrubbed

4 cloves garlic, unpeeled

3 strips (3 inches long) orange zest

3 sprigs fresh thyme

Kosher salt and freshly ground white or black pepper

2 tablespoons olive oil

2½ cups homemade or reduced-sodium chicken
    broth, or water

2 teaspoons honey

⅓ cup fresh orange juice

2 tablespoons red-wine vinegar

1 tablespoon prepared horseradish

½ cup sour cream

A few teaspoons cream or water as needed

Fresh dill sprigs, for garnish (optional)

Heat the oven to 375°F. Put the beets and garlic on a large sheet of heavy-duty aluminum foil. Scatter on the orange zest and thyme, season with salt and pepper, and drizzle with the olive oil. Fold up the sides of the foil and crimp to make a tight packet. Slide the foil packet onto a baking sheet and into the oven. Bake for 1 hour. Open the packet carefully (to avoid the steam) and check that the beets are tender by piercing one with the tip of a sharp knife. The knife should slide in easily; if it doesn't, reseal the package and continue baking. Set aside to cool for 15 to 20 minutes. Using paper towels, rub the skins off the beets and cut the beets into chunks. Peel the garlic cloves. Discard the thyme and orange zest, saving any juices collected in the foil.

Drop about one-third of the beet chunks, the garlic, and any collected juices into a blender. Add some of the chicken broth and the honey. Before turning on the blender, vent the lid by removing the pop-out center if there is one, or just open the lid a bit and drape a clean dishtowel over the vented lid. Blend to a smooth purée and transfer to a bowl. Continue in batches, puréeing all the beets. Stir in the orange juice and vinegar. Season to taste with salt and pepper. Cover and refrigerate to chill the soup thoroughly. Meanwhile, stir the horseradish into the sour cream. If the sour cream is too stiff (it should be the consistency of lightly whipped cream), stir in a few teaspoons cream or water to loosen it. Refrigerate until serving time.

To serve, ladle the soup into cups or bowls and spoon a bit of the horseradish sour cream onto each serving. Garnish with fresh dill, if you like.

Other recipe ideas

SAUTÉED BEETS WITH GREENS Stir-fry tender greens like spinach or watercress with chopped fresh ginger and garlic. Add roasted beet slices or wedges to the pan; deglaze with a little orange juice and cider vinegar. Serve warm.

BEEF TENDERLOIN WITH BEETS AND BLUE CHEESE Arrange a bed of roasted beet slices on a serving plate and top with a bit of really good blue cheese and a seared filet mignon.

CITRUS-MARINATED ROASTED BEET SALAD Marinate roasted beet wedges in a mix of orange and lemon juice, fresh thyme, olive oil, salt, and pepper. Serve on a bed of arugula, garnished with toasted hazelnuts.

DID YOU KNOW? Beets are one of the sweetest vegetables around, with even more sugar than carrots or sweet corn.

Belgian Endive

The juicy-crisp texture and bittersweet flavor of Belgian endive brings a welcome snap and freshness to winter, and the graceful shape and subtle color add elegance to salads and appetizers. When cooked, Belgian endive becomes meltingly tender, rich, and nutty—almost like a different vegetable.

PICKING THE BEST

At the market, endive should be snow-white, with just a little yellow at the tips; the ribs and bases should not show any browning. White heads of Belgian endive are most common, but you may run across red-edged heads, too. These taste the same as white, and heat will dull their purply-red hue, so take advantage of their color in salads.

KEEPING IT FRESH

Heads of endive (or chicons, as they're sometimes called) that have been in the light too long will start to turn green and may taste bitter; the amount of time depends on how they've been handled, so the best approach is to keep them in the dark. When you get them home, wrap the heads in plastic and tuck them into the vegetable crisper. Plan to use them within a few days.

PREPARING

To use endive raw, pull off any wilted or brown leaves and wipe the rest of the head with a damp paper towel. Wait until just before serving to slice raw endive, as its cut edges brown rapidly. For interesting endive shapes, slice the head on a sharp diagonal, turning as you go. Stop cutting when you get to the tiniest center leaves and the core, which should be discarded.

Endive that will be grilled, broiled, or braised benefits from a short steam first; put a few slices of lemon in the water and steam whole, trimmed heads for 5 to 10 minutes.

HOW TO USE IT

Endive's succulent, bittersweet leaves are wonderful as part of a salad, and their delicate spears make a natural vehicle for savory spreads, dips, and fillings, so Belgian endive is a standard in the hors d'oeuvre repertoire. But Belgian endive is also lovely when cooked; grilling or braising the whole heads or sautéing a chiffonade of endive will bring out a nutty complexity that's hidden in the raw form.

RECIPES

Pancetta-Wrapped Endive with Salsa Verde

SERVES 4

FOR THE SALSA VERDE

1 cup tightly packed flat-leaf parsley leaves

¼ cup sliced shallots (2 small)

1 to 2 cloves garlic, chopped; more to taste

¼ cup plus 2 tablespoons excellent-quality extra-virgin olive oil

1 tablespoon white-wine vinegar

Grated zest of ½ lemon

1 hard-cooked egg

1 tablespoon capers, rinsed, drained, and chopped

Salt and freshly ground black pepper

FOR THE ENDIVE

4 medium heads Belgian endive, steamed for 10 minutes and cooled

2 tablespoons extra-virgin olive oil

1 lemon, halved

Salt and freshly ground black pepper

16 slices pancetta, about ⅛ inch thick

Make the salsa verde: In a food processor, combine the parsley, shallots, garlic, oil, vinegar, and lemon zest. Add the egg; pulse briefly until just chopped. Stir in the capers. Taste and season with pepper and salt, if necessary. Cover and refrigerate for an hour or so before serving to let the flavors develop. About 15 minutes before serving, take the salsa verde out of the refrigerator and let it come to room temperature.

Cook the endive: Cut the steamed endive in half lengthwise. Cut out and discard the tiny center leaves and the core. Brush the endive with 1 tablespoon of the olive oil and season with a squeeze of lemon and sprinkling of salt and pepper. Wrap each endive half loosely with two slices of pancetta (the slices may unravel as you work with them; this is fine). Brush again with a little olive oil. Heat a grill or broiler. Arrange the wrapped endive on the grill over glowing (not flaming) coals or close to the broiler and cook, turning several times, until the pancetta is crisp and browned and the endive is heated through, about 8 minutes. Arrange on a platter and spoon the salsa verde around the endive. Serve immediately.

Smoked Salmon on Belgian Endive with Crème Fraîche and Chives

MAKES ABOUT 35 TO 40 HORS D'OEUVRES

4 large heads Belgian endive, preferably a mix of green and red endive

⅓ cup crème fraîche (available in the specialty cheese section of some supermarkets)

¼ pound thinly sliced smoked salmon, cut crosswise into ¼-inch-wide strips

Freshly ground black pepper

½ medium lemon

1 small bunch fresh chives, sliced diagonally into ¼-inch segments

Discard any damaged outer endive leaves. Trim the base and separate the leaves. You should end up with 35 to 40 large leaves (save the small inner leaves for a salad). Arrange the leaves on a baking sheet.

Put the crème fraîche in a squeeze bottle or a small piping bag. (You can also make a piping bag by trimming one corner of a small zip-top bag.) Pipe a small dollop of crème fraîche on each endive leaf. Gently arrange a small pile (about 4 strips) of the sliced salmon on top of the crème fraîche. Season the salmon with some black pepper and a little squeeze of lemon juice. Sprinkle a few chives on top (you may not need them all), arrange the leaves on a platter, and serve.

Other recipe ideas

ENDIVE-ORANGE SALAD Toss sliced endive with fresh or canned orange segments, watercress, and a simple balsamic vinaigrette.

BRAISED ENDIVE AND CARROTS Braise endive by halving heads lengthwise and browning them, cut side down, in a sauté pan until deep golden brown, along with diced carrots, onions, and celery. Add chicken stock and simmer, covered, until tender.

ENDIVE-SPINACH SAUTÉ Slice endive crosswise and sauté over high heat in olive oil and butter with chopped fresh spinach, minced garlic, and a dash of crushed red pepper flakes. Serve with a squeeze of lemon.

Brassica oleracea cvs.

Brussels Sprouts

The world is divided into two camps over Brussels sprouts: those who hate them and those who adore them. Fortunately, more people are discovering the nutty, sweet flavor of Brussels sprouts as well as their versatility in the kitchen.

KEEPING IT FRESH

If you buy a stalk, cut off the sprouts and put them in a plastic bag in the crisper drawer. Store sprouts in the fridge for up to two weeks in the coldest part and be sure they're not too moist or they'll mold. The longer they're stored, the more the outer leaves will yellow, so just peel them off before cooking.

PREPARING

The trick to cooking sprouts perfectly is to deal with their density. To maximize their nuttiness and down-play any cabbagey flavors, cut sprouts into the size and shape that works best with your cooking method. No matter how you decide to cut, cook, and flavor your sprouts, they'll need their ends trimmed first with a sharp paring knife. Then be sure to pull off any tough-looking, damaged, or yellow leaves to expose the prettier surface below. See how to cut sprouts on p. 295.

HOW TO USE

Brussels sprouts adapt to a surprising number of cooking methods; you can even eat them raw, thinly sliced and tossed with dressing as a salad. Quarters are best for roasting. The oven's heat penetrates them well; plus, they have a lot of surface area so they brown well.

Shredding is perfect for a quick sauté. This method gives you the "leafiest" texture; most of the shreds aren't attached to the core, so they fluff up. Slicing is great for braising. The liquid cooks them evenly and relatively quickly, and the flavors of the braising liquid integrate deliciously with the slices.

PICKING THE BEST

Choose sprouts with tight heads with little decay or yellowing; most sprouts, though, will have a few outer leaves that aren't perfect, and you'll often see sprouts whose outer leaves have been munched by insects, but that doesn't seem to affect the quality of the inner sprout. Sprouts that have seen some frost will be really sweet, while sprouts that are loose and ruffly have most likely been grown in too much heat and their flavor won't be as intensely sweet and nutty.

If you're lucky, you can find the whole stalk, which is gorgeous in a sculptural way (but a pain to store).

PRESERVING OPTIONS

To freeze Brussels sprouts, blanch first for 3 to 5 minutes, depending on the size. Cool in an ice bath, drain, and dry, and then store in airtight freezer bags.

Fall

.... RECIPES ....

Brussels Sprouts Braised with Pancetta, Shallot, Thyme, and Lemon

SERVES 6 TO 8

¼ pound pancetta, cut into ¼-inch dice (about ½ cup)

1 tablespoon olive oil

½ cup small-diced carrot (2 small)

⅓ cup minced shallot (2 to 3 medium)

⅛ teaspoon crushed red pepper flakes

2 pounds Brussels sprouts, trimmed and cut lengthwise through the core into ¼-inch-thick slices

Kosher salt and freshly ground black pepper

One 14-ounce can reduced-sodium chicken broth

1 bushy 3-inch sprig fresh thyme

2 tablespoons chopped oil-packed sun-dried tomato

1 tablespoon unsalted butter

1 teaspoon lightly packed finely grated lemon zest

In a 12-inch skillet over medium heat, cook the pancetta in the olive oil, stirring frequently, until the pancetta has rendered much of its fat and is nicely browned, 4 to 5 minutes. Increase the heat to medium high, stir in the carrot, shallot, and red pepper flakes and cook to soften the vegetables, 1 to 2 minutes. Add the sprouts, season lightly with salt and pepper, stir to coat with the fat, and cook, stirring, until the sprouts wilt slightly and a few brown lightly, 2 to 3 minutes.

Add the broth and thyme, cover with the lid slightly ajar, and adjust the heat to a lively simmer. Cook the sprouts until they're just barely tender, 4 to 6 minutes. Remove the lid, increase the heat to medium high, and cook, stirring frequently, until all the liquid has evaporated and the sprouts are quite tender (but not mushy), about 3 minutes. Turn off the heat, gently stir in the sun-dried tomato, butter, and lemon zest. Season to taste with salt and pepper.

DID YOU KNOW? Brussels sprouts have more protein than most green vegetables. Combined with a whole grain, they make a complete protein, making them a good choice for a vegetarian main dish.

Creamy Brussels Sprout Gratin

SERVES 6

2 pounds Brussels sprouts, ends trimmed and outer leaves removed; sprouts halved lengthwise

3 tablespoons unsalted butter, melted

Kosher salt and freshly ground black pepper

1 cup coarse fresh breadcrumbs (from a baguette or other white bread)

¾ ounce (¼ cup) finely grated Gruyère

1¼ cups heavy cream

Heat the oven to 425°F. Put the Brussels sprouts in a shallow baking dish that will hold them in a snug single layer (a 9x13-inch rectangle or slightly smaller oval is good). Toss with 2 tablespoons of the melted butter, ¾ teaspoon salt, and several grinds of pepper. Spread them evenly in the dish and roast, tossing once or twice, until browned in spots and tender when pierced with a knife, 25 to 30 minutes.

While the sprouts roast, combine the breadcrumbs with the remaining 1 tablespoon melted butter and ⅛ teaspoon salt in a small bowl. Mix in the Gruyère.

When the Brussels sprouts are tender and browned, pour the cream over them and continue baking until the cream has a saucy consistency and coats the sprouts, 5 to 7 minutes. Remove the pan from the oven. Set the oven to broil and position a rack 6 inches below the broiler. Sprinkle on the breadcrumb mixture. Broil the gratin until the crust is deep golden brown, about 5 minutes.

Other recipe ideas

LEMON-KISSED BRUSSELS SPROUTS Sauté Brussels sprout leaves (slice the inner core) in olive oil; finish with lemon and chopped parsley.

DILLED BRUSSELS SPROUTS Steam sprouts until tender; toss with melted butter and chopped dill.

PENNE WITH PINE NUTS, BRUSSELS SPROUTS, AND CARAMELIZED ONION Make a pasta dish with penne, quartered sautéed Brussels sprouts, caramelized onion, pine nuts, and lemon zest. Loosen with a bit of pasta water and finish with grated Parmesan.

Brassica oleracea cvs.

Cabbage

When properly treated, cabbage is sweet, mild, and delicious. It's also extremely nutritious—high in vitamin C and many antioxidants. Although cheap and plentiful year-round, cabbage is king in late fall, as those grown in cool weather and touched by frost are likely to be sweeter than those grown in warm weather.

PICKING THE BEST

Cabbage is available year-round in one variety or another, but its flavor is enhanced by cold weather, which turns the starch in the plant to sugar, making the vegetable sweeter.

There are three different types of European cabbage: green (also called Dutch white), red (which is really purple and has a slightly peppery flavor), and Savoy, which has deep blue-green, crenellated leaves. Napa, or Chinese, cabbage is also commonly available and can be used in most recipes that call for cabbage. Napa cabbage has ruffled, thin, light-green leaves that are as tender as lettuce and crunchy white stems that are similar in texture to green cabbage, with a hint of celery flavor. Napa's more delicate texture makes it a great choice for slaws and salads.

With any variety, look for firm, compact heads with no signs of browning. European cabbages should feel hard and heavy. Napa cabbage, on the other hand, will be light in comparison. If you plan to stuff the cabbage, avoid those whose leaves have small cracks.

KEEPING IT FRESH

Keep heads sealed in plastic wrap and stored in the crisper drawer. If you want to eat the cabbage raw, use it within 4 days. If you're planning to cook it, cabbage will keep for up to a couple of weeks, though Savoy cabbage should be used within 4 or 5 days no matter what the final preparation, as it's more fragile.

PREPARING

For all varieties of cabbage, remove any wilted outer leaves before slicing or shredding. Slice the cabbage in half lengthwise and remove its tough core, unless you're trying to preserve whole leaves for stuffing, in which case you should cut the core from the whole head.

HOW TO USE IT

Cabbage makes a wonderful salad—generally called a slaw—when shredded and tossed with a bright dressing, but its sweetest character comes out with cooking. Steaming, braising, and stir-frying are excellent ways to prepare cabbage. The longer the cabbage cooks, however, the stronger the sulfurous elements become, so whatever method you use, cook just until tender.

Grilling and roasting also brings out the sweet side of cabbage. Try cutting it into narrow wedges, coat in olive oil, salt, and pepper, then grill or roast until tender and beginning to char.

Green

Savoy

Red

Bok choy

Mexican-Style Slaw with Jícama, Cilantro, and Lime

SERVES 6 TO 8

1 small or ½ medium red or green cabbage (or use a
    mix of both, about 1½ pounds), bruised outer
    leaves removed, cored, and cut into 6 wedges
1 tablespoon kosher salt, plus more to taste
1 medium jícama (about 1 pound), peeled and
    quartered
4 scallions (white and green parts), thinly sliced on
    the diagonal (about ½ cup)
¼ cup chopped fresh cilantro
¼ cup plus 2 tablespoons mayonnaise
¼ cup fresh lime juice, plus more to taste
1 jalapeño, cored, seeded (if you like), and minced

Thinly slice the cabbage in a food processor using the
4mm slicing disk or by hand; you should have about
6 packed cups. Put the cabbage in a colander and toss
it with 1 tablespoon salt. Lay a plate that fits inside
the colander on top of the cabbage and set a heavy
can or jar on top of the plate. Drain the cabbage in
the sink or over a bowl for 2 hours.

If using a food processor, switch to the grating disk
and grate the jícama or cut it into very thin (julienne)
strips by hand; you should have about 2 cups. Put the
jícama in a large bowl and toss in the scallion and
cilantro.

In a small bowl, whisk the mayonnaise, lime juice,
and jalapeño.

Turn the cabbage out onto a clean dishtowel or
paper towels and pat it thoroughly dry. Toss the
cabbage with the jícama and the lime mayonnaise.
Season to taste with more salt and lime juice if
needed.

Sweet-Sour Red Cabbage

SERVES 6

1 tablespoon olive oil
6 ounces applewood-smoked bacon (about 7 slices),
    cut into julienne (about 1½ cups)
1 large yellow onion (12 ounces), thinly sliced (about
    2 cups)
1 small head red cabbage (about 2 pounds) cored,
    cut into eighths, and thinly sliced crosswise
    (about 8 cups)
1 cup packed dark brown sugar
¼ cup red-wine vinegar
¾ teaspoon kosher salt; more as needed
Freshly ground black pepper

In a 5- or 6-quart Dutch oven, heat the oil over high
heat, add the bacon, and cook, stirring occasionally,
until its fat is rendered and the bacon is crisp, 3 to
4 minutes. Add the onion and cook, stirring
frequently, until soft and lightly colored, about
3 minutes. Add the cabbage and cook, stirring
regularly, until just wilted, about 5 minutes. Add the
brown sugar and vinegar, stir well, and let cook until
the cabbage is wilted but still has a bit of crunch left
to it, about 5 minutes. Season with ¾ teaspoon salt
and several grinds of pepper. Adjust the acidity or
sweetness with a touch more vinegar or sugar if you
like, and add more salt and pepper if needed.

Stir-Fried Napa Cabbage with Garlic, Fresh Chile, and Basil

SERVES 4

1 medium-small head Napa cabbage (about 1¾ pounds)
1 tablespoon canola oil
3 medium cloves garlic, coarsely chopped (about
    1 tablespoon)
1 tablespoon fish sauce
1½ teaspoons sugar
¼ teaspoon kosher salt, plus more to taste
½ medium serrano chile, coarsely chopped (don't seed)
¼ cup roughly torn fresh basil leaves
2 to 3 teaspoons fresh lime juice
2 medium scallions (green part only), thinly sliced on
    an extreme diagonal, for garnish

Slice the cabbage in half lengthwise. Position one half cut side up and slice it across the middle at the point where the ruffled, leafy top gives way to white stem. Remove the core, slice the stem end lengthwise into 1½-inch-thick wedges, and cut the wedges crosswise into 1½-inch pieces (the leaves will separate). Cut the leafy half in the same way. Keep the leaves and stems separate. Repeat with the remaining half cabbage. You should have about 5 cups stems and 4 cups leaves.

Heat a wok or a 12-inch skillet over high heat for about 45 seconds and then add the oil, swirling it to coat the pan. When the oil is hot and shimmering, add the garlic and the white stems. Stir-fry until the stems brown lightly in spots and begin to release some liquid, about 2 minutes. Add the fish sauce, sugar, salt, and chile and toss. Continue to stir-fry until the stems are barely tender, about 2½ minutes.

Add the cabbage leaves, stirring quickly to move them to the bottom of the pan. As soon as the stems are just tender and the tops are barely wilted, 30 to 40 seconds more, remove from the heat and stir in the basil and 2 teaspoons lime juice. Season to taste with salt, garnish with the scallion, and add more lime juice, if you like. Serve immediately.

Caramelized Cabbage on Creamy Polenta

SERVES 6

2 tablespoons plus ½ teaspoon extra-virgin olive oil; more for the pan

¼ pound chopped pancetta

2 cloves garlic, minced

1 small sprig rosemary, chopped

2 pounds green, white, or Savoy cabbage, cored and thinly shredded

2 teaspoons kosher salt, plus more to taste

Freshly ground black pepper

About 3 tablespoons dry white wine (or water); more as needed

A few drops of balsamic vinegar

1 cup medium-coarse cornmeal, preferably organic stone-ground

1 tablespoon unsalted butter

2 ounces finely grated Asiago or Pecorino Romano

Prepare the cabbage: Heat 2 tablespoons of the olive oil in a wide, deep saucepan over medium heat. Add the pancetta, garlic, and rosemary and sauté until the pancetta and garlic soften, about 4 minutes. Add the cabbage, ½ teaspoon of the salt, pepper to taste, the wine, and ¼ cup water; toss to coat thoroughly. Cover and cook over medium heat for about 1 hour; check about every 5 minutes and add a little more water or white wine whenever the cabbage seems too dry or begins to brown too fast (the cabbage should stew slowly and brown lightly). After about 1 hour, uncover and cook, stirring, until the cabbage is meltingly tender, lightly caramelized, medium brown, and somewhat dry to the touch, about 5 to 10 minutes. Add the balsamic vinegar, taste, and adjust seasonings.

Meanwhile, prepare the polenta: Heat the oven to 350°F. In an oiled 3-quart nonstick ovenproof skillet, combine the cornmeal, 4 cups water, the remaining ½ teaspoon olive oil, and the remaining 1½ teaspoons salt; stir briefly. Bake, uncovered, for 40 minutes. Remove the pan from the oven, give the polenta a good stir, and return the pan to the oven to bake for another 5 minutes. Stir in the butter and half of the cheese. Pour the polenta into a greased 9-inch heatproof dish, cover evenly with the cabbage, and scatter the remaining cheese on top. Bake until the tips of the cabbage are brown and crisp, 10 to 15 minutes. Serve hot.

Other recipe ideas

BRAISED SAVOY CABBAGE Sauté thick wedges of Savoy cabbage in butter until lightly colored, then simmer in chicken or vegetable broth with a bay leaf and fresh thyme until tender.

STUFFED CABBAGE LEAVES WITH LAMB AND FETA Stuff blanched cabbage leaves with a mixture of ground lamb, rice, fresh oregano, mint, and feta cheese. Bake in a light tomato broth.

SESAME-GINGER SLAW Make an Asian slaw by tossing shredded cabbage with soy sauce, rice vinegar, a touch of Asian sesame oil, and some sesame seeds and grated fresh ginger.

Daucus carota var. sativum cvs.

Carrots

This familiar root vegetable is the workhorse of the kitchen. Along with onions and celery, carrots form the aromatic base called a mirepoix that starts off so many soups and stews. When raw, carrots are crisp and refreshing. When cooked, their sweetness intensifies and they become tender, delicious as a solo player or an accommodating partner for other ingredients.

Purple Dragon **Rainbow**

PICKING THE BEST

Though most carrots are orange, this member of the parsley family comes in many shapes and sizes, from purple to white, slender to chubby, tapered to conical, even round. Most "baby" carrots at the supermarket are actually mature carrots whittled down. They can be convenient, since they require little prep, but they won't have the sweetness of true immature carrots, which you can find at farmer's markets. Your best guarantee of freshness is to buy carrots in bunches, with green tops still attached. Even when large, carrots with fresh tops should still be tender, juicy, and full of flavor.

Look for firm roots and fresh, dark greens. When buying packaged carrots, look for plump, firm, fresh-looking roots with no shaggy hair-like protrusions.

KEEPING IT FRESH

Once you get carrots home, cut off the green tops, if still attached, so they don't draw moisture from the roots. Store carrots in plastic in the refrigerator; though they do keep well, they lose sweetness and flavor the longer they're stored; try to use them within 2 weeks. Peeled carrots will dry out faster than unpeeled.

PREPARING

There's no need to peel young carrots; the skin packs a lot of flavor as well as vitamins. As carrots mature, their skin becomes a little bitter, so peel off just a thin layer. Very mature carrots can have a woody and fibrous core; remove it by cutting the carrots lengthwise and then cutting along the sides of the core where it meets the outer orange part of the carrot.

HOW TO USE IT

Use carrots in any dish in which you want an earthy sweetness. When raw, carrots bring a terrific crunchy texture. Cooked carrots are a natural addition to stews, soups, and braised dishes. A tiny dice of carrots is nice folded into a risotto, and when puréed, carrots make lovely bases for soups or even soufflés. Roasted carrots, on their own or tossed with other roasted roots, make a wonderful side dish.

PRESERVING OPTIONS

Carrots make tasty pickles, especially baby carrots, which look so appealing in the canning jar. You can also freeze carrots, in thick slices or as a cooked purée. Cut raw carrots into slices, blanch for about 2 minutes, cool, drain, and then pack into airtight freezer bags.

RECIPES

Carrot and Coriander Soup

SERVES 8

3 ounces (6 tablespoons) unsalted butter

2 yellow onions, thinly sliced

3 pounds carrots, peeled and cut into 1-inch pieces

1 bunch cilantro (about 3 ounces), stems attached, washed well, a handful of leaves reserved for garnish

1 jalapeño, cored, halved, and seeded

1 teaspoon salt

1 tablespoon coriander seeds, ground

6 to 8 cups homemade or reduced-sodium chicken broth or water

½ cup crème fraîche or sour cream, for garnish

In a large saucepan, melt 4 tablespoons of the butter over medium-high heat. Add the onion and sauté until soft, about 5 minutes. Add the carrots, cilantro (except for the reserved leaves), jalapeño, salt, and ground coriander. Continue to cook the vegetables for about 10 minutes, stirring occasionally. Add the broth and simmer until the vegetables are completely tender, about 35 minutes. Purée the soup in batches in a blender until smooth. (Be careful to fill the blender no more than one-third full and hold a towel over the lid while you turn it on). For less heat, remove half of the jalapeño before puréeing.

Stir in the remaining 2 tablespoons butter and taste for seasoning. If the soup seems too thick, add a little water. Garnish with a drizzle of crème fraîche and the reserved cilantro leaves.

Sweet Pickled Baby Carrots

MAKES 18 TO 20 PICKLED CARROTS

Kosher salt

¾ pound baby carrots with their tops on (18 to 20 carrots, about 6 inches long and ½ inch thick at the wide end)

2 tablespoons coriander seeds

1 cup dry white wine

1¼ cups honey

1 cup Champagne vinegar

½ cup sherry vinegar

Bring a medium saucepan of salted water to a boil over high heat. Fill a large bowl with ice water.

Meanwhile, peel the baby carrots and remove all but about ½ inch of the green stems. Boil the carrots until barely tender, about 5 minutes. Immediately drain the carrots and then immerse them in the bowl of ice water.

In a small saucepan, toast the coriander seeds over medium heat just until fragrant and lightly browned, 3 to 5 minutes. Add the white wine and boil until reduced to about ¼ cup, 6 to 10 minutes.

In a medium saucepan, heat the honey over medium-high heat until it bubbles, about 3 minutes. Add the Champagne and sherry vinegars, and then the coriander and wine mixture; simmer for 5 minutes. Watch carefully and reduce the heat as necessary to prevent a boil-over.

Arrange the carrots upright in a clean 1-quart canning jar or other nonreactive container and pour the honey mixture over top. Let cool to room temperature. Cover and refrigerate for at least 4 hours but preferably 24 hours before serving the pickles. They will keep, refrigerated, for 2 to 3 weeks.

Other recipe ideas

ROASTED CARROTS AND SHALLOTS Cut carrots into thick julienne, toss with sliced shallots, a splash of olive oil, fresh thyme, salt, and pepper, and roast until tender and slightly browned.

SPICED CARROT STIR-FRY Make an Indian stir-fry with shredded carrots, cabbage, and minced jalapeño, finished with toasted cumin seeds, ground coriander, and a squeeze of lime juice.

BRAISED SWEET-AND-SOUR CARROTS Braise whole small carrots or long chunks in butter or olive oil, a little water or broth, and a bit of honey and Dijon mustard. Braise until tender and then let the liquid reduce to a syrupy, sweet-tangy glaze.

CREAMY CARROT PURÉE Make a mashed carrot purée by boiling carrots and perhaps parsnips and mashing as you would potatoes. Enrich the purée with butter or cream and season with a dash of nutmeg and ground ginger.

Apium graveolens var. rapaceum cvs.

Celeriac

Celeriac looks like a hairy softball, but its flavor is light and like a cross between celery and parsley. Also called celery root, it's delicious raw and cooked.

PICKING THE BEST

Choose those about the size of a baseball; larger ones can be woody or spongy inside. It should be firm and heavy with no signs of sprouting or shriveling. If its parsley-like leaves are still attached, they should look fresh, not wilted.

KEEPING IT FRESH

Keep celeriac dry, cool, and in the dark, where it can last 8 to 12 days before it begins to show any signs of deterioration. Keep it refrigerated once you peel or cut it.

PREPARING

To trim, cut off the leaves (if there are any) and the top and bottom of the root and then slice away the knobby skin until the inner white part of the root appears. Expect a good amount of trim loss due to the uneven surface of the root. Like a potato, peeled celery root turns brown, so drop it in a bowl of cold water or wait to peel until just before you need it.

HOW TO USE IT

Try it diced, shredded, or julienned in salads or add it to a soup or stew or to a creamy gratin. For a delicious twist on mashed potatoes, replace up to half of the potatoes with cubed celeriac and boil together until both are tender.

RECIPES

Silky Leek and Celeriac Soup

SERVES 6 TO 8

3 tablespoons unsalted butter

2 medium leeks (white and light green parts),
    trimmed, halved lengthwise, cut crosswise into
    thin half-moon slices, rinsed and drained

1 medium yellow onion, thinly sliced

1 teaspoon kosher salt, plus more to taste

1½ pounds celeriac (about 1 large)

¾ cup crème fraîche

¼ cup heavy cream; more as needed

Freshly ground black pepper

¼ cup thinly sliced fresh chives

In a heavy 4-quart or larger pot, melt the butter over medium-low heat. Add the leeks, onion, and a big pinch of salt and cook, stirring occasionally, until very soft and light golden but not brown, 15 to 20 minutes. Reduce the heat to low if you see signs of browning.

Meanwhile, peel the celeriac with a sharp knife (expect to slice quite a bit off the exterior). Halve the peeled celeriac lengthwise and cut each half into 1-inch-thick wedges. Cut each wedge crosswise into ¼-inch slices. You should have about 5 cups.

Add the celeriac, 1 teaspoon salt, and ½ cup water to the leeks. Cover and cook until the celeriac is tender, 10 to 15 minutes. (Check occasionally; if all the water cooks off and the vegetables start to brown, add another ½ cup water.) Add 4½ cups water, bring to a simmer, and continue to cook for another 20 minutes. Let cool slightly.

Purée the soup (with an immersion blender or in small batches in a stand blender) to a very smooth consistency. Cool completely and then store in the refrigerator at least overnight or up to 2 days.

About an hour before serving, put the crème fraîche in a bowl and stir in enough cream until the mixture reaches the consistency of yogurt. Leave the mixture at room temperature until you're ready to serve the soup. (Cold cream will cool the soup.)

Reheat the soup. (Gradually thin it with as much as 1 cup water if needed.) Taste and add salt as needed. Ladle the soup into shallow bowls. Top each with a spoonful of crème fraîche (it should float on top of the soup), a pinch of pepper, and a sprinkle of chives.

Celeriac and Yukon Gold Purée

SERVES 8

1½ pounds celeriac (1 large or 2 small), peeled
    and roughly chopped

1½ pounds Yukon Gold or russet potatoes, peeled
    and cut into chunks

1 tablespoon plus 1½ teaspoons coarse salt

¾ cup milk or half-and-half

3 tablespoons unsalted butter

2 tablespoons grated fresh or prepared horseradish,
    or to taste

Fresh lemon juice

Freshly ground white pepper

Put the celeriac and potatoes in a pot, cover with water by at least an inch, and add 1 tablespoon of salt. Bring to a boil. Reduce the heat to medium, cover partway, and cook until tender, 20 to 25 minutes. Drain. Return the vegetables to the pot and heat on medium for 1 to 2 minutes, stirring to evaporate excess water. Rinse a small saucepan in cold water (this will make the pan easier to clean later); pour in the milk or half-and-half. Bring to just below a simmer over medium heat; set aside. Force the vegetables through a ricer or food mill and return them to the boiling pot. Beat in the butter with a wooden spoon. Add the milk to the potatoes a little at a time, beating vigorously after each addition. Stir in horseradish and lemon juice to taste. Add the remaining 1½ teaspoons salt, season with pepper, and serve.

Other recipe ideas

CLASSIC CÉLERI RÉMOULADE Grate raw celeriac and mix with a flavorful homemade mayonnaise to make a traditional French salad. Serve with country terrine, carrot salad, and potato salad.

CELERIAC-POTATO MASH WITH ROASTED GARLIC Boil equal amounts of celeriac and potato, then mash with some roasted garlic, butter, and cream or milk to make a rustic mash.

APPLE-CELERIAC PURÉE Stew chunks of celeriac and apple together in a little chicken broth and a bay leaf, then purée for a lightly sweet side dish to pork.

Escarole

Treviso

Radicchio

Frisée

Cichorium intybus and cvs.

Chicories

Most of the time, we're not attracted to foods that are bitter, but there are a few exceptions, and chicory is one. Members of the chicory family, which includes a range of greens that are eaten both raw and cooked, balance an assertive bitterness with a touch of sweet that makes them complex, intriguing, and often exactly the right thing to pair with richer foods. And chicories' textures—crunchy and succulent—give these greens great versatility.

PICKING THE BEST

You should choose your chicory based on what you plan to do with it. For cooking, you'll want a sturdier member, such as escarole or radicchio; for salads, choose a more tender variety—though all of these greens are substantial in texture. Belgian endive is also a chicory, though many people don't realize it; see more information on p. 180.

Here are the varieties you'll find most often.

- **Escarole:** A broad-leaved chicory, with wide, succulent stems and leaves that look more crumpled than curly. Like all chicories, it has a bitter flavor, though somewhat less so than curly endive. Other names are common chicory, broad chicory, or Batavian endive. Great for braising or wilting into soups.
- **Curly endive:** A hearty, narrow-leaved chicory, with narrow stems and frilly, very curly leaves; it's also called chicory and curly chicory. Good both cooked and raw.
- **Frisée:** Essentially baby curly endive. Its tender leaves are finer and its flavor is milder than its more mature cousin.
- **Radicchio:** Looks different from its cousins because of the striking garnet-red color, usually with creamy white ribs, and its tight round head. The bittersweet flavor is similar to other chicories.

- **Treviso:** An elongated radicchio, with a looser head and slightly less intensely magenta leaves.

When choosing escarole, avoid heads with especially thick or tough-looking outer leaves. With curly endive, the stem end shouldn't show signs of browning, nor should the outer leaves look wilted or have black tips. The pale center leaves are the best part, so choose a head with lots of them. Frisée is all about the heart, so look for heads with deep-green outer leaves and a large white to pale-yellow heart. For radicchio and Treviso, look for tightly formed heads and no browning on outer leaves.

KEEPING IT FRESH

Store chicories in a plastic bag in the crisper drawer in your refrigerator and use within a few days.

PREPARING

Remove any blemished outer leaves from any chicory. For larger varieties such as escarole and for radicchio, cut out the core. Wash leaves in a few changes of water (escarole in particular can be quite sandy). If cooking, you can leave water clinging to the leaves; otherwise dry them well in a salad spinner. Depending on the dish you'll make, tear the chicory into bite-sized pieces or leave slightly larger. Radicchio can look nice when cut into chiffonade, or to grill it, cut into thick wedges; cut Treviso in half lengthwise for the grill.

HOW TO USE IT

Chicories are prepared in a variety of different ways, depending on the type. Escarole can be eaten raw in salads, but its hearty leaves benefit from sautéing, stir-frying, braising, and wilting into soups. Curly endive is usually eaten raw, but as with escarole, cooking mellows its assertively bitter flavor. Frisée is a favorite of French cooks for salads, especially when paired with a warm bacon vinaigrette. Radicchio is a bold addition to a mixed green salad, adding color as well as strong flavor, and both radicchio and Treviso are delicious when brushed with olive oil and grilled until slightly wilted and browned, then served with a garlicky dressing.

SURPRISING PAIRINGS

One of the best ways to address the bitterness of chicory is by pairing it with another ingredient that's its equal in assertiveness: anchovies. Anchovy dressings are a classic Italian complement to salads made from chicory relatives, and the Italians seem to be chicory's biggest fans. Other salty partners that have a similar taming effect include bacon and salty cheeses, such as feta and Parmigiano-Reggiano.

The famous chicory coffee of New Orleans is a blend of coffee and the ground roasted root from a chicory plant. The custom was thought to have been brought to New Orleans by the Acadians who migrated from France via Nova Scotia. During the French revolution, coffee was scarce and the roasty, mellow flavor of chicory root was discovered to be a fine way to stretch the precious beans.

RECIPES

Frisée Salad with Oranges and Pistachios

SERVES 4

1 large or 2 small heads frisée, rinsed, dried, and torn into bite-sized pieces (about 6 cups)
2 navel oranges or blood oranges
2 tablespoons sherry vinegar or red-wine vinegar
1 teaspoon honey
3 tablespoons finely diced red onion
⅓ cup extra-virgin olive oil
Kosher salt and freshly ground black pepper
½ cup pistachios, toasted

Put the frisée in a large salad or mixing bowl. Finely grate the zest of one of the oranges into a small bowl. Slice the skin from both oranges and cut the orange sections away from the dividing membranes; put the sections in another bowl.

Add the vinegar, honey, and onion to the zest, whisk in the oil, and season to taste with salt and pepper. Add just enough of the dressing to the frisée to coat it lightly. Mound the frisée on four salad plates, scraping any red onion remaining in the bowl over the frisée. Arrange the orange slices on top, scatter with the pistachios, and serve immediately.

Spicy Sausage, Escarole, and White Bean Stew

SERVES 3 TO 4

1 tablespoon extra-virgin olive oil
1 medium yellow onion, chopped
¾ pound hot Italian sausage, casings removed
2 medium cloves garlic, minced
Two 15-ounce cans cannellini beans, rinsed and drained
1 small head escarole, chopped into 1- to 2-inch pieces, washed, and lightly dried
1 cup homemade or reduced-sodium chicken broth
1½ teaspoons red-wine vinegar, plus more to taste
Kosher salt
¼ cup freshly grated Parmigiano-Reggiano

Heat the oil in a heavy 5- to 6-quart pot over medium heat. Add the onion and cook, stirring occasionally, until tender, 5 to 6 minutes. Add the sausage, raise the heat to medium high, and cook, breaking up the sausage with a wooden spoon until lightly browned and broken into 1-inch pieces, 5 to 6 minutes. Add the garlic, cook for 1 minute, then stir in the beans. Add the escarole in batches; using tongs, toss with the sausage mixture to wilt and make room for more.

When all the escarole is in, add the chicken broth, cover the pot, and cook until the beans are heated through and the escarole is tender, about 8 minutes. Season to taste with vinegar and salt. Transfer to bowls and sprinkle each portion with Parmigiano.

Quick Chicken Sauté with Walnuts, Curly Endive, and Orange Pan Sauce

SERVES 2

2 medium boneless, skinless chicken breast halves (12 ounces total), cut into ¾-inch chunks
Kosher salt and freshly ground black pepper
2 tablespoons plus 1 teaspoon olive oil
6 ounces curly endive (curly chicory), washed, dried, and chopped into 2-inch pieces (about 6 cups, loosely packed)
2 cloves garlic, minced
¼ teaspoon coriander seeds, crushed
¼ cup water or homemade or reduced-sodium chicken broth
½ cup orange juice, preferably freshly squeezed
1 tablespoon good-quality white-wine vinegar
1 tablespoon unsalted butter
2 tablespoons minced fresh flat-leaf parsley
2 tablespoons coarsely chopped toasted walnuts

Season the chicken with salt and pepper. Heat 1 tablespoon of the oil in a medium sauté pan over medium-high heat. Add the endive and cook, stirring frequently, until deep green but still crisp-tender, about 90 seconds. Transfer to a medium bowl.

Heat 1 tablespoon oil in the pan and add the chicken. When the underside of the chicken has turned deep golden brown (after about 1 minute), turn it with a metal spatula. Turn occasionally for even browning until almost cooked through, 3 to 5 minutes, and transfer to the bowl of endive.

Reduce the heat to medium, heat the remaining 1 teaspoon oil in the pan, and add the garlic and coriander. Cook until fragrant, about 30 seconds. Add the water, orange juice, and vinegar. Scrape up and blend in any browned bits in the pan. Simmer

vigorously until the sauce has thickened a bit, 2 to 3 minutes. Stir in the butter, then the chicken and endive and any juices; season with salt and pepper to taste, and sprinkle with parsley and walnuts.

Green Beans and Radicchio with Shaved Parmesan

SERVES 4

2½ tablespoons extra-virgin olive oil
12 ounces slender green beans, trimmed and halved
1 medium yellow onion, halved and thinly sliced
Kosher salt and freshly ground black pepper
3 cups ½-inch strips radicchio (about 6 ounces)
1 large clove garlic, minced
1 tablespoon fresh lemon juice
Shavings of Parmigiano-Reggiano, for garnish

Heat a 12-inch skillet over medium-high heat. Pour in 2 tablespoons of the oil and swirl to coat the pan. When the oil is shimmering but not smoking, add the beans in an even layer. Scatter onion on top. Season with salt and pepper and cook undisturbed for 2 minutes. Add the radicchio and sauté, stirring occasionally, until it has begun to brown and the green beans are crisp-tender, about another 6 minutes. If the vegetables are cooking too fast, lower the heat to medium. Stir in the garlic, cooking for about another minute. Transfer to a serving bowl. Drizzle with lemon juice and the remaining ½ tablespoon oil; toss gently. Season to taste with salt and pepper, garnish with Parmigiano shavings, and serve.

Other recipe ideas

WALDORF-STYLE ESCAROLE SALAD Make a hearty salad with diced apple, celeriac, and torn pieces of escarole, all tossed in a mustardy vinaigrette and topped with blue cheese and walnuts.

GRILLED CHICKEN FRISÉE CAESAR Toss frisée in a zesty Caesar-style dressing and serve with grilled boneless chicken thighs and rustic croutons.

BACON-BRAISED CHICORIES Cook a few strips of good bacon, sauté any of the chicories in the reserved bacon fat, then deglaze with some sherry vinegar. Season with a touch of hot sauce, ground black pepper, and crumble the bacon on top.

Brassica oleracea cvs.

Collard Greens

You may think of collards as just part of traditional Southern cuisine, but once you taste them, you'll be figuring out ways to work them into any recipe that calls for greens. Generously sized and easy to prepare, collards have an earthy sweetness and a silky but chewy texture. And collards are extremely nutritious, with significant amounts of vitamins, minerals, and phytonutrients.

KEEPING IT FRESH

While greens tend to last longer unwashed, you're ten times more likely to use the greens before they go bad if you make them recipe-ready before storing them. Store washed and dried collards in plastic bags with the air pressed out for up to 5 days.

PREPARING

Whether you wash when you bring them home from the store or only just before cooking, do it thoroughly, as collards can be gritty. Trim out the center rib by slicing around it with a knife. Stack the leaves together, roll tightly, and cut across into ribbons, thick or thin depending on your recipe.

HOW TO USE IT

Collards will be tough and leathery unless patiently simmered. The assertive flavors of these greens also mellow with cooking and blend with the aromatics with which they're cooked. A few drops of vinegar also work to soften the edge a bit. Collards eventually become silky and tender, though they'll retain a touch of toothiness. Blanch until tender, then sauté or mix with a cream sauce and bake into a gratin. Or simply braise with some olive oil or bacon fat and season with garlic and lemon. Traditional Southern recipes finish collards with a touch of sugar, vinegar, and hot sauce or cayenne.

PICKING THE BEST

Collards usually come in bunches of large, paddle-shaped leaves. Choose those that are an even, rich dusty green with no signs of yellowing. They should feel supple with no cracking; avoid any that are slimy where the stems are tied together.

PRESERVING OPTIONS

Collards freeze well. Wash thoroughly, trim, and then cut into strips. Blanch about a pound at a time for 3 to 4 minutes, drain well, and then seal in airtight freezer bags.

RECIPES

Creamy Collards with Smithfield Ham

SERVES 8 TO 10

¼ cup olive oil

1 cup finely chopped onion

1 tablespoon finely chopped garlic

1½ cups chopped Smithfield ham or other country-cured ham, or prosciutto

2 cups homemade or reduced-sodium chicken broth

2 large heads (about 3 pounds total) collard greens, washed, stemmed, and cut into ¼-inch strips

2 cups heavy cream

Salt and freshly ground black pepper

Heat the olive oil in a large pot over medium-high heat. Add the onion and garlic; sauté until translucent, about 5 minutes. Add the ham; sauté for about 1 minute. Add the broth and collard greens; cover and cook, stirring occasionally, until the collards are tender, about 15 minutes. (The greens will diminish in volume as they cook.) Add the cream and cook until it reduces and thickens slightly, another 10 to 15 minutes. Season with salt and pepper to taste.

Quick-Sautéed Collard Ribbons

SERVES 3

1 tablespoon malt vinegar

2 teaspoons pure maple syrup

1½ pounds collard greens (about 30 leaves)

2 tablespoons extra-virgin olive oil

4 small cloves garlic, lightly smashed and peeled

Pinch of crushed red pepper flakes

½ teaspoon kosher salt

In a small bowl, whisk the malt vinegar and maple syrup.

Trim the stem from each collard leaf with a sharp knife, dividing the leaf completely in half lengthwise as you cut away the stem. Discard the stems; wash and dry the leaves.

Stack half of the leaves and roll them up tightly crosswise into a cigar shape. Using a very sharp knife, cut the collard "cigar" crosswise into ¼-inch-thick slices. Use your fingers to unfurl the slices, which will be tightly curled together. Repeat with the second half of the leaves.

In a 12-inch nonstick skillet, heat the olive oil and the garlic over medium-high heat. Cook, stirring and flipping the garlic, until it's fragrant and just lightly browned, about 3 minutes. Remove and discard the garlic. Add the red pepper flakes, stirring to distribute in the hot oil, and immediately add the collards and salt. Using tongs, stir and toss the collards until they're coated with the oil, and continue tossing until they're slightly wilted, about 1 minute. Most of the greens will have turned a bright green, with some beginning to turn a darker green. Don't overcook, as they'll become tough. Take the pan off the heat, drizzle on the maple-vinegar mixture, stir well, and transfer to a shallow serving platter. Serve immediately.

Other recipe ideas

VEGETARIAN TACOS Slice collards into ribbons and braise with plenty of onion and garlic; cook until all liquid has evaporated so the greens aren't drippy. Fill tortilla shells, then top with salsa and crumbled feta.

SMOKY BRAISED COLLARDS For a smoky but baconless side dish, braise collards in olive oil with onion, garlic, and smoked paprika; finish with a squeeze of lemon juice.

STUFFED PHYLLO APPETIZER Simmer collards until tender, then chop and fold into a light béchamel sauce. Season with lemon and fresh herbs such as cilantro, dill, parsley, and mint. Use as a stuffing for phyllo triangles or a phyllo-crusted pie.

Vaccinium macrocarpon cvs.

Cranberries

It's hard to imagine the American Thanksgiving feast without the tart, bracing flavor of cranberries, whether transformed into the jellied sauce from the can or a freshly made zesty cranberry relish. But the crunchy burgundy berries can do more than accompany turkey to the table—they shine in cakes, pies, and more.

PICKING THE BEST

Look for round, plump cranberries with smooth skin and no bruises; the redder, the better.

KEEPING IT FRESH

Cranberries have a short season, but fortunately they keep well, so it's easy to stock up. You can store fresh cranberries in the refrigerator's crisper drawer for up to 4 weeks, or freeze them for up to a year.

PREPARING

Other than picking out any soft or shriveled berries, cranberries don't need any sort of preparation before using.

HOW TO USE IT

Because they're so tart, cranberries are rarely used raw, though some holiday relishes and slaws pair tart raw cranberries with sweeter ingredients to temper the bite. Most recipes call for simmering the berries with sugar and spices, so they'll soften and develop winey, appley flavors in addition to the sour. Beyond sauces, use cranberries in salads, quick breads, and chutneys.

PRESERVING OPTIONS

Cranberries take well to freezing, which is great because they're plentiful around the holidays but often hard to find later, so stock up while you can. You can freeze them in their original packaging, or you can wash, dry, and pick through the berries first (discard any dark, mushy ones) and then transfer them to a heavy-duty freezer bag.

Use frozen cranberries like fresh cranberries in recipes. There's no need to thaw the berries—just put them in a colander, rinse in cold water, pat dry with a towel, and use—but you may need to increase cooking time slightly.

DID YOU KNOW?

Somehow people have gotten the idea that cranberries grow in water, which is not true and which, if it *were* true, would surely diminish the fruit's intense flavors. Cranberry bogs are sandy-bottomed flats, which are flooded only briefly at harvest time; the berries float and are corralled with booms for easier gathering.

Cranberry Upside-Down Cake

SERVES 12

8 ounces (1 cup) very soft unsalted butter; more
for the pan

1 cup very firmly packed light brown sugar

¼ teaspoon ground cinnamon

2 cups cranberries, fresh or frozen (thawed, rinsed,
and dried), at room temperature

1 cup granulated sugar

1 large egg yolk, at room temperature

2 large eggs, at room temperature

²/₃ cup sour cream, at room temperature

1 teaspoon pure vanilla extract

½ teaspoon salt

7 ounces (1¾ cups) cake flour

1 teaspoon baking powder

¼ teaspoon baking soda

Position a rack in the lower third of the oven and
heat the oven to 350°F. Lightly butter the bottom and
sides of a 9-inch round cake pan with sides at least
2½ inches high. (A springform pan will work; set it on
a foil-lined baking sheet to catch any leaks.)

Put 4 tablespoons of the butter in the buttered
pan. Put the pan in the oven until the butter melts,
about 5 minutes. Remove the pan from the oven
and stir in the brown sugar and cinnamon until
well combined. Spread the brown sugar mixture
evenly over the bottom of the pan and spread the
cranberries evenly over the sugar.

Put the remaining 12 tablespoons butter in a
medium bowl. Using a wooden spoon, cream the
butter with the granulated sugar and egg yolk until
blended, about 20 seconds. Switch to a whisk and stir
in the eggs one at a time. Whisk until the batter is
smooth and the sugar begins to dissolve, about
30 seconds. Whisk in the sour cream, vanilla, and salt.
Sift the cake flour, baking powder, and baking soda
directly onto the batter. Using the whisk, combine
the ingredients until the mixture is smooth and free
of lumps.

Spread the batter evenly over the cranberry
mixture in the cake pan. Bake until the center of the
cake springs back when gently touched and a skewer
inserted in the center comes out with only moist

crumbs clinging to it, 50 to 65 minutes. Set the pan
on a rack to cool for 5 to 10 minutes (the cranberry
syrup in the bottom of the pan will be too thick if you
wait longer). Run a knife between the cake and sides
of the pan. Invert the cake onto a serving plate and
remove the pan. Let cool for at least another
15 minutes before serving. This cake is best served
warm and fresh.

Cranberry-Orange Muffins

MAKES 12 MUFFINS

1½ cups fresh cranberries, picked through and rinsed

9 ounces (2 cups) unbleached all-purpose flour; more
for the pan

2 ounces (½ cup) cake flour

2 teaspoons baking powder

1 teaspoon ground ginger

½ teaspoon baking soda

½ teaspoon salt

5 ounces (10 tablespoons) unsalted butter, softened
at room temperature; more for the pan

¾ cup plus 2 tablespoons granulated sugar

2 large eggs, at room temperature

1½ teaspoons finely grated orange zest (using a
rasp-style zester, this is the zest of 1 small orange)

1 teaspoon pure vanilla extract

1 cup buttermilk, at room temperature

¼ cup fresh orange juice

2 tablespoons turbinado sugar (such as Sugar in
the Raw®)

Position a rack near the center of the oven and heat
the oven to 425°F. Generously butter a standard
12-cup muffin tin, including the top rim, and dust
the pan with flour. Tap out any excess.

Using a food processor, coarsely chop the
cranberries. In a medium bowl, mix the two flours,
baking powder, ginger, baking soda, and salt.

In the bowl of a stand mixer fitted with the paddle
attachment, beat the butter and granulated sugar
on medium speed until light and fluffy, about 2
minutes. Scrape the bowl. Beat in the eggs one at a
time, mixing for at least 30 seconds at medium speed
and scraping the bowl after each addition. Beat in

the orange zest and vanilla. With the mixer on low speed, briefly beat in one-third of the flour mixture, then add ½ cup of the buttermilk. When combined, mix in another one-third of the flour; then mix in the remaining ½ cup buttermilk and the orange juice, and finally mix in the rest of the flour. Scrape the bowl and beat the batter just until smooth, another 10 seconds. Using a rubber spatula or a wooden spoon, fold the cranberries into the batter.

Spoon the batter evenly into the muffin tin (each cup will be quite full). Sprinkle the tops of the muffins generously with the turbinado sugar. Bake until the tops are golden and a skewer inserted an inch into the top of a muffin comes out clean, 15 to 18 minutes. Let the muffins cool in the pan for 5 minutes and then turn them out onto a wire rack to cool completely. These muffins are best eaten the day they're made.

Ginger-Spice Cranberry-Apple Streusel Pie

SERVES 8

FOR THE STREUSEL

4½ ounces (1 cup) unbleached all-purpose flour

¾ cup packed light brown sugar

½ cup chopped lightly toasted walnuts

¼ teaspoon salt

3 ounces (6 tablespoons) unsalted butter, melted

FOR THE FILLING

4 tart baking apples, such as Granny Smith or Pink Lady (1½ to 2 pounds)

6 ounces fresh or thawed frozen cranberries (1¾ cups)

¾ cup plus 6 tablespoons sugar

3½ tablespoons unbleached all-purpose flour

1 tablespoon finely chopped crystallized ginger

¼ teaspoon ground cardamom

¼ teaspoon ground cinnamon

1 blind-baked All-Butter Piecrust (recipe follows)

Position a rack in the center of the oven, set a heavy-duty rimmed baking sheet on the rack, and heat the oven to 350°F.

Make the streusel: In a medium bowl, combine the flour, sugar, walnuts, and salt. Using your fingers, blend the butter into the flour mixture. Set aside.

Make the filling: Peel, quarter, and core each apple. Cut each quarter lengthwise into ¼-inch-thick slices

and then cut each slice crosswise at ¼-inch intervals to make tiny rectangles. In a food processor, pulse the cranberries with ¾ cup of the sugar until coarsely chopped. In a large bowl, combine the remaining 6 tablespoons sugar with the flour, ginger, cardamom, and cinnamon, breaking up ginger clumps with your fingers. Toss in the cranberry mixture and apples.

Mound the filling into the piecrust. Sprinkle the streusel topping over the apple mixture, pressing the streusel between your fingers into small lumps as you sprinkle.

Put the pie on the heated baking sheet and bake until the streusel is deeply browned and the filling is bubbling vigorously at the edges of the pie, 65 to 75 minutes. Check every 20 minutes, and if the pastry edge or the streusel browns before the filling is done, loosely cover the top or edges of the pie as needed with aluminum foil.

Transfer to a rack and let cool completely before serving. The pie can be stored at room temperature for up to 2 days.

All-Butter Piecrust

MAKES ONE 9-INCH PIECRUST

6¾ ounces (1½ cups) unbleached all-purpose flour; more for rolling

1 teaspoon sugar

⅜ teaspoon table salt

4 ounces (8 tablespoons) cold unsalted butter, preferably European style, cut into ¾-inch pieces

3 to 4 tablespoons ice water

Make the dough: Put the flour, sugar, and salt in a medium bowl and stir with a rubber spatula or a fork to combine. Add the butter to the bowl. Rub the cold chunks of butter between your fingertips, smearing the butter into the flour to create small (roughly ¼-inch) flakes of fat.

Drizzle 3 tablespoons ice water over the flour mixture. Stir with the spatula or a fork, adding 1 tablespoon more water if necessary, until the mixture forms a shaggy dough that's moist enough to hold together when pressed between your fingers. With well-floured hands, gently gather and press the dough together, and then form it into a disk with smooth edges. Wrap the dough in plastic and chill for at least 1 hour, preferably 2 to 4 hours, before rolling.

Roll the dough: Let the chilled dough sit at room temperature to soften slightly—it should be cold and firm but not rock hard. Depending on how long the dough was chilled, this could take 5 to 20 minutes. When ready to roll, lightly flour the countertop or other surface (a pastry cloth, silicone rolling mat, or parchment on a counter also works great) and position the rolling pin in the center of the dough disk. Roll away from you toward 12 o'clock, easing the pressure as you near the edge to keep it from becoming too thin. Return to the center and roll toward 6 o'clock. Repeat toward 3 and then 9 o'clock, always easing the pressure at the edges and picking up the pin rather than rolling it back to the center.

Continue to "roll around the clock," aiming for different "times" on each pass until the dough is 13 to 14 inches in diameter and about ⅛ inch thick. Try to use as few passes of the rolling pin as possible. After every few passes, check that the dough isn't sticking by lifting it with a bench knife (dough scraper). Reflour only as needed—excess flour makes a drier, tougher crust. Each time you lift the dough, give it a quarter turn to help even out the thickness.

Line the pie plate: Gently transfer the dough to a 9-inch pie plate, preferably metal, by folding it in half and unfolding it into the plate. Do not stretch the dough as you line the pan or it will spring back when baked. Gently lift the outer edges of the dough to give you enough slack to line the sides of the pan without stretching the dough. Trim the overhanging dough to 1 inch from the edge of the pan. Roll the dough under itself into a cylinder that rests on the edge of the pan.

Crimp the edge: To crimp the edge, have one hand on the inside of the edge, and one hand on the outside, and use the index finger of the inside hand to push the dough between the thumb and index finger of the outside hand to form a U or V shape. Repeat around the edge of the pie plate, creating a crimped edge whose individual flutes are about an inch apart. As you are going along, if you notice that the edge is not perfectly symmetrical and that the amount of dough you'll have to crimp seems sparse in places, take a bit of trimmed scrap, wet it with a drop or two of water, and attach it to the sparse area by pressing it firmly into place.

Prick the sides and bottom of the crust all over with a fork. Refrigerate until firm, about 1 hour or overnight. This will relax the dough and help prevent the edges from caving in.

Blind-bake the crust: Position a rack in the center of the oven and heat the oven to 425°F. Line the chilled piecrust with foil and fill it with dried beans or pie weights. Bake for 15 minutes; remove the foil and the beans or weights. Reduce the oven temperature to 375°F. Bake until the bottom looks dry but is not quite done and the edges are light golden, 5 to 7 minutes more. Let cool on a rack while you prepare the filling.

Cranberry Citrus Compote

MAKES 5 CUPS

24 ounces fresh cranberries
Finely grated zest of 1 lemon
Finely grated zest of 1 orange
2 shallots, finely chopped (about 4 tablespoons)
2 cups sugar
½ cup orange juice
½ cup thinly sliced scallion greens (3 large)

Heat the oven to 350°F. Pick through the cranberries to remove stems or bad berries. Combine the cranberries, lemon zest, orange zest, shallot, and sugar in a bowl and mix thoroughly. Turn into a 3-quart glass baking dish and drizzle the orange juice over the cranberry mixture. Bake, stirring occasionally, until the sugar is dissolved and a few berries have popped open, about 30 minutes. Remove from the oven, let cool thoroughly (the pectin in the excess liquid will firm up when cool), cover, and refrigerate. (You can do this up to 1 week ahead.)

Remove the compote from the refrigerator early on the day of serving to bring it to room temperature. Fold in the scallion and transfer to a serving bowl.

Other recipe ideas

SAGE, WALNUT, AND CRANBERRY STUFFING Add chopped fresh cranberries and some dried cranberries to a bread stuffing for poultry. Season with chopped fresh sage, onion, and toasted walnuts.

APPLE-CRANBERRY CRISP Toss fresh cranberries with diced apples, sugar, cinnamon, and fresh ginger and bake with a streusel topping until browned and bubbling. Serve with vanilla bean or ginger ice cream.

Pachyrhizus erosus and cvs.

Jícamas

This South American tuber, also called yam bean root, looks a little like a squashed softball with rough, papery brown skin and not much else to attract attention. But once you get beneath the skin, jícama (pronounced HEE-ka-ma) boasts a crisp, juicy flesh—like a very crunchy, unsweet apple or a water chestnut—that makes it a stand-out for snacks, salads, and slaws.

PICKING THE BEST
Pick up a few jícamas to find one that feels very heavy for its size; jícama should always be firm with un-wrinkled (though slightly rough) skin.

KEEPING IT FRESH
Store jícama in a cupboard as you would a potato for up to a month; it doesn't need refrigeration until it's been peeled or cut.

PREPARING
Cut jícama in half with a large knife and then peel off the skin and about ⅛ inch of the more fibrous flesh below the skin with a paring knife. Once peeled, it's very easy to slice and dice.

HOW TO USE IT
Jícama is most often used raw. In Mexico, where this tuber originates, it's frequently sliced into sticks, sprinkled with chili powder and lime juice, and eaten as a snack. But diced jícama adds fantastic crunch to salads, and you can sauté, stir-fry, or simmer jícama much as you would turnip.

Jícama, Avocado, Radish, and Orange Salad with Cilantro

SERVES 6 TO 8

4 oranges

1 teaspoon cumin seeds

1 clove garlic

Kosher salt

5 tablespoons fresh lime juice, plus more to taste

Large pinch of cayenne

¼ cup extra-virgin olive oil

1 small jícama (about 1¼ pounds)

8 small red radishes, cut into very thin round slices

5 scallions (white and light green parts), cut diagonally into thin slices

Freshly ground black pepper

2 large ripe but firm avocados

1 cup packed fresh cilantro leaves

Finely grate 2 teaspoons zest from the oranges and set the zest aside. With a sharp paring knife, slice the ends off the oranges. Stand each orange on one of its cut ends and pare off the rest of the peel in strips, making sure to remove all of the pith. Working over a small bowl, carefully cut the orange segments away from the connective membrane. Squeeze the membranes over the bowl to get any remaining juice.

Put the cumin seeds in a small dry skillet and toast over medium heat until slightly browned and aromatic, about 1 minute. Remove from the skillet and let cool. Grind the seeds to a fine powder in a mortar and pestle or an electric spice mill. Using a mortar and pestle or the flat side of a chef's knife, mash the garlic to a paste with a pinch of salt. Put the garlic paste and cumin powder in a small bowl (or keep it in the mortar) and whisk in the 2 teaspoons orange zest, 3 tablespoons orange juice (from the bowl of orange segments), the lime juice, and the cayenne. Let the mixture sit for 5 to 10 minutes and then whisk in the olive oil.

Meanwhile, peel the jícama and it cut into ⅛-inch-thick matchsticks 2 to 3 inches long. In a large bowl, combine the jícama, radishes, and scallion. Season with salt and pepper and toss with about two-thirds of the vinaigrette. Set aside for 5 to 10 minutes to let the flavors mingle.

Just before serving, thinly slice the avocados diagonally. Lay half of the avocado slices in a shallow bowl and season with salt and pepper. Drizzle some of the remaining vinaigrette on the avocado. Add the cilantro and orange segments to the bowl of jícama and toss gently. Taste and adjust the seasoning with more salt, pepper, and lime juice if needed. Put the jícama salad on top of the sliced avocado and tuck the remaining slices of avocado into the salad. Season the top slices with salt and drizzle with the remaining vinaigrette. Serve immediately.

Fresh Cherry Relish and Goat Cheese Crostini

MAKES 18 CROSTINI

1 cup fresh sweet cherries (about 5½ ounces), pitted and finely chopped

½ cup finely diced jícama

1 medium scallion (white and green parts), very thinly sliced

1 teaspoon chopped fresh mint

½ teaspoon red-wine vinegar

Pinch of cayenne; more to taste

Kosher salt and freshly ground black pepper

2½ ounces (⅓ cup) soft fresh goat cheese

2½ ounces (⅓ cup) ricotta cheese

Eighteen ½-inch-thick baguette slices, toasted

In a medium bowl, stir the cherries, jícama, scallion, mint, vinegar, and cayenne. Season to taste with salt, black pepper, and more cayenne.

In a small bowl, mix the goat and ricotta cheeses with a pinch each of salt and pepper. Lightly spread cheese over each baguette toast and top with relish.

Other recipe ideas

JÍCAMA SLAW Grate jícama and carrot and toss together in a dressing made from lime juice, cumin, salt, a touch of sugar, and some smoked paprika for a zesty slaw.

MELON-JÍCAMA SALAD Toss cantaloupe chunks with diced jícama, finely diced red onion, and minced jalapeño; dress in lime juice with sugar and salt.

Brassica oleracea cvs.

Kale

Kale is like cabbage with an attitude: a little peppery and a bit sweet, with a slight mineral edge. Its blue-green leaves have substantial texture that doesn't get mushy. Kale is also a nutritional powerhouse, with high levels of beta-carotene and vitamins A, C, and K, as well as iron and calcium.

PICKING THE BEST

Kale is usually sold in bundles. Choose deeply colored leaves, with no signs of yellowing or bruising. If it's secured by a twist-tie or band, check around it for slime.

There are three basic types of kale:

- **Russian kale:** Flatter leaves with spiky edges and a sweeter flavor are the hallmarks of this variety.
- **Scotch kale:** With exuberantly ruffled, dark green, almost blue, leaves, Scotch kale has a deep, spicy flavor.
- **Tuscan or black kale:** Also known as lacinato, cavolo nero, or dinosaur kale, this type has elongated, very dark blue-green leaves with a pebbled texture. The flavor can be quite sweet and the leaves are more tender and quick-cooking than other varieties.

KEEPING IT FRESH

Store kale unwashed in an unclosed plastic bag in the refrigerator's crisper drawer, where it will keep for several days. If you need to store it longer, wrap the bundle in slightly damp paper towels before putting it in a plastic bag to help prolong its freshness. But try to use kale within 5 to 7 days, because the longer you keep it, the stronger its flavor will become and the more its nutrients will fade.

PREPARING

Remove the tough stems and central ribs from all but the smallest leaves by cutting them out with a knife or simply tearing the leaf away from the rib (see Swiss Chard, p. 308). Cut the leaves into ribbons or chop them.

Wash kale in a deep sink or a very large bowl of cold water, gently swirling to encourage any soil to float off. Kale can harbor little insects such as aphids, so always take a look on the back side of the leaves to be sure any critters have washed away. Lift out the leaves and shake off the excess water. For most preparations, it's fine to leave some droplets clinging to the kale.

HOW TO USE

Tiny, fresh kale leaves can be tender enough to eat raw in salads, but cooking kale with some liquid yields nicely tender results. Kale's hardy texture requires more cooking time than a quick-wilting green such as spinach or chard. Figure on a good 15 to 20 minutes or more, depending on the variety. Braising, steaming, sautéing, and simmering in soups are among the best cooking methods for kale. Cooked kale also makes an excellent ingredient for dishes like creamy gratins and rich savory tarts.

PRESERVING OPTIONS

Freeze kale while it's in season and you'll have good greens throughout the year. Wash, trim, and roughly chop the kale, then blanch it in boiling water for 1 minute. Drain thoroughly and pack into freezer bags, pushing out all the air (or use a vacuum food-sealer system). Use within 6 months for best quality.

Tuscan, or black

Curly

Red Russian

Black Kale with Ham, Garlic, and Onion

SERVES 8

3 pounds kale, preferably black Tuscan cavolo nero, washed

Kosher salt

3 ounces (6 tablespoons) unsalted butter

6 ounces smoked ham, cut into ¼-inch dice (about 1 cup)

1½ cups thinly sliced yellow onion (from about 1 medium onion)

6 cloves garlic, thinly sliced

1½ cups homemade or reduced-sodium chicken or vegetable broth

Freshly ground black pepper

Red-wine vinegar (optional)

Remove the tough stems from the kale leaves by slicing a narrow "V" up into each leaf to remove the entire stem. Wash the leaves well in cold water and drain in a colander. Stuff into large (gallon-size or bigger) zip-top bags and put in the freezer for at least 2 hours or up to a month.

Fill an 8-quart pot with 2 inches of water and bring it to a boil over high heat; add a good pinch of salt and the frozen kale (right out of the freezer). Cover with the lid slightly ajar and cook on high heat, turning occasionally, until tender, about 20 minutes. The kale should still have a little bite but shouldn't be stringy or tough. Drain in a colander and press with the back of a large spoon to squeeze out as much excess liquid as possible. When the kale is cool enough to touch, chop it into small pieces.

Melt 3 tablespoons of the butter in the 8-quart pot over medium-high heat. Add the ham and cook until it starts to brown a little, about 3 minutes. Reduce the heat to medium. Add the onion and garlic and a pinch of salt; cover and cook, stirring occasionally, until softened, about 5 minutes. You don't want the onion or garlic to brown; if they start to, lower the heat. Add the broth, bring to a boil, reduce the heat to maintain a gentle simmer, and cook for 5 minutes. Return the kale to the pot, stir in the remaining 3 tablespoons butter, season generously with pepper (13 turns of a pepper mill should do), and cook gently until the flavors are well blended, about 7 minutes. Taste and adjust the seasonings as necessary.

Transfer to a serving bowl and serve immediately with a slotted spoon. Offer red-wine vinegar for sprinkling on individual portions, if you like.

Kale and White Bean Soup with Rustic Croutons

SERVES 4

¼ cup extra-virgin olive oil

1 medium onion (6 ounces), diced

2 ounces very thinly sliced pancetta, diced (about ½ cup)

1 tablespoon minced garlic

1 medium to large bunch kale (about 14 ounces), washed, thick stems cut away, and leaves sliced across into ¾-inch-wide strips (about 9 to 10 cups)

1 teaspoon coarse salt

Freshly ground black pepper

2 cups homemade or reduced-sodium chicken broth

1 cup cooked or canned cannellini, navy beans, or other white beans, rinsed and drained

1 tablespoon fresh lemon juice

¼ cup grated Parmigiano-Reggiano

2 cups Rustic Croutons (recipe follows)

Heat the olive oil in a 4-quart low-sided soup pot or Dutch oven over medium to medium-high heat. Add the onion and pancetta and sauté until the onion is softened and both are browned, about 12 minutes. Add the garlic, stir, and sauté until fragrant, 30 seconds to 1 minute. Add the kale and stir thoroughly to coat the leaves (and to deglaze the pan slightly with their moisture). Season with ½ teaspoon of the salt and a few grinds of fresh pepper. Add the broth, stir well, and bring to a boil; cover the pot, lower to a simmer, and cook until the kale is almost completely tender, 10 to 25 minutes. Uncover the pot, add the beans, and simmer for another 2 to 3 minutes. Add the lemon juice and turn off the heat. Ladle the soup into four shallow soup bowls and top each with 1 tablespoon of the cheese and a quarter of the croutons.

RUSTIC CROUTONS

MAKES 2 CUPS

2 tablespoons extra-virgin olive oil

2 cups lightly packed ¾-inch bread cubes from crusty
bread, like ciabatta

Salt

Heat the oil in a nonstick skillet over medium-high
heat. Add the bread cubes and stir to coat with the
oil. Season with salt and sauté, stirring constantly, until
crisp and browned on most sides, 2 to 4 minutes.

Braised Kale with Pancetta

SERVES 2

2 tablespoons olive oil

¼-inch slice pancetta, diced (about ¼ cup)

1 small onion, chopped

Pinch of crushed red pepper flakes

1½ pounds kale, stemmed, leaves roughly torn

1½ cups homemade or reduced-sodium chicken broth

1 small clove garlic, minced

Freshly ground black pepper

In a large, heavy saucepan, heat the oil over medium-
high heat. Add the pancetta, onion, and red pepper
flakes; sauté until the onion is deep golden, about
5 minutes. Add the kale; toss with tongs to coat the
leaves with oil. Add the chicken broth and bring to a
boil. Cover, reduce the heat to medium low, and simmer until the leaves are quite tender, about 10 minutes
(thicker-leaved varieties will need longer, so check,
adding water or broth if needed, and taste a leaf).

Stir in the garlic, raise the heat to high, and boil
uncovered until the pan is dry. Season with a bit of
pepper (you probably won't need salt) and serve.

Warm Salad of Autumn Greens
with Plum Vinaigrette

SERVES 12

FOR THE PLUM VINAIGRETTE

5 tablespoons Damson plum preserves

¼ cup Champagne vinegar or white-wine vinegar

1 tablespoon Dijon mustard

1 cup canola or peanut oil

1 tablespoon chopped shallot

Kosher salt and freshly ground pepper

FOR THE GREENS

One 10-ounce bag spinach

1 bunch young kale, preferably Tuscan

1 large or 2 small heads frisée or escarole

3 to 4 tablespoons olive oil or peanut oil

¾ cup (about 3 ounces) roasted, skinned hazelnuts,
roughly chopped, or 1 pound chestnuts, roasted,
peeled, and quartered

Kosher salt and freshly ground black pepper

In a blender or food processor, pulse the preserves,
vinegar, and mustard until smooth. Continue pulsing
and slowly add the oil until incorporated. Add the
shallot and salt and pepper to taste; pulse briefly.

Pull off or cut away any tough stems from the
spinach and kale, and cut the kale into strips about
½ inch wide. Cut the bottoms off the frisée or escarole.
Mix all the greens, wash thoroughly, and spin dry.

In a very large sauté pan (preferably nonstick),
heat about 1 tablespoon of the olive or peanut oil
over medium-high heat and add one-third of the
greens, one-third of the nuts, and salt and pepper
to taste. Sauté 1 to 2 minutes, stirring all the time,
until the leaves are slightly wilted. Drizzle a little of
the vinaigrette on them, toss lightly with tongs, and
transfer the nuts and greens to a serving platter.
Repeat with the remaining greens in two more
batches, adding only enough oil to the pan as needed
to sauté. Serve immediately.

Other recipe ideas

BRAISED KALE WITH SUN-DRIED TOMATOES Braise
roughly chopped kale with plenty of good olive oil
and a little water or broth and salt and pepper; add
chopped garlic and chopped oil-packed sun-dried
tomatoes in the last few minutes of cooking. Finish
with a touch of balsamic vinegar.

KALE CAESAR SALAD Thoroughly wash and trim
a head of Tuscan kale. Slice into ¼-inch strips and
dry in a salad spinner. Toss with a good Caesar or
other assertive, lemony dressing, and top with some
croutons and shaved Parmesan.

MASHED KALE AND POTATOES Steam chopped kale
until tender, then fold into mashed potatoes and
season well with salt, pepper, and nutmeg to make a
version of Irish colcannon.

Brassica oleracea cvs.

Kohlrabi

People often comment on kohlrabi's funny looks ("sputnik-like!"), but its crisp, juicy texture and unusual flavor quickly take center stage. This underappreciated member of the brassica family combines the earthy sweetness of cabbage and the crunchy bite of a turnip, with just a hint of radish-like heat.

PICKING THE BEST

Kohlrabi is a bulbous stem that grows just above ground, with leafy stalks protruding upward from various parts of the bulb. Both bulb and leaves are edible and are best cooked separately. You can find purple and green kohlrabi, although both are white inside and taste essentially the same. Look for bulbs 3 inches in diameter or less (about the size of a medium turnip). They're more tender and delicate in flavor than larger ones and usually don't require peeling. Large bulbs tend to be tough and woody, with a hard outer layer.

KEEPING IT FRESH

Cut the leafy stalks off the bulbs and refrigerate them separately in zip-top bags. If stored properly, the bulbs can last for a few weeks. The leaves, however, should be consumed within 2 or 3 days.

PREPARING

Larger kohlrabi can be woody, so use a sharp knife to peel it, paring until you are left with just a light green or white bulb. Cut the kohlrabi in half and cut away any brown spots or spongy parts. Cut into chunks or slices or julienne according to your recipe.

HOW TO USE IT

Use kohlrabi bulbs raw—shredded or thinly sliced—to add crunch to slaws and salads. Or cook them in a variety of ways. They're tasty sautéed or roasted (cut them into thin slices or bite-sized wedges first) or when added to your favorite braises and stews. You can also boil the bulbs until tender and mash them. When cooked, kohlrabi retains some of its crunchy texture but the flavor mellows quite a bit. Treat the leafy tops as you would kale or collard greens: Sauté them in oil or add them to soups and stews in the last 15 minutes or so of cooking.

Kohlrabi-Radish Slaw with Cumin and Cilantro

SERVES 8

3 tablespoons white-wine vinegar

1 teaspoon Dijon mustard

1 teaspoon clover honey

¼ teaspoon cumin seeds, toasted and coarsely
    ground in a mortar and pestle

¼ teaspoon kosher salt, plus more to taste

Freshly ground black pepper

5 tablespoons canola oil

5 radishes, grated (about 1 cup)

3 medium carrots, grated (about 1½ cups)

2 small unpeeled kohlrabi bulbs (purple, green,
    or both), trimmed and cut into ⅛-inch-thick
    matchsticks (3 cups)

½ medium head green cabbage (about 1 pound),
    thinly sliced (5 cups)

⅓ cup chopped fresh cilantro

In a small bowl, whisk the vinegar, mustard, honey,
cumin, ¼ teaspoon salt, and a pinch of pepper.
Gradually whisk in the oil until combined.

Put the radishes, carrot, kohlrabi, cabbage, and
cilantro in a large bowl. Pour the dressing over the top
and toss to combine. Season with salt and pepper.

Toasted Israeli Couscous Salad with Mint, Kohlrabi, Cucumber, and Feta

SERVES 4 TO 6

¾ teaspoon kosher salt; more as needed

1 cup Israeli couscous

½ medium English cucumber, peeled and finely diced
    (1 cup)

1 small unpeeled kohlrabi bulb (purple or green),
    trimmed and finely diced (1½ cups)

½ cup coarsely chopped fresh mint leaves; additional
    sprigs for garnish

¼ cup extra-virgin olive oil

2 tablespoons fresh lemon juice; more as needed

1 teaspoon finely grated lemon zest

¼ teaspoon freshly ground black pepper, plus more
    to taste

1 cup small-diced feta cheese

In a large saucepan, bring 2 quarts well-salted water
to a boil.

Meanwhile, in a medium skillet over medium heat,
toast the couscous, stirring frequently, until golden
brown, about 7 minutes. Cook the couscous in the
boiling water until tender, about 10 minutes. Drain
and rinse under cold running water until cool; drain
well. Pour the couscous into a large bowl. Stir in the
cucumber, kohlrabi, and mint.

In a small bowl, mix the oil, lemon juice and zest,
¾ teaspoon salt, and pepper. Stir in the feta. Add the
feta mixture to the couscous, season to taste with
salt, pepper, and lemon juice, and mix well. Transfer
to a serving bowl and garnish with the mint sprigs.

Other recipe ideas

LEMON-CAPER KOHLRABI SALAD Make a salad of
finely sliced kohlrabi and thinly sliced onion tossed
in a lemony vinaigrette mounded on lightly dressed
greens. Garnish with capers.

PICKLED KOHLRABI Make a quick refrigerator pickle
with thick batons of kohlrabi in a rice-vinegar brine.

INDIAN-SPICED STEWED KOHLRABI Simmer
diced kohlrabi and chopped kohlrabi greens with
diced tomato, onion, garlic, mild green chile, a little
tamarind paste, and Indian spices to make a curry.

KOHLRABI FRITTERS Shred kohlrabi, bind with an
egg and some flour, season, and fry in hot oil to
make fritters.

White button

Cremini

Portabella

Hen of the Woods

Shiitake

Mushrooms

Mushrooms are a mysterious ingredient in a cook's repertoire. Even button mushrooms, which are cultivated, have a woodsy allure that brings to mind a treasure foraged from the forest. The flavor of a mushroom is varied, too, from meaty to nutty to lobstery sweetness. Cooked correctly, mushrooms can add a layer of flavor and texture to any dish.

PICKING THE BEST

Grocery stores carry cultivated mushrooms and often a few varieties of wild mushrooms (some of which are cultivated) as well. Farmer's markets are a great source for rarer and more seasonal varieties of truly wild mushrooms. Here are several common varieties:

- **Black trumpets (wild):** A type of chanterelle with a buttery, woodsy flavor, these are great baked in gratins or tossed with pasta. Look for them from early summer to early winter.
- **Button or white mushrooms (cultivated):** Somewhat nutty and creamy when raw, white mushrooms become earthy and rich when cooked. Use them in soups, stews, and pasta sauces, or sauté some with butter and a little garlic to serve over a grilled steak.
- **Chanterelles (wild):** With a distinct apricot-like flavor, chanterelles are one of the few mushrooms that can be paired with acidic ingredients without losing their flavor. They're delicious with game or shellfish. They're in season early summer through early winter.
- **Cremini (cultivated):** Simply young portabellas; they're firmer with a more intense flavor. Use them in risotto or braise them in a bit of cream to make a simple pasta sauce.
- **Enoki (cultivated):** These look like white bobby pins. Try them raw in salads or as a garnish for soups. They have a mild flavor that isn't particularly distinctive.
- **Hen of the woods (wild):** Also called maitake, these shaggy-headed mushrooms are firm, earthy, and very nutty. They're delicious sautéed.

- **Morels (wild):** These earthy yet delicate mushrooms pair well with light meats such as chicken or veal. Like most mushrooms, morels love butter, cream, and grains such as rice and polenta. Look for them from early spring into July.
- **Oyster mushrooms (cultivated):** These mushrooms have subtle flavor, so are best when paired with other simple ingredients. Sauté lightly to serve with poultry or fish, or combine with pasta, polenta, or rice.
- **Porcinis (wild):** Also called bolete, these have pale silken flesh and a meaty texture. They are wonderful when slowly braised or added to a risotto, and there may be no better mushroom for grilling.
- **Portabellas (cultivated):** Simply cremini grown to gargantuan proportions, portabellas have dense and fibrous flesh. Grilling and roasting intensify portabellas' flavor and are excellent ways to cook them.
- **Shiitake (cultivated and wild):** Distinctive, slightly smoky mushrooms that adapt well to other strong flavors. They're commonly used in Asian cooking and can be enjoyed raw or cooked. Shiitake stems tend to be fibrous, so unless the mushrooms are young and tender, don't eat the stems.

Whether your mushrooms are wild or cultivated, choose those that are firm and slightly moist with no signs of decay. The best ones will feel heavy for their size. They should have a woodsy scent and look fresh and alive; as mushrooms decay, the can develop a slightly fishy odor, so definitely take a sniff.

KEEPING IT FRESH

Warm air and water will cause mushrooms to decay, so keep them cool and dry. Store your mushrooms in a basket or an open paper bag in the refrigerator and don't clean them until you're ready to use them. They should last 4 or 5 days.

PREPARING

Begin by trimming the stem, where there's usually a concentration of dirt from the forest floor. Don't actually wash wild mushrooms, which generally have irregular shapes that trap water and can become soggy, but instead wipe them clean with a damp cloth or scrape them with a paring knife. Don't hesitate to quickly rinse off any stubborn bits of dirt, but if you do, cook the mushrooms immediately after or they'll start to decay. For cultivated mushrooms, washing is actually quicker and less tedious than wiping, and the grit the mushrooms leave behind is impressive. Plus, any moisture will be released in cooking. Simply fill a large bowl with water, plunge the mushrooms in for a moment, swirl them around, and then lift them out; drain them in a strainer and pat them dry if you like.

HOW TO USE IT

Some mushrooms can be eaten raw, but most should be thoroughly cooked; many mushrooms, particularly wild ones, have proteins that can be difficult to digest unless thoroughly cooked. (And, of course, never eat a wild mushroom that hasn't been positively identified by an expert—if you're a beginner forager, always verify your find before sampling.)

A fresh mushroom is mostly water. The good news is that the water contains a high concentration of flavor. When you cook mushrooms, cook them long enough so that all their water is released, and then keep cooking them until the liquid has evaporated. The flavors will become concentrated and the textures slightly crisp, not slippery.

When seasoning mushrooms, be subtle. The flavors of different mushrooms themselves can be easily overwhelmed. Garlic and mushrooms are a great combination, but garlicky mushrooms all taste the same. Go easy with acidic ingredients, such as vinegar, wine, and lemon juice. While they may enhance the overall flavor of a dish, they tend to diminish the taste of the mushrooms themselves.

RECIPES

Grilled Portabella and Goat Cheese Sandwiches

SERVES 4

1 cup tightly packed fresh basil leaves

½ cup pitted green olives, such as Manzanilla, coarsely chopped

1 tablespoon walnuts or pine nuts

1 small clove garlic, coarsely chopped

½ cup plus 2 teaspoons extra-virgin olive oil

Kosher salt and freshly ground black pepper

8 small to medium portabella mushrooms, stemmed, gills removed, and wiped clean

4 soft round rolls, such as Portuguese or kaiser, split in half

4 ounces fresh goat cheese, crumbled

Heat a panini or sandwich press according to the manufacturer's instructions. (Alternatively, heat a nonstick grill pan over medium-high heat.)

While the press is heating, put the basil, olives, nuts, and garlic in a food processor and process until finely chopped. With the motor running, add 6 tablespoons of the olive oil in a slow, steady stream through the feed tube and continue to process until thick and smooth. Season the pesto to taste with salt and pepper.

Brush the mushrooms with 2 tablespoons of the olive oil and sprinkle with salt and pepper. Put them on the press, pull the top down, and cook until softened and browned, 3 to 5 minutes (or cook in the grill pan, flipping once). Transfer to a plate and let cool slightly.

Spread the pesto on the bottom halves of the rolls. Put 2 mushrooms on each and then some goat cheese. Top the sandwiches with the other halves of the rolls. Brush both sides of the sandwiches with the remaining 2 teaspoons oil.

Put the sandwiches on the press, pesto side up, pull the top down, and cook until browned and crisp and the cheese is melted, 5 to 7 minutes, depending on how hot your machine is. (If using a grill pan, put a heavy pan on top of the sandwiches and cook, turning the sandwiches over once.) Carefully remove from the press and serve.

Stuffed Mushrooms with Pancetta, Shallots, and Sage

MAKES 30 HORS D'OEUVRES

35 to 40 cremini mushrooms (about 1½ pounds), about 1½ to 2 inches wide

3 tablespoons unsalted butter; more for the baking dish

1½ ounces pancetta, finely diced (¼ cup)

5 medium shallots, finely diced

2 teaspoons chopped fresh sage

Pinch of crushed red pepper flakes

½ teaspoon kosher salt; more for seasoning

⅔ cup coarse fresh breadcrumbs (preferably from a day-old rustic French or Italian loaf)

¼ cup freshly grated Parmigiano-Reggiano

Freshly ground black pepper

2 to 3 tablespoons extra-virgin olive oil, for drizzling

Position a rack in the center of the oven and heat the oven to 425°F. Trim and discard the very bottom of the mushroom stems. Remove the mushroom stems and finely chop them, along with five of the largest mushroom caps.

Heat a medium sauté pan over medium heat for 1 minute and add 2 tablespoons of the butter. When it has melted, add the pancetta and cook until it starts to render some of its fat, 1 to 2 minutes. Add the shallot, sage, and red pepper flakes; cook gently until the shallot is tender, about 4 minutes (reduce the heat if the shallot begins to brown). Stir in the chopped mushroom stems and ½ teaspoon salt. Cook, stirring frequently, until the mixture is tender, about 3 minutes. Add the remaining 1 tablespoon butter. When it has melted, transfer the mushroom mixture to a bowl and stir in the breadcrumbs and Parmigiano. Season to taste with salt and black pepper and let cool slightly.

Butter a shallow baking dish large enough to hold the mushrooms in one layer. Arrange the mushrooms in the dish and season the cavities with salt. Stuff each cavity with a rounded teaspoonful of the filling, or more as needed. The filling should form a tall mound. (You may have leftover filling; if you have extra mushrooms, keep stuffing until you run out of filling.) Drizzle the mushrooms with the olive oil and bake until the mushrooms are tender and the breadcrumbs are golden brown, 20 to 25 minutes. Transfer to a platter and serve warm.

Wild Mushroom Risotto

SERVES 2 AS A MAIN COURSE

3 cups homemade or reduced-sodium chicken broth; more if needed

1 ounce dried porcini mushrooms, soaked for 30 minutes in 1 cup warm water; mushrooms chopped, soaking liquid strained and reserved

2 ounces (4 tablespoons) unsalted butter

¾ cup arborio rice

2 cups assorted fresh wild mushrooms, cleaned, trimmed, and coarsely chopped

⅔ cup dry white wine

Kosher salt

¼ cup chopped fresh flat-leaf parsley

2 tablespoons freshly grated Parmigiano-Reggiano

Heat the chicken broth along with the reserved strained porcini soaking liquid; lower the heat to a simmer. In a medium, heavy saucepan over medium-high heat, melt 2 tablespoons of the butter. Stir in the rice, toasting just until it starts to sizzle and pop, about 1 minute. It should not color. Stir the porcini and the fresh mushrooms into the rice. Stir in the wine.

When almost all the liquid has disappeared, after about 2 minutes, add just enough hot broth to cover the rice. Lower the heat to maintain a vigorous simmer, stirring occasionally. When the broth is almost gone, add enough to cover the rice, along with a pinch of salt. Check on the risotto every 3 or 4 minutes, giving it an occasional stir to make sure it isn't sticking to the bottom of the pan and adding just enough broth to cover the rice when the liquid has almost disappeared.

Continue this way until the rice is just al dente, about 20 minutes total cooking time. Bite into a grain; you should see a white pin-dot in the center. Take the risotto off the heat. Add the remaining 2 tablespoons butter; stir vigorously for a few seconds. Add the parsley, Parmigiano, and more salt, if needed. The risotto should be moist and creamy, not runny. Stir in more broth to loosen the risotto, if you like. Serve immediately.

Morel Sauce

MAKES ABOUT 2½ CUPS

2 ounces dried morels, preferably small

3 tablespoons unsalted butter

¼ cup finely diced shallot

1 large clove garlic, minced

1 cup dry Marsala

2 cups heavy cream

½ teaspoon kosher salt, plus more to taste

1 tablespoon fresh lemon juice

1 tablespoon thinly sliced fresh chives

1 tablespoon minced fresh tarragon or thyme

Freshly ground black pepper

In a small saucepan, bring 2 cups water to a boil over high heat. Turn off the heat, add the morels, cover, and soak until soft and rehydrated, 30 minutes. Lift them out with a slotted spoon and gently press on them with another spoon to squeeze excess liquid back into the pot. Cut any large ones in half and set the mushrooms aside. Strain the soaking liquid through a sieve lined with a coffee filter and return it to the (rinsed) saucepan. Over medium-high heat, reduce the soaking liquid to ¼ cup, about 10 minutes.

Melt the butter in a 3-quart saucepan over medium heat. Add the shallot and cook, stirring often, until soft and golden brown, 2 minutes. Add the garlic and cook for 1 minute, then add the morels. Reduce the heat to low and cook, stirring often, until heated through, about 2 minutes. Add the Marsala and increase the heat to bring to a simmer. Cook until the mixture begins to dry out, 8 to 10 minutes. Add the reduced soaking liquid, cream, and salt. Simmer until the sauce thickens slightly, about 10 minutes. Add the lemon juice and herbs, then season to taste with salt and pepper. (You can keep the sauce warm for up to 30 minutes before serving on pasta, polenta, or a seared beef filet mignon.)

Wild Mushroom Soup with Sherry and Thyme

SERVES 6

2 tablespoons unsalted butter

2 tablespoons olive oil

1 medium onion, cut into medium dice (about 1½ cups)

4 cloves garlic, minced

¾ pound fresh wild mushrooms, wiped clean, trimmed (stems removed from shiitake), and thinly sliced (to yield about 4½ cups)

2 tablespoons plus 1 teaspoon fresh thyme leaves

½ teaspoon kosher salt, plus more to taste

½ teaspoon freshly ground black pepper, plus more to taste

4 cups homemade or reduced-sodium chicken or vegetable broth

¼ cup half-and-half

3 tablespoons dry sherry

1 tablespoon soy sauce

Melt the butter and olive oil in a 5-quart or larger stockpot over medium-high heat. Add the onion and cook until it's beginning to brown (resist the urge to stir too often), about 4 minutes. Stir in the garlic and cook for 1 minute. Add the mushrooms, 2 tablespoons of the thyme, and the salt and pepper; cook until the mushrooms become limp, 2 to 4 minutes.

Add the broth, scraping up any browned bits in the pot with a wooden spoon. Bring to a boil over high heat, reduce the heat to maintain a simmer, and cook until the mushrooms are tender, 7 to 10 minutes. Remove from the heat and let cool slightly. Transfer about half of the soup to a stand blender and process until smooth. (Be careful to fill the blender no more than one-third full and hold a towel over the lid while you turn it on.) Return the mixture to the pot and stir in the half-and-half, sherry, and soy sauce. Add more salt and pepper to taste, if needed, and reheat. Garnish each serving with a small pinch of the remaining 1 teaspoon thyme.

Other recipe ideas

HUNGARIAN RAGOÛT Sauté a mix of cremini and some wild mushrooms until nicely browned and tender. Add a generous amount of sour cream and lots of good, fresh paprika and a touch of caraway and simmer until creamy (don't boil). Serve over wide egg noodles.

ROASTED HALIBUT AND MUSHROOMS Sauté a mix of wild mushrooms until just golden, then season with fresh thyme. Put a thick fillet of halibut in a small roasting pan, pile the mushrooms around it, dot with butter, and roast at around 450°F until the halibut is done. Finish with some lemon juice.

CHANTERELLE SALAD Sauté chanterelles in olive oil until nicely browned. Toss with frisée, shredded radicchio, cooked pancetta, and toasted hazelnuts in a sherry-vinegar dressing.

Cooking with Dried Mushrooms

Dried mushrooms can taste luxurious, but they're also convenient and affordable. Their flavor is more intense than their fresh equivalent, and the texture is meaty. Like fresh mushrooms, they're terrific in everything from soups to sauces to sautés.

Before using dried mushrooms in a recipe, even if it's a soup or a stew, it's best to rehydrate them in hot water. First, it plumps up the mushrooms, and, as a bonus, the soaking liquid creates a flavorful broth, which you can incorporate into a dish as you would any other broth. Second, soaking also helps remove grit from the mushrooms that would otherwise spoil your dish.

Once the mushrooms have steeped, add them to braises, stews, or sauces, sautéing them with aromatics like shallot, garlic, or onion. Because they're moist, mushrooms don't exactly brown, but the quick toss in hot oil intensifies their flavor. Add the mushroom soaking liquid and finish cooking the dish.

To keep your mushroom mix economical, mix shiitake with other mushrooms, particularly when using a pricey variety like morels. Shiitake's flavor complements that of other mushrooms, and shiitakes are more affordable than most.

The quality of dried mushrooms can vary greatly. Look for mushrooms that have a nice size and shape, and avoid overly shriveled or crushed specimens.

For long-term storage, seal dried mushrooms in two heavy-duty zip-top freezer bags and put them in the freezer. For short-term storage (a month or less), seal the mushrooms in an airtight container or a zip-top bag and store in a cool, dark place.

Nuts

You may not think of nuts as part of the produce world, because we eat them once they're dried and crunchy, but indeed a nut is an agricultural product for which season and freshness are key. And nuts are as versatile as any fruit or vegetable—they add flavor and texture whether as a salty snack, an accent in a salad or pilaf, or in a creamy sauce or crunchy candy.

PICKING THE BEST

Most grocery stores offer an array of nuts to choose from, and if you're lucky, you may find local producers bringing nuts in the fall to your farmer's market.

- **Almonds:** At their peak harvest in November, just in time for holiday baking. Use them whole, sliced, slivered, chopped, or ground in cakes, cookies, candies, tarts, pies, and puddings. Their milky, mild flavor pairs beautifully with vegetables and fish, too. Marcona almonds are a Spanish variety that's wider and flatter than a regular almond and is most often sold fried in olive oil and sprinkled with salt.
- **Black walnuts:** Native to America and more closely related to hickory nuts than to English walnuts. Their flavor is strong; in small amounts, they add exotic interest to cakes and cookies. Their shells are rock-hard, so they're always sold shelled in broken pieces.
- **Brazil nuts:** Deliciously rich meat. Most often cracked and eaten after dinner, they're also good in fruitcakes, cookies, and candies. Use them to stuff dates or prunes. For easy slicing or chopping, first simmer shelled Brazil nuts in water for 5 minutes.
- **Cashews:** Tan and shaped like a kidney bean. Cashews are native to Brazil (though they're also grown in India and the West Indies) and are high in fat and have a buttery texture and an almost sweet flavor.
- **English walnuts:** The walnuts we see most often. Easy to shell, but they turn rancid quickly, so shell only as you use them. Delicious after dinner with cheese, pears, apples, and a glass of port. Authentic Italian pesto often includes walnuts as well as pine nuts.

- **Hazelnuts:** Also called filberts, they're delicious ground in pastries, cakes, tarts, and ice cream. Hazelnut and chocolate together are a classic European combination called gianduia. Add chopped hazelnuts to a winter fruit salad, or serve whole hazelnuts with soft cheese like Camembert or Brie.
- **Macadamia nuts:** A subtle, rich nut, with a creamy texture. Native to Australia, they're grown almost exclusively in Hawaii and are often sold whole but out of their extremely hard shell. Delicious but pricey, they go especially well with tropical flavors, as well as coffee and chocolate. Use chopped in breads, cakes, cookies, pies, or serve with drinks, lightly toasted and salted.
- **Peanuts:** Great roasted and eaten out of hand. They're also an essential ingredient in cuisines in warmer parts of the globe. Be cautious when substituting them for other nuts in baked goods. The strong flavor that stands up so well to hot chiles in Thai and Chinese cooking can overwhelm other ingredients.
- **Pecans:** A native American nut with a rich, sweet flavor and tender, almost crumbly crunch. Try some finely chopped in a pie dough recipe. Toss into a salad of romaine and blue cheese, sprinkle over candied yams, or fold into a poultry stuffing.
- **Pine nuts:** Tender and buttery. Cheaper to buy these tiny nuts in bulk in the produce section (where the turnover is better) rather than in jars in the Italian dry goods section of the grocery store.
- **Pistachios:** A beautiful jade green color. The flavor is buttery and quite sweet, and pistachios are often used for desserts, especially for flavoring ice cream.

Brazil nut

Walnut

Chestnut

Almond

Hazelnut

KEEPING IT FRESH

Store all nuts in a cool, dry place. Shelled nuts, unless vacuum-packed in cans, should be tightly wrapped. Macadamia nuts have a high oil content, so they're very perishable and should be refrigerated in an air-tight container. Pine nuts are also best stored in the fridge for up to a few weeks or frozen up to 3 months.

PREPARING

A light roasting in a moderate oven until fragrant and lightly golden will accentuate the flavor of most nuts. Just be careful not to overdo it because darkly roasted nuts will be bitter and dry. Roasted nuts turn rancid more quickly than raw ones, so use them within a few days after roasting.

Skinning isn't always a must; it's more a matter of aesthetics. If grinding almonds or hazelnuts for pastry, the skins incorporate into the mixture, and many cooks like the look of tiny specks of skin. With coarsely chopped nuts like hazelnuts, which have a loose skin, pieces of skin tend to separate from the nut, so skinning them results in a cleaner look and taste.

Grinding is easiest to do in an inexpensive drum-type nut or cheese grater. Nuts have a high fat content, so if you use a food processor, pulse briefly and pay close attention or you'll end up with nut butter.

Shelling peanuts doesn't require a nut cracker, but for hard-shelled nuts, the best option is an old-fashioned hinged nut cracker. A nut pick helps coax out reluctant walnut or pecan meats. And freezing Brazil nuts for a few hours seems to make their hard shells easier to crack.

HOW TO USE IT

A big bowl of mixed nuts on the table to crack seems to stimulate after-dinner conversation, but as an ingredient, nuts add rich flavor and crunchy texture to both sweet and savory dishes—tossed whole into salads, chopped for breads and piecrusts, ground for Southeast Asian sauces, stirred into cake or cookie batters, and folded into ice cream.

PRESERVING OPTIONS

Nuts keep well in the freezer for up to 3 or 4 months, as long as they're tightly wrapped. They can get a bit flabby, so only freeze untoasted nuts and then give them a light toasting before use.

············· RECIPES ·············

Chocolate Nut Upside-Down Cake

SERVES 8 TO 10

FOR THE CARAMEL TOPPING

¾ cup packed dark brown sugar

2½ ounces (5 tablespoons) unsalted butter; more for the pan

1¼ cups toasted assorted unsalted nuts (such as slivered almonds, walnut halves, and roughly chopped hazelnuts)

FOR THE CAKE

6 ounces (1⅓ cups) unbleached all-purpose flour

1½ ounces (½ cup) unsweetened natural cocoa powder

¾ teaspoon baking powder

¼ teaspoon baking soda

¼ teaspoon table salt

5 ounces (10 tablespoons) unsalted butter, at room temperature

1 cup sugar

1 teaspoon pure vanilla extract

3 large eggs

½ cup buttermilk

Heat the oven to 350°F and lightly butter the sides of a 9x2-inch round cake pan.

Make the caramel topping: In a small saucepan, combine the brown sugar, butter, and 3 tablespoons water. Cook over medium heat, stirring often, until the butter is melted and the mixture is smooth. Bring to a boil and pour into the prepared pan, swirling to coat the bottom evenly. Scatter in the nuts evenly and gently press them in.

Make the cake: Sift together the flour, cocoa powder, baking powder, baking soda, and salt. In a medium bowl, beat the butter with an electric mixer until smooth. Gradually add the sugar; continue beating until fluffy. Beat in the vanilla. Add the eggs one at a time, beating briefly after each addition. Sprinkle half of the flour mixture over the butter and mix on low speed just until the flour disappears. Add the buttermilk and mix until just blended. Gently mix in the remaining flour. Scoop spoonfuls of batter onto the nuts and gently spread the batter evenly in the pan. Lightly tap the pan on the counter to settle the ingredients.

Bake until a toothpick inserted in the center comes out clean, about 45 minutes. Immediately run a paring knife around the inside edge of the pan. Set a flat serving plate on top of the pan and invert the cake. Let the inverted pan rest for about 3 minutes to let the topping settle. Gently remove the pan and serve slightly warm or at room temperature.

Green Beans with Smoked Paprika and Marcona Almonds

SERVES 4

Kosher salt

¾ pound green beans, trimmed and cut on the diagonal into 2-inch lengths (3 cups)

½ cup thinly sliced shallot (about 2 medium)

1 tablespoon extra-virgin olive oil

1½ teaspoons granulated sugar

⅓ cup coarsely chopped Marcona almonds

¼ teaspoon sweet or hot Spanish smoked paprika (pimentón de la Vera)

Bring a large pot of well-salted water to a boil. Cook the beans in the water until just tender, 4 to 5 minutes. Drain and run under cold water to cool. Drain well.

Put the shallot and olive oil in a cold 12-inch skillet and set the pan over medium-high heat. Cook until the shallot begins to turn golden, stirring to break it into rings, about 2 minutes. Sprinkle the sugar over the shallot and stir constantly until golden all over, about 45 seconds. Add the almonds, stir well, and immediately add the beans and smoked paprika. Cook, stirring, until heated through, 2 to 3 minutes. Season to taste with salt and serve.

Sole Fillets with Toasted Pine Nuts, Lemon, and Basil

SERVES 2

4 small sole or flounder fillets (about 3 ounces each)

Salt and freshly ground black pepper

5 tablespoons extra-virgin olive oil

¼ cup fresh lemon juice

½ cup toasted pine nuts

¼ cup chopped fresh basil

Season the fillets with salt and pepper. Heat 4 tablespoons of the olive oil in a large skillet over high heat. Sauté the fillets on one side (in batches if necessary) until the edges begin to turn opaque (about 2 minutes) and then turn them over and cook for 1 to 2 minutes to finish. Transfer the fillets as they're cooked to a warm plate. When all the fillets are cooked and removed from the pan, carefully pour the lemon juice into the pan, scrape up any browned bits, and boil the juice to reduce it to about 1 tablespoon, about 1 minute. Add the pine nuts and basil and remove the pan from the heat. Put the fillets on serving plates and spoon the contents of the pan over all. Drizzle with the remaining 1 tablespoon olive oil.

Brown Rice Salad with Basil and Pistachios

SERVES 6 TO 8

1 cup uncooked long-grain brown rice

½ cup golden raisins

¼ cup plus 2 tablespoons mild-tasting olive oil

¼ cup red-wine vinegar

½ cup raw unsalted pistachio nuts

1 small red onion, finely diced

4 medium to large cloves garlic, finely diced

One 15½-ounce can chickpeas, drained and rinsed

1 medium red bell pepper, cored, seeded, and finely diced

1 teaspoon kosher or fine sea salt, plus more to taste

1 teaspoon crushed red pepper flakes

½ cup firmly packed fresh basil leaves, cut into thin strips (chiffonade) (see how on p. 301)

Fill a medium saucepan with water and bring it to a boil over high heat. Add the rice and return to a boil. Cook, uncovered, until the rice grains are cooked and tender but still a little chewy, 20 to 25 minutes. Drain the rice through a sieve and rinse with cold water to stop the cooking. Set aside.

While the rice is cooking, purée the raisins, ¼ cup of the oil, and the vinegar in a blender, scraping the jar as needed, to make a thick, smooth vinaigrette.

Heat a 10-inch skillet over medium-high heat and toast the pistachios, stirring frequently, until they brown in spots and give off a strong nutty aroma, about 2 minutes. Transfer to a cutting board. When cool enough to touch, chop them coarsely.

Heat the remaining 2 tablespoons oil in the same skillet over medium-high heat until very hot. Stir-fry the onion and garlic until honey brown, 2 to 3 minutes. Scrape this into a large bowl along with the pistachios, vinaigrette, chickpeas, bell pepper, salt, and red pepper flakes. Add the rice to the bowl and fold the ingredients together. The salad can be served at room temperature or chilled. Just before serving, fold in the basil, taste, and season with more salt, if you like.

Traditional Peanut Brittle

MAKES ABOUT 2 POUNDS
Unflavored vegetable oil for greasing the slab
¾ teaspoon baking soda
½ teaspoon salt
1 teaspoon pure vanilla extract
2 cups sugar
¾ cup light corn syrup
1½ cups raw peanuts (Spanish or blanched)
2 tablespoons unsalted butter, softened

Generously oil an 18-inch-square marble slab (or an inverted baking sheet) and a thin metal spatula. Sift the baking soda and salt onto a small sheet of waxed paper. Measure the vanilla extract into a small container. Set all of these near your work area, along with a pair of rubber gloves.

In a heavy 4-quart deep saucepan, combine the sugar, corn syrup, and ½ cup water. Stir over medium-low heat until the sugar dissolves, 10 to 12 minutes. When the solution is clear and begins to boil, increase the heat to high and stop stirring. Put a candy thermometer in the solution, holding it with a mitt to protect your hand. When the mixture registers 265°F on the thermometer, 8 to 10 minutes later, add the nuts and stir gently to disperse them through the mixture. Continue cooking, stirring occasionally, until the mixture reaches the hard-crack stage, 305° to 310°F, about another 5 minutes. Remove the pan from the heat. Stir in the softened butter, the vanilla extract, and then the baking soda and salt. The mixture will begin to foam.

Stir just until the mixture foams evenly, and without delay pour it onto the oiled marble slab. The mixture should spread to about 14 inches in diameter. Slip the oiled spatula under the hot candy to loosen the edges and bottom. Put on the gloves and as soon as the candy is firm enough on the bottom to be picked up (the top won't be hard yet), lift the edges and turn the entire piece of brittle over. With gloved hands, stretch the brittle to extend it so it's as thin as you can get it, about 17 inches in diameter. Let the candy cool undisturbed for at least 1 hour and then break it into small pieces. Store the brittle in airtight containers for up to 10 days.

Fettuccine with Artichokes, Hazelnuts, and Cream

SERVES 4 AS A MAIN COURSE OR 8 AS A FIRST COURSE
½ lemon
Kosher salt
2 tablespoons unsalted butter
2 tablespoons extra-virgin olive oil
1 small yellow onion, minced
4 large artichoke bottoms, halved
Freshly ground black pepper
1 cup homemade chicken broth (or equal parts water and reduced-sodium broth)
1 cup heavy cream
½ cup coarsely chopped toasted hazelnuts
2 tablespoons minced fresh flat-leaf parsley; more for garnish
1 pound dried fettuccine

Squeeze the lemon into a small bowl of water; as you trim the artichoke bottoms, you'll put them in the lemon water to prevent darkening. Put a large pot of salted water on to boil over high heat. Heat the butter and olive oil in a 12-inch skillet over moderately low heat. Add the onion and cook until softened, about 10 minutes. Meanwhile, cut each artichoke half into very thin wedges (about 8 per half). Return the wedges to the lemon water. When the onion is soft, drain the artichokes and add them to the skillet. Season with salt and pepper; stir to coat. Cover and reduce the heat to low. Cook until the artichokes are tender, 20 to 30 minutes. Check occasionally to be sure they're not burning or sticking; adjust the heat accordingly and add a tablespoon or two of water if necessary to prevent burning.

Add the broth, cream, hazelnuts, and parsley to the skillet and bring to a simmer over medium-high heat.

Simmer until thickened slightly, 8 to 10 minutes. Taste and adjust the seasonings.

While the sauce is reducing, cook the pasta in the boiling water until al dente. Set aside 1 cup of the pasta water, drain the pasta, and return it to the warm pot. Add the sauce to the pasta and toss well. If the sauce is too thin, return the pot to medium heat and cook until the pasta absorbs most of it. If the pasta seems dry, moisten with some of the reserved water. Serve immediately in warm bowls, garnishing each portion with a little more parsley.

Brussels Sprouts with Toasted Hazelnut Butter

SERVES 6 TO 8

FOR THE BUTTER

⅓ cup hazelnuts (about 1 ounce)

2 ounces (4 tablespoons) unsalted butter, softened at room temperature

2 teaspoons finely grated lemon zest

1½ teaspoons lightly chopped fresh thyme

½ teaspoon honey

¼ teaspoon kosher salt

FOR THE BRUSSELS SPROUTS

¼ cup extra-virgin olive oil

1¾ pounds Brussels sprouts, trimmed and quartered or cut into 6 wedges if very large (about 6 cups)

1½ teaspoons kosher salt, plus more to taste

½ cup reduced-sodium chicken broth

Make the butter: Heat the oven to 400°F. Put the hazelnuts on a small rimmed baking sheet. Roast in the oven until they are a deep golden brown (the skins will be visibly splitting), 5 to 6 minutes. Wrap the nuts in a clean kitchen towel, let cool for a couple of minutes, and then take the skins off by rubbing the nuts together in the kitchen towel while still warm. Don't worry about getting off all of the skins.

Let the nuts cool for about 10 minutes. Finely chop ¼ cup of the nuts in a small food processor. The nuts should be very finely ground but not so much that they turn into nut butter. Coarsely chop the remaining nuts and set aside for a garnish.

Put the finely chopped nuts, butter, lemon zest, thyme, honey, and salt in a small bowl and mix with a spatula until well combined. Set aside or refrigerate if not using right away.

Cook the Brussels sprouts: Heat the oil in a 12-inch skillet over medium-high heat. Add the Brussels sprouts and 1½ teaspoons salt and stir well. Reduce the heat to medium and cook, stirring occasionally and then more frequently as the sprouts begin to brown, until all of the sprouts are golden brown on most sides and have lost their raw color (they will still feel firm), 15 to 18 minutes. Add the broth and immediately cover the pan. Cook until the broth has reduced to a few tablespoons, about 2 minutes. Uncover, raise the heat to high, and boil off most of the remaining liquid, 1 to 2 minutes. Take the pan off the heat and add the hazelnut butter in spoonfuls; toss well. Season to taste with salt.

Transfer the sprouts to a warm serving dish and garnish with the reserved hazelnuts.

Other recipe ideas

HOMEMADE NUTTY GRANOLA Toss whole almonds, hazelnuts, or pecans (don't use more than one type of nut, for even cooking) with vegetable oil, honey or maple syrup, dry milk powder, salt, and spices. Spread on rimmed baking sheet pans and toast in a 325°F oven until dry and crisp.

SPINACH AND PINE NUTS Sauté fresh spinach in olive oil with a few crushed red pepper flakes until just wilted and tender; drain off any excess liquid. Toss with golden raisins and a handful of lightly toasted pine nuts.

ALMOND CHEESECAKE Add lightly toasted and finely chopped almonds to the graham cracker crust for a cheesecake, then flavor the cheesecake filling with a touch of almond extract. Serve with a fresh peach compote.

Pastinaca sativa cvs.

Parsnips

A parsnip may lack the color of its cousin the carrot, but its flavor is powerful—at once earthy and sweet, with a hint of a spice, almost cinnamony. And cooking with parsnips is a pleasure because they respond beautifully to so many methods.

PREPARING

Whether to peel parsnips depends on how you plan to use them. For a rustic dish, such as roasted or fried parsnips, peeling isn't necessary because you won't notice the skin once the parsnip is browned. But for a more refined treatment, such as a puréed parsnip soup, it's nice to peel them so that there won't be any bits of skin in the finished soup. If you don't peel your parsnip, scrub the outer skin thoroughly to remove any dirt or small roots.

For best flavor, remove the core of larger parsnips, which can be flavorless and stringy. To remove the core from an uncooked parsnip, first cut the root in half lengthwise, and then again into lengthwise quarters. Use the tip of a sharp knife to cut out the dark, heavy-grained core. If you're cooking the parsnip whole, you can easily remove the core after it has been cooked. Just slice the parsnip lengthwise and scoop out the core with a spoon.

HOW TO USE IT

Raw parsnips cut into paper-thin rounds are an interesting addition to a vegetable platter. Grated parsnips add crunch and variety to a green salad and pair especially well with slightly bitter greens. When cooked, a parsnip's starchy insides soften, and their flavor becomes more intense. Steaming works best for young, tender roots because it preserves their delicate flavor. The larger roots have a stronger flavor that stands up well to frying and roasting; when roasting meats, add parsnips to the pan during the last hour of cooking.

PICKING THE BEST

With parsnips, bigger isn't necessarily better. Larger roots do have a rich, deep flavor, but they also often have a woody texture, especially at the core. When buying parsnips, examine them as you would a carrot. They should feel heavy and firm, not limp. Look for parsnips with tight skins; avoid those that are shriveled or that have cracks or large bruises.

KEEPING IT FRESH

Refrigerate your parsnips in a plastic bag until you're ready to use; they'll keep this way for several weeks.

PRESERVING OPTIONS

You can freeze parsnips by cutting them into small cubes, blanching for 2 minutes, draining well, and then sealing in airtight freezer bags.

Parsnip and Parmesan Soup

SERVES 5 TO 6

2 ounces (4 tablespoons) unsalted butter

1½ pounds parsnips, peeled, trimmed, and cut into
½-inch dice (a scant 4 cups)

6 ounces shallots, cut into ¼-inch dice (about
1¼ cups)

8 cloves garlic, minced

1 tablespoon finely chopped fresh oregano, plus tiny
sprigs for garnish

1½ teaspoons kosher salt, plus more to taste

½ teaspoon freshly ground black pepper, plus more
to taste

4½ cups homemade or reduced-sodium chicken or
vegetable broth

1½ ounces (½ cup) freshly grated Parmigiano-
Reggiano

2 teaspoons soy sauce

2 teaspoons fresh lemon juice

Melt the butter in a 5-quart or larger stockpot set
over medium heat. While the butter is still foaming,
add the parsnips and cook until lightly browned, 7 to
10 minutes (resist the urge to stir too often or they
won't brown). Stir in the shallots, garlic, chopped
oregano, salt, and pepper, and cook until the shallot
is very limp and the entire mixture is beginning
to brown, 8 to 10 minutes. Add the broth, using a
wooden spoon to scrape up any browned bits in the
pot. Bring to a boil, reduce the heat to maintain a
low simmer, and cook until the parsnips are very soft,
6 to 8 minutes. Remove from the heat and let cool
somewhat.

Purée the soup using a stand or hand-held
immersion blender (you'll need to work in batches if
using a stand blender—be careful to fill the blender
no more than one-third full and hold a towel over
the lid when you turn it on). Return the soup to the
pot and stir in the Parmigiano, soy sauce, and lemon
juice. Taste and add more salt and pepper if needed.
Reheat the soup and garnish each serving with an
oregano sprig.

Mashed Parsnips with Lemon and Herbs

SERVES 4

Kosher salt

2 pounds medium parsnips, peeled, cored, and cut
into 1½- to 2-inch pieces

¼ cup crème fraîche

2 tablespoons unsalted butter

Finely grated zest of 1 small lemon, plus 1 tablespoon
juice

Salt and freshly ground black pepper

1 tablespoon chopped fresh chives, mint, parsley, dill,
or a mix

Bring a large pot of salted water to a boil. Add the
parsnips and cook until tender when pierced with a
fork, 12 to 15 minutes. Drain the parsnips in a colander
and let them steam under a clean kitchen towel for
about 5 minutes.

Return the parsnips to the pot and mash them
with a potato masher, keeping them rather rough.
Stir in the crème fraîche, butter, lemon zest, and juice.
Season to taste with salt and pepper. Transfer to a
warm serving bowl and sprinkle with the chopped
herbs.

Other recipe ideas

ROOT VEGETABLE RISOTTO Steam finely diced
parsnips, turnips, and carrots and add to a risotto
flavored with pancetta and sage.

MOROCCAN LAMB STEW Toss chunks of parsnip
into a savory lamb stew along with some prunes,
chickpeas, and Moroccan spices. Finish with chopped
fresh cilantro and toasted sliced almonds.

ROASTED PARSNIP SIDE DISH Cut parsnips into
julienne and roast with julienned carrots until the
vegetables are tender and starting to brown, then
toss in a shallot-and-herb vinaigrette.

Red Bartlett

Starkrimson

Anjou

Beurre Bosc

Pyrus communis cvs.

Pears

Pears aren't flashy; in fact, they're quite subtle in color and flavor. But when their flavor and texture are at their peak, pears are pretty amazing—creamy, smooth flesh and sweet juice, so abundant it runs down your chin. And pears like to be cooked, working well in sweet and savory dishes.

PICKING THE BEST

Pears come in a range of sizes and shapes, and their colors range from a russeted dun to green to almost apple-red. Most pears are good for snacking, but some are better for cooking than others.

- **Anjou:** Juicy and very sweet, it becomes creamy when ripe. It appears in October and is available well into the early summer.
- **Bartlett:** A ripe Red Bartlett is bright red; a ripe Bartlett is bright yellow. Aromatic and sweet, this pear is perfect eaten raw. It's the first pear to appear in late August.
- **Bosc:** These come into season in September and can be available well into spring. The dense, grainy flesh has an elegant, aromatic flavor that's perfect for cooking.
- **Comice:** This very sweet, very juicy pear is wonderful raw. Its season starts in early September and lasts into December.
- **Forelle:** The slightly crunchy texture of this pear, which appears in September, means it holds up well when cooked, but it's also delicious raw and in salads.
- **Seckel:** The smallest of pears, it has extremely sweet, very dense, crisp flesh, and it's lovely poached or roasted. Its season is September through December.

All pears are picked when the fruit is mature but not yet ripe because, left to ripen on the tree, they would develop deposits of lignin, which makes the flesh grainy. If the pears are very hard when you buy them, they may need several days to ripen. You can hasten the process by storing them in a closed paper bag.

The best way to judge ripeness is to gently press the neck of the fruit near the stem with your thumb; if the flesh gives, the pear is ready to eat. And use your nose, too—a ripe pear will give off a delicious, sweet aroma. For cooking, pears should generally be "firm-ripe," or just at the beginning of the ripening window.

KEEPING IT FRESH

Once ripe, pears will stay in good shape for a couple of days, but for longer storage, hold them in the refrigerator. Ripe pears should be handled delicately because their tender skin and flesh will bruise at the lightest bump.

PREPARING

Pears are simple to prepare. Many have skin that's delicate enough to leave on when using in salads or sliced on a galette or tart. But if the skin feels tough or grainy, peel it with a vegetable peeler. Halve the pear lengthwise and cut out the soft core and few seeds; some pears have a fibrous core that runs to the stem, so remove that, too. A melon baller does a neat job of coring pears; or use the smallest paring knife you have, cutting only with the tip of the blade.

HOW TO USE IT

The subtle, sweet flavor of a pear is delicious both raw and cooked, and pears adapt beautifully to both savory and sweet dishes. You can use a pear anywhere you would use an apple, provided that a softer texture is acceptable (think of it this way: if an apple is like gingham, a pear is more like silk taffeta).

PRESERVING OPTIONS

Pears freeze well enough to use in baked goods or for pear sauce, but as they're delicate, handle them gently. Peel, core, and chunk or slice the pears. To prevent browning, toss with a mixture of ½ teaspoon (1,500mg) ascorbic acid (also known as Fruit-Fresh) dissolved in 3 tablespoons water. Spread out on a tray and freeze until hard, then pile into airtight freezer bags.

RECIPES

Grilled Brie, Turkey, and Pear Sandwiches

SERVES 4

½ ripe pear, cored and thinly sliced
1 teaspoon fresh lemon juice
1½ cups (about 8 ounces) shredded cooked turkey or chicken
1½ teaspoons lightly chopped fresh thyme leaves
Eight ½- to ¾-inch-thick slices artisan-style whole-grain sandwich bread
2 tablespoons Dijon mustard
8 ounces Brie, sliced
4 teaspoons unsalted butter, softened

In a small bowl, toss the pear slices with the lemon juice. Heat a large skillet or griddle over low heat.

Meanwhile, toss the turkey and thyme in a medium bowl. Spread each bread slice with mustard. Arrange half of the Brie on four slices of the bread. Layer the pears over the Brie. Mound the turkey mixture on top of the pears, layer on the remaining Brie, and top with the remaining bread slices, mustard side down.

Lightly spread the tops of the sandwiches with half of the butter and set them, buttered side down, in the heated skillet (if necessary, cook the sandwiches in two batches). Set a large heavy skillet right on top of the sandwiches and put 2 pounds of weights (canned goods work well) in the empty skillet. Cook the sandwiches until golden brown on one side, about 4 minutes.

Remove the weights, butter the sandwich tops, and turn the sandwiches over. Replace the skillet and weights and continue to cook until the second side is golden brown and the cheese is oozy, about 4 minutes longer. Cut the sandwiches in half and serve.

Butterscotch Baked Pears

SERVES 4

4 firm-ripe pears
½ lemon
3 ounces (6 tablespoons) butter, cut into pieces
¼ cup granulated sugar
¼ cup firmly packed dark brown sugar
⅔ cup heavy cream
1 teaspoon pure vanilla extract
½ teaspoon salt
1 tablespoon Scotch whisky (optional)

Heat the oven to 375°F. Peel the pears, cut them in half lengthwise, and, using a melon baller, scoop out the cores. Rub them all over with the lemon half to prevent browning.

In a heavy 10-inch ovenproof skillet, melt the butter. Add the granulated sugar and brown sugar and stir to dissolve. Arrange the pears in the pan, cut side down, in a single layer. Bake the pears uncovered, basting occasionally with the liquid in the pan, until they begin to soften and color slightly. Depending on the pears' ripeness, baking time can range from 20 to 60 minutes. Remove the pears with a slotted spoon and set aside.

Transfer the pan to a burner and boil the mixture left behind over medium-high heat until it reaches a rich, golden brown and smells like caramel, 2 to 5 minutes. Slowly whisk the cream into the caramel until smooth. Add the vanilla, salt, and Scotch, if using. Serve the sauce over the warm pears.

Pear Clafoutis with Almonds

SERVES 6

3 tablespoons unsalted butter; more for the pan
2 medium pears (about 12 ounces total)
2 tablespoons pear eau de vie, such as Poire William
3 large eggs
⅓ cup sugar
1½ ounces (⅓ cup) unbleached all-purpose flour
Pinch of freshly grated nutmeg
1 teaspoon pure vanilla extract, or seeds from ½ split vanilla bean
¼ cup heavy or whipping cream
½ cup whole milk
¼ cup sliced almonds

Position a rack in the center of the oven and heat the oven to 350°F. Butter a 9-inch cake pan or pie plate.

Peel the pears and cut them in half. Remove the core and any fibers and cut the halves into ¼-inch slices. Put the slices in the prepared cake pan. Sprinkle them with the pear eau de vie and toss to coat; spread them in a fairly even layer.

In a large bowl, whisk the eggs and sugar until lightly frothy and the sugar is dissolved. Sprinkle or sift in the flour and nutmeg and add the vanilla. Whisk until smooth. Gradually add the cream and milk, whisking just until smooth. Melt 2 tablespoons of the butter and stir it into the batter. Pour the batter over the fruit, sprinkle the almonds on top, and dot the surface with bits of the remaining 1 tablespoon butter.

Bake until evenly puffed and brown and a skewer comes out clean, about 40 minutes. Serve warm.

What Are Asian Pears?

The pears that we're used to eating in the United States are not the pear that's prized in Asia. Asian pears are cousins to the familiar Bartlett and its kin, but this fruit is similar to an apple—rounder and crisper, yet with the delicacy and honeyed perfume of a good pear.

Asian pears are usually round and firm to the touch when ripe. They ripen on the tree, so they're ready to eat right after harvest. They're very crisp, juicy, and only slightly sweet. You'll often see them individually wrapped or cradled in foam netting to protect their delicate skin. The most popular Asian pear varieties in the U.S. is 20th Century, which is round with smooth yellow skin, or the bronze-toned Hosui pear.

Choose smooth, unblemished, and very fragrant Asian pears. Unlike their European cousins, Asian pears are excellent keepers—store them for up to a week at room temperature or up to 3 months in the refrigerator.

Gingerbread-Pear Cobbler

SERVES 12 TO 16

FOR THE PEAR LAYER

5¼ pounds ripe pears (about 12 medium), peeled, cored, and cut into ⅛- to ¼-inch-thick slices (Bosc or Anjou pears work well)

¾ cup sugar

2 tablespoons fresh lemon juice (from 1 lemon)

1½ teaspoons minced lemon zest (from 1 lemon)

2 tablespoons minced crystallized ginger (about 1 ounce)

1½ tablespoons unbleached all-purpose flour

2 tablespoons unsalted butter, at room temperature, cut into small pieces; more for the pan

FOR THE GINGERBREAD BISCUIT LAYER

9 ounces (2 cups) unbleached all-purpose flour

5½ tablespoons sugar

1 tablespoon ground ginger

2½ teaspoons baking powder

2 teaspoons ground cinnamon

¾ teaspoon ground cloves

½ teaspoon salt

¼ teaspoon baking soda

3 ounces (6 tablespoons) vegetable shortening

2½ tablespoons unsalted butter, at room temperature

2 large eggs

6 tablespoons whole milk

⅓ cup molasses

¾ teaspoon pure vanilla extract

FOR THE TOPPING

½ cup sliced almonds

2 tablespoons sugar

Make the pear layer: Position a rack in the center of the oven and heat the oven to 400°F. Lightly butter a 10x15x2-inch baking dish.

In a large bowl, gently toss the sliced pears with the sugar, lemon juice, and lemon zest. Make sure the lemon juice completely coats the pears to keep them from browning. Sprinkle the crystallized ginger and flour over the top. Stir until evenly incorporated, breaking apart any ginger pieces that may be stuck together. Spread the pear mixture evenly in the prepared pan and dot with the softened butter pieces.

Make the biscuit layer: In a medium bowl, stir the flour, sugar, ground ginger, baking powder, cinnamon, cloves, salt, and baking soda with a fork. With the fork, work in the shortening and the softened butter until the size of small peas.

In a small bowl, whisk the eggs, milk, molasses, and vanilla extract. Make a well in the center of the dry ingredients and pour the egg mixture into the well. Stir just until the dry ingredients are completely blended. Dollop the batter by heaping tablespoonfuls onto the pears to create a cobbled effect, taking care to space the dollops about 1 inch apart. (Though the batter will cover only about half of the pear layer, don't spread it out. It will rise and spread to cover most of the pears as it bakes. If you run out of space to dollop the batter before it's all used, distribute what remains among the existing dollops.)

Add the topping and bake: Sprinkle the nuts and sugar evenly over the cobbler. Bake until the pears are tender and the topping is golden brown, 35 to 40 minutes. If needed, rotate the pan midway through the baking to allow the top to brown evenly. Let rest for at least 20 minutes before serving. Serve warm.

Cauliflower with Brown Butter, Pears, Sage, and Hazelnuts

SERVES 8 TO 10

3 ounces (6 tablespoons) unsalted butter

1 medium head cauliflower, cut into small florets about ¾ inch wide

½ cup toasted, skinned, and chopped hazelnuts

8 fresh sage leaves, thinly sliced crosswise

1 teaspoon kosher salt, plus more to taste

½ teaspoon freshly ground black pepper

2 large ripe pears, cored and thinly sliced

2 tablespoons chopped fresh flat-leaf parsley

In a 12-inch skillet over medium-high heat, melt the butter until light brown and bubbly. Add the cauliflower, hazelnuts, and sage. Cook for 2 minutes, stirring occasionally. Season with 1 teaspoon salt and ½ teaspoon pepper and continue cooking, stirring occasionally, until the cauliflower is browned and crisp-tender, another 6 to 7 minutes.

Remove the pan from the heat. Add the pear slices and parsley. Gently toss to combine and warm the pears. Season to taste with more salt. Serve hot or at room temperature.

Arugula Salad with Pears, Prosciutto, and Aged Gouda

SERVES 4

2 tablespoons white-wine vinegar

½ teaspoon Dijon mustard

¼ teaspoon kosher salt

⅛ teaspoon freshly ground black pepper

¼ cup extra-virgin olive oil

5 to 6 ounces arugula, any large stems removed and leaves washed and dried (6 loosely packed cups)

2 medium pears, peeled if you like, cored, and cut into 1-inch chunks

4 thin slices prosciutto, cut crosswise into ½-inch-wide ribbons

3 ounces aged Gouda, cut into 2-inch-long sticks (1 cup)

1 ounce walnuts, toasted and coarsely chopped (¼ cup)

In a small bowl, whisk the vinegar, mustard, salt, and pepper. Gradually whisk in the oil.

In a large bowl, toss the arugula and pears with half of the dressing. Portion onto four plates, scatter the prosciutto and cheese on top of each salad, and drizzle with a little of the remaining dressing. Sprinkle on the nuts and serve immediately.

Glazed Pork Roast with Carrots, Parsnips, and Pears

SERVES 4 TO 6

One 2-pound center-cut boneless pork loin roast

Kosher salt and freshly ground black pepper

1½ tablespoons Dijon or grainy mustard

1½ tablespoons honey

2 tablespoons roughly chopped fresh sage

½ pound carrots (3 or 4), peeled

½ pound parsnips (3 or 4), peeled

2 firm but ripe Bosc pears, quartered, cored, and stemmed

1½ tablespoons olive oil; more for the pan

Position a rack in the center of the oven and heat the oven to 400°F. Lightly oil the bottom of a medium roasting pan or 15x10-inch Pyrex dish and set the pork in the center. Season the pork with salt and pepper.

In a small bowl, mix the mustard, honey, and half of the sage; spread on the top and sides of the pork. If the carrots and parsnips are thick (about 1 inch or larger around), cut them in half or quarters lengthwise so that they're all roughly the same thickness (about ½ inch thick at their thickest part). Toss the vegetables and pear wedges with the olive oil and the remaining sage, season with salt and several grinds of pepper, and arrange around the pork.

Pour ½ cup water into the pan and roast in the center of the oven until an instant-read thermometer inserted in the center of the roast registers 145°F, 30 to 45 minutes. (The cooking time will vary widely depending on the thickness of the roast; start checking early, and check frequently once the temperature reaches 130°F.) Transfer the pork to a carving board. (If the vegetables and pears aren't fully tender by the time the pork is done, return them to the oven until tender, 5 to 10 minutes more.) Let the pork rest for 5 minutes before slicing thinly. Serve with the vegetables, pears, and pan juices.

Other recipe ideas

PEAR-CHERRY CHUTNEY Make a sweet-sour pear chutney by simmering chopped pears and onion, dried sour cherries, and an equal amount of sugar and cider vinegar. Serve with roast pork or over a triple-cream cheese.

ROQUEFORT-PEAR CANAPÉS Fill whole Belgian endive leaves with some crumbled Roquefort cheese, a few toasted pecan pieces, and a little pepper, and top with a sliver of ripe pear.

PEAR-BRANDY TURNOVERS Sauté diced pears in butter and brown sugar, and flavor with a splash of brandy; let cool. Cut squares of thawed frozen puff pastry, put a few spoonfuls of pear filling in the center, fold into a triangle, pinching the seams well, and bake until the pastry is browned and the filling is hot and bubbly. Serve with ice cream.

Diospyros kaki and cvs.

Persimmons

A ripe persimmon is an exotic treat—the honeyed flavor and silky texture are luxurious. Easily mistaken for underripe tomatoes, these round, orangy-red fruits are popular the world over. Depending on the variety, persimmons can have smooth, custard-like flesh that tastes of banana and mango or firmer flesh with notes of apricots and a mellow sweetness.

crisp flavor reminiscent of apricots, while the Hachiya has tropical fruit notes and is very rich and sweet. American persimmons, a third type, grow wild. They're small, about the size of a plump cherry; you'll find lots of old American recipes for persimmon pudding made with these wild fruits.

With either variety, look for fruit that's plump, heavy for its size, and vibrantly colored, with glossy skin. Avoid those with bruises, blemishes, or cracks.

KEEPING IT FRESH
Keep unripe fruit at room temperature, preferably in a brown paper bag, to help it ripen. If persimmons are already ripe and soft when you buy them, eat them right away or store in the refrigerator for no more than 2 days.

PREPARING
Remove the core for both eating and cooking. The skin is edible, though you may want to peel it because it can be a little waxy. Cut the fruit into wedges, slices, or cubes, or if it's a very ripe Hachiya, simply spoon out the pudding-like pulp.

HOW TO USE IT
You can eat persimmons out of hand or add them to sweet dishes such as puddings, breads, cookies, and ice cream. They're also delicious in savory preparations like salsas and relishes, in salads, or sautéed as a side dish for roasted pork or lamb.

PICKING THE BEST
Persimmon varieties are divided into two categories, astringent and nonastringent. Astringent varieties, such as the acorn-shaped Hachiya, are tannic and sour when underripe; they should be eaten when very ripe and jelly-soft. Fuyu is the most common nonastringent variety. Shaped like pincushions, they are smaller than Hachiyas and have fewer tannins, so they can be eaten both underripe and soft. The Fuyu has a subtle,

Fuyu Persimmon and Fennel Salad with Hazelnuts

SERVES 6

6 tablespoons fresh orange juice

2 tablespoons white-wine vinegar

2 tablespoons minced shallot

2 teaspoons finely grated orange zest

¼ teaspoon kosher salt, plus more to taste

½ cup extra-virgin olive oil

4 medium ripe Fuyu persimmons, peeled, quartered, cored, and thinly sliced

2 medium bulbs fennel, trimmed, cored, and very thinly sliced or shaved with a mandoline or vegetable peeler

⅓ cup lightly packed fresh flat-leaf parsley leaves, coarsely torn if large

Freshly ground black pepper

½ cup toasted, skinned hazelnuts, chopped

½ cup shaved Parmigiano-Reggiano

Put the orange juice, vinegar, shallot, zest, and ¼ teaspoon salt in a small bowl and let sit for 15 to 30 minutes to soften the shallot and meld the flavors. Gradually whisk in the oil.

In a large bowl, toss the persimmons, fennel, and parsley with enough of the vinaigrette to coat (you may not need all of it). Season to taste with salt and pepper. Portion onto six salad plates and sprinkle with the hazelnuts and Parmigiano.

Other recipe ideas

PERSIMMON GRANITA Purée a few soft, ripe persimmons (either variety) and strain the pulp. Season with a bit of sugar and lemon or orange juice, and freeze to make a persimmon ice.

CREAMY PERSIMMON FOOL Lightly sweeten some whipped cream and flavor with a touch of brandy. Fold in Hachiya persimmon purée and some chopped crystallized ginger.

FUYU PERSIMMON-HABANERO CHUTNEY Simmer chopped firm Fuyu persimmon with some finely chopped onion, minced fresh ginger, and minced habanero in cider vinegar sweetened with dark brown sugar and spiced with some cloves, coriander, and a cinnamon stick until thick.

PERSIMMON TEA BREAD Flavor a quick bread with persimmon purée, chopped dried cranberries or sour cherries, and some chopped toasted pecans.

DID YOU KNOW? The leaves of the persimmon tree fall while the fruit is still on the tree, creating a stunning sight on a fall day—bare branches laden with rich, burnt-orange globes.

Idaho

Purple Peruvian

Red boiling

Russian
Banana

French fingerling

Yukon Gold

Solanum tuberosum cvs.

Potatoes

It's hard to imagine that there's anyone on earth who doesn't love potatoes. Mild and starchy, they're the epitome of comfort food, readily absorbing the flavors of other ingredients around them, from a simple pat of butter to complex and vibrant Indian curry spices. The price is always right with a potato, too, and at most markets, the cook has the choice of anything from a marble-size creamer to a burly russet weighing in at close to a pound.

PICKING THE BEST

All potatoes should feel heavy and firm, never soft, wrinkled, or blemished. Try not to buy potatoes in plastic bags since it's hard to evaluate them, and avoid potatoes that are tinged with green, which indicates the presence of solanine, produced when potatoes are exposed to light, either in the field or after harvest. This mildly poisonous alkaloid has a bitter flavor and can cause an upset stomach.

In order to choose the right type of potato, you need to know what you plan to do with it.

For baking, mashing, and french fries: Potatoes such as russets, Idahoes, and Russet Burbanks are high in starch and low in moisture. They have thick skins, so they bake to perfection and make the fluffiest mashed potatoes. When you eat these potatoes, you can sense their abundance of starch, as they feel granular and dry on your tongue. The moisture-absorbing quality of high-starch potatoes also makes them good thickeners in soups. But that same quality prevents these potatoes from holding together during cooking, so they're not ideal for any dish where you want the potato to hold its shape: scalloped potatoes, whole roasted, or hash browns.

High-starch potatoes are your best bet for frying. Starch granules on the outside immediately swell in the heat; as the outside cooks and browns, the surface seals, preventing the french fry from absorbing lots of cooking fat so you get a french fry with a crisp and golden exterior and a dry, fluffy interior.

Multi-purpose: Yukon Golds, with their slightly nutty flavor, and Yellow Finns, with their golden skin and flesh, have less starch and a creamier texture than high-starch potatoes. You can mash these medium-starch potatoes, but expect the result to be creamy rather than light and fluffy. Some cooks also prefer the in-between starch content of these potatoes for pan-fried potatoes and potato salads.

For salads, gratins, and roasting: Red-skinned potatoes and round whites are high-moisture, low-starch potatoes, sometimes called "waxy." When you slice into one of these potatoes, the flesh looks translucent and firm. These potatoes hold their shape and don't fall apart easily when handled, and they contain more sugar than other types, so turn deliciously brown during cooking. These qualities make them suited equally well for boiling, roasting, or sautéing. Waxy potatoes are also ideal for scalloped potatoes because their slices retain their shape and texture during cooking, instead of disintegrating into the surrounding sauce. Because of their low starch content, these varieties only lightly absorb salad dressing, so use them if you like a potato salad that's chunky, rather than creamy.

• **Fingerlings:** Small and slender and somewhat

resembling fingers (hence the name), fingerlings are low-starch potatoes that hold their shape well, making them a good, albeit petite, all-purpose potato. Though they come in a variety of colors (tan and red as well as purple), all have thinner skin and denser flesh than round potatoes. Fingerling varieties include Russian Banana, Butterfinger, Rose Finn Apple (which has rose-pink skin and yellow flesh that's blushed with red), and Ruby Crescent.

- **Purple potatoes:** Purple potatoes (sometimes called blue potatoes), including purple Peruvian fingerlings, stand slightly apart in taste and texture. They have a nice earthy flavor but also a relatively low moisture content, which makes them drier, almost like a russet. This means that purple potatoes are more likely to fall apart when cooked, so you need to pay extra attention when braising or boiling them for salads. They're at their best sautéed or roasted, because they become wonderfully crisp on the outside and dry and soft inside.

KEEPING IT FRESH

Potatoes should be stored in a dark, cool (45° to 50°F), dry place, with good air circulation—so not in plastic bags. If the temperature is too cold, however, some of the potatoes' starches will turn into sugars. Not only does this taste unpleasant, but the extra sugars also lead to overbrowning during cooking. If a potato winds up in cold storage, you can convert the sugars back to starches by storing it at room temperature for a few days.

PREPARING

Potatoes are a breeze to prepare. Rinse them, scrubbing lightly if they seem dusty. Peel potatoes when the skins are thick or if you want a pristine appearance, though many cooks like to leave in some skin for nutrition and texture, and potatoes cooked in their skins will be more flavorful, hold their shape better, and absorb less water. Check for blemishes or green spots and cut them out with a paring knife; when cutting away the green, be sure to remove at least $1/8$ inch of flesh below the green tinge. You can peel potatoes a couple of hours ahead of using, but they brown quickly, so keep them in a bowl of cold water with a splash of lemon juice added.

HOW TO USE IT

The only cooking method that doesn't work with a potato is *not* cooking it—there is little pleasure to be found in a raw potato, though some people claim to like eating them like apples. Depending on the variety of potato, steaming and boiling enhance their creaminess (and mashing with cream and butter takes that a step further), baking makes them fluffy, braising lets them soak up flavors, and any type of frying—whether as a slender french fry, chunky hash browns, or finely grated rösti potatoes—gives them an irresistible golden crunch.

PRESERVING OPTIONS

Raw or cooked, potatoes don't freeze well at home, but there are a few potato dishes that do freeze well, including twice-baked potatoes, which have a higher fat content because of the added butter. You can also freeze mashed potatoes and reheat them in the oven, microwave, or double-boiler, but they won't retain their fluffy texture.

DID YOU KNOW?

According to the Idaho Potato Commission, potatoes and onions release gases that interact and make each spoil more quickly, so don't store them together.

Mustard and Rosemary Roasted Potatoes

SERVES 4 TO 6

⅓ cup plus 1 tablespoon Dijon mustard

¼ cup olive oil

1 tablespoon dry vermouth or other dry white wine

2 cloves garlic, minced

1 tablespoon chopped fresh rosemary

1 teaspoon coarse salt

Freshly ground black pepper

2 pounds waxy potatoes, cut into ¾- to 1-inch dice

Heat the oven to 400°F. In a large bowl, whisk the mustard, olive oil, vermouth, garlic, rosemary, salt, and a few grinds of pepper. Add the potatoes and toss to coat. Dump the potatoes onto a large rimmed baking sheet and spread them in a single layer. Roast, tossing with a spatula a few times, until the potatoes are crusty on the outside and tender throughout, 50 to 55 minutes. Serve hot.

Potatoes Fondantes

SERVES 4 TO 6

2 pounds baby Yukon Gold potatoes (20 to 25 potatoes, 1½ to 1¾ inches in diameter)

1 sprig fresh rosemary

2 cups homemade or reduced-sodium chicken broth; more as needed

2 tablespoons good-quality extra-virgin olive oil

1 tablespoon unsalted butter

1 teaspoon kosher salt (less if the broth is salty)

1 to 2 tablespoons thinly sliced fresh chives

Fleur de sel or other sea salt, for serving (optional)

Trim the potatoes of any eyes or damaged areas and wash well in cold water. Arrange as many potatoes as will fit in one layer in a 10-inch nonstick skillet (there should be a little room to spare; save any extra potatoes for another use). Add the rosemary, broth, oil, butter, and salt. Bring to a boil over high heat. Reduce the heat to medium, cover the pan but leave the lid a tad ajar, and boil until the potatoes are tender when pierced with a fork, about 20 minutes. The liquid should still halfway surround the potatoes; if it doesn't, add more broth or water until it does.

Remove the pan from the heat and press on each potato with a ¼-cup measure just until it cracks open. Set the pan over medium-high heat and cook, uncovered, until all the liquid has evaporated and the potatoes have browned on one side, about 10 minutes. Gently turn the potatoes and brown the other side, another 4 to 5 minutes.

Remove the pan from the heat and let the potatoes rest for 5 minutes before transferring them to a serving platter. Sprinkle with the chives and serve immediately, passing the fleur de sel so diners can sprinkle some on if they want.

Yukon Gold Gruyère Galette

SERVES 4 TO 6

¼ cup finely chopped shallot (from about 2 large)

3 tablespoons extra-virgin olive oil, plus ½ teaspoon for the pan (or use olive-oil spray for the pan)

1 pound Yukon Gold potatoes (about 2 large or 3 medium), unpeeled and scrubbed

1 heaping teaspoon very lightly chopped fresh thyme

Kosher salt

½ cup finely grated Parmigiano-Reggiano (about 1½ ounces, grated on a box grater's small holes)

1 cup finely grated Gruyère (about 3½ ounces)

Combine the shallot and 3 tablespoons of the oil in a small saucepan and bring to a simmer over medium heat. Reduce to a low simmer; cook the shallot until nicely softened (don't let it brown), about 2 minutes. Remove from the heat and let cool completely.

Position a rack in the center of the oven and heat the oven to 400°F. Rub the bottom and inside edge of a 7½-inch tart pan with a removable bottom with the remaining ½ teaspoon olive oil or spray with olive-oil spray. Put the tart pan on a rimmed baking sheet lined with foil.

Slice the potatoes as thinly as possible (about 1/16 inch) with a chef's knife. Discard the ends. Put the potato slices in a mixing bowl, add the shallot and olive oil along with the thyme, and toss well to thoroughly coat the potatoes.

Cover the bottom of the tart pan with a layer of potato slices, overlapping them slightly. Start along the outside edge of the tart pan and, making slightly overlapping rings, move inward until the bottom is covered with one layer of potatoes. Sprinkle the potatoes with salt (a generous 1/8 teaspoon) and then sprinkle about one-quarter of the Parmigiano and about one-quarter of the Gruyère over all. Arrange another layer of potatoes, season with salt, sprinkle with cheese, and repeat two more times, until you have four layers of potatoes. Top the last layer with more salt and any remaining cheese.

Bake the galette until the top is a reddish golden brown and the potatoes are tender in all places (a fork with thin tines should poke easily through all the layers), 45 to 50 minutes. The bottom will be crisp and the sides brown.

Let the galette cool in the pan for 10 to 15 minutes. It will then be cool enough to handle but still plenty hot inside for serving. Have a cutting board nearby. Run a paring knife around the edge of the galette to loosen it and carefully remove the tart ring by gently pressing the tart bottom up. Slide a very thin spatula under and all around the bottom layer to free the galette from the pan bottom. Use the spatula to gently slide the galette onto the cutting board. Cut into four or six wedges, or as many as you like.

Potato Stir-Fry with Mint and Cilantro

SERVES 6

2 pounds red potatoes (about 6 medium), peeled and cut into 3/4-inch cubes (about 5 cups)

3 tablespoons canola oil

1 tablespoon yellow mustard seeds

24 curry leaves (optional)

1 small whole dried red chile

2 teaspoons ground coriander

2 teaspoons cumin seeds

1/2 teaspoon ground turmeric

2 medium cloves garlic, minced

1 jalapeño (seeds and ribs removed if you prefer a milder flavor), finely chopped

1 medium red onion, finely chopped

2 teaspoons kosher salt, plus more to taste

1/2 teaspoon cayenne (optional)

2/3 cup fresh mint leaves, finely chopped

1/2 cup loosely packed fresh cilantro sprigs, finely chopped

Juice of 1/2 lemon (1 to 2 tablespoons)

Put the potatoes in a medium bowl, cover with cool water, and set aside.

Heat the canola oil and the mustard seeds in a large wok or 12-inch skillet over medium-high heat until the mustard seeds start to sizzle and pop, 1 to 2 minutes (use a splatter screen, if you have one, so the seeds don't pop out of the pan). Add the curry leaves (if using), chile, coriander, cumin seeds, and turmeric, and cook, stirring occasionally, until the cumin browns and the curry leaves are crisp, 1 to 1½ minutes. Stir in the garlic and jalapeño and cook until the garlic is fragrant, about 30 seconds.

Drain the potatoes and add them to the pan along with the onion. Cook, stirring occasionally, until the potatoes are translucent around the edges, 2 to 3 minutes. Cover, reduce the heat to medium low, and cook, stirring and scraping the bottom of the pan every 5 minutes, until the potatoes are just tender, 12 to 15 minutes. (Reduce the heat to low if the potatoes seem to be burning.)

Add the salt and cayenne (if using) and cook for 30 seconds. Stir in the mint, cilantro, and lemon juice, cover the pan, and let the potatoes sit off the heat for 10 minutes. Scrape up the browned bits and stir them into the potatoes. Taste, add more salt if needed, and serve.

Creamy Potato Salad with Radishes, Lemon, and Dill

SERVES 6

2 pounds smallish waxy potatoes, unpeeled and scrubbed

Kosher salt

2 inner ribs celery and their tender leaves, finely chopped (about 1/2 cup)

3/4 cup thinly sliced radishes (about 6 small radishes)

3 scallions (white and light green parts), chopped

2 tablespoons chopped fresh dill

1/4 cup heavy cream, well chilled

1/2 cup mayonnaise

1½ teaspoons Dijon mustard

1½ tablespoons fresh lemon juice

2 teaspoons grated lemon zest

Freshly ground pepper (black or white)

Put the potatoes in a medium saucepan, cover with water by an inch or two, add a large pinch of salt, and bring to a boil. Reduce the heat to medium, partially cover, and cook until the potatoes are tender, about 20 minutes. Test for doneness by spearing a potato with a thin metal skewer. It should penetrate easily into the center of the potato and then slide right out. If the skewer lifts the potato out of the pot when you withdraw it, continue cooking a little longer. Drain the potatoes and let them cool. You can drain them on a cooling rack set over or in your sink, which will avoid squashing the tender potatoes (as often happens with a colander) and also lets the potatoes cool quickly.

When the potatoes are at room temperature, cut them into ¾-inch chunks and put them in a mixing bowl. Add the celery, radishes, scallion, and dill, and fold gently to distribute; set aside.

In a small bowl, whisk the cream until frothy but not at all stiffened. Whisk in the mayonnaise and mustard. Add the lemon juice, zest, ½ teaspoon salt, and pepper to taste. Pour the dressing over the salad and fold it in with a rubber spatula. Taste for seasoning, and add more salt and pepper if needed. Serve, or cover and chill for up to a day.

Braised Fingerling Potatoes with Fennel, Olives, and Thyme

SERVES 4

3 tablespoons extra-virgin olive oil

¾ pound fingerling potatoes (7 or 8 medium), cut lengthwise into ¼-inch-thick slices

¼ teaspoon kosher salt, plus more to taste

1 small bulb fennel, trimmed and halved lengthwise, then cut lengthwise into ½-inch-thick slices

1 medium sweet onion, thinly sliced

½ cup homemade or reduced-sodium chicken broth

3 sprigs fresh thyme, plus 2 teaspoons chopped fresh thyme, for garnish

¼ cup pitted Niçoise olives

Freshly ground black pepper

Heat the oven to 375°F. Heat 1½ tablespoons of the oil in a 10-inch straight-sided ovenproof sauté pan over medium-high heat. Add the potatoes and ¼ teaspoon salt and cook, stirring occasionally, until the potatoes begin to brown, about 7 minutes. Transfer the potatoes to a plate.

Add the remaining 1½ tablespoons oil and the fennel to the pan with a pinch of salt and cook, stirring occasionally, until lightly browned, about 5 minutes. Add the onion to the pan and cook, stirring often, until it starts to soften and lightly brown, 2 minutes more. Add the broth and bring to a boil. Gently nestle the potatoes into the fennel-onion mixture and add the thyme sprigs. Cover the pan and braise in the oven until the potatoes and fennel are tender, about 20 minutes.

Uncover the pan, add the olives, and continue to braise until most of the liquid has evaporated and the vegetables are meltingly tender, another 10 minutes. Remove from the oven, discard the thyme sprigs, and season to taste with salt and pepper. Garnish with the chopped thyme and serve.

Other recipe ideas

POTATO FRITTERS Gently mix leftover mashed potatoes with flaked cooked (or canned) salmon, tuna, or chopped shrimp and some chopped scallions, fresh herbs, grated lemon zest, and lots of black pepper. Shape into small patties and fry gently. Serve with more lemon and a small green salad.

SPANISH TORTILLA Fry sliced Yukon Golds in lots of olive oil until tender. Gently mix the potatoes with beaten eggs and some sautéed onion, then pour into a hot skillet and cook as you would a frittata, flipping halfway through cooking. Let cool to room temperature before cutting into squares to serve.

OVEN-ROASTED POTATO WEDGES Cut starchy potatoes like russets into thick wedges, season generously with salt, pepper, and chopped thyme. Roast in a hot oven until browned and tender and serve with a romesco sauce for dipping.

Cydonia oblonga cvs.

Quinces

Quinces look like rustic, lumpy yellow pears, often covered in pale fuzz, but their fragrance is as heady as a love potion, perfumey and complex. Not edible raw, quince flesh turns a delicate pink when cooked, which just enhances its appeal.

PICKING THE BEST
Choose quince that are large and fully yellow; greenish fruit may be underripe. Take a sniff—ripe quince will smell fruity and floral.

KEEPING IT FRESH
If your quince isn't completely yellow, store it on the counter until totally ripe, yellow all over, and quite fragrant. Once ripe, use quince quickly or it will turn mealy. Store ripe quince in a loose plastic bag in the refrigerator for up to 2 weeks.

PREPARING
Peel quince as you would an apple or pear; this can be a bit tricky because of their uneven shape. Use a large knife to cut it in half lengthwise, taking care because the fruit is hard and you'll need to use a bit of force. If using halved, cut out the seeds and core from the center using a stiff sharp knife (when raw, quince is generally too hard to use a melon baller for this); for quarters, chunks, or slices, simply slice away the center seed portion.

HOW TO USE IT
Quince really can't be eaten raw—it's very high in tannin which makes it unpalatably astringent, and it's also quite hard. Poaching is ideal because you can slowly tenderize the fruit while creating a flavorful poaching liquid to use in desserts; you should poach sliced quince before using in tarts, galettes, or strudels. You can slow-roast halved quinces, keeping them covered so they don't dry out, or add wedges or chunks to braised lamb or pork.

PRESERVING OPTIONS
Quince is very high in pectin and therefore makes excellent jams and jellies, as well as quince paste, called membrillo in Spain and Portugal.

Spiced Quince and Apple Sauce

MAKES ABOUT 4 CUPS

2 medium quinces, peeled, quartered, and cored

¼ cup sugar, plus more to taste

4 large sweet apples, such as Jonagold, peeled,
    quartered, and cored

One 3-inch cinnamon stick

½ vanilla bean, split

½ star anise

Put the quinces, ¼ cup sugar, and 1 cup water in a
heavy medium saucepan. Bring to a boil, reduce the
heat, and simmer, covered, stirring occasionally, until
the quinces turn pink and are beginning to soften,
about an hour. Add the apples, cinnamon stick,
vanilla bean, and star anise to the pan and continue
simmering, covered and stirring occasionally, for
another 45 minutes, or until all the fruit is very
tender. Taste for sweetness, and add a bit more sugar
if needed. Remove from the heat and let cool, then
fish out the spices and discard. Mash with a potato
masher or put through a food mill using a medium
disk. Serve slightly warm or cold.

Other recipe ideas

SAUTÉED QUINCE AND LEEKS Sauté sliced leeks in
butter until tender, then add slices of quince and
keep cooking until the quince is tender. Season with
some fresh rosemary and serve alongside seared
duck breast or pork chop.

SPANISH MEMBRILLO Cook chopped quince and
sugar until very thick. Pour into a mold and let set up
into a thick sweet paste, called membrillo. Slice and
serve with cheeses, especially manchego.

SPICED QUINCE GALETTE Simmer sliced quince in a
sugar syrup with a cinnamon stick, a chunk of ginger,
and a vanilla bean until tender; drain any excess
syrup, then spread the quince on a sheet of puff
pastry and bake until golden brown.

SEASONAL RELISH Simmer fresh cranberries with
finely diced quince, brown sugar, a few cloves, and
a tiny bit of cayenne until you have a chunky purée;
serve with roast turkey.

Brassica napus var. napobrassica

Rutabagas

Rutabagas aren't sexy, but their sweet yet snappy flavor—with hints of cabbage (their cousin)—gives them a well-deserved place at the table. Like all roots, they're good keepers and make delicious contributions to stews and braises.

PICKING THE BEST
Rutabagas are sometimes called swedes, yellow turnips, or wax turnips and can easily be confused with actual turnips. But rutabagas usually have yellow flesh and purple-tinged yellow skin, and they're bigger than turnips. Choose firm rutabagas that feel heavy for their size. The ideal size is under 4 inches in diameter.

KEEPING IT FRESH
If the greens are still attached when you buy your rutabaga, remove them before storing the bulb in a plastic bag in the refrigerator for up to 2 weeks.

PREPARING
Rutabagas are often sold coated in food-grade wax, which keeps them from drying out during winter storage, so a paring knife—rather than a vegetable peeler—is the best option for peeling. Before peeling a rutabaga, trim off the top and bottom; this gives you a flat surface on which to stand the vegetable and will eliminate wobbling. Cut into chunks, slices, or dice, depending on your recipe.

HOW TO USE IT
You can eat rutabagas raw, for example grated into a slaw-style salad, but generally they're cooked. Steam or boil, then mash; slice and add to a gratin or casserole; dice and toss into soups or stews; and toss chunks with oil and herbs and roast, either alone or with other root vegetables.

PRESERVING OPTIONS
You can freeze rutabagas by cutting into cubes, blanching for about 3 minutes, draining well, and then packing into airtight containers. Or make mashed rutabaga and freeze, tightly sealed.

RECIPES

Potato and Rutabaga Gratin with Blue Cheese

SERVES 6 TO 8

3 cups heavy cream

2 cloves garlic, peeled and smashed

1 bay leaf

2 hearty sprigs fresh thyme

Pinch of freshly grated nutmeg

3 tablespoons melted unsalted butter; more butter for the foil

1 medium rutabaga (about 1½ pounds), peeled, quartered, and very thinly sliced

2 to 3 russet potatoes (about 1½ pounds), peeled and very thinly sliced

Salt and freshly ground black pepper

4 ounces blue cheese, such as Maytag, Roquefort, or Bleu d'Auvergne, crumbled

3 tablespoons fresh breadcrumbs, toasted

Heat the oven to 375°F. Rinse a small saucepan in cold water (this will make the pan easier to clean later), add the cream, garlic, bay leaf, thyme, and nutmeg. Bring to just below a simmer over medium heat, remove from the heat, cover, and set aside to infuse for about 30 minutes.

Brush a large gratin dish or 3-quart flameproof casserole dish with a little of the melted butter. Arrange half of the rutabaga slices in the bottom of the dish, followed by half of the potato slices. Season with salt and pepper. Dot the surface with the blue cheese. Continue with another layer of rutabaga slices and a final layer of potatoes. Season the top with salt and pepper. Strain the seasoned cream over the top. In a small bowl, combine the breadcrumbs with the remaining melted butter and sprinkle over the top. Butter the dull side of a large sheet of foil and cover the gratin.

Bake for 40 minutes, remove the foil, and continue to bake until the top is browned, the sides are bubbly, and the potatoes are tender when pierced, another 30 to 40 minutes. Let rest for 10 minutes before serving.

Roasted Medley of Winter Roots

SERVES 6

½ pound parsnips, peeled and cut into 2-by ½-inch sticks

3 to 4 carrots, peeled and cut into 2-by ½-inch sticks

2 medium rutabagas, peeled and cut into ¾-inch dice

3 medium beets, peeled and cut into ¾-inch dice

10 to 12 cloves garlic

12 to 15 small white boiling onions, or 1 cup pearl onions (walnut size), peeled

3 sprigs fresh rosemary or thyme

3 small bay leaves

2½ tablespoons melted unsalted butter

1½ tablespoons vegetable oil

Salt and freshly ground black pepper

Heat the oven to 400°F. Dump the vegetables into a large, low-sided roasting pan or onto a heavy rimmed baking sheet; they should be just one layer deep. Toss in the herbs and drizzle on the butter and oil. Season with salt and pepper and toss to coat the vegetables evenly. Roast, tossing with a spatula a few times, until the vegetables are very tender and browned in spots, about 50 minutes. Discard the bay leaves. Serve warm.

Other recipe ideas

CREAMY HOT RUTABAGA PURÉE Simmer rutabagas until tender, then mash with salt, pepper, butter, and a bit of crème fraîche and freshly grated horseradish.

APPLE-RUTABAGA GRATIN Arrange a bed of caramelized onions in a baking dish, then layer slices of rutabaga with sliced apples on top. Season with some fresh thyme and bake until tender.

AUTUMN LAMB WITH RUTABAGA AND PEAR Braise lamb shanks with herbs and white wine, adding diced rutabaga about halfway through the cooking. Finish by folding in chunks of sautéed pear.

Ipomoea batatas cvs.

Sweet Potatoes

Sweet potatoes are beloved at the Thanksgiving table, but their earthy-sweet flavor and moist texture are welcome any time of year. They're rich in beta-carotene and vitamin C, helping us feel a little less guilty about indulging our starch cravings. And they're delicious whether baked, fried, sautéed, or braised in soups and stews.

they bruise easily. If baking them, look for uniformly sized ones so they'll cook at the same pace.

KEEPING IT FRESH

Stored in a dark, cool place with good air circulation, they'll keep for months. Although they'll get drier, they're still perfectly good. Baked sweet potatoes keep well in the fridge for a week or longer, so you can have them on hand to mash or use as twice-baked, in a soup, or just warmed up whole and brightened with a knob of herb butter or a spoonful of pesto.

HOW TO USE IT

Baking and roasting are perfect methods to bring out the toffee notes of sweet potatoes, but you can also fry them, slice and layer them in a gratin, or steam and mash them. They're most often used as a side dish, but of course sweet potato pie is a classic dessert.

SURPRISING PAIRINGS

Sugary accents such as marshmallows and brown sugar may be common, but a fantastic partner for a sweet potato is a fresh or dried chile. The spicy heat balances the sweetness, and the husky chile flavor brings a welcome complexity.

PICKING THE BEST

Sweet potatoes have thin, edible skins and come in a variety of colors. Orange is the most common and is usually moister and sweeter than yellow. You might even find purple varieties popping up at your grocery store. Whichever variety you choose, make sure they're firm and unblemished, and handle them with care, as

PRESERVING OPTIONS

You can bake sweet potatoes ahead and freeze them to reheat later. Wrap whole cooked potatoes in their skins individually in plastic wrap, then seal in airtight freezer bags.

DID YOU KNOW?   Although sweet potatoes are often labeled as "yams," they're not related to a true yam, which is starchy and dry with white flesh and thick dark skin.

Sweet Potato, Ham, and Goat Cheese Salad

SERVES 4

1 medium yellow onion, halved lengthwise and cut into ½-inch wedges

1 medium sweet potato, peeled and cut into ¼-inch rounds

½ cup extra-virgin olive oil

1¼ teaspoons chopped fresh rosemary

¾ teaspoon kosher salt, plus more to taste

½ teaspoon freshly ground black pepper, plus more to taste

¾ pound ham steak (preferably one labeled "ham with natural juices"), cut into ¾-inch cubes (2 cups)

2 tablespoons pure maple syrup

2 tablespoons balsamic vinegar

5 ounces mesclun salad mix

4 ounces fresh goat cheese, crumbled

Position a rack in the center of the oven and heat the oven to 450°F. Line a rimmed baking sheet with foil. On the baking sheet, toss the onion, sweet potato, 2 tablespoons of the oil, 1 teaspoon of the rosemary, ½ teaspoon salt, and ¼ teaspoon pepper and spread in a single layer. Roast until the vegetables start to become tender, about 15 minutes.

In a small bowl, toss the ham with the maple syrup. Push the vegetables on the baking sheet aside to make room for the ham and bake until the ham and onion are browned in places, about 10 minutes.

Meanwhile, in a small bowl, whisk the remaining 6 tablespoons oil with the vinegar, the remaining ¼ teaspoon rosemary, and ¼ teaspoon each salt and pepper. In a large bowl, toss the mesclun with ¼ cup of the vinaigrette. Season to taste with salt and pepper.

Portion the mesclun onto four plates. Top with the roasted vegetables and ham. Sprinkle each salad with some of the goat cheese. Drizzle with the remaining vinaigrette and serve.

Twice-Baked Sweet Potatoes with Chipotle Chile

SERVES 4

4 small sweet potatoes of similar size (about 3 pounds total), scrubbed

1 to 2 teaspoons olive oil or vegetable oil

¼ cup sour cream; more for serving

½ chipotle chile in adobo, minced to a paste, plus more to taste

2 tablespoons unsalted butter, softened

1 teaspoon kosher salt

1 lime, cut into quarters

Heat the oven to 425°F. Put the potatoes on a foil-lined baking sheet spaced as far apart as possible; rub with oil. Bake until a fork slips easily into the center of the potato, 50 to 55 minutes. Set on a rack to cool but leave the oven on.

When the potatoes are cool enough to handle, slice off about the top third (lengthwise) of each potato. Peel off and discard the skin from this top section and put the flesh in a medium bowl. Scoop out the rest of the flesh of each potato, leaving about ¼ inch of potato attached to the skin to help retain its structure. Put the potato flesh in the bowl.

Beat the sweet potato flesh, sour cream, chile paste, butter, and salt with an electric hand mixer on medium speed just until smooth. Taste and, if you want more heat, mince more chipotle to a paste and add it. Mound the mixture into the potato skins and set them in a baking pan. Bake the stuffed potatoes at 425°F until hot, 20 to 25 minutes. Serve with the lime wedges and more sour cream.

Other recipe ideas

SWEET POTATO GRATIN WITH RYE CRUMBS AND GRUYÈRE Make a potato gratin by layering alternating slices of sweet potato and russet potato with cream and grated Gruyère. Top with mustardy rye breadcrumbs and bake.

INDIAN-SPICED SWEET POTATO SOUP Purée roasted sweet potato, then simmer with ginger and curry spices; top with chopped apple, mint, and yogurt.

Beta vulgaris ssp. cicla and cvs.

Swiss Chard

A big, ruffly bunch of Swiss chard is one of the prettiest sights on a market display, whether the striking white and green of traditional Swiss chard or the day-glo pink, yellow, and red stems of varieties such as Bright Lights. But Swiss chard isn't just pretty—it's delicious, too, with an intense earthiness and a touch of minerality and a powerful dose of nutrition, including impressive amounts vitamins K, A, and C.

Bright Lights

Red

Green

Remove any twist ties from the greens. Lay the greens in the bags between the towels, close the bag tightly and refrigerate. The Swiss chard should stay fresh for 5 to 7 days this way.

PREPARING

Greens harbor grit, so they need thorough washing before cooking. Discard any yellowed or slimy leaves, and trim away tough stem ends. Cut out the stems by running a sharp knife along both sides of the stem, in a V cut, but don't discard the stems (see p. 308). Rinse and cut stems crosswise into slices or chunks, depending on your final recipe. Stack the leaves together and cut into ribbons, thin or thick, depending on your recipe. To wash the leaves, fill a large bowl with cool water and swish the Swiss chard around. Lift out the leaves and empty the silty water; repeat a few more times until no more grit shows up in the water. Let the Swiss chard dry on dishtowels or in a colander.

HOW TO USE IT

Swiss chard doesn't have the robust texture of some other greens such as kale or collards, so it's best with a thorough but light cooking method. One of the best ways to cook it is to simply wilt it and then season with oil, butter, and some aromatics to serve as a side dish, or use the wilted Swiss chard in soups, gratins, savory tarts, or pastas.

PICKING THE BEST

Choose Swiss chard with supple, glossy leaves and shiny stems that have moist, not split, ends.

KEEPING IT FRESH

Whether you clean the Swiss chard before you store it or just before cooking, you need to keep it barely moist but not wet enough to encourage rot. Line the largest zip-top bags you can find with paper towels.

PRESERVING OPTIONS

Swiss chard leaves freeze well, but the texture of Swiss chard stems doesn't fare well, so trim and discard. Blanch the leaves for a minute or two, then dry and seal in airtight freezer bags.

Bulgur Salad with Wilted Swiss Chard and Green Olives

SERVES 6 TO 8

1½ cups medium bulgur

1 tablespoon plus 1 teaspoon kosher salt, plus more to taste

1½ pounds Swiss chard (about 1 large or 2 small bunches), stemmed

¼ cup fresh lemon juice (from 1 to 2 lemons)

2 medium cloves garlic, minced and mashed to a paste with a pinch of salt

1 large shallot, finely diced

½ pound whole green olives, such as Picholines, rinsed well in warm water, pitted, and very coarsely chopped (1 cup)

½ cup coarsely chopped fresh cilantro

½ cup coarsely chopped fresh flat-leaf parsley

½ cup extra-virgin olive oil

Freshly ground black pepper

Bring a large pot of water to a boil. Put the bulgur and 1 teaspoon salt in a large bowl. Add 2¼ cups of the boiling water and cover the bowl. Let sit until the water has been absorbed and the bulgur is tender, about 1 hour.

Add 1 tablespoon salt to the remaining boiling water, add the Swiss chard, and cook until tender, 2 to 3 minutes. Drain the Swiss chard and run under cold water to cool. Thoroughly squeeze the chard to remove the excess liquid and chop to the same size as the chopped herbs. Lightly toss the Swiss chard so it doesn't remain in clumps when combined with the bulgur.

Combine the lemon juice, garlic, and shallot, and let sit for at least 15 minutes.

Gently fold the lemon juice mixture, chard, olives, cilantro, parsley, and olive oil into the bulgur. Season to taste with salt and pepper. Serve warm or at room temperature.

Swiss Chard with Lemon, Fennel, and Parmigiano

SERVES 8

4 large bunches Swiss chard (about 3½ pounds)

Kosher salt and freshly ground black pepper

2 cups thinly sliced fennel bulb, plus ½ cup chopped fronds (fronds optional)

2 medium lemons

6 tablespoons extra-virgin olive oil

6 medium cloves garlic, peeled and thinly sliced

½ cup freshly shaved Parmigiano-Reggiano (shave with a vegetable peeler)

Cut the chard stalks off just below each leaf and thinly slice the stalks. Chop the chard leaves into large pieces. Keep the stalks and leaves separate.

Bring a large, wide pot of salted water to a boil. Add the sliced fennel and chard stalks and cook for 3 minutes. Add the chard leaves and cook until tender, 3 to 5 minutes. Drain in a colander. Rinse and dry the pot.

Finely grate the zest from the lemons and set aside. Cut the top and bottom ends off the lemons, then stand each on a cut end and slice off the peel to expose the flesh. (Try to remove all of the bitter white pith.) Cut the lemon segments from the membranes, letting them drop into a small bowl.

Heat the oil and garlic in the pot over medium heat. When the garlic begins to sizzle, add the fennel fronds (if using) and the lemon segments and cook, stirring often, for 1 minute. Add the chard leaves and stems and fennel and cook, stirring, until heated through. Stir in the lemon zest and season to taste with salt and pepper. Serve, sprinkled with the Parmigiano.

Other recipe ideas

GARLICKY SWISS CHARD Sauté chard in fruity olive oil with minced garlic and slivered sun-dried tomatoes. Finish with hot sauce and a squeeze of lemon.

HEARTY PORTUGUESE SOUP Cook sliced onion, sliced Swiss chard stems, and garlic until fragrant, then add potatoes and some broth; cook until tender. Add a chiffonade of Swiss chard leaves, and browned chorizo sausage.

Brassica rapa cvs.

Turnips

Turnips may be a humble root vegetable, but they shine in the cold months, bringing an intriguing complexity to seasonal dishes. In frosty weather, the turnip plant converts more of the starch in the root into sugar, balancing its peppery upfront flavor; its open-grained texture does a remarkable job of absorbing the flavors of other ingredients during cooking.

PICKING THE BEST

Don't confuse turnips with their larger and sweeter cousins rutabagas (though the two can often be substituted for one another). Turnips are usually white-fleshed, with white or white and purple skin, while rutabagas have yellow flesh. You'll see a wider range of turnip shapes and sizes at farmer's markets; be on the lookout—usually during the spring—for tiny white Japanese or baby turnips, which are tender, silky, and sweet.

Look for turnips that feel firm and heavy for their size, whether large or small, with crisp flesh. Avoid turnips that are soft or flabby, or have brown, moist spots, which are signs of rot. Turnips tend to get woody as they grow, so the best ones are less than 4 inches in diameter.

KEEPING IT FRESH

Store turnips in a plastic bag in the refrigerator for up to a week for thin-skinned Japanese types or 2 weeks for sturdier varieties. If the turnips still have their greens attached, remove them before storing, because they can draw moisture out of the roots. If the turnip greens look fresh, they can be delicious, so store them separately, wrapped in a plastic bag with the air pressed out.

PREPARING

For baby or Japanese turnips, simply trim the roots and tops and rinse. For bigger turnips, peel off the skin and, on gnarly ones, the outer layer of flesh. Plan to cook the turnips shortly after peeling, because their cut surfaces can discolor and develop off flavors if allowed to stand.

HOW TO USE IT

You can think of turnips as you would most root vegetables—good for mashing, braising, roasting, or adding to stews and soups. Roasting is especially good at bringing out turnips' sweetness. Small turnips are delicious raw, either grated or cut into thin slices; they'd make an earthy-sweet change of pace on a crudité platter or as part of a salad, perhaps paired with radishes.

PRESERVING OPTIONS

You can freeze turnips by cutting them into ½-inch dice, blanching for 2 minutes, draining, and then packing into airtight freezer bags.

Slow-Sautéed Turnips and Carrots

SERVES 4

1½ tablespoons olive oil, preferably fruity and full flavored

1½ tablespoons unsalted butter

3 leeks (white and pale green parts only), halved lengthwise if large, cut into ½-inch rings, separated, well washed, and well drained (2 cups)

2 medium turnips (1 pound total), peeled and cut into ½-inch wedges (2¾ cups)

5 to 6 carrots (¾ pound total), peeled and sliced ⅜ inch thick on the diagonal (2 cups)

Salt and freshly ground black pepper

1 tablespoon coarsely chopped fresh tarragon or basil

2 teaspoons chopped fresh flat-leaf parsley

Set a heavy 9- to 10-inch skillet over high heat with the olive oil and butter. When the butter has melted, stir in the leeks, turnips, and carrots, and cook for 1 minute, stirring once or twice. Season with salt, cover, reduce the heat to medium low, and cook for 5 minutes. Uncover and cook at a medium sizzle, stirring occasionally, until the carrots and turnips are almost completely tender and are nicely—but lightly—browned, about 25 minutes. (After about 15 minutes, the vegetables should be just starting to brown, so lower the heat if they're cooking too quickly.)

Reduce the heat to very low and continue cooking until tender, about 5 minutes more. Turn off the heat, season to taste with pepper and more salt, if necessary. Gently fold in the tarragon or basil. Transfer to a warm serving dish, sprinkle with the parsley (or fold it in as well), and serve.

DID YOU KNOW? Turnips greens are edible—delicious, even—with a taste similar to collards, kale, or other hardy greens. Your best bet for good turnip greens is your own garden or the farmer's market, however, because they need to be fresh and not wilted. If you'd like to cook the greens, cut them off the turnips as soon as you get home and store them separately.

Cider-Glazed Turnips and Apples with Sage and Bacon

SERVES 4 TO 6

1½ pounds (about 9 small) turnips

4 slices bacon, cut into ½-inch pieces

2 tablespoons unsalted butter

1 cup apple cider

2 teaspoons sugar

1½ teaspoons kosher salt, plus more to taste

1 large firm, sweet apple such as Pink Lady or Braeburn

2 teaspoons chopped fresh sage

Freshly ground black pepper

Peel the turnips and cut them in half lengthwise. Cut each half into wedges 1 inch thick at the widest point.

Put the bacon pieces in a large skillet and set over medium heat. Cook, stirring occasionally, until crisp, about 8 minutes. Transfer to a plate lined with paper towels. Pour off the bacon fat from the pan and set the pan back on the burner. Add the butter and, when melted, add the turnips, apple cider, sugar, and salt. Bring to a boil over high heat. Cover the pan with the lid slightly askew, reduce the heat to medium high, and cook at a steady boil, shaking the pan occasionally, until the turnips are just tender but not soft (a paring knife should enter a turnip with just a little resistance), 8 to 10 minutes. Meanwhile, peel and core the apple and cut it into ½-inch slices.

Uncover the pan, add the apples and sage, and continue to boil, stirring occasionally, until the liquid has reduced to a sticky glaze, 2 to 3 minutes. The turnips should be soft and the apples should be crisp-tender. (If not, add a few tablespoons of water and continue to cook for another 1 to 2 minutes.) Toss in the cooked bacon and season to taste with black pepper and more salt if necessary.

Other recipe ideas

LAMB STEW WITH TURNIPS AND FENNEL Add baby turnips or turnip chunks to a spring lamb stew, along with fennel and new potatoes.

LEMON-PARMESAN TURNIPS Braise baby turnips in chicken broth until tender, then toss with grated Parmesan and lemon zest.

Cucurbita spp. and cvs.

Winter Squash

When stacks of hard winter squash start appearing at farmer's markets and roadside stands, you know that autumn is truly here. The dozens of different squash varieties in an array of green, orange, gold, and red displace the waning season's zucchini, tomatoes, and eggplant—inspiration to shift over to cold-weather cooking with the sweet, nutty flesh of a winter squash.

PICKING THE BEST

From single-serving-sized sweet dumpling to the behemoth Hubbard or pumpkins, squash varieties are as much about outer beauty as eating qualities. Most squash taste similar, with subtle differences in texture and sweetness. Here are some favorites:

- **Acorn:** These squash can be white, gold, or green. The white and gold have pale flesh, a grainy texture, and a bland, faintly nutty, sometimes acrid flavor. The green is most popular, with orange-yellow flesh and a sweet, nutty flavor and smooth texture that purées beautifully.

- **Butternut:** The finely grained, deep orange flesh has a rich, full, nutty-sweet flavor. Butternut, which weighs 1 to 2 pounds, is ideal for mashing, puréeing, and baking in gratins.

- **Delicata:** Perfect for serving two people, delicata often weighs less than a pound. These small squash have yellow or cream-colored skin with dark green stripes. Because of their thin, edible skin, they don't have a long shelf life, so inspect them carefully for bruises and cuts and store them at room temperature for no more than 2 weeks. Their moist flesh tastes like a combination of roasted corn and lemon zest and it becomes richer when roasted or sautéed.

- **Hubbard:** Probably the largest squash you'll find at the market, these teardrop-shaped behemoths are often sold in manageable chunks, so you can buy only what you need. They have thick skin that ranges from dark green to beautiful bluish gray and a dense, smooth, bright-gold flesh with an intense vegetable flavor that isn't as sweet as other squashes.

- **Kabocha:** A Japanese variety, these squat medium-sized squash have a rough, dark-green skin that's sometimes mottled with orange or faint white stripes. Their starchy yellow-orange flesh holds its shape when cooked in liquid, so they're great steamed or added to stews and braises. Their sweet, nutty flavor marries well with Asian ingredients like soy sauce, ginger, and sesame oil.

- **Rouge vif d'etampes:** With dark orange flesh that turns lighter orange around the seed cavity, it's slightly grainy with a fine flavor, making it a favorite for gratins and soups. Also known as French pumpkin, it can weigh from 2 to 20 pounds.

- **Spaghetti:** Named for the crisp spaghetti-like strands of their cooked flesh, these football-sized squash are more about texture than flavor. Once cooked, they make an unexpected ingredient in shredded vegetable salads or a great stand-in for spaghetti. Their mild flavor pairs well with just about any dressing or sauce.

- **Sugar pumpkin:** These small, round pumpkins have sweet, less fibrous flesh than your typical jack o' lan-

Swan White acorn

Delicata

Kabocha

Long Island
Cheese

Acorn

Carnival

tern pumpkins (which are not meant for eating), so these are good all-purpose cooking pumpkins.

- **Sweet dumpling:** When the skin turns creamy yellow streaked with orange, sweet dumplings are at their peak of flavor. The pale yellow-gold flesh is slightly grainy, with a distinctly nutty flavor. A small squash, often weighing less than a pound, sweet dumpling can be stubborn and difficult to cut through.

No matter which variety, choose squash that feel solid and heavy. As winter squash lose freshness, they dry out and become lighter, even spongy. The skin should be hard with no signs of softness.

KEEPING IT FRESH

Winter squash are great keepers. Protected from easy spoilage by their hard skin, most winter squash will last a month or longer stored in a cool, dry place—in the basement or garage or on a kitchen counter. Hubbards can be stored for up to 5 months. Don't store squash for long at temperatures lower than 50°F, however, because they deteriorate. Once the squash has been cut open, it should be wrapped tightly in plastic, refrigerated, and used within 3 or 4 days.

PREPARING

The biggest challenge with winter squash is cutting one open. Use a large, sharp knife and watch where your fingers are placed! See how to cut winter squash on p. 309. Winter squash with less formidable skins, such as delicata and butternut, can be sliced into halves or rounds. Once a winter squash is cut open, remove the seeds and any particularly fibrous strings surrounding the seed cavity by scraping out with a spoon. You can leave the skin on for baking or steaming the squash, but otherwise peel it before cooking, using a sturdy vegetable peeler or a sharp paring knife.

HOW TO USE IT

Winter squash are extremely versatile, though rarely eaten without cooking. Puréed for a soup or cubed and roasted with fresh herbs, they can be prepared many ways and adapted to recipes for almost every course.

PRESERVING OPTIONS

To freeze winter squash up to 6 months, steam or roast it, then cut into chunks or mash. Freeze in airtight freezer bags.

Butternut Squash Ravioli with Rosemary Oil

SERVES 6

½ pound butternut squash, peeled, seeded, and cut into ½-inch dice (1½ cups)

¼ cup extra-virgin olive oil

1 tablespoon plus ½ teaspoon kosher salt

1 clove garlic, minced

1½ teaspoons minced fresh rosemary

¼ cup heavy cream

¼ cup freshly grated Parmigiano-Reggiano; more for serving

Freshly ground black pepper

36 square or round wonton wrappers

Put the squash, ⅔ cup water, 1 tablespoon of the oil, and a scant ½ teaspoon salt in a large, deep sauté pan. Turn the heat to high until the water simmers; cover and steam the squash until it's just tender and the water has just evaporated, 5 to 6 minutes; check often. Stir in the garlic and ½ teaspoon of the rosemary; sauté until fragrant, about 1 minute. Transfer to a food processor and add the cream, Parmigiano, and a few grinds of pepper. Process, scraping the bowl as needed, until the mixture is mostly smooth.

While the squash cools slightly, wash the sauté pan and fill it with 2 quarts water and 1 tablespoon salt; bring to a simmer over medium-high heat.

With a large wire rack and a small bowl of water close by, lay six wonton wrappers on a clean, dry countertop. Drop a rounded teaspoon of filling in the center of each wrapper. Brush the edges of each wrapper with a little water. Fold each wrapper to create a triangle or half moon, pushing out any air bubbles and pressing the edges to seal completely. Transfer the ravioli to the wire rack; repeat with the remaining wonton wrappers and filling, making sure the countertop is dry after each batch.

Heat the remaining 3 tablespoons oil and 1 teaspoon rosemary in a small skillet or saucepan over medium heat. When the rosemary starts to sizzle, take the pan off the heat.

Drop half of the ravioli into the simmering water in the sauté pan. Cook until the wrapper over the filling starts to wrinkle and the ravioli turn translucent, 3 to 4 minutes. With a large slotted spoon, transfer six ravioli to each of three pasta plates. Repeat to cook the remaining ravioli. Drizzle each portion of the ravioli with 2 teaspoons of the pasta cooking water and 1 teaspoon of the rosemary oil, sprinkle with a little Parmigiano, and serve immediately.

Beef Ragù over Spaghetti Squash with Garlic Bread

SERVES 4

¼ baguette, halved lengthwise

1½ tablespoons unsalted butter, melted

6 medium cloves garlic

½ teaspoon kosher salt; more as needed

¼ teaspoon freshly ground black pepper, plus
    more to taste

1 small (2½-pound) spaghetti squash, halved
    lengthwise and seeded

1 tablespoon extra-virgin olive oil

1 pound lean ground beef

1 small yellow onion, finely chopped

One 15-ounce can crushed tomatoes

¼ cup coarsely chopped fresh basil

¼ cup freshly grated Parmigiano-Reggiano

Heat the oven to 375°F. Arrange the bread cut side up on a foil-lined baking sheet. Brush it with the butter. Peel and chop the garlic. Divide the garlic in half and sprinkle one-half with a generous pinch of salt. Using the flat side of a chef's knife, mince and mash the garlic and salt together to form a smooth paste. Spread each piece of bread evenly with garlic paste and season with salt and pepper. Bake until light golden brown and crisp, 12 to 14 minutes. Cut each piece in half to make 4 pieces total, and cover with foil to keep warm.

Meanwhile, arrange the spaghetti squash in a single layer in the bottom of a large, wide pot. (Don't worry if the squash halves don't lie completely flat in the pot.) Add ½ inch of water, cover the pot, and bring to a boil. Reduce to a simmer and cook until the squash is tender enough to shred when raked with a fork but still somewhat crisp, 15 to 20 minutes. Transfer the squash to a plate and set aside until cool enough to handle.

While the squash cooks, heat the oil in a 12-inch skillet over medium-high heat. Add the beef, the remaining chopped garlic, the onion, ½ teaspoon salt, and ¼ teaspoon pepper; cook, stirring to break up the meat, until just cooked through, 5 to 6 minutes. Drain and discard the fat if necessary. Add the tomatoes, basil, and ¼ cup water; stir well and bring to a boil. Reduce the heat to medium low and simmer for 10 minutes. Season to taste with salt and pepper.

With a fork, rake the squash flesh into strands, transfer to plates, and season to taste with salt. Ladle the beef ragù over the squash and garnish with the Parmigiano. Serve with the garlic bread.

Roasted Hubbard Squash Soup with Hazelnuts and Chives

SERVES 8 TO 10

3 tablespoons extra-virgin olive oil

3 large cloves garlic

1 tablespoon coriander seeds

1½ teaspoons fennel seeds

1½ teaspoons dried sage

1 small (5½- to 6-pound) Hubbard squash, halved
    lengthwise and seeded

2 tablespoons unsalted butter

1 large leek (white and light green parts only),
    halved lengthwise and thinly sliced crosswise and
    thoroughly rinsed

2 medium carrots, cut into small dice

1 teaspoon kosher salt; more as needed

5 cups homemade or reduced-sodium chicken or
    vegetable broth

1 bay leaf

2 teaspoons fresh lemon juice

Freshly ground black pepper

½ cup hazelnuts, toasted, skinned, and chopped

2 tablespoons thinly sliced chives

Several small pinches of Espelette pepper or cayenne

Position a rack in the center of the oven and heat the oven to 400°F. Line a heavy-duty rimmed baking sheet with parchment.

In a mortar and pestle, pound the oil, garlic, coriander seeds, fennel seeds, and sage until they resemble a coarse paste. Rub the spice mixture on the flesh of the squash halves. Set them cut side down on the prepared pan and roast until tender when pierced with a fork, about 1 hour. Let cool, cut side up. When cool enough to handle, scrape the flesh away from the rind—you'll need about 5 cups.

Melt the butter in a 5- to 6-quart Dutch oven over medium heat. Add the leek, carrot, and a big pinch of salt and cook, stirring occasionally, until the leek is softened, 8 to 10 minutes. Add the squash, broth, bay leaf, and 1 teaspoon salt and bring to a boil over high heat. Reduce the heat to a low simmer, cover, and cook for 30 minutes to develop the soup's flavor.

Remove the bay leaf and allow the soup to cool slightly. Purée the soup in batches in a blender. (Be careful to fill the blender no more than one-third full and hold a towel over the lid while you turn it on.) Return the soup to the pot and add the lemon juice. Season to taste with salt and pepper. Garnish with the chopped hazelnuts, chives, and Espelette pepper or cayenne.

Soy-Braised Kabocha Squash

SERVES 4 TO 6

¼ cup reduced-sodium chicken or vegetable broth

3 tablespoons reduced-sodium soy sauce

1 tablespoon sugar

1 tablespoon rice wine (sake) or dry sherry

2 tablespoons vegetable oil

4 scallions, thinly sliced, green and white parts separated

1 tablespoon minced garlic

1 tablespoon minced fresh ginger

½ medium kabocha squash, peeled, seeded, and cut into ¾-inch chunks (3½ to 4 cups)

Combine the broth, soy sauce, sugar, rice wine, and ⅓ cup water in a small bowl. Stir to dissolve the sugar and set aside.

Heat the oil in a wok or 12-inch skillet over medium heat until hot. Add the white parts of the scallions, the garlic, and ginger and cook, stirring constantly, until fragrant but not brown, 30 seconds. Add the squash, increase the heat to medium high, and cook, stirring occasionally, until the squash begins to soften and the aromatics brown slightly, about 3 minutes.

Reduce the heat to medium, add the soy sauce mixture, and stir, scraping the pan with the spoon to loosen any browned bits. Cover and simmer until the squash is just tender when pierced with a fork, 4 to 6 minutes. Transfer to a serving dish and garnish with the scallion greens.

Roasted Acorn Squash with Five Flavor Variations

SERVES 2

1 acorn squash (about 1¼ pounds)

¼ teaspoon coarse salt

Seasonings from the variations below

MAPLE SEASONING

1½ tablespoons unsalted butter, softened

2 tablespoons pure maple syrup

2 tablespoons chopped pecans (optional; add during last 10 minutes of cooking) or 1½ teaspoons minced fresh ginger (optional)

BROWN SUGAR SEASONING

1½ tablespoons unsalted butter, softened

1½ tablespoons brown sugar

APPLE CIDER SEASONING

1½ tablespoons unsalted butter, softened

2 tablespoons apple cider mixed with 1 tablespoon honey and a pinch of ground cinnamon

ORANGE CURRY SEASONING

1½ tablespoons unsalted butter, softened

2 tablespoons orange juice mixed with 1 tablespoon honey, 1 teaspoon minced fresh ginger, and a big pinch of curry powder

PARMESAN THYME SEASONING

2 tablespoons olive oil

1 tablespoon freshly grated Parmigiano-Reggiano

¼ teaspoon chopped fresh thyme

Heat the oven to 400°F. Slice a thin piece off both ends of the squash, including the stem. Cut the squash in half crosswise (perpendicular to the ribs). Scoop out the seeds with a sturdy spoon.

Line a rimmed baking sheet, jellyroll pan, or shallow baking dish with foil or parchment. (If you're only cooking two halves, be sure to use a small pan that the squash will fit into somewhat snugly.) If you use foil, rub it with butter to keep the squash from sticking.

Set the squash halves on the prepared baking sheet and smear the flesh all over with the softened butter (for the Parmesan Thyme Squash, just drizzle the olive oil all over). Sprinkle with the salt. Sprinkle or drizzle the remaining ingredients over the top edge of the squash and into the cavity (most of the liquid will pool up there).

Roast the squash halves until nicely browned and very tender (poke in several places with a fork to test), about 1 hour and 15 minutes for small to medium squash; larger squash may take longer. Don't undercook. Serve warm with a spoon.

Butternut Squash and Potato Gratin with Walnut Crust

SERVES 9

1 butternut squash (about 2 pounds), peeled
2 Idaho potatoes (about 1¼ pounds total), peeled
Kosher salt and freshly ground black pepper
6 tablespoons grated Parmigiano-Reggiano
1 cup heavy cream
½ cup finely chopped walnuts
½ cup fresh breadcrumbs combined with
    2 tablespoons melted unsalted butter

Heat the oven to 350°F. Grease an 8-inch-square (2-quart) glass or ceramic baking dish. Cut the squash in half lengthwise and scrape out the seeds and fibers. Slice the squash and potatoes about ⅛ inch thick (use a mandoline if you have one). Line the bottom of the baking dish with a layer of squash (overlapping slightly), season lightly with salt and pepper, sprinkle with a little of the Parmigiano, and drizzle with a little of the cream. Cover with a layer of potato slices, season with salt, pepper, Parmigiano, and cream. Repeat with the remaining squash and potatoes until the dish is full, ending with a top layer of squash, seasoned and topped with any remaining cheese and cream. (You may have extra squash.) Press down lightly to distribute the cream and compact the layers. The last layer of squash should be just sitting in the cream, but not covered by it. Cover the dish with foil and bake until the vegetables feel tender when poked with a thin, sharp knife (check the middle layer), about 1 hour and 10 minutes.

Combine the walnuts and buttered breadcrumbs. Remove the gratin from the oven, sprinkle with the breadcrumb-nut mixture, and bake until the top is lightly browned, 5 to 10 minutes. Let sit in a warm place for 20 minutes before serving so that liquids will set and tighten the gratin. Cut into 9 squares and serve.

Delicata Squash with Caramelized Shallots and Sherry

SERVES 4

1¼ pounds delicata squash (1 large)
2 tablespoons olive oil
¼ cup dry sherry (such as fino)
½ teaspoon kosher salt; more as needed
Freshly ground black pepper
1 tablespoon unsalted butter
1 cup thinly sliced shallot (2 to 3 large)
4 teaspoons finely chopped fresh sage

Heat the oven to 350°F. Peel the squash, leaving the skin in the crevices. Trim the ends. Cut the squash in half lengthwise and scoop out the seeds. Slice the halves crosswise ½ inch thick.

Heat 1 tablespoon of the oil in a 10-inch skillet over medium-high heat. Add half of the squash in a single layer and cook without moving until the slices begin to brown, about 2 minutes. Flip and cook until the second side begins to brown, 1 to 2 minutes. Transfer to a 9x13-inch baking dish. Repeat with the remaining squash. Arrange the squash in a single layer in the dish. Sprinkle with 2 tablespoons of the sherry, ½ teaspoon salt, and a few grinds of pepper.

Heat the remaining 1 tablespoon oil and the butter in the skillet over medium heat. Add the shallot and a pinch of salt; cook, stirring frequently, until the shallot is deep golden brown on the edges, 3 to 5 minutes. Take the pan off the heat; add the sage and remaining 2 tablespoons sherry, scraping up the browned bits from the pan. Scatter the shallots on the squash.

Cover the pan with foil and bake until the squash is tender when pierced with a fork, 25 to 30 minutes. Season to taste with salt and pepper.

Other recipe ideas

ROASTED SQUASH SALAD Dice butternut or other fine-grained winter squash, toss with olive oil and rosemary, salt, and pepper, and roast until tender. Arrange on a bed of frisée dressed with a Dijon-maple vinaigrette; top with crumbled bacon.

CURRIED WINTER SQUASH Simmer cubes of winter squash with cumin, coriander, and ginger plus canned tomatoes, chickpeas, and diced green chiles in coconut milk. Serve over rice with chopped cilantro.

Winter

- Avocados
- Bananas
- Bean Sprouts
- Ginger
- Grapefruit
- Kiwi
- Lemons
- Limes
- Mangos
- Oranges and Mandarins
- Passionfruit
- Pineapple
- Pomegranates
- Sunchokes

Avocados

Beneath the almost reptilian skin of an avocado lies vibrant, two-toned yellow-green flesh that's unlike any other fruit. It's smooth, buttery, and rich rather than sweet and juicy, making it perfect as a luscious condiment or dip.

Zutano

Hass

know an avocado is ready to eat when it gives a little when pressed. Avocados might need a few days at room temperature to ripen, so plan ahead.

KEEPING IT FRESH

To ripen, leave avocados at room temperature, or put in a bag with a banana to speed things up. Once ripe, refrigerate and they'll last a few more days. Exposed flesh discolors quickly, so use or serve soon after preparing. Lemon or lime juice slows the discoloration, as will storing it tightly wrapped in the refrigerator.

PREPARING

Slice in half lengthwise around the pit. Twist the two halves in opposite directions, then pull apart. Carefully but firmly lodge the blade of a chef's knife into the pit and use the knife to twist the pit out. (Scrape the pit from the knife against the edge of the sink.)

There are several ways to remove the flesh from the skin. Hold the avocado in the palm of your hand and, using a large spoon, carefully scoop out the flesh. You can also slice or dice the flesh before you scoop it out, just be sure not to pierce the skin. Cut in diagonal slices or, if cubes are your goal, make a second set of diagonal slices perpendicular to the first (see p. 295). Carefully scoop out the slices or cubes.

HOW TO USE IT

Use avocados raw—they get bitter when cooked. They're excellent mashed into guacamole or other sauces, puréed and mixed with yogurt or buttermilk for a chilled soup, or diced and tossed in salsas or salads.

PRESERVING OPTIONS

Avocado purée freezes well for use in sandwiches and dips. For every two puréed avocados, add 1 tablespoon lemon juice. Pack into airtight containers, with 1 inch of headspace, and freeze for up to 5 months.

PICKING THE BEST

Of the several varieties of avocado available commercially, the Hass and the Fuerte are the most common. The Hass has rough skin that ranges from dark green to purply black. The Fuerte is larger with smoother, emerald-green skin. Look for fruit that is average to large, oval-shaped, and heavy for its size. Hass avocados will turn dark green to nearly black as they ripen, but other varieties retain their light-green skin even when ripe. Avocados only ripen once picked. You'll

RECIPES

Avocado, Mango, and Pineapple Salad with Pistachios and Pickled Shallots

SERVES 4 TO 6

1 medium shallot (1 to 2 ounces), sliced into very thin rings

2 tablespoons Champagne vinegar or rice vinegar

¼ teaspoon kosher salt; more as needed

3 tablespoons extra-virgin olive oil

1 teaspoon red-wine vinegar

2 cups baby arugula or watercress

¼ cup roasted, salted pistachios, coarsely chopped

1 tablespoon thinly sliced fresh mint

1 tablespoon thinly sliced fresh basil

Freshly ground black pepper

3 medium firm-ripe avocados (6 to 7 ounces each), pitted, peeled, and sliced lengthwise ¼ inch thick

2 kiwis, peeled, halved, and sliced ¼ inch thick

1 medium mango, pitted, peeled, and sliced lengthwise ¼ inch thick

½ medium pineapple, peeled, cored, and cut into ½-inch dice (about 2 cups)

In a medium bowl, toss the shallot with the Champagne vinegar and a pinch of salt and set aside for 10 minutes, stirring once. Drain the shallot into a small bowl and reserve the vinegar. Whisk the olive oil and red-wine vinegar into the shallot vinegar.

In a medium bowl, toss 1 tablespoon of the vinaigrette with the pickled shallots, arugula or watercress, pistachios, mint, basil, ¼ teaspoon salt, and a few grinds of pepper. Arrange the avocado, kiwi, mango, and pineapple on a platter. Drizzle with the remaining vinaigrette and season to taste with salt and pepper. Top with the arugula mixture and serve immediately.

Spiced Shrimp and Avocado Toasts

MAKES 16 CANAPÉS

16 large shrimp (about ½ pound), peeled, deveined, rinsed, and patted dry

¾ teaspoon kosher salt

Freshly ground black pepper

1 teaspoon chili powder, plus more to taste

2 tablespoons extra-virgin olive oil

2 small ripe avocados (about 12 ounces total)

1 tablespoon fresh lime juice; more for sprinkling

3 tablespoons chopped fresh cilantro, plus 16 whole leaves for garnish

16 thin slices toasted baguette

Season the shrimp with ¼ teaspoon salt, a few grinds of pepper, and 1 teaspoon chili powder. Set a heavy 10-inch skillet over medium-high heat for 1 minute. Add the oil and shrimp and sauté, stirring occasionally, until the shrimp are opaque and firm to the touch, about 2 minutes. Transfer to a cutting board.

Pit the avocados and scoop the flesh into a small bowl. Add 1 tablespoon lime juice, the chopped cilantro, and a pinch of chili powder. Mash with a fork until relatively smooth and season with a heaping ½ teaspoon salt and a few grinds of pepper. Slice the shrimp in half lengthwise.

To assemble, spread the mashed avocado over the toasts. Top each with two halved pieces of shrimp and a cilantro leaf, sprinkle with lime juice and salt, and serve.

Other recipe ideas

BLACK BEAN AND AVOCADO QUESADILLA Stuff a cheese and black bean quesadilla with diced avocado.

TOMATILLO-AVOCADO SALSA Stir mashed avocado into puréed tomatillo, scallion, garlic, and Serrano chile; season with salt and hot sauce.

ENHANCE A SANDWICH Stack a BLT with some sliced avocado, add some finely diced avocado to a tuna sandwich, or add a layer of sliced avocado to a grilled cheese before you grill it.

Musa acuminata cvs.

Bananas

Sweet with a honey-like flavor, bananas have a comforting custardy texture, and their peel-and-eat nature makes them a convenient snack. But they are also nutritious, with large amounts of potassium, vitamin C, vitamin B6, and fiber.

PICKING THE BEST

There aren't a lot of choices in "regular" bananas—they're almost all the same variety—but you can find some options, especially at Hispanic markets.

- **Baby:** Also called niño or ladyfinger bananas, these have a firm texture and luscious flavor, and their petite size is visually appealing.
- **Cavendish:** Reliable and easy to harvest, this is the most widely available commercial variety. Some agricultural experts think the dominance of this variety makes the world supply vulnerable to disease.
- **Plantains:** In the same family as bananas, but they're larger, with more starch and very little sweetness. They're cooked like a vegetable rather than eaten raw.
- **Red:** With reddish purple skin and slightly pink, creamy flesh, they're often sweeter than yellow bananas, with a touch of raspberry flavor. When ripe, their skins should have a purple hue.

Look for bananas with no cracks or bruises. Buy them tinged with green if you don't plan to eat them right away—they will keep ripening at room temperature. To choose a fully ripe banana, look for one that's completely yellow with a few black spots freckling the skin. It should give slightly when touched, peel easily, and have a fruity, fragrant aroma.

KEEPING IT FRESH

If you find yourself with too many ripe bananas on your hands, you can refrigerate them for a few days. The skin may turn black but the flesh will be fine.

PREPARING

For baking, simply mash the peeled bananas with a fork or purée in a food processor. For grilling or sautéing, use a ripe but still firm banana and slice it lengthwise in half or cut long slices on the diagonal. For stews and braises, just cut into chunks. When using bananas raw, as in a salad or relish, toss the pieces with lemon juice to keep them from discoloring.

HOW TO USE IT

Bananas are mostly eaten out of hand, but very ripe ones are delicious in a smoothie or a batter for quick breads and muffins. Green or barely ripe bananas are delicious in savory dishes such as Caribbean stews and curries, chutneys, and salsas. Firm-ripe bananas caramelize beautifully on the grill or in a sauté pan.

Plantains, with their firmer, starchier consistency, can be baked, grilled, boiled, sautéed, mashed like potatoes, or fried into delicious chips.

PRESERVING OPTIONS

Bananas darken when cooked or exposed to air, so are difficult to preserve beyond freezing (whole or sliced) or drying chips in a food dehydrator. Freezing turns the bananas rather mushy, so they're best used in baked goods and smoothies once thawed.

Plantain

Ecuadorian baby

Costa Rican Red

Common

Brown-Butter Banana Cake with Chocolate Chips

SERVES 12

8 ounces (1 cup) unsalted butter; more for the pan

1⅓ cups sugar

3 large eggs

1 cup finely mashed ripe bananas (2 medium)

1 teaspoon pure vanilla extract

½ teaspoon salt

7½ ounces (1⅔ cups) unbleached all-purpose flour; more for the pan

1¼ teaspoons baking soda

⅔ cup mini semisweet chocolate chips

Position a rack in the center of the oven and heat the oven to 350°F. Butter and flour a 10-cup decorative tube or Bundt pan. Tap out any excess flour.

Melt the butter in a medium saucepan over medium-low heat. Once the butter is melted, cook it slowly, letting it bubble, until it smells nutty or like butterscotch and turns a deep golden hue, 5 to 10 minutes. If the butter splatters, reduce the heat to low. Remove the pan from the heat and pour the browned butter through a fine sieve into a medium bowl and discard the bits in the sieve. Let the butter cool until it's very warm rather than boiling hot, 5 to 10 minutes.

Using a whisk, stir the sugar and eggs into the butter. (Since the butter is quite warm, you can use cold eggs for this.) Whisk until the mixture is smooth (the sugar may still be somewhat grainy), 30 to 60 seconds. Whisk in the mashed bananas, vanilla, and salt. Sift the flour and baking soda directly onto the batter. Pour the chocolate chips over the flour. Using a rubber spatula, stir just until the batter is uniformly combined. Don't overmix.

Spoon the batter into the prepared pan, spreading it evenly with the rubber spatula. Bake until a skewer inserted in the center comes out with only moist crumbs clinging to it, 42 to 45 minutes. Set the pan

on a rack to cool for 15 minutes. Invert the cake onto the rack and remove the pan. Let cool until just warm and then serve immediately or wrap well in plastic and store at room temperature for up to 5 days.

Banana-Caramel Tart

SERVES 12

One 14-ounce can sweetened condensed milk (preferably Eagle® brand)

6 ounces (1⅓ cups) unbleached all-purpose flour

¼ cup plus 2 teaspoons sugar

½ teaspoon salt

4 ounces (½ cup) unsalted butter, cut into ⅜-inch dice and chilled well

1 pint (2 cups) heavy cream

1 large egg yolk

4 ripe bananas

¼ teaspoon instant coffee granules

½ teaspoon pure vanilla extract

Make the caramel: Fill the base pan of a double boiler (or a medium saucepan) halfway with water. Bring to a boil and then reduce the heat to medium for an active simmer (just shy of a boil). Pour the sweetened condensed milk into the double boiler's top insert (or into a stainless-steel bowl that fits snugly on top of the saucepan) and set over the simmering water. Every 45 minutes, check the water level in the pot and give the milk a stir. Replenish with more hot water as needed. Once the milk has thickened to the consistency of pudding and has turned a rich, dark caramel color, 2½ to 3 hours, remove from the heat, let cool, and cover.

Make the crust: Meanwhile, combine the flour, ¼ cup of the sugar, and salt in a food processor. Pulse to combine. Add the butter pieces and gently toss to lightly coat with flour. Blend the butter and flour mixture with about five 1-second pulses (count "one one-thousand" with each pulse) or until the mixture is the texture of coarse meal with some of the butter

DID YOU KNOW? A cluster of bananas is called a hand. A single banana is called a finger. And if you're tired of picking those bitter stringy bits off the flesh of the fruit, peel it from the bottom instead of the top.

pieces the size of peas. In a small bowl, whisk 2½ tablespoons of the cream with the egg yolk and pour over the flour mixture. Process continuously until the mixture turns golden in color and thickens in texture yet is still crumbly, about 10 seconds.

Transfer the mixture to a medium-large bowl and press the mixture together with your hand until it comes together into a ball. Shape the dough into an 8-inch-wide disk and put it in the center of an 8½- to 9-inch fluted tart pan with a removable bottom. Beginning in the center of the dough and working out toward the edges, use your fingertips to gently press the dough evenly into the bottom and up the pan sides. The edges should be flush with the top edge of the pan. If you find a spot that's especially thick, pinch away some of the dough and use it to bulk up a thin spot. Cover with plastic wrap and freeze for 1 hour.

Position a rack in the center of the oven and heat the oven to 400°F. Right before baking, line the dough with aluminum foil and cover with pie weights or dried beans. Bake on the lower oven rack for 20 minutes. Carefully lift the foil (along with the weights) out of the tart pan, lower the oven temperature to 375°F, and bake until the crust is deep golden brown, about 15 minutes. Transfer the tart pan to a wire rack to cool to room temperature.

Assemble the tart: Spread the caramel over the crust using a rubber spatula or offset spatula. If the caramel has cooled and is too firm to spread easily, reheat it over simmering water in the double boiler until loosened but not hot. Slice each banana in half lengthwise and arrange the halves on top of the caramel in a circular pattern. To fit the banana halves snugly in the center of the pan, cut them into smaller lengths.

Put the coffee granules in a small zip-top bag. Press a rolling pin back and forth over the granules to crush them into a powder.

In a chilled medium stainless-steel bowl, beat the remaining heavy cream, the vanilla, and the remaining 2 teaspoons sugar with an electric mixer at medium-high speed until it holds soft peaks when the beaters are lifted. Spoon the whipped cream over the bananas, sprinkle with the coffee powder, remove the pan sides, and serve.

Open-Faced Chocolate Banana-Cream Sandwiches

SERVES 6

1 cup heavy cream
½ teaspoon sugar
2 ounces (4 tablespoons) unsalted butter
3 slightly underripe bananas, peeled and sliced
    ½ inch thick on the diagonal
2 tablespoons dark rum
1 tablespoon honey
Pinch of kosher salt
½ cup chopped semisweet chocolate or morsels
    (about 3½ ounces)
6 digestive tea biscuits (such as Carr's®)

Whip the cream with the sugar to medium-soft peaks in a medium bowl; refrigerate.

Melt 3 tablespoons of the butter in a 10-inch sauté pan over medium-high heat until the milk solids in the butter start turning brown. Add the bananas in a single layer and cook without stirring until they brown, about 1 minute. Flip with a spatula and brown the other side. Add the rum and then add the honey, the remaining 1 tablespoon butter, and the salt. Stir and flip very gently until the bananas are evenly coated. Take off the heat and keep warm.

Melt the chocolate over a double boiler or in the microwave. Stir in 2 to 3 tablespoons water to thin the chocolate to a pourable consistency.

Set the biscuits on six dessert plates, spoon the bananas on them, and drizzle with the melted chocolate. Top with a dollop of the cream and serve immediately.

Other recipe ideas

GRILLED CARAMEL BANANAS Split ripe but firm bananas lengthwise, brush with melted butter, then grill until soft and slightly browned. Drizzle with caramel sauce and serve with ice cream.

BREAKFAST SMOOTHIE Purée ripe bananas, yogurt, frozen strawberries, and a splash of orange juice.

BANANA-PEACH SABAYON Arrange thickly sliced bananas and peaches in a gratin pan, top with some rum-flavored sabayon, and broil until lightly browned.

Vigna radiata

Bean Sprouts

Thick mung bean sprouts, often used in stir-fries, are perhaps the most well-known, but sprouts from lentils, radishes, or soy beans have a delicious earthy flavor and a crisp texture. While the flavor of most sprouts is delicate to bland, the texture is uniquely appealing: succulent and crisp for the thicker mung bean sprouts, light and springy for the more delicate varieties.

Clover

Mung bean / Pea

Alfalfa

ing roots, sliminess, or a musty odor are all signs that sprouts may be over the hill. To avoid risk of food-borne illness, the USDA recommends that sprouts be stored at 32°F, which is colder than most grocery store produce shelves. If the sprouts on display don't look fresh, ask if there are more in the cooler, which will be at a colder temperature.

KEEPING IT FRESH
If not using sprouts that day, rinse them in a colander under cold water, transfer them to a zip-top bag lined with paper towels, and store in the crisper. If you need to keep them more than a couple of days, try storing them submerged in a covered container of ice water in the refrigerator, changing the water and adding more ice daily. This can keep sprouts fresh for up to 5 days.

PREPARING
Whether for eating raw or for cooking, all you need to do is wash and dry them as you would a salad green.

HOW TO USE IT
Mung bean sprouts show up in many Asian soups and stir-fries, generally just tossed in toward the end of cooking; cooking for more than a few minutes will make sprouts soggy. The more delicate sprouts, such as alfalfa sprouts, should only be used fresh and are most often used as a garnish for sandwiches or salads, but they could also make a fine topping for grilled fish or chicken.

PICKING THE BEST
Look for sprouts that have crisp white roots with yellow and light green leaves, ideally with their seed buds still attached. Sprouts are very perishable, and darken-

DID YOU KNOW? You can grow your own sprouts, from mung, adzuki, or garbanzo beans, alfalfa and other grain seeds, lentils, peppery vegetables such as radishes, and lots more. You simply need to follow a process of soaking, rinsing, and draining—usually with the help of a sprouting container—and within a few days, you can have your own very fresh sprouts.

RECIPES

Quick Shrimp Pad Thai

SERVES 2

3 ounces dried wide (pad thai) rice noodles

2 tablespoons fish sauce

2 tablespoons sugar

1 tablespoon soy sauce

1 teaspoon hoisin sauce

1 teaspoon chile-garlic sauce (such as Lee Kum Kee®
  brand)

1 teaspoon vegetable oil

1 teaspoon minced garlic

6 ounces medium shrimp (51 to 60 per pound),
  peeled and deveined (to yield 1 cup)

One 4-ounce can fire-roasted whole green chiles
  (such as Ortega® brand), drained and sliced into
  long, very thin slivers (to yield ½ cup)

1½ cups bean sprouts

2 tablespoons crushed unsalted roasted peanuts

⅓ cup coarsely chopped fresh cilantro

10 fresh mint leaves, torn into small pieces

1 lime, cut into wedges, for serving

Submerge the rice noodles in a bowl of very warm
(110°F) water and soak until they're pliable but still
rather firm, about 30 minutes. Meanwhile, prep
the rest of the ingredients. Drain the noodles in a
colander (no need to pat dry).

In a small bowl, combine the fish sauce, sugar, soy
sauce, hoisin sauce, and chile-garlic sauce.

Once the noodles are drained, heat the oil in a
large (12-inch) skillet or stir-fry pan over high heat
until very hot. Add the garlic, stir, and immediately
add the shrimp. Stir-fry until the shrimp turn pink
and firm, 2 to 3 minutes. Add the fish sauce mixture.
Stir to mix for about 20 seconds, then add the chile
slivers and the noodles. Stir-fry until the noodles
are tender and the liquid is absorbed, 1 to 2 minutes.
If the noodles are too firm, add 1 tablespoon water
and cook for another minute. Add the bean sprouts
and stir-fry until they're slightly limp, 1 to 2 minutes.
Transfer to a serving platter or individual plates and
garnish with the peanuts, cilantro, and mint. Serve
immediately, with lime wedges on the side.

Other recipe ideas

CRUNCHY SPROUT AND CABBAGE SLAW
Toss sprouts into an Asian-style slaw made with
Napa cabbage, julienned carrots, sliced scallion,
chopped peanuts, sliced jalapeño, cilantro, mint, and
lime juice with a touch of peanut oil.

SPROUT-TOPPED GRILLED CHICKEN SANDWICH Layer
good artisan bread with slices of grilled chicken,
some roasted red pepper, and shredded Monterey
Jack cheese. Broil until the cheese bubbles, and then
top with sprouts that are dressed with soy sauce,
grated fresh ginger, and rice vinegar.

SOOTHING ASIAN CHICKEN SOUP Season chicken
soup with fresh ginger and garlic and add finely
sliced bok choy and some bean sprouts; simmer for a
few minutes, then drizzle with Asian sesame oil.

Ginger

Fresh ginger's light spiciness, tangy freshness, warmth, and mellow sweetness complement a range of dishes, from sweet to savory. It can be a dominant flavoring, or it can work in conjunction with other flavors; it works in ethnic dishes as well as familiar comfort foods.

PICKING THE BEST

Ginger's character varies with age. Young ginger (harvested after 6 months) is tender, juicy, and sweet, while older ginger (harvested between 10 and 12 months) is more fibrous and spicy. Look for young ginger in Asian markets. It will have thin, papery skin and pink-tinged tips. Fibrous older ginger can be used in braised dishes and broths.

Avoid discolored or moldy ginger. Look for ginger—the pieces with multiple knobs are called "hands"—with thin, smooth, unblemished skin. If you break off a knob, the texture should be firm, crisp, and not overly fibrous (making it easier to slice), with a fresh, spicy fragrance.

KEEPING IT FRESH

There are many opinions on how to store ginger. In our test kitchen, we found unpeeled ginger stored in a zip-top bag stayed fresh and wrinkle-free for 8 weeks. Or submerge peeled in vodka; dry well before using, then peel away the outermost layer to remove any alcohol.

PREPARING

With very young ginger, leave the skin on. For more mature ginger, remove it, unless you're just slicing the ginger to infuse into a liquid, where it will be removed. Instead of a peeler, use the edge of a spoon to scrape off the skin. It takes a bit more effort than a paring knife or a peeler, but it's less wasteful.

Slice ginger into planks or matchsticks, or chop, mince, grate, or purée it, depending on use.

HOW TO USE IT

Ginger's flavor fades as it cooks, so for more oomph, add some or all at the end of cooking.

Thin slivers of ginger become irresistibly crisp and chewy when roasted with other vegetables, while small bits of minced ginger in pilafs, stir-fries, or salads provide bursts of warm, spicy flavor. Use planks or slices to infuse flavor into a broth.

For only flavor, grate the ginger using a rasp-style grater; grating eliminates any ginger fibers.

PRESERVING OPTIONS

Freeze a whole hand of fresh ginger in an airtight zip-top freezer bag for up to 4 months, or slice into coins, wrap in plastic, and retrieve only the amount you need. The texture will be slightly mushy but the flavor is fine for adding to cooked dishes.

Gingery Sautéed Carrots

SERVES 2 TO 3

1 tablespoon pure maple syrup

2 teaspoons fresh lime juice

2 tablespoons unsalted butter

1 tablespoon extra-virgin olive oil

1 pound carrots, trimmed, peeled, and cut into sticks about 4 inches long and ⅓ inch wide

¾ teaspoon kosher salt

1 tablespoon minced fresh ginger

Combine the maple syrup, lime juice, and 1 tablespoon water in a small dish and set near the stove. Set a shallow serving dish near the stove, too.

In a 10-inch straight-sided sauté pan, heat 1 tablespoon of the butter with the olive oil over medium-high heat. When the butter is melted, add the carrots and season with the salt. Toss with tongs to coat well. Cook, gently tossing occasionally at first and then more frequently, until most of the carrots are well browned and tender when pierced with a fork, 6 to 9 minutes (if the carrots aren't fully tender but look like they're burning, reduce the heat to medium).

Reduce the heat to low, add the remaining 1 tablespoon butter and the ginger and cook, stirring and scraping the bottom of the pan with a heatproof rubber spatula, until the butter has melted and the ginger is fragrant, 15 to 20 seconds. Carefully add the maple syrup mixture and cook, stirring, until the liquid reduces to a glazy consistency that coats the carrots, 15 to 20 seconds.

Immediately transfer the carrots to the serving dish, scraping the pan with the spatula to get all of the gingery sauce. Let sit for a few minutes and then serve warm.

Ginger Ice Cream

MAKES 3½ CUPS; SERVES 4

2 cups heavy cream

1 cup whole milk

2 ounces fresh ginger, peeled and roughly chopped (to yield a generous ⅓ cup)

¾ cup sugar

5 large egg yolks

½ teaspoons pure vanilla extract

In a heavy saucepan, combine the cream, milk, ginger, and half of the sugar. Stir and bring to a boil over medium-high heat. Remove from the heat and let stand for 1 hour to allow the ginger to infuse into the cream and milk. Reheat the mixture until hot but not boiling (175°F on an instant-read thermometer).

Meanwhile, use a whisk or hand-held mixer to beat the remaining sugar and the yolks in a medium bowl until thick and pale yellow, about 2 minutes. Whisk about ½ cup of the hot cream mixture into the yolk mixture, and then stir the warmed yolk mixture back into the remaining cream. Heat the mixture slowly over medium low, stirring constantly, until it's thick enough to coat the back of a wooden spoon and a line drawn on the spoon with a fingertip remains intact (180°F on an instant-read thermometer).

Remove from the heat and strain through a fine-mesh sieve into a medium bowl. Stir in the vanilla. Set the bowl in a larger bowl filled with ice water and stir the custard occasionally until it reaches room temperature. Cover the bowl and refrigerate until cold (about 40°F), about 1 hour. Freeze in an ice-cream maker, following the manufacturer's instructions.

Other recipe ideas

FRESH GINGER SYRUP Infuse a sugar syrup with fresh ginger slices. Add the syrup to iced tea or fresh lemonade, or pour it over fresh or poached fruit.

ALL-PURPOSE GINGER MARINADE Make a quick marinade by combining minced ginger, minced garlic, soy sauce, and Asian sesame oil.

CRUNCHY GINGER GARNISH Fry thin matchsticks of ginger until crisp to top sautéed fish.

Citrus x paradisi and cvs.

Grapefruit

Nothing beats the zing of plain, unadulterated grapefruit for breakfast. But the juicy flesh and perfumed zest of this sweet-tart fruit also add a real spark to all kinds of dishes, from salads to desserts. Grapefruit is so juicy that it's like two treats in one: enjoy the segments first, then squeeze the rinds to release a refreshing juice as a chaser.

Pomelo

Red

Look for firm fruit that feels heavy for its size, with plump, glossy skin. Generally the thinner the skin, the juicier the fruit.

KEEPING IT FRESH
Store grapefruit at room temperature for up to a week or in the produce drawer of your refrigerator for up to 3 weeks.

PREPARING
To eat as a snack, peel the skin from the flesh and separate the segments with your hands, or cut in half along the equator and cut around the membrane of each segment to eat with a spoon. To release the segments with no membrane attached, see the technique on p. 304. Grapefruit zest is a nice addition to certain salads and salsas, but it is more bitter than other citrus skin, so you may want to blanch it several times to tame the harshness before adding it to your recipe. And beware of grapefruit pith, which is intensely bitter (it's used to flavor tonic water).

HOW TO USE IT
Eating out of hand is the most obvious—and highly satisfying—way to enjoy grapefruit, but tossing segments into salads, salsas, or pan sauces is an easy way to add juicy bright flavor to food. A twist of grapefruit zest makes a nice change from lemon or lime in drinks where a little bitterness is welcome.

PICKING THE BEST
Grapefruit falls into two basic types, based on the color of the flesh: white and pink (which includes red). This flesh color is not an indication of sweetness, which is more attributed to the season—grapefruit picked early are sour, but the same variety will turn sweeter as the season progresses; the peak of sweetness and flavor happens around March. Regardless of color, the varieties are all similar, with the main difference being the number (or lack) of seeds.

PRESERVING OPTIONS
Candying the peel is a great way to preserve the bright flavor of grapefruit. Use as a garnish for iced tea, lemonade, or cocktails, or chop and add to cake batters, fillings, frostings, salad dressings, pan sauces, braises, or stews.

Broiled Grapefruit with Honey, Vanilla, and Cardamom

SERVES 4

2 large grapefruit

2 tablespoons honey

1 teaspoon pure vanilla extract

Seeds of 1 cardamom pod, ground in a mortar (or a pinch of ground cardamom)

Position a rack about 4 inches below the broiler and heat the broiler on high. With a serrated knife, cut the grapefruit in even halves at the equator. Using a small paring knife or a grapefruit knife, cut each section away from the surrounding membrane. Set the grapefruit halves in a shallow broiler-safe pan (such as an enameled baking dish or a heavy-duty rimmed baking sheet). If necessary, trim a thin slice off their bottoms so they sit level.

In a small bowl, combine the honey and vanilla. Drizzle the honey mixture over the grapefruit halves. Dust each with a bit of the cardamom. Broil until bubbling and lightly browned in spots, 4 to 6 minutes. Remove from the oven and let cool slightly. Serve warm or at room temperature.

Grapefruit Upside-Down Cake with Rosemary

MAKES ONE 10-INCH CAKE

8 ounces (2 cups) slivered almonds, toasted

2 tablespoons coarsely chopped fresh rosemary

2 tablespoons honey

2 teaspoons pure vanilla extract

12 ounces (1½ cups) unsalted butter; more for the pan

2 cups sugar; more for the pan

4½ ounces (1 cup) unbleached all-purpose flour

10 large egg whites

2 grapefruit, peel and pith removed, sectioned, and drained on a paper towel

In a food processor, pulverize the toasted almonds to a fine powder and set aside. Finely chop 1 tablespoon of the coarsely chopped rosemary.

In a small bowl, stir together the finely chopped rosemary, the honey, and vanilla and set aside. In a heavy medium saucepan, melt the butter with the remaining 1 tablespoon rosemary. Cook until the butter begins to brown and has a nutty, slightly smoky aroma, about 10 minutes; don't let it burn. Let cool to room temperature.

Butter the bottom and sides of a 10-inch round springform pan with 3-inch sides. Line the bottom with a round of parchment; butter the parchment and dust it lightly with sugar. In a large bowl, mix the sugar, flour, and almonds. In another bowl, beat the egg whites to soft peaks. Strain the butter into the dry ingredients. Add the honey mixture; mix thoroughly. Fold in the egg whites until incorporated.

Position a rack in the center of the oven and heat the oven to 350°F. Arrange the grapefruit sections in one layer on the bottom of the prepared pan. Pour the batter over the fruit. Bake until the cake is well risen, firm on top, and a toothpick stuck into the center comes out clean, 65 to 75 minutes. (You may want to put a piece of foil on the oven's lower shelf to catch any drips.) Let the cake cool in the pan on a rack for 15 minutes. Set a serving plate over the cake pan and invert the cake onto the plate. Gently lift off the pan. Slice and serve warm.

Other recipe ideas

GRAPEFRUIT-CABBAGE SLAW Toss finely shredded cabbage and thinly sliced fresh chile in some salt and grapefruit juice; let sit until slightly wilted, then top with grapefruit segments and chunks of avocado; drizzle with olive oil.

HERBED GRAPEFRUIT-MANGO SALSA Combine grapefruit sections, diced mango, chopped red bell pepper, lime and grapefruit juice, olive oil, and lots of chopped herbs (basil, cilantro, or mint) to make a salsa for grilled chicken, fish, or meat.

WINTER CITRUS AND VANILLA BEAN SALAD Simmer simple syrup with a vanilla bean, lemon zest, and a little grapefruit zest, then pour over grapefruit and orange segments (include some blood oranges if you can) and let steep for at least 20 minutes.

Actinidia deliciosa and cvs.

Kiwi

Kiwi is an odd little fruit, which is part of its appeal. Small, egg-shaped, and covered in a fine layer of soft brown hair, a kiwi has flesh that's bright green and studded with tiny, black edible seeds. Kiwis' bright, tropical, and decidedly sweet-tart flavor make them perfect for snacking as well as for livening up a fruit salad. A bonus: A small kiwi delivers about the same amount of vitamin C as an orange.

PICKING THE BEST

It's better to select a slightly firm kiwi and then let it ripen and soften a bit before using rather than picking ones that feel quite soft in the store—they're often bruised and overripe. Ideally the flesh will yield just slightly when pressed, like a ripe pear.

Kiwi has a smaller, smoother relative as well, called hardy kiwi or kiwiberry. These are about the size of a grape, have no fuzz on the skin, and are generally sweeter than regular kiwi.

KEEPING IT FRESH

Allow unripe kiwis to soften at room temperature; put them in a bag with a banana to speed things up. Store ripe kiwis loosely covered in a plastic bag in the refrigerator for 3 to 5 days.

PREPARING

There are two ways to eat kiwi. The fuzzy brown skin is not edible, so you can either halve the kiwi and scoop out the flesh with a spoon, or you can peel and slice the fruit. Hardy kiwis need nothing more than a rinse.

HOW TO USE IT

While you could cook a kiwi, the delicate flesh is really best raw, used in fruit salad, salsas, or on top of a fruit tart or other pastry.

PRESERVING OPTIONS

You can use kiwi in jams and preserves, but for the best texture and color, mix with other fruit such as strawberries. And kiwi freezes well in slices or when crushed and sweetened to be used later in jams.

Grilled Mixed Fruits with Island Spices and Dark Rum

SERVES 4

¼ teaspoon ground cinnamon

¼ teaspoon ground allspice

⅛ teaspoon ground ginger

Pinch of ground nutmeg

Pinch of ground cloves

½ cup dark rum

1 tablespoon brown sugar

½ tablespoon honey

2 tablespoons pineapple juice (canned is fine)

Juice from ½ lime

1 medium pineapple, peeled, eyes removed, and cored

6 ounces firm-ripe strawberries, hulled

3 firm-ripe mangos, pitted and peeled

3 kiwis, peeled

½ cup confectioners' sugar

Combine the cinnamon, allspice, ginger, nutmeg, and cloves; set aside. In a small bowl, combine the rum, brown sugar, honey, pineapple juice, and lime juice; set aside.

Leave small fruits, such as strawberries, whole; cut others into 1- to 1½-inch cubes. Thread the fruit on skewers, alternating contrasting colors. Sprinkle the spices over the kebabs. Shortly before grilling, baste the kebabs with half of the rum marinade and dust generously with confectioners' sugar to promote caramelization. Grill over a moderately hot fire until the fruit begins to show grill marks. Turn and continue to grill until the fruit has softened and browned nicely. Take care not to burn the strawberries. Drizzle the remaining marinade over the kebabs and serve immediately.

Tropical Salsa

MAKES 4½ CUPS

1 cup diced mango (1 large mango)

1 cup diced papaya (1 large papaya)

⅓ cup diced kiwi (2 small kiwis)

1 cup diced pineapple

⅓ cup diced red bell pepper

¼ cup diced red onion

¼ cup packed fresh cilantro leaves, minced

1 or 2 jalapeños, cored, seeded, and minced

1 tablespoon fresh lime juice

Pinch of salt

Pinch of cayenne

Combine all the ingredients in a large bowl and toss gently. Taste and adjust the seasonings.

Other recipe ideas

KIWI-LIME SORBET Purée kiwis, sweeten with simple syrup, and flavor with lime juice, then freeze to make a sorbet or granita.

MIXED GREENS WITH KIWI Toss chunked kiwis into a green salad for a refreshing burst of flavor. Dress with a light raspberry vinaigrette.

TROPICAL PAVLOVA Top the meringue base of a pavlova with slices of kiwi, mango, and strawberries.

DID YOU KNOW? Kiwi contains an enzyme similar to the one in papayas and pineapple that prevents gelatin from setting. The enzymes can also create off flavors when it's in contact with dairy products for a long time, such as in a frozen dessert. So if you plan to use kiwi in ice cream or frozen cream pies, for example, you need to cook it first; freezing does not inactivate the enzyme.

Meyer

Lisbon

Citrus limon and cvs.

Lemons

The bracing tartness of lemon seems just the thing we crave during the winter months, which is when lemons and other citrus are at their best and most abundant. It's hard to conceive of cooking without a cheerful lemon at our side—the zest full of heady perfume and the juice ready to give a bright edge to whatever we squeeze it over or into.

PICKING THE BEST

Most lemons are one of two varieties, Lisbon and Eureka, which are the most common varieties grown in California and Arizona. The two are virtually identical and have a common flavor profile—the tart, acidic flavor we associate with lemons. A third supermarket variety, Bearss, is grown in Florida and is also quite similar in flavor.

Look for lemons that seem heavy for their size, promising more juice, and select ones with plump, glossy skin—indications that the rind will be rich in flavorful oils.

Meyer lemons are not true lemons but believed to be a cross between a lemon and a mandarin or orange. Meyer lemons are thinner- and smoother-skinned, rounder in shape, and have a deeper yellow-orange hue. They spoil easily, also, so be sure there are no patches of softness or mold on your Meyers. Though not exactly sweet, Meyers are less acidic than regular lemons, and their zest and juice have herbal, even floral undertones that can add a wonderful nuance to any recipe calling for lemons. Since they are more delicate, Meyer lemons are harder to ship and are rare at supermarkets, but during their season (winter to early spring), they can often be found at specialty grocers.

KEEPING IT FRESH

If you use lemons daily, you can simply keep them in a basket right on your kitchen counter. For longer storage, store lemons in the refrigerator in a plastic bag, but don't crowd them because they're prone to molding.

PREPARING

Lemons yield two flavorful components—the fragrant zest and the tangy juice. To zest a lemon, use a rasp-style grater, which easily turns a lemon rind into a pile of tiny, feather-light bits without digging into the bitter white pith. You can also use a citrus zester with four or five small holes for making long, thin strips, or use a sharp vegetable peeler and a knife to make strips or to mince zest.

For juicing, a plastic or wooden reamer is a fine choice, but a citrus press is an even more efficient tool. As with limes, if you roll your fruit on the counter with medium pressure before cutting and juicing, it will yield more juice.

HOW TO USE IT

Use lemon in anything that wants a lift, from apple pie filling to zucchini bread. The zest carries much of the "lemony" flavor, with the juice delivering the acidic zing. If you want to preserve the flavor, add grated

271

zest near the end of cooking, but you can add a strip of pared zest early to a stew or sauce and let the flavor infuse slowly. Lemon segments also are a nice addition to rich sauces for fish or chicken, and very thin slices of whole lemons are delicious when roasted until crisp.

If you're substituting Meyer lemons for regular lemons, your recipe may need less sugar than usual or a bit more acid from a regular lemon or some vinegar.

SURPRISING PAIRINGS

While lemon partners with virtually any flavor and is a natural with fresh herbs, there is a lovely affinity between lemon and rosemary. This citrus-herb pairing works in savory dishes but also in sweet; a lemon-rosemary granita or lemonade is super-refreshing summer fare.

PRESERVING OPTIONS

Lemons are a bit too tart to make marmalade on their own but can be combined with other citrus. Lemon juice freezes well, if you find yourself with a surfeit of lemons. And look to North Africa for a brilliant way to turn fresh lemons into a preserved zesty condiment.

.... RECIPES ....

Lemon Pudding Cakes

SERVES 8

Softened butter for the ramekins

2 ounces (4 tablespoons) unsalted butter, melted and
cooled slightly

1 cup sugar

3 large eggs, separated, at room temperature

¼ cup unbleached all-purpose flour

¼ plus ⅛ teaspoon salt

1¼ cups whole milk, at room temperature

⅓ cup fresh lemon juice, at room temperature

1 tablespoon finely grated lemon zest

Lightly sweetened whipped cream, for serving
(optional)

Position a rack in the center of the oven and heat the oven to 350°F. Butter eight 6-ounce ceramic ovenproof ramekins or Pyrex custard cups and arrange them in a baking dish or roasting pan (a 10x15-inch or two 8x8-inch Pyrex dishes work well).

In a large bowl, whisk the melted butter with ⅔ cup of the sugar and the egg yolks until smooth and light, about 1 minute. Add the flour and salt and pour in just enough milk to whisk the flour smoothly into the egg yolk mixture. Then whisk in the remaining milk and the lemon juice until smooth. The mixture will be very fluid.

Put the egg whites in a large bowl. Beat with an electric mixer (a hand-held or a stand mixer fitted with the whisk attachment) on medium speed until the whites begin to foam, 30 to 60 seconds. Increase the speed to high and beat just until the whites hold soft peaks when the beater is pulled away, another 1 to 2 minutes. Reduce the mixer speed to medium. With the mixer running, very slowly sprinkle in the remaining ⅓ cup sugar; this should take about a minute. Stop the mixer and scrape the bowl. Beat on high speed until the whites hold medium-firm peaks when the beater is pulled away, about another 30 seconds.

Scrape one-third of the egg whites into the egg yolk mixture, sprinkle the lemon zest on top, and whisk until combined. Gently incorporate the remaining whites into the batter, using the whisk in a folding/stirring motion. The batter will still be thin.

Portion the mixture evenly among the ramekins; the cakes don't rise much, so you can fill the ramekins to within 1/8 inch of the top. Pull out the oven rack and put the baking dish full of ramekins on the rack. Pour warm water into the dish to reach halfway up the sides of the ramekins. Bake until the tops of the cakes are light golden and slightly puffed, and when touched with a finger, they should feel spongy and spring back a bit but hold a shallow indentation, 25 to 30 minutes. Using tongs, carefully transfer the ramekins to a rack. Let cool to room temperature and then refrigerate for at least 2 hours and up to 24 hours before serving, with whipped cream if you like.

Lemon Curd

MAKES ABOUT 2 CUPS

3 ounces (6 tablespoons) unsalted butter, softened at room temperature

1 cup sugar

2 large eggs

2 large egg yolks

2/3 cup fresh lemon juice

1 teaspoon grated lemon zest

In a large bowl, beat the butter and sugar with an electric mixer, about 2 minutes. Slowly add the eggs and yolks. Beat for 1 minute. Mix in the lemon juice. The mixture will look curdled, but it will smooth out as it cooks.

In a medium heavy-based saucepan, cook the mixture over low heat until it looks smooth. (The curdled appearance disappears as the butter in the mixture melts.) Increase the heat to medium and cook, stirring constantly, until the mixture thickens, about 15 minutes. It should leave a path on the back of a spoon and will read 170°F on a thermometer. Don't let the mixture boil.

Remove the curd from the heat; stir in the lemon zest. Transfer the curd to a bowl. Press plastic wrap on the surface of the lemon curd to keep a skin from forming and chill the curd in the refrigerator. The curd will thicken further as it cools. Covered tightly, it will keep in the refrigerator for a week and in the freezer for 2 months.

Lemon-Rosemary Sorbet

MAKES 3½ CUPS

1½ cups sugar

1½ cups water

½ cup finely chopped fresh rosemary

1⅓ cups fresh lemon juice

3 tablespoons vodka

In a saucepan, combine the sugar and water over high heat. Stir occasionally until the sugar is completely dissolved and the syrup is simmering, about 5 minutes. Remove from the heat. You should have about 2 cups syrup.

Combine the warm syrup with the rosemary, lemon juice, and vodka. Stir well to combine, and then let the mixture cool to room temperature. For faster freezing, transfer the cooled mixture to the refrigerator to chill there first.

Strain the mixture and then freeze it in an ice-cream maker, following the manufacturer's instructions.

Other recipe ideas

LEMON GREMOLATA GARNISH Chop together the zest of a lemon with plenty of parsley and garlic until everything is finely minced. Add a generous grind of black pepper and strew over roasted or braised meats, pasta dishes, and just about anything grilled.

LEMON-ANCHOVY SAUCE Make a finishing sauce for broiled or grilled fish by mixing minced anchovies, grated garlic, lemon zest and juice, a little olive oil, and some freshly ground pepper. Drizzle a couple of teaspoons over each serving of fish.

LEMON-ROASTED CHICKEN Stuff the cavity of a whole chicken with lemon quarters and herbs before roasting. Then stir the lemon quarters through the pan drippings before making a pan sauce.

Citrus aurantifolia and cvs.

Limes

Limes entice first by their deep green color and next by their perfume, which is citrusy yet very floral. Keeping a few limes in the fridge ensures that you can perk up the flavor of anything from a cool glass of water to a spicy salsa.

Persian

Key

PICKING THE BEST

There are two main varieties of this small green citrus fruit: the Persian lime and the Key lime. The most common and widely available is the Persian lime, which is about the size of a small lemon with thin green skin. The Key lime, which is much rarer, is smaller, more acidic, and has a strong, citrusy aroma. Key limes have thinner skin, which tends to be yellow-green or completely yellow when ripe.

For both types of lime, look for ones that seem heavy for their size, promising more juice. Also keep an eye out for plump, glossy skin—indications that the rind will be rich in flavorful oils. Choose Persian limes that are about 2 inches in diameter, fragrant, and plump, with smooth, medium-green skin. Choose Key limes that are about 1½ inches in diameter with smooth greenish-yellow or yellow skin and a strong lime aroma.

KEEPING IT FRESH

If you plan to use limes within a day or two, you can store them at room temperature. For storage beyond a couple of days, keep them somewhere cool and dry, preferably in a basket or net bag to allow for air circulation, which prevents mold. And store limes in the refrigerator for up to 2 weeks.

PREPARING

To remove the fragrant green zest, use a rasp-style grater, which easily shreds the thin rind into feather-light bits without digging into the bitter white pith beneath.

For juicing, a plastic or wooden reamer is a fine choice, but a citrus press is even more efficient if you're juicing a lot of limes. If you roll the lime on the counter with medium pressure before cutting and juicing, it will yield more juice.

HOW TO USE IT

Limes are mostly used for their juice, but the zest contains flavorful oils and therefore adds both flavor and fragrance to dishes. Add zest at the end of cooking to preserve its flavor. Juice can be added at any point in cooking, but generally a spritz of lime juice to finish is the best approach.

SURPRISING PAIRINGS

Not really a surprise to anyone who's had a margarita, but salt and limes have a wonderful affinity. The salt could take the form of soy sauce or fish sauce, as well as regular salt, which is why limes integrate so well into many Asian cuisines. Thai limeade, which is sweet but with a decidedly salty edge, is addictively refreshing.

PRESERVING OPTIONS

You can preserve limes in the same way you would make preserved lemons to use in stews, tagines, and salads. Limes also make a zesty marmalade. If you have an abundance of limes, you can juice them and freeze the juice in ice cube trays or other small containers.

DID YOU KNOW?

Wild limes are a different fruit. Native to Southeast Asia, they're small, bright green citrus fruits with bumpy, wrinkled skin. Both the peel and the pulp deliver vibrant citrus flavor and are deeply aromatic, but even the leaves are good for cooking. Used widely in Southeast Asian cuisine, especially in curries, wild lime leaves give dishes a refreshing, lingering lift that is intensely floral and citrusy. Until recently these were most commonly called kaffir limes, but that term is deemed derogatory in some languages, so wild or Asian lime is now used.

Grilled Corn on the Cob with Lime-Cayenne Butter

SERVES 8 TO 10

4 ounces (½ cup) unsalted butter
Juice of 1 lime
1 teaspoon kosher salt
½ teaspoon cayenne
8 to 10 ears sweet corn

Melt the butter in a small saucepan and stir in the lime juice, salt, and cayenne. Keep warm.

Peel off all but one or two layers of the corn husks. Pull the remaining husks down, but not off, and remove the bulk of the silks (the rest will come off easily after they char). Pull up the husks; it's okay if some kernels peek through.

Prepare a hot charcoal fire or heat a gas grill to high. Put the corn on the grate while the coals are still red-hot (cover a gas grill). Grill the corn, turning often, until the outer layer of husk is completely charred. Depending on your fire, this could take from 5 to 10 minutes. You can push the corn to a cooler spot if you're grilling other things for your meal, or transfer the grilled corn to a platter and keep it warm in the charred husks.

Just before serving, peel off the husk and brush away any remaining silks. Brown the kernels on the grill briefly, turning the corn frequently to develop a roasty color and a little additional smoke flavor, about 1 minute. (If the corn spends too long on the grill without the protection of the husk, the kernels will become dry and a bit chewy.)

Brush the warm lime-cayenne butter on the hot grilled corn and serve immediately.

Creamy Lime Ricotta Tart
in a Gingersnap Crust

SERVES 12

One 15-ounce container whole-milk ricotta (about
   1½ cups)

3 ounces cream cheese, at room temperature

¾ cup sugar

2 tablespoons unbleached all-purpose flour

¼ teaspoon salt

3 large egg yolks

1 tablespoon finely grated lime zest

1 tablespoon lime juice

1 Press-in Cookie Crust (made with gingersnaps),
   baked and cooled (recipe follows)

Strips of lime zest, for garnish

Position a rack in the center of the oven and heat the oven to 350°F. In a medium bowl, combine the ricotta and cream cheese. Using an electric mixer, beat on medium speed until well blended and no lumps remain, about 3 minutes. Add the sugar, flour, and salt and continue beating until well blended, about 1 minute. Add the egg yolks, lime zest, and lime juice. Beat until just incorporated. Use a rubber spatula to scrape the filling into the crust and spread the filling evenly.

Bake the tart until the filling just barely jiggles when the pan is nudged, 30 to 35 minutes. Let cool completely on a rack. Refrigerate the tart in the pan until chilled and firm, 2 to 3 hours. Serve garnished with strips of lime zest.

Press-In Cookie Crust

MAKES A CRUST FOR ONE 9½-INCH TART

1 cup finely ground cookies (ground in a food
   processor); choose from one of the following:
   about 25 chocolate wafers, 8 whole graham
   crackers, 20 gingersnaps, or 35 vanilla wafers

2 tablespoons sugar

1½ ounces (3 tablespoons) unsalted butter, melted

Position a rack in the center of the oven and heat the oven to 350°F. Have ready an ungreased 9½-inch fluted tart pan with a removable bottom.

In a medium bowl, mix the cookie crumbs and sugar with a fork until well blended. Drizzle the melted butter over the crumbs and mix with the fork or your fingers until the crumbs are evenly moistened. Put the crumbs in the tart pan and use your hands to spread the crumbs so that they coat the bottom of the pan and start to climb the sides. Use your fingers to pinch and press some of the crumbs around the inside edge of the pan to cover the sides evenly and create a wall a scant ¼ inch thick. Redistribute the remaining crumbs evenly over the bottom of the pan and press firmly to make a compact layer. (Use a metal measuring cup with straight sides and a flat base for this task.)

Bake the crust until it smells nutty and fragrant (crusts made with lighter-colored cookies will brown slightly), about 10 minutes. Set the baked crust on a rack and let cool. The crust can be made up to 1 day ahead of filling and stored at room temperature, wrapped well in plastic.

Tandoori Chicken

SERVES 4 TO 6

FOR THE MARINADE

One 2-inch piece fresh ginger, peeled

4 large cloves garlic

¼ teaspoon turmeric

1 teaspoon chili powder

1½ teaspoons salt

½ teaspoon cumin seeds, ground

¾ cup plain low-fat yogurt

1 tablespoon fresh lime juice

A few drops of red food coloring or tandoori coloring
   (optional)

FOR THE CHICKEN

2 to 3 pounds boneless chicken thighs and breasts

2 ounces (4 tablespoons) melted butter or olive oil

FOR THE GARNISH

½ mild onion, thinly sliced

½ cup chopped fresh cilantro leaves

1 or 2 fresh green chiles, thinly sliced

1 lime, cut into wedges

Make the marinade: In a blender or food processor, blend the ginger and garlic to a fine paste (you may need to add a little water to make a paste). Add the turmeric, chili powder, salt, cumin, yogurt, lime juice, and food coloring, if using; process until combined.

Prepare the chicken: Remove the skin from the chicken, leaving some fat. Make a few slits in each piece and transfer to a nonreactive dish large enough for the pieces to lie flat. Pour the marinade over the chicken and stir to coat the chicken thoroughly. Seal with plastic, refrigerate, and marinate for at least 4 but no more than 12 hours, turning the chicken once.

Grill the chicken: Prepare a charcoal grill with an even layer of coals or heat a gas grill to medium high. While the grill is heating up, take the chicken out of the refrigerator. When the charcoal is red-hot, lay the chicken pieces on the grill about 2 inches apart. Baste with any remaining marinade. Cover the grill, leaving the vents half-open on a charcoal grill.

After about 5 minutes, remove the grill lid and turn over the chicken pieces; they should look slightly charred. Replace the lid and continue cooking for another 5 to 7 minutes. Uncover the chicken, baste it with the melted butter, turn it over, and leave it uncovered for the rest of the cooking time. Baste after 2 or 3 minutes and test for doneness—the meat should feel firm when you press it.

Transfer the chicken to a large platter. Arrange the onion, cilantro, chiles, and lime wedges over the chicken and seal the platter with foil. Let the chicken rest for 10 minutes to absorb the garnish flavors.

Other recipe ideas

VIETNAMESE DIPPING SAUCE Make a tangy dipping sauce for spring rolls by mixing lime juice, sugar, fish sauce, garlic, chile paste, and a bit of water.

LIME MERINGUE PIE Substitute lime juice for lemon juice in your favorite lemon meringue pie recipe.

TANGY WATERMELON CHUNKS Squeeze lime juice over chunks of watermelon, sprinkle with salt and chile powder, and serve as a snack.

Mangifera indica and cvs.

Mangos

A sensuous fruit, with its vivacious orange flesh, juicy consistency, and exotic perfume, mango is also one of the world's most popular fruits. Delicious eaten as is, mangos transform themselves beautifully into smoothies and frozen desserts as well as savory dishes.

kidney-shaped, and a rich golden yellow when ripe. Choose firm fruit; the skin should be tight around the flesh. A green variety will just begin to show some yellow or red in the skin. As a final test, smell the mango. It should have a faintly sweet aroma, especially around the stem. No perfume generally means no flavor, but if the fruit smells sour or like alcohol, it's past its prime.

KEEPING IT FRESH

Unripe mangos should not be stored below 55°F, since the cold will make them ripen unevenly and give them off flavors. To ripen a mango, keep it at room temperature. When ripe, the fruit will become more aromatic, its skin will take on a blush, and its flesh will yield gently to the touch. To speed up the ripening process, put a few mangos in a paper bag with a banana. When fully ripe, you can refrigerate them, but only for up to 3 days.

PREPARING

Mangos must be peeled but the flesh is slippery so it's hard to peel the fruit while it's whole. The easiest method is to cut away each rounded half (or "cheek"), leaving behind the flat center pit. You can then cut the cheeks into slices or cubes and cut the flesh away from the skin; for more instruction, see p. 302.

PICKING THE BEST

There are over 1,000 mango varieties, but the most common in the U.S. have a tough, thin skin that starts out green and becomes yellow with red mottling as the fruit ripens. Mangos' fragrant flesh is deep orange and extremely juicy—though it can be fibrous—with an exotic, sweet-tart flavor.

A variety that's recently entered the American market is Champagne, also known as Manila or Ataulfa mango. It's worth seeking out because of its extremely smooth, nonfibrous flesh and small, "snackable" size. It's about the size of an avocado, slightly flattened and

HOW TO USE IT

Mangos are best raw, which preserves their bright flavor. Use them in fruit salads, desserts, smoothies, or in savory salsas and salads.

PRESERVING OPTIONS

Very ripe, juicy mangos may be frozen in chunks or slices as is. Less ripe mangos should be frozen with sugar or sugar syrup. Seal in airtight freezer bags.

Mango-Lime Granita

MAKES 16 SMALL SERVINGS

1½ ripe mangos (1½ pounds total), peeled
1 teaspoon finely grated lime zest
¾ cup sugar
1 tablespoon fresh lime juice

Cut the mango flesh away from the pit and chop coarsely into 1-inch pieces; you should have 2 to 2½ cups packed fruit. In a food processor, combine the mango and lime zest. Process until completely smooth, 1 to 2 minutes, stopping to scrape down the sides with a rubber spatula as needed. Transfer the purée to a medium bowl and add 2 cups water, the sugar, and the lime juice. Stir with a large spoon or whisk until the sugar has thoroughly dissolved.

Pour the purée into a 9-inch-square shallow baking pan. This pan size works best because it provides a large surface area, a key point in speeding up the freezing process. To further hasten freezing, use a metal pan (metal conducts cold well).

Put the pan in the freezer and stir every 30 minutes, being sure to scrape the ice crystals off the sides and into the middle of the pan, until the mixture is too frozen to stir, about 3 hours, depending on how cold your freezer is (some granitas can freeze in as little as 1 hour). Use a large dinner fork to stir and scrape; the tines are perfect for breaking up ice crystals.

Cover the pan with plastic and freeze overnight. When ready to serve the granita, place a fork at the top of the dish and pull it toward you in rows, moving from left to right and rotating the pan as well. Scrape up the shaved ice and fill chilled glasses or bowls.

Baby Greens with Mango and Marinated Onion

SERVES 6 TO 8

½ cup very thinly sliced red onion (about ½ a small onion)
⅓ cup red-wine vinegar
Kosher salt and freshly ground black pepper
2 tablespoons plain seasoned rice vinegar
2 tablespoons canola or grapeseed oil
2 tablespoons extra-virgin olive oil
8 to 10 ounces (6 to 8 large handfuls) baby greens or mesclun, well washed and dried
2 medium ripe mangos, peeled, pitted, and finely diced (about 2 cups)

In a small bowl, combine the onion and red-wine vinegar with a little salt and pepper. Set aside for at least 20 minutes or up to 90 minutes.

In a small bowl, combine the seasoned rice vinegar, canola or grapeseed oil, and the olive oil. Just before serving, generously season the greens with salt and pepper, whisk the dressing, and toss the greens with just enough of the dressing to lightly coat. Divide the salad among salad plates. Drain the onion. Arrange the onion and mangos over the greens. Serve immediately.

Other recipe ideas

TROPICAL BEURRE BLANC Cut a mango into tiny dice and add to a lime-butter sauce, along with some chopped cilantro and a dash of hot sauce. Serve over fish.

ICE CREAM SUNDAES WITH GRILLED MANGO AND PINEAPPLE Thread chunks of mango and pineapple on skewers, brush with butter, and grill. Serve with ice cream and spiced caramel sauce.

THAI RICE PUDDING Serve sliced mango with rice pudding made with Thai sticky rice and coconut milk.

DID YOU KNOW?

Green mango is the tart, unripe fruit. Powdered dried green mangos, called amchur, is used in Indian cooking the way lemon is used in Western cooking, but adding tang without liquid. Tart amchur powder is used in soups, lentil dals, vegetable dishes, and chutneys, and as a meat tenderizer.

Citrus sinensis and cvs., Citrus reticulata and cvs.

Oranges and Mandarins

Do you want to brighten a gloomy winter's day? Then start to peel an orange, tangerine, or clementine—the fragrant oils in the skin alone will fill the room with a sweet, refreshing scent. The sweetest members of the citrus family, like all citrus, are at their best in colder months—providing a welcome hit of color and freshness to winter salads, snacks, and desserts.

PICKING THE BEST

This family of sunny orange fruit is wide, but with a few exceptions, most subvarieties of these oranges aren't labeled at the market. That's because the differences have little to do with flavor and more to do with when the fruit matures during the year—only a grower would know one from the other.

- **Blood oranges:** These have a much sweeter flavor and less acidity than navels or Valencias, with overtones of raspberries or strawberries. Their thin skins may be blushed with red, and the flesh is a distinctive blood-red. If you want sweetness, blood oranges are the way to go, especially if paired with slightly bitter ingredients, such as radicchio. At the market, you might find varieties like Moro or Tarocco. Moros have dark-purple flesh and a deep-reddish rind. Taroccos (sometimes called half-blood oranges because they aren't as red as the Moro) have a blushed rind.
- **Navel oranges:** Navel oranges get their name from a second, smaller orange that develops at the base. (This undeveloped twin looks a little like a belly button.) Seedless, with thick skins, navels are the best eating oranges. Though a little less juicy than Valencias, they're virtually interchangeable when it comes to cooking. At the store, most navels are labeled simply "navel," but you might see some called Cara Cara; these have dark-pink flesh, an orange exterior, and a sweet, mildly acidic flavor.

- **Valencia oranges:** Originally from Spain, these are thin-skinned and almost seedless. They're your best bet when you need lots of juice, but Valencia oranges are also a great choice for any recipe that calls for sweet oranges.

Then there are all the hybrid relatives between oranges and mandarins and other citrus; these varieties are usually distinguished by loose, easy-to-peel skin and flowery flavor. Here are a few favorites.

- **Clementines:** These have a deeper flavor than other tangerines and are bursting with juice. The glossy-skinned, petite fruits are virtually seedless. They're in markets from late November through April.
- **Dancy tangerines:** Sweet and mellow-tasting, these have a reddish-orange peel that easily gives way to deep orange flesh. Look for them in December and January.
- **Honey tangerines:** Aromatic, with a distinctive, rich flavor, honey tangerines are slightly flat with thin, glossy skins and sweet, very juicy flesh. They're sold from January to April.
- **Satsumas:** Very juicy and virtually seedless, with a mild, sweet flavor, satsumas are the first tangerine variety to appear in the markets. Look for them from mid-October through December.

Navel

Tangelo

Cara Cara

Blood

- **Tangelos:** Almost as large as an orange, these are hybrids of mandarins and grapefruit. Sometimes called a honeybell or Minneola, they're extremely juicy and can be recognized by their distinctive knobby end.
- **Temple oranges:** Also called tangors, these are a cross between tangerines and oranges. They're quite juicy and have a somewhat spicy, almost tart flavor. Look for them from January through March.

No matter what variety, look for oranges and mandarins that are firm and heavy for their size, good indications of juiciness. Choose fruit with no blemishes or soft areas, and avoid ones that look dry.

KEEPING IT FRESH

Oranges and their cousins are fine if stored at room temperature for a few days, but they'll last longer and taste better if refrigerated; they'll hold there for up to a couple of weeks.

PREPARING

How you prepare an orange depends on what you intend to do with it. To capture the aromatic oils in the skin, you can use a fine rasp-style grater and grate the zest to add to dishes. For long-cooked dishes, you can add a long strip of zest that you pare away with a paring knife or vegetable peeler; it's easy to retrieve after its flavors have infused into the dish. Be sure to scrape or slice away any bitter white pith that's attached to the zest before you use it.

For eating out of hand, just cut the orange into wedges; to garnish a drink or fruit salad, a slice looks pretty—just be sure to flick out any seeds. The most time-consuming, but useful, method for oranges and other citrus is to cut out just the succulent flesh, eliminating skin, pith, and the membrane between the segments. See how on p. 304.

HOW TO USE IT

Almost every part of the fruit is usable in the kitchen: the flesh, the juice, and the aromatic skin. Only its seeds and the spongy white pith between the skin and the flesh are not of use. The vibrant fresh flavor of oranges does change with heat, however, so the best showcase for an orange and its kin is in uncooked preparations or dishes in which the orange is just barely cooked.

······················· **RECIPES** ·······················

Pan-Roasted Chicken Breasts with Orange-Brandy Sauce

SERVES 6

FOR THE CHICKEN

2 cups fresh navel or Valencia orange juice

2 tablespoons finely grated orange zest

6 tablespoons plus ¼ teaspoon kosher salt

Six 6- to 7-ounce boneless, skin-on chicken breast halves

2 tablespoons extra-virgin olive oil

Freshly ground black pepper

FOR THE SAUCE

3 tablespoons unsalted butter

1 medium shallot, minced

2 tablespoons brandy

1 cup fresh navel or Valencia orange juice

½ cup reduced-sodium chicken broth

1 navel or Valencia orange, cut into segments, segments cut into thirds

1 tablespoon chopped fresh flat-leaf parsley

Kosher salt and freshly ground black pepper

Brine the chicken: Combine the orange juice, zest, 6 tablespoons salt, and 4 cups water in a large bowl or pot; stir to dissolve the salt. Add the chicken breasts and refrigerate for 2 to 3 hours.

Cook the chicken: Position a rack in the center of the oven and heat the oven to 400°F. Remove the chicken from the brine and pat it dry with paper towels.

Heat the olive oil in a 12-inch ovenproof skillet over medium-high heat until shimmering hot. Add the chicken, skin side down, in a snug single layer and cook until the skin is golden brown, 3 to 5 minutes. Turn the chicken, season with ¼ teaspoon salt and a few grinds of pepper, and put the pan in the oven. Roast the chicken until an instant-read thermometer registers 165°F in the center of the thickest breast, about 15 minutes. Remove from the oven, transfer the chicken to a carving board, tent with foil, and let rest while you make the sauce.

Make the sauce: Pour the juices from the skillet into a heatproof measuring cup. Let the fat rise to the surface and then spoon it off.

Melt 2 tablespoons of the butter in the skillet over medium-high heat. Add the shallot and cook, stirring, until soft, 1 to 2 minutes. Remove from the heat and add the brandy. Return the pan to the heat and cook, scraping the bottom of the pan, until the brandy has almost evaporated, about 30 seconds. Increase the heat to high and add the orange juice. Boil until thick and syrupy and reduced to about ⅓ cup, about 5 minutes. Add the chicken broth, pan juices, and any juices from the carving board. Boil until reduced to about ¾ cup, about 3 minutes.

Swirl in the orange segments, then turn off the heat, and swirl in the remaining 1 tablespoon butter and the parsley until the butter is melted. Season to taste with salt and a few grinds of pepper.

To serve, cut the chicken on the diagonal into thin slices and arrange on 6 serving plates. Drizzle with the sauce.

Sear-Roasted Halibut with Blood Orange Salsa

SERVES 4

FOR THE SALSA

¾ cup fresh navel or Valencia orange juice (from 2 medium oranges)

3 small blood oranges, cut into segments, segments cut in half

2 tablespoons minced red onion

1 tablespoon chopped fresh cilantro

1 tablespoon extra-virgin olive oil

1 tablespoon finely grated navel or Valencia orange zest (from 2 medium oranges)

Kosher salt and freshly ground black pepper

FOR THE HALIBUT

1 teaspoon finely grated navel or Valencia orange zest (from 1 small orange)

1 teaspoon chopped fresh thyme

1½ teaspoons kosher salt

½ teaspoon freshly ground black pepper

Four 6-ounce skinless halibut fillets

3 tablespoons olive oil

Position a rack in the center of the oven and heat the oven to 425°F.

Make the salsa: In a small saucepan, boil the orange juice over medium heat until reduced to ¼ cup, 8 to 10 minutes. Let cool.

In a medium bowl, combine the reduced orange juice, blood orange segments, onion, cilantro, olive oil, and orange zest. Season to taste with salt and pepper.

Cook the halibut: In a small bowl, mix the orange zest, thyme, salt, and pepper. Rub the mixture all over the halibut fillets. Heat the oil in a 12-inch ovenproof skillet over medium-high heat. When the oil is shimmering hot, arrange the fillets in the pan. Sear for about 2 minutes without moving; then use a thin slotted metal spatula to lift a piece of fish and check the color. When the fillets are nicely browned, flip them and put the pan in the oven.

Roast until the halibut is just cooked through, 3 to 5 minutes. Remove the pan from the oven and transfer the halibut to serving plates. Spoon some of the salsa over each fillet.

Fresh Oranges with Caramel and Ginger

SERVES 4 TO 6

5 seedless oranges, such as navel, including some blood oranges if possible

2 tablespoons chopped crystallized ginger

⅓ cup sugar

8 to 10 mint leaves, very thinly sliced

Finely grate the zest (use a rasp-style grater if you have one) from one of the oranges to get 2 teaspoons zest. Cut the tops and bottoms off each orange, being sure to cut into some of the flesh; reserve the tops and bottoms. Cut the peel off the sides, exposing the flesh by cutting under the pithy membrane. Discard the peels cut from the sides. Cut each orange in half vertically, trim out the pithy core, and then slice each piece crosswise into ¼-inch half moons. Arrange the slices on a large, shallow serving dish or deep platter.

Combine the grated zest and crystallized ginger on a cutting board and chop them together until they're well mixed. Scatter the ginger and zest evenly over the oranges.

Put 2 tablespoons water in a small, heavy-based saucepan and pour the sugar on top. Bring to a boil over high heat, lower the heat to medium high, and boil without stirring until the syrup has turned a deep medium brown, 5 to 8 minutes. Watch the pan carefully during the last few minutes, as the caramel goes quickly from brown to burnt. Using a heavy pot holder to hold the pan, immediately drizzle the caramel over the oranges, getting a bit of caramel on each slice. Scatter the mint over the oranges. Squeeze the juice from the reserved ends of the oranges over all. If you serve right after assembly, you'll get bits of crunchy caramel with the orange slices; if you let it sit for a couple of hours, the caramel will dissolve and blend with the orange juices to make a toasty syrup. Both ways are very appealing.

Orange Layer Cake

SERVES 8 TO 10

FOR THE FILLING

⅔ cup sugar

3 tablespoons unbleached all-purpose flour

1 cup fresh orange juice (from about 3 large or 4 medium oranges), without pulp

2 large egg yolks

2 tablespoons salted butter

FOR THE CAKE

10⅛ ounces (2¼ cups) unbleached all-purpose flour; more for the pans

2½ teaspoons baking powder

1 teaspoon salt

⅓ cup salted butter; more for the pans

⅓ cup vegetable shortening

2 teaspoons grated orange zest (from about 1 large orange)

1½ cups sugar

3 large eggs

1 cup fresh orange juice (from about 3 large or 4 medium oranges), without pulp

FOR THE FROSTING

6 ounces (12 tablespoons) salted butter, at room temperature

4½ cups (about 18 ounces) confectioners' sugar

Dash of salt

1 teaspoon grated orange zest

5 tablespoons fresh orange juice

FOR THE GARNISH

1 or 2 small oranges, sliced thin, slices cut halfway through on one side, and laid on paper towels to drain

7 or 8 sprigs fresh mint (pick pairs of leaves)

Make the filling: Combine the sugar and the flour in a heavy-based saucepan. Whisk just to mix. Add the orange juice and egg yolks and whisk vigorously again to combine. Put the saucepan over medium-high heat and cook, whisking constantly, until the mixture boils (3 to 4 minutes). Cook for another 1 minute, stirring constantly (the mixture will thicken noticeably and become less cloudy). Be sure it boils for 1 minute so that the filling will thicken enough to support the cake. Remove from the heat and stir in the butter. Transfer to a bowl, cover with plastic wrap (lay the wrap directly on the filling's surface), and refrigerate. Chill thoroughly before using.

Make the cake: Position a rack in the center of the oven and heat the oven to 350°F. Sift together the flour, baking powder, and salt. Butter two 9x1½-inch round cake pans and line the bottom of each with a round of parchment. Lightly flour the sides and bottom of each pan.

In an electric mixer fitted with the paddle attachment, cream the butter, shortening, and zest. Gradually add the sugar, creaming until the mixture is light and fluffy. Scrape down the sides of the bowl. Add the eggs, one at a time, mixing well between additions and scraping down the sides.

Add the sifted dry ingredients alternately with the orange juice to the creamed mixture, beating well on low speed after each addition. Pour equal amounts of the batter into the two prepared cake pans. Tap the pans on the counter before putting them in the oven to remove any air bubbles and to even the batter. Bake until a toothpick inserted in the middle comes out clean, about 28 minutes. Let the cake layers cool in the pans on a rack for 10 minutes and then loosen the layers by running a knife between the cake and the edge of the pan. Remove the layers from the pans and put them on a rack to continue cooling.

Make the frosting: Cream the butter in the mixer. Add the confectioners' sugar and salt and combine thoroughly. Add the orange zest and mix to combine. Add the orange juice and mix on high speed until well blended, scraping down the sides. It will be light and creamy. Refrigerate if not using right away.

Assemble the cake: When all the components are cool, put one cake layer on a cake stand or a cardboard cake round. Spread the orange filling over the cake to make a ¼-inch layer. You'll have about ⅓ cup extra filling; serve it alongside the cake, if you like. Put the second layer on top of the first and refrigerate the cake until the filling has chilled again and firmed up, about 45 minutes.

Loosen the frosting by beating with a spatula (if it's very stiff, beat it with an electric mixer). Using an icing spatula, spread just a very thin layer of frosting over the whole cake (this is called a "crumb coat" because it secures loose crumbs) and refrigerate the cake to let the frosting firm up, about 10 minutes. Put on the final coat of frosting, taking care to work gently, as the top layer of the cake tends to slide around slightly because of the filling. If it slides, just push it back. Create a pattern on the frosting using the icing spatula (heat it up under warm water and dry it). Transfer the cake (on its cardboard or by lifting it with spatulas) to a cake plate or pedestal.

Garnish the cake: Twist the orange slices into S-shapes and put seven or eight around the top of the cake. Tuck a pair of mint leaves into each orange twist.

Clementine Granita

SERVES 4

¾ cup sugar

2 tablespoons finely chopped clementine zest (from 2 to 3 medium clementines)

Kosher salt

3 cups fresh clementine juice, with pulp (from 18 to 20 medium clementines, or about 4 pounds)

In a small saucepan, stir the sugar, zest, a pinch of salt, and ¾ cup water. Bring to a boil over medium heat and cook, stirring, until the sugar dissolves and the syrup is clear, about 2 minutes. Set aside to cool slightly as you juice the clementines.

Stir the juice and syrup together, pour into a small metal pan, such as a loaf pan, cover with plastic, and freeze for 2 hours. Stir the mixture with a spoon, breaking up the portions that have become solid, and return to the freezer. Stir every 30 minutes until the mixture is evenly icy and granular, about another 2 hours.

Cover and return to the freezer until ready to serve. To serve, scrape with a spoon to loosen the mixture, and spoon into small bowls or glasses. (Note: If you have an ice-cream maker, this recipe works equally well as a sorbet.)

Candied Orange Zest

MAKES 1½ CUPS

½ cup lemon, orange, or lime zest, or a combination (use a vegetable peeler to remove the zest in strips; avoid getting too much white pith), thinly sliced

½ cup sugar; more for dredging

1 teaspoon fresh lemon juice

2 tablespoons light corn syrup

Put the zest in a small saucepan and cover with cold water. Bring to a quick boil and drain. Repeat the process. (This blanching removes some of the zest's bitterness.) Put the drained zest in the saucepan again and add the sugar, ¼ cup water, and the lemon juice. Bring to a boil and add the corn syrup. Boil until the mixture reaches 240°F on a candy thermometer, about 5 minutes. Pour into a sieve, let drain, and then let cool slightly. Spread the zest on a baking sheet and let cool completely, 20 to 30 minutes. Dredge the zest in sugar, if you like. Store in an airtight container for up to 4 days.

Other recipe ideas

HONEY-SPICED CLEMENTINES Make a syrup by bringing 1 part water to a boil with 1 part honey and 1 part sugar, along with some spices such as cardamom pods, cloves, or star anise. Simmer thickly sliced clementines or oranges in the syrup for about 10 minutes, then let sit overnight. Pack into clean canning jars and refrigerate for up to 3 months.

ORANGE-PECAN WILD RICE SALAD Toss cooked wild rice with chopped oranges or clementines, scallion, toasted pecans, and lots of parsley. Dress it with a vinaigrette made with olive oil and lemon and orange juices.

TANGERINE BUTTER SAUCE Simmer fresh tangerine or orange juice until it's reduced and syrupy. Whisk in some cold butter until the sauce is thick. Season with salt, white pepper, and some grated lemon zest, adding a little lemon juice for brightness as needed. Drizzle the sauce over steamed vegetables, sautéed or grilled sole or halibut, or use as a dipping sauce for steamed artichokes.

Passiflora edulis and cvs.

Passionfruit

The eggplant-colored orb of a passionfruit is like an inside-out Fabergé egg—a dull, leathery exterior, but inside, jewel-like seeds and heady, fragrant pulp. Though not really suitable for snacking on, the pulp or juice of passionfruit adds an exotic, tropical flavor to fruit salads, sorbets, and those frozen blender drinks that make us feel like we're on vacation in the tropics.

KEEPING IT FRESH

Keep ripe passionfruit wrapped in a plastic bag in the refrigerator for up to a week.

PREPARING

When you're ready to use them, cut them in half with kitchen shears over a fine strainer set in a bowl to catch the juices. Then scoop out the seedy flesh and press it through the strainer with a flexible rubber spatula or the back of a spoon. The seeds are edible, but most recipes call for only the strained pulp.

HOW TO USE IT

Rather than a fruit you'd eat out of hand, passionfruit has tasty pulp and juices; these are what you're after. Use in sauces, compotes, and to flavor glazes for cakes and pastries; the juice makes delicious drinks and sorbets. The edible seeds are peppery and crunchy, however, so you can use the pulp and seeds together as a condiment or an accent to a plate of fresh fruit.

SURPRISING PAIRINGS

Passionfruit and dark chocolate make a fantastic pairing. The citrus notes in the fruit play off the fruitiness of good dark chocolate, and the tropical perfume just makes it all the more intriguing. Consider chocolate-passionfruit truffles or a passionfruit coulis for a flourless chocolate cake.

PICKING THE BEST

Passionfruit get uglier as they ripen, so choose ones that have wrinkly or dimpled skin and feel heavy for their size. The best indicator of ripeness is the gentle sloshing sound they make when shaken. Avoid buying fruits with soft spots or surface mold; they're too far gone. If you can find only underripe ones, let them sit out at room temperature for a few days to ripen.

PRESERVING OPTIONS

Passionfruit freezes well. You can either wrap the whole fruit in plastic to be scooped out later or scoop out the pulp into airtight freezer bags.

RECIPES

Passionfruit and Citrus Salad with Coconut Meringues

SERVES 2

1 kiwi, peeled and sliced

1 ripe mango, pitted, peeled, and diced

1 blood orange, peeled and segmented

½ ripe star fruit, sliced

½ cup diced fresh pineapple

3 tablespoons fresh orange juice

1 tablespoon fresh lime juice

½ teaspoon sugar, preferably superfine; more to taste

2 ripe passionfruit

Coconut meringues (store-bought or homemade), for garnish

Candied orange zest, for garnish (optional; see the recipe on p. 285)

Combine the kiwi, mango, blood orange, star fruit, and pineapple in a bowl. Stir together the orange juice, lime juice, and sugar; pour this mixture over the fruit. Split the passionfruit and either the spoon the pulp and seeds over the mixed fruit, or strain the pulp to remove the seeds and then pour over the fruit. Portion into serving dishes, and garnish each with one or two coconut meringues and candied orange zest, if using.

Passionfruit Sorbet

SERVES 6

1 cup passionfruit pulp (from about 12 passionfruit); reserve 2 tablespoons seeds for garnish, if you like

3 cups tangerine juice (from about 8 large tangerines)

½ to ¾ cup sugar

Mix the passionfruit pulp with the tangerine juice. Put the sugar in a small saucepan with 1 cup of the mixed juice and heat until the sugar dissolves. (If you want a tart taste, use the smaller amount of sugar; for a sweeter sorbet, add more.) Add the sugar mixture to the remaining juice and refrigerate until thoroughly chilled. Add the seeds, if desired. (The seeds won't change the flavor, but they look dramatic and add a slight crunch.) Freeze the mixture in an ice-cream maker according to the manufacturer's instructions and serve when ready. If you don't have an ice-cream maker, put the mixture in a bowl in the freezer and stir every half hour until frozen. Before serving, put the freezer-made sorbet in a food processor with the dough blade. Process just long enough to break up the ice crystals for a slushy texture, about 30 seconds.

Other recipe ideas

PASSIONFRUIT VINAIGRETTE Whisk passionfruit juice with honey, canola oil, sesame oil, black pepper, and shallots for a delicious dressing for grilled chicken.

BUTTERY PASSIONFRUIT POUND CAKE Flavor a rich, buttery pound cake by pouring a glaze made from passionfruit juice and sugar over the top.

TROPICAL FRUIT TART Make a fresh fruit tart with lots of tropical fruits, decorate with passionfruit seeds, which are dark and crunchy, then drizzle with the bright orange juice for some perfume and flavor.

Ananas comosus and cvs.

Pineapple

Fresh pineapple's intense aroma and spunky acidity are wonderful winter pick-me-ups, and while it's most often eaten raw, pineapple loves heat and develops a deep, caramelly sweetness when cooked. The sweet-tart flavor of pineapple works beautifully alongside a wide range of companion flavors and ingredients.

PICKING THE BEST

Two common varieties are Golden Ripe and Hawaiian Jet. Golden Ripes should have an overall golden hue; intensely sweet, they're best for eating plain and using in blender drinks. Hawaiian Jets have a greenish cast even when ripe; they're not as sweet, tend to keep longer, and are best for grilling or using in cooked desserts.

There are a few ways to tell if a pineapple is ready to eat. Sniff it: A ripe one has a sweet fragrance with no hint of fermentation. Squeeze it: If it's rock hard, it's probably unripe. If there's a little bit of give, the pineapple is probably nice and ripe. Pass on fruit with soft spots. Another clue: A juicy pineapple will feel heavy for its size, but check to make sure that juice isn't leaking from the bottom, indicating that the fruit is breaking down. Also, the top leaves should be bright and crisp looking.

KEEPING IT FRESH

A ripe pineapple will start to deteriorate if you leave it at room temperature. For best flavor, stash your pineapple in the fridge until you're ready to eat it. Once you've cut into it, wrap well in plastic for storage.

PREPARING

No matter how you cut the pineapple, you'll start by cutting off the top and bottom with a large knife. Then depending on your recipe, you'll cut the flesh into strips, chunks, or rings. See how on p. 306.

HOW TO USE IT

Pineapple is luscious eaten on its own, but it's also a good addition to smoothies, fruit salads, cakes and muffins, chutneys, and more. Pineapple's relatively sturdy texture makes it a good candidate for grilling. Roasted pineapple can be the base for a range of fruit desserts. There are a few things to consider when cooking with pineapple. When roasting pineapple, taste the fruit first. If it's especially sweet, you may want to use a bit less sugar. Also, pineapple is quite juicy, so when you're using fresh chunks in a baking recipe, it's a good idea to drain them in a strainer and then set them on a few layers of paper towels.

PRESERVING OPTIONS

You can freeze fresh pineapple, peeled and cut into chunks, strips, or crushed; there's no need to blanch first.

Grilled Steak Salad with Pineapple-Ginger Dressing

SERVES 4

FOR THE DRESSING

5 tablespoons pineapple juice

1 tablespoon soy sauce

1 tablespoon peanut oil

1 tablespoon Asian sesame oil

2 teaspoons fresh lime juice

½ teaspoon honey

½ teaspoon finely grated fresh ginger

1 small clove garlic, minced

Large pinch of crushed red pepper flakes

¼ cup small-diced fresh pineapple

1 tablespoon finely chopped fresh cilantro

FOR THE STEAK

1 pound flank steak

1½ tablespoons vegetable oil; more for the grill

1 teaspoon kosher salt

1 teaspoon freshly ground black pepper

FOR THE SALAD

6 ounces torn butter lettuce (about 6 lightly
   packed cups)

1 medium cucumber, seeded and thinly sliced

3 radishes, thinly sliced

Kosher salt and freshly ground black pepper

¼ cup thinly sliced scallion (white and light
   green parts)

Heat a gas grill to medium high.

Make the dressing: In a small bowl, whisk the pineapple juice, soy sauce, peanut oil, sesame oil, lime juice, honey, ginger, garlic, and pepper flakes to blend. Stir in the pineapple and cilantro.

Cook the steak: Rub the steak with the oil and season with the salt and pepper. Clean and oil the grill grates. Grill the steak, covered, until it has nice grill marks on one side, 5 to 6 minutes. Flip and reduce the heat to medium. Cook, covered, until done to your liking, another 4 to 5 minutes for medium rare. Transfer to a cutting board and let rest for 5 to 10 minutes.

Assemble the salad: In a large bowl, toss the lettuce, cucumber, and radishes with about half of the dressing. Season to taste with salt and pepper. Divide among 4 large plates.

Thinly slice the steak across the grain and drape it over the greens. Drizzle some of the remaining dressing over the beef, sprinkle with the scallions, and serve.

Other recipe ideas

GRILLED PINEAPPLE WITH CARAMEL AND PECANS Cut thick rings of fresh pineapple, grill until slightly softened and golden brown, then serve with a scoop of vanilla ice cream, a drizzle of caramel sauce, and crushed toasted pecans.

ROASTED PINEAPPLE MUFFINS Roast wedges of pineapple with a little butter and brown sugar, then dice and use in a blueberry muffin recipe in place of all or half the berries.

PINEAPPLE SALSA Make a relish of chopped fresh pineapple, minced hot chile, finely diced red onion, and chopped cilantro, then use it to top tacos.

Punica granatum and cvs.

Pomegranates

Maybe pomegranates seem so special because of the inverse relationship between effort and reward—you have to work hard to get to the fruit of a pomegranate, but once you do, the bittersweet, exotic, and crunchy seeds taste all the better. A pomegranate's sculptural shape makes you want to have a bowlful on the table just for looks alone, and the fruit has an ancient allure—many scholars think the "apple" in the biblical story of Adam and Eve might really have been a pomegranate.

PICKING THE BEST

Pomegranates are approximately the size of an orange with a flared, spiky crown at one end and red, leathery skin. Cutting into one reveals hundreds of ruby-colored seeds (called arils) packed in compartments separated by tough, shiny membranes. Each aril is made up of a tiny, edible seed surrounded by a translucent sac of juice (usually pink or deep red) that has a bright, sweet-tart flavor.

Choose pomegranates that are heavy for their size with bright, fresh-looking skin that's free of blemishes, cracks, and splits.

KEEPING IT FRESH

Whole pomegranates keep well at room temperature (away from sunlight) for several days, and for up to 3 months refrigerated in plastic bags. The seeds can be refrigerated for up to 3 days. For longer storage, freeze the seeds in single layers on trays and transfer them to airtight containers, where they'll keep for 6 months in the freezer. Pomegranate juice can be refrigerated for up to 3 days and frozen for up to 6 months.

PREPARING

With their bright sweet-sour flavor and ruby color, pomegranate seeds make a beautiful and flavorful garnish, but they can be a real mess to get out using the traditional method of cutting open the fruit and scooping out the seeds. Some of the seeds invariably burst, staining everything they touch, and there always seem to be little pieces of membrane clinging tenaciously to the seeds. Scoring the fruit, then pulling it apart and coaxing out the seeds in a bowl of cool water helps contain the mess. See the instruction on p. 307.

HOW TO USE IT

Pomegranate seeds add a bright jewel-like accent to salads, cakes, and tarts, as well as a sweet-tart hit of flavor, which is lovely with rich meats such as duck breast with a pan sauce or fragrant Middle Eastern lamb tagine.

RECIPES

Chicken Paillards with Avocado and Pomegranate Salsa

SERVES 4

FOR THE CHICKEN

Four 4- to 6-ounce boneless, skinless chicken breast halves

¼ cup fresh lemon juice

3 tablespoons extra-virgin olive oil

1 tablespoon pomegranate molasses (available at Middle Eastern and other specialty stores)

¾ teaspoon kosher salt

¼ teaspoon freshly ground black pepper

FOR THE SALSA

1 large lemon

½ medium pomegranate

3 small scallions (white and light green parts), thinly sliced

2 medium firm-ripe avocados (6 to 7 ounces each), pitted, peeled, and cut into ¼-inch dice

2 tablespoons extra-virgin olive oil

2 teaspoons chopped fresh flat-leaf parsley

1 teaspoon finely diced seeded jalapeño

1 teaspoon pomegranate molasses

½ teaspoon kosher salt, plus more to taste

Prepare the chicken: Pound each chicken breast between pieces of plastic wrap until about ⅜ inch thick. In a shallow bowl, stir the lemon juice, 2 tablespoons of the olive oil, the pomegranate molasses, salt, and pepper. Add the chicken, turn to coat well, cover, and refrigerate for at least 20 minutes and up to 1 hour.

Make the salsa: Finely grate the zest from the lemon and then squeeze out 1 tablespoon juice. Pick the seeds out of the pomegranate, discarding any pith, and put them in a bowl. Add the lemon zest and juice, scallions, avocado, olive oil, parsley, jalapeño, pomegranate molasses, and salt. Fold gently with a rubber spatula. Season to taste with more salt.

Cook the chicken: Heat ½ tablespoon of the olive oil in 12-inch skillet over medium heat. Add 2 of the chicken breasts and cook until lightly browned, about 3 minutes. Flip and cook until lightly browned on the other side and cooked through, about 3 minutes

more. Transfer the chicken to a plate and cover to keep warm. Repeat with the remaining ½ tablespoon oil and 2 chicken breasts. Serve the chicken with the salsa spooned over the top.

Citrus Pomegranate Compote with Mint

SERVES 8

4 blood oranges

4 tangerines

3 grapefruits

Seeds of 2 large pomegranates

Granulated sugar (optional)

1 teaspoon chopped fresh mint

Fresh mint leaves, for garnish

Use a thin, sharp knife to cut away all the peel and white pith of the citrus fruits. Reserve the peels. Then, holding the fruit over a bowl to catch any juice, cut along the dividing membranes of the sections toward the center of the fruit, and release the segments into the bowl. Squeeze the membranes over the fruit in the bowl. Twist the reserved peels over the bowl to release their aromatic oils.

Add the pomegranate seeds. Taste and add a bit of sugar, if you like. Stir in the chopped mint. Chill until ready to serve. Garnish with fresh mint leaves.

Other recipe ideas

WINTER SALSA Make a stunning salsa by combining pomegranate seeds with blood orange segments, minced jalapeño, diced red onion, a drizzle of honey, and a squeeze of fresh lime juice.

POMEGRANATE PARFAIT Make a pretty dessert by combining a packet of unflavored gelatin dissolved in a little water with some simple syrup, some prosecco or sweet white wine, and plenty of pomegranate seeds. Pour into pretty glasses, chill until firm, and serve with spice cookies.

POMEGRANATE-ARUGULA-RICOTTA SALAD Sprinkle pomegranate seeds over a salad of arugula, ricotta salata, and toasted almonds. Dress with a vinaigrette made with a touch of pomegranate molasses.

Helianthus tuberosus and cvs.

Sunchokes

The sunchoke is a bit of a mystery—it looks a lot like ginger but has an intriguing, subtly sweet, nutty flavor, reminiscent of potato and jícama. Also called Jerusalem artichokes (even though they're not related), there's a distinct hint of artichoke as well.

KEEPING IT FRESH

Wrap sunchokes in paper towels and store them in a plastic bag in the refrigerator vegetable drawer for up to a week.

PREPARING

Peeling sunchokes is optional. The thin peel has a slightly chewy texture, but it's not unpleasant, and you may find the effort of peeling their knobby surfaces isn't worth the return.

The cut surfaces of sunchokes, like those of potatoes, tend to oxidize and turn pink. To prevent this, submerge cut sunchokes in lemon water until ready to cook.

HOW TO USE IT

Sunchokes can be scrubbed, sliced, and eaten raw as a crisp addition to salads and crudité platters, or used as a substitute for water chestnuts or jícama. Sunchokes become tender and slightly starchy when cooked, so they're delicious roasted, steamed, boiled, or fried. To roast them, cut into chunks, toss with a little oil, season, and add to a roasting pan with a whole chicken or a pork or beef roast during the last half hour of cooking. You can steam or boil whole sunchokes until tender and then mash them roughly or serve them whole. For a creamy soup (the one instance where you may want to peel sunchokes so the soup has a smooth texture), simmer cut-up sunchokes in broth and milk or cream until tender and then purée. And to make addictive sunchoke chips, fry thin slices in peanut oil.

However you prepare them, keep the seasoning mild and minimal to allow the sunchokes' subtle flavor to shine.

PICKING THE BEST

Choose firm, smooth-skinned sunchokes without sprouts or bruises. Avoid those that feel soft, wrinkled, or moist.

DID YOU KNOW? Sunchokes aren't artichokes at all, even though their more common name is Jerusalem artichoke. They're actually the tubers of a variety of sunflower, which is why sunchoke or sunflower choke is a better name for them. "Jerusalem" is thought to be a corruption of *girasole*, which is the French word for sunflower.

RECIPES

Pan-Roasted Sunchokes and Artichoke Hearts with Lemon-Herb Butter

SERVES 4 TO 6

2 tablespoons extra-virgin olive oil

1 pound medium sunchokes, scrubbed and cut lengthwise into ¾-inch-thick wedges

½ teaspoon kosher salt, plus more to taste

8 ounces frozen quartered artichoke hearts, thawed

2 tablespoons finely chopped shallot

3 tablespoons dry vermouth

1 tablespoon fresh lemon juice

2 tablespoons cold unsalted butter, cut into small pieces

1 tablespoon chopped fresh flat-leaf parsley

2 teaspoons chopped fresh tarragon

Freshly ground black pepper

Position a rack in the upper third of the oven and heat the oven to 400°F.

In a 12-inch ovenproof skillet, heat the oil over medium-high heat until shimmering hot. Add the sunchokes and ¼ teaspoon salt; cook, flipping as needed, until well browned on both cut sides, 2 to 3 minutes per side. Add the artichoke hearts and ¼ teaspoon salt; cook, stirring occasionally, until lightly browned, 2 to 3 minutes.

Move the skillet to the oven and roast until the sunchokes are tender, about 20 minutes. With a slotted spoon, transfer the vegetables to a bowl and cover to keep warm.

Set the skillet over medium heat, add the shallot, and cook, stirring with a wooden spoon, until softened and lightly browned, 1 to 2 minutes. Add the vermouth and cook, stirring and scraping the bottom of the pan to loosen any browned bits, until the vermouth has almost evaporated.

Reduce the heat to low, add the lemon juice, and then add the butter one piece at a time, swirling the pan to melt the butter before adding the next piece. Stir in the parsley and tarragon. Return the vegetables to the pan and toss to reheat and coat in the butter. Season to taste with salt and pepper before serving.

Mushrooms, Asparagus, and Sunchokes with Hazelnuts

SERVES 4

⅓ cup hazelnuts

¼ cup walnut oil

⅔ pound sunchokes, peeled and sliced into 1-inch sticks

⅔ pound asparagus (about 14 medium spears), rinsed, tough stems snapped off, and cut into 1-inch lengths

1 cup quartered wild mushrooms, or a mix of wild and domestic

1 teaspoon chopped fresh thyme (or ½ teaspoon dried)

½ teaspoon salt

¼ teaspoon freshly ground black pepper

¼ cup balsamic vinegar; more or less to taste

Heat the oven to 400°F. Spread the nuts on a small baking sheet and toast for 6 to 8 minutes, or until their skins turn dark and crack. Pour the nuts into a clean dishtowel, fold the towel in half, let the nuts cool slightly, and rub the towel against them to remove their skins. Chop the nuts coarsely and set aside.

In a large skillet, heat the walnut oil over medium-high heat. Add the sunchokes, asparagus, and mushrooms. Sauté, stirring often, for 1 to 2 minutes. Sprinkle the vegetables with the thyme, salt, pepper, and vinegar. Reduce the heat slightly, cover the pan, and continue cooking for 1 to 2 minutes, shaking or stirring occasionally until the vegetables are crisp-tender. At the last moment, toss in the chopped hazelnuts. Serve immediately.

Other recipe ideas

HERBED SUNCHOKE PURÉE Mash steamed or boiled sunchokes, enrich with butter and good olive oil, and shower with fresh herbs.

STEAK WITH MUSHROOM-SUNCHOKE TOPPING Sauté slices of sunchoke with a mix of mushrooms, minced shallot, rosemary, and thyme. Serve over sliced steak.

Prepping Produce

Artichokes

PREPARING ARTICHOKE BOTTOMS

1 Fill a large bowl with cold water and add the juice of one lemon. Pull back the outer leaves of each artichoke until they break at the base.

2 Remove the leaves until you reach the pale yellow-green, tender inner leaves. With a sharp knife, slice off all but 1 inch of the stem.

3 Cut across the leaves just above where they join the base. Discard these, but reserve the outer leaves for steaming another time, if you like.

4 With a small knife, pare the stem and the base, removing any dark green parts. If you like, cut the stem and base in half.

5 With a melon baller or a spoon, scoop out and discard the hairy artichoke and prickly leaves inside. Immediately drop the trimmed artichoke into the lemon water to retard browning.

TRIMMING BABY ARTICHOKES

1 Snap off and discard the outer leaves until you reach the tender, pale green interior cone of leaves.

2 With a paring knife, trim the stem to within 1 to 1½ inches of the base. Trim around the base to smooth off the nubbins left by the outer leaves, then trim off the fibrous outer layer of the stem.

3 Cut ½ to 1 inch off the tip of the leaf cone, then cut the artichoke in half lengthwise.

4 To keep the artichokes from browning, float them in a bowl of lemon water until you're ready to cook them.

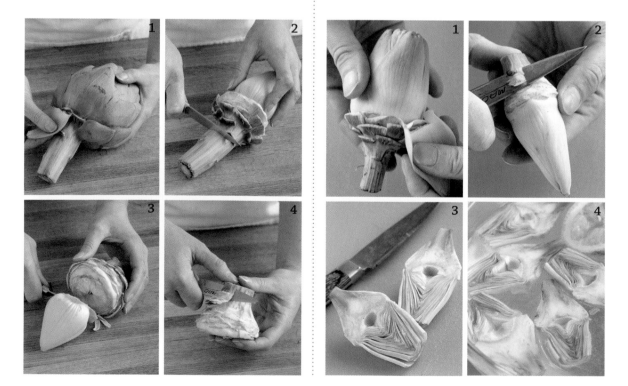

Avocados

SLICING

1 Just before serving, cut the avocado in half lengthwise and remove the pit. Using a paring knife, cut the avocado diagonally into ¼-inch (or wider) slices, without piercing through the skin. If dice is your goal, make a second set of diagonal slices perpendicular to the first.

2 To remove the sliced or diced avocado from its skin, hold the avocado in the palm of your hand and, using a large spoon, carefully scoop out the slices.

Brussels sprouts

TRIMMING

1 Trim the base of the core to expose a fresh surface.

2 Peel off and discard the outer layer of leaves, or more if necessary due to insect damage. Rinse the sprouts well.

3 When cooking the sprouts whole, score an X in the base of the core. Heat will penetrate the core so the sprouts cook evenly.

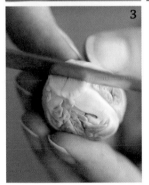

Cabbage

TRIMMING AND CORING

1 Peel away and discard any tough outer leaves.

2 Cut the cabbage into quarters through the base.

3 Cut the core out of each quarter. You're now ready to slice.

Chiles, dried

TOASTING

Be prepared to work quickly and ventilate well, as chile smoke is irritating and may cause you to cough and sneeze. Heat a heavy-duty skillet (such as cast iron) over medium-high heat until you can feel the heat radiate from the surface. Working with one type of chile at a time, add it to the skillet. Flip or stir frequently for even toasting, until lightly charred—not scorched. Immediately transfer to a cool container.

Chiles, fresh

ROASTING

For one or two peppers, on a gas stove:

Coat each chile with a little vegetable oil. Roast directly on the grate of the gas stove over high heat, turning occasionally until it's charred all over.

For a batch of peppers, on gas or charcoal grills, gas or electric stoves:

Coat each chile with a little vegetable oil. Grill over a hot charcoal fire or gas grill, covered. Or put the oiled chiles on a foil-lined baking sheet and broil as close to the element as possible, turning the chiles so they char evenly.

Put the charred chiles in a bowl while they're still hot and cover with plastic. Let them rest until they're cool enough to handle, 15 to 30 minutes. Pull on the stem: the seed core will pop out. Cut the chile open, flick out any seeds, and turn skin side up. With a paring knife, scrape away the charred skin. Don't rinse the chiles—you'll dilute their flavor.

Corn

CUTTING KERNELS FROM THE COB

To cut corn kernels off the cob, first cut the ear of corn in half crosswise. This gives you a flat end on which to stand the half-cob (and means the kernels don't have as far to fall and won't bounce as much). Then stand a half-cob cut end and slice down the length of the ear between the kernels and cob. Try to get as much of the kernel as you can, but don't cut too close to the cob or you'll have tough bits on the kernels. Rotate the cob and repeat until all the kernels are cut.

If you're not using the kernels immediately after cutting them from the cob, preserve their sweetness by blanching them in boiling water for 1 to 2 minutes. Drain, let cool, and store in a covered container in the fridge for up to 5 days. Or freeze the blanched kernels in a single layer on a baking sheet until hard, then store in an airtight container in the freezer, where they'll keep for up to 3 months.

Eggplant

BASIC METHOD FOR CHAR-ROASTING EGGPLANT

To start, pierce the eggplant with a skewer and cook it whole and unpeeled directly over a grill flame until the skin is blackened all over and the flesh is thoroughly soft, 15 to 20 minutes. Char-roasting can get messy, so if you're trying this over an indoor gas flame, line the burner trays with foil or try broiling the pierced eggplant instead. Peel off the blackened skin, drain the flesh in a colander, and squeeze out all of the moisture.

As an alternative to char-roasting, pierce the eggplant in several places and roast it whole and unpeeled on a baking sheet at 350°F until it's quite soft and starting to collapse, almost an hour. Peel and drain it as you would for char-roasting.

Favas

PREPARING

1 To shell favas, break open the pods. Sometimes you can slide your finger along one side, opening the seam as you would a zipper, but other times you just have to break the pod apart in pieces.

2 Blanch the favas in boiling water for 1 minute, drain, and cool under running water.

3 Favas have one end that's slightly flattened and slightly wider, with a scar where it was attached to the shell. Grasp the fava between your fingers with the scar facing up, and with the thumbnail of your other hand, tear into the scar end and peel back. Pinch gently and the fava will slide right out.

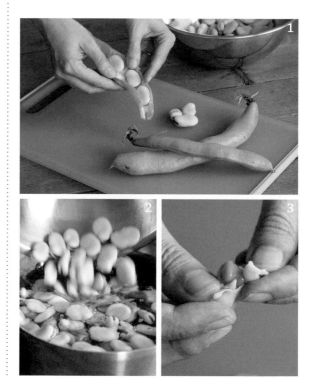

Fennel

TRIMMING AND CORING

1 To prep fennel, trim off and discard the stalks and fully expanded leaves, or save them to use in stocks. Save the dense, tight, baby leaves for mincing and garnishing the finished dish. If the outer layer of the bulb is in good shape and isn't too fibrous, use it; otherwise, break it off and use it for stock. Carefully trim off a thin slice of the root end, leaving the rest of the core intact to hold together wedges or vertical slices.

2 For diced or slivered fennel, cut the bulb lengthwise in half or quarters.

3 Cut away the dense inner core. Slice or dice as your recipe specifies.

Garlic

ROASTING

1 Separate a head of garlic into individual cloves. Don't peel the cloves, but do rub off any flaky or papery skin. Use a paring knife to nip off the stem end of each clove. You want the peel to stay on, but it's fine if a little comes off.

2 Put the cloves in the center of a square of aluminum foil, drizzle with a little olive oil, and use your fingers to rub the oil evenly on the cloves. Add fresh herb sprigs for aroma, if you like.

3 Gather the foil into a beggar's pouch and set the pouch directly on the rack of a 350°F oven. Roast until the garlic becomes very soft and lightly browned, about 1 hour. You can roast two heads' worth of cloves in one pouch, but for more than that, make another pouch.

4 Open the pouch and let the cloves sit until they're cool enough to handle. Squeeze each clove gently at the untrimmed end and the roasted flesh should slide right out in one piece.

Ginger

PEELING AND CUTTING

1 Peel ginger unless you plan on discarding it before serving. Try using the edge of a metal spoon to scrape off the skin. It takes a bit more effort than a paring knife or a peeler, but it's less wasteful and it lets you maneuver around the knobs and gnarls.

2 **Planks:** Diagonally slice the ginger across the fibers to cut it into planks, which you can use to infuse flavor into liquid. Cutting planks is also the first step to making matchsticks or a mince.

3 **Matchsticks:** To cut ginger into julienne-style matchsticks, stack the ginger planks and slice them into thin strips.

4 To take the ginger to the chopped or minced stage, turn the stack of matchstick pieces 90 degrees and chop to the consistency you want.

Grated: To grate ginger, use a rasp-style grater. It does an amazing job of grating even the most fibrous knob of ginger into a juicy, paste-like consistency.

Hazelnuts

SKINNING

There are two ways to skin hazelnuts. For both methods, let the nuts cool completely before using or before storing in a sealed container in the freezer for up to 3 months.

The toasting method

Spread the nuts in a single layer on a baking sheet and toast in a 375°F oven until the skins are mostly split and the nuts are light golden brown (the skins will look darker) and fragrant, about 10 minutes. Don't overtoast or the nuts will become bitter. Wrap the hot nuts in a clean dishtowel and let them sit for 5 to 10 minutes. Then vigorously rub the nuts against themselves in the towel to remove most of the skins. This may take a lot of rubbing, so be persistent.

The blanching method

For every ½ cup of hazelnuts, bring 1½ cups water to a boil. Add 2 tablespoons baking soda and the nuts; boil for 3 minutes—expect the water to turn black and watch out for boilovers. Run a nut under cold water and see if the skin slips off easily. If not, boil the nuts a little longer until the skins slip off. Cool the nuts under cold running water, slip off the skins, blot dry, and then toast in a 375°F oven.

Herbs

PICKING PARSLEY

Rather than picking the leaves individually, "shave" them right off the bunch. Hold a rinsed bunch of parsley with the leaves facing away from you. Graze a chef's knife along the length of the bunch, starting near the base of the leaves and keeping the blade almost parallel to the stems. As long as you have a sharp blade, the leaves (and some of the more tender stems) will come right off.

SLICING AND MINCING BASIL

1 **Fine shreds:** Stack leaves on top of one another and roll into a tight tube. (For smaller leaves, bunch as tightly together as possible before cutting.) Cut the rolled leaves using a single swift, smooth stroke for each slice. The width is up to you. This is known as a chiffonade.

2 **Minced:** Turn the chiffonade slices (keeping them together with a gentle pinch) and make a few perpendicular cuts as wide or as narrow as you like.

Don't go back over the basil as you might when finely chopping parsley or it will get bruised.

Leeks

CLEANING

Since leeks are grown with soil piled all around them, there is plenty of opportunity for dirt and grit to settle between their onion-like layers. The easiest way to clean a leek is to trim the root end and the dark green tops and cut it in half lengthwise (or, if you want to retain the appearance of whole leeks in your dish, just cut about two-thirds of the way through the stalk). Hold the leek root end up under cold running water and riffle the layers as if they were a deck of cards. Do this on both sides a couple of times until all the dirt has been washed out.

Lettuce/Salad Greens

WASHING

Whether you grow your own lettuce or buy it, be sure to wash it well. Nothing ruins a salad like gritty greens. Swish the leaves in a large bowl of cool water, let them sit so the grit settles to the bottom, and then lift out the leaves. Repeat until no grit remains and then spin dry.

Mangos

DICING

1 Balance the mango on one of its narrow sides, and then slice off one of the wide sides of the fruit. Try to cut as close to the seed as possible, usually about ¾ inch from the center. Repeat with the other wide side and then slice off the remaining strips of fruit from the narrow sides.

2 To dice the wide pieces of mango, cup one in your palm and use a paring knife to score the fruit into the dice size you want. Try to cut down to but not through the skin, and hold the mango with a kitchen towel to protect your hand in case the knife does pierce the mango skin.

3 Use your fingertips to pop the mango inside out and then use the paring knife to slice the cubes away from the skin.

4 To dice the narrow strips of mango, simply trim away the skin and cut.

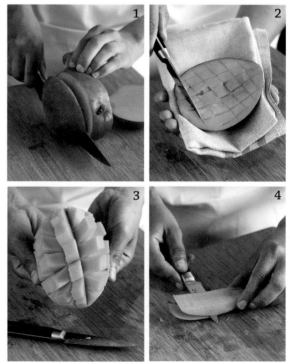

Melons

PEELING

1 Cut off the melon's top and bottom ends.

2 Stand the melon on one of the cut ends and slice off the remaining skin in strips, taking care to hug the curves so that you're trimming only the skin and not the flesh. A flexible knife works well for this.

3 Cut the melon in half, scoop out the seeds, and then cut up the flesh as you like.

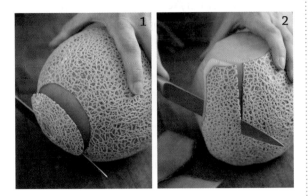

Onions

DICING

1 Trim the ends but leave much of the root intact. Cut the onion in half from end to end and peel each half. Lay one half on its cut side. Make parallel vertical cuts from the root to the stem end, but not completely through the root end. Space the cuts as wide as you want your dice.

2 Make one or two horizontal cuts, keeping the knife parallel to the cutting board, again being careful not to cut through the root end. Whether you make one or two horizontal cuts depends on the size of the onion.

3 Make a series of cuts perpendicular to the previous cuts, again spacing them as wide as you want the dice to be. Keep the fingers of your guiding hand curled so you don't cut your fingertips.

4 When you get close to the root end and the cutting becomes awkward, flip the onion root side up, as shown, and slice across it one or two times. Flip the onion back to its previous orientation. The top is now flat and easier to dice. Finish dicing down to the root. Discard the root and repeat with the other onion half.

Oranges

CUTTING SEGMENTS

1 Cut off the top and bottom of the orange, slicing off enough to expose a circle of the orange's flesh.

2 With a paring knife, slice off a strip of peel from top to bottom. Try to get all of the white pith, but leave as much of the flesh as possible. Continue all the way around.

3 To make segments (a.k.a. suprêmes), use a paring knife to cut on either side of each membrane, freeing the orange segment in between. Work over a bowl to catch the juice.

4 To make slices, cut the orange crosswise in the desired thickness.

Parsnips

CORING

After trimming the ends and peeling the parsnip, quarter it lengthwise. Hold a sharp paring knife parallel to the cutting board and slowly run the knife between the core and the tender outer part of the parsnip. The core curves with the shape of the parsnip, so you won't be able to get it all, but that's fine—just remove as much as you can without sacrificing too much of the tender part.

Passionfruit

When ready to use, cut the passionfruit in half with kitchen shears over a fine-mesh strainer set in a bowl to catch the juices. Then scoop out the seedy flesh and press it through the strainer. A ripe passionfruit yields about 1 tablespoon pulp with seeds or ½ tablespoon strained pulp.

Peaches

PEELING

To peel peaches for pies, canning, or other purposes, have ready a pot of boiling water, a bowl of ice water, a paring knife, and a slotted spoon. Work with one piece of fruit at a time because leaving them in the ice water for too long makes them harder to peel. This method works for tomatoes, too.

1 With the paring knife, lightly score an X into the flower end of the fruit.

2 Drop the fruit into the boiling water for 15 to 20 seconds.

3 Use the slotted spoon to briefly dip the fruit into the ice water (shocking them this way stops the cooking).

4 Starting at the X, use the paring knife to help you peel off the skin. It should come off easily; if not, repeat the boiling and shocking steps.

PITTING

1 Using a paring knife, start at the stem end of the fruit and cut through to the pit. Run the knife all the way around the fruit, keeping the blade up against the pit, finishing where you started.

2 Hold the fruit in your hands and gently twist each half in opposite directions until one half comes free from the pit. Set that half aside.

3 Remove the pit from the remaining half by loosening one end with your finger or the tip of a knife.

4 If the pit doesn't come free, don't force it—you'll only damage the flesh if you force out the pit. Instead, cut off a few sections from the half. You will then be able to wiggle the pit free.

Pineapples

TRIMMING AND CORING

1 Begin by trimming the leaves and the base. Set the pineapple on its side. Using a large chef's knife, cut along the shoulder of the fruit, about an inch below the long pointy leaves, to remove all traces of the fibrous top. Then slice off about ½ inch of the base so the fruit will stand upright.

2 Remove the rind. Stand the pineapple on a cutting board and cut off vertical strips of rind, following the contours of the fruit and cutting deep enough to remove the dark, prickly spots known as eyes. After removing all the rind, go back and trim away any remaining eyes.

3 For rings, cut the peeled, uncored pineapple into thin or thick rounds. Punch out the core from each slice using a small, round cookie cutter (or use the tip of a paring knife).

4 For wedges, chunks, or bite-sized pieces, cut the fruit lengthwise into quarters. Cut away the woody core by slicing along the length of each piece just under the core. Then slice into wedges or chunks.

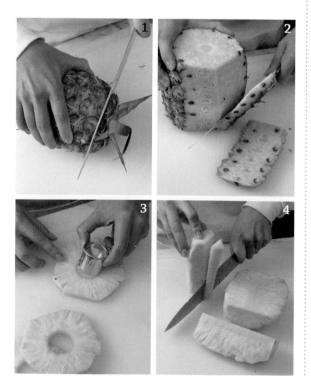

Plums

CUTTING INTO WEDGES

1 Find the indentation running down the length of the plum. With your knife parallel to the indentation, cut the flesh away from the pit in two pieces and set them aside.

2 Trim the remaining flesh from each side of the pit—these are two of your wedges.

3 Slice the two larger pieces into four wedges each, for a total of ten wedges.

Pomegranates

GETTING OUT THE SEEDS

1 Cut off the "crown" end of the fruit, exposing the seeds below.

2 Lightly score the fruit from stem to crown end in several places, breaking through to the white, pithy membrane beneath the skin.

3 Soak the fruit in a large bowl of cool water for 5 minutes. Working under water, break the fruit apart into sections, freeing the seed clusters from the membranes. The pomegranate seeds sink to the bottom of the bowl, and the membranes float.

4 Skim off and discard the membranes. Drain the seeds and lay them on paper towels to dry.

Sweet peppers

CUTTING

1 With a sharp chef's knife, cut off the top of the pepper just below the shoulder so that you remove the entire stem end, exposing the ribs inside the pepper. Squarely cut off the narrow bottom. Reserve the trimmed ends. The pepper will now be shaped like a cylinder.

2 Set the pepper on one end and, with the tip of your knife, make one neat vertical slice to open the cylinder.

3 Set the pepper skin side down and work the knife along the inside of the pepper (with the blade parallel to the work surface), removing the ribs and seeds while unrolling the pepper so that it lies flat.

4 You now have a neat rectangle of bell pepper that you can julienne or dice. You can trim and chop the reserved ends as well.

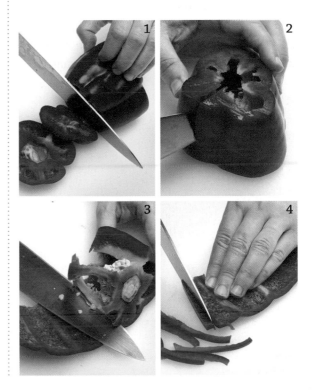

Sweet peppers

ROASTING

There are two simple methods to roast peppers to bring out their deep, rich flavor and soft texture.

Slow-roasting in the oven: Put the peppers on a rimmed baking sheet and roast them in a 400°F oven, turning occasionally, until they get browned all over, 45 to 60 minutes. Remove the peppers from the oven, cover with a dishtowel, and set aside to cool. Seed, peel, and cut the peppers as you like. The long cooking time results in soft and juicy pepper pieces.

Roasting over a flame: This is the quicker of the two cooking methods. It results in a slightly firmer pepper, which is what you want to add body to pastas and side dishes like relishes. For this method, first heat a gas grill to high or prepare a charcoal grill fire. Cut the tops and bottoms from the peppers and cut the peppers into three or four flat pieces, discarding the tops, seeds, and ribs. Grill the pepper sides and bottoms skin side down until blistered and charred all over, 6 to 8 minutes. (You can also char them over the flame of a gas stove or under a broiler.) Put the peppers in a bowl and cover with a plate. Let sit until cool enough to handle. Peel the charred skin and discard. Don't be too concerned if flecks of skin remain attached. Cut the peppers as you like.

Swiss chard

TRIMMING THE RIBS

Separate, but don't discard, chard stems from the leaves by running a sharp knife along both sides of the stem.

Tomatoes

SEEDING AND DICING

Best for round tomatoes

1 Core the tomato and cut it in half crosswise with a serrated knife to expose the seed chamber. Gently squeeze out the seeds, using a finger or a small table knife to help empty the chambers. Lay the seeded tomato halves, cut side down, on a cutting board.

2 Holding the serrated knife parallel to the cutting board, cut the tomato halves horizontally into slices that are as thick as you want your dice to be. Next, cut each stack of tomato slices into strips as wide as you want your dice, and then slice these strips crosswise into dice.

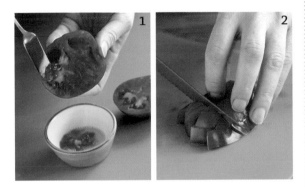

Best for plum tomatoes

1 Cut a thin slice from the bottom to create a flat surface on which to stand the tomato. Cut wide strips from the top, curving down to the bottom, to separate the flesh from the inner seed core. Cut all the flesh away in this manner, leaving the seedy core of the tomato; discard the core.

2 Cut each strip of flesh lengthwise as wide as you want your dice to be, and then cut these strips crosswise into dice.

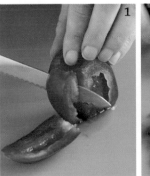

Winter squash

CUTTING INTO PIECES

1 Prick the squash several times with a fork and microwave for 3 minutes; it will soften slightly, making it easier to cut open. Or bake the whole squash directly on the rack in a 350°F oven until slightly softened and the skin begins to change color, about 10 minutes.

Set the squash on a towel on a cutting board to prevent it from slipping, and push the tip of a sharp chef's knife into the squash near the stem. Carefully push the knife through the squash to the cutting board to cut off the stem.

2 Cut lengthwise through half of the squash, starting with the tip of your knife in the center of the squash. If the knife sticks, don't try to pull it out; this is dangerous, since it may come out suddenly. Instead, tap the handle with a rubber mallet or meat tenderizer until the knife cuts through the squash.

3 Rotate the squash and cut through the other side the same way.

4 Push the halves apart with your hands. With a soupspoon, scrape the seeds and stringy bits away from the flesh and discard.

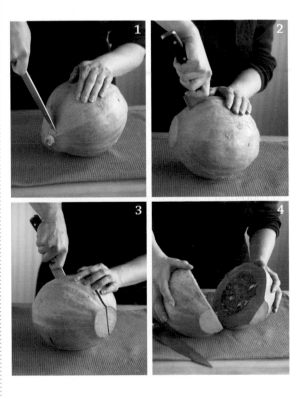

Freezer Know-How

If you have a vegetable garden in the backyard, or even if you're just a farmer's market junkie, you know you can't possibly use up the season's bounty of fruits and vegetables, so learning to freeze well is a great way to preserve the fresh flavors of fruits and veggies at their peak. Here's a handy guide for freezing all the season's favorites.

Freezing

THREE EASY STEPS FROM FRESH TO FROZEN

1 Prepare your fruits or vegetables as advised in this book. Create a level area in your freezer to fit a rimmed baking sheet. If you're strapped for space, use something smaller—like a cake pan—and repeat the freezing steps below as needed.

2 Arrange the prepared fruits or vegetables in a single layer, making sure they don't touch. (If you like, you can line the baking sheet with parchment, foil, or waxed paper.) Freeze until solid, 60 to 90 minutes, depending on the size and your freezer's temperature.

3 Transfer to heavy-duty freezer bags. Press out as much air from the bag as possible (if you have a vacuum sealer, use it), seal, and date the bag. Store in the back of the freezer (the coldest part) until ready to use. To thaw, transfer the amount you need to a bowl or plate and thaw in the refrigerator.

Using Your Frozen Produce

Freezing is a great way to preserve flavor, but don't expect fruits and vegetables that have been frozen to have the same texture as fresh ones. That's why it's better to cook with them than eat them out of hand. Here are some ideas:

FRUITS

Frozen: Use in pie or galette fillings and in smoothies.

Partially frozen (5 to 10 minutes out of the freezer at room temperature): Use in sauces, smoothies, cake batters, and pancakes, and as garnishes.

Thawed: Use in sauces, smoothies, and jams.

VEGETABLES

Frozen: Use in soups, braises, and stews, and steamed.

Thawed: Use in sautés, stir-fries, and purées.

A couple of exceptions: Tomatoes should always be thawed and drained before using in soups, braises, stews, and sauces (don't use in sautés or stir-fries). Corn on the cob can be steamed frozen but should be thawed before grilling.

Freezer Basics

FREEZER TEMP

Set your freezer at 0°F or colder (use a freezer thermometer to check). Many home freezers are opened and closed frequently, causing the temp to fluctuate. This makes fruits and vegetables thaw and refreeze. To prevent this, stash frozen fruits and veggies as far from the door as possible.

FREEZING TIME

Use fruits and vegetables stored in a stand-alone freezer (infrequently opened chest or upright) within 10 to 12 months. For a frequently opened freezer compartment, use within 3 months.

Blanching Vegetables

Most vegetables benefit from blanching before freezing. The process stops the enzymes' aging action while slowing vitamin and nutrient loss. It also brightens and sets the vegetables' color. In general, fruits don't need blanching (unless it's to remove the peel). Here's how to blanch:

1 Bring a large pot of water to a rolling boil (about 2 quarts per 2 to 3 cups of vegetables).

2 Working in small batches, add the vegetables. Allow the water to return to a boil and cook very briefly, about 2 minutes.

3 Using a large slotted spoon, scoop out the veggies and immediately rinse them in cold water or immerse them in a large bowl of ice water to stop the cooking. Remove and dry thoroughly before freezing.

Metric Equivalents

LIQUID/DRY MEASURES	
U.S.	**METRIC**
¼ teaspoon	1.25 milliliters
½ teaspoon	2.5 milliliters
1 teaspoon	5 milliliters
1 tablespoon (3 teaspoons)	15 milliliters
1 fluid ounce (2 tablespoons)	30 milliliters
¼ cup	60 milliliters
⅓ cup	80 milliliters
½ cup	120 milliliters
1 cup	240 milliliters
1 pint (2 cups)	480 milliliters
1 quart (4 cups; 32 ounces)	960 milliliters
1 gallon (4 quarts)	3.84 liters
1 ounce (by weight)	28 grams
1 pound	454 grams
2.2 pounds	1 kilogram

OVEN TEMPERATURES		
°F	**Gas Mark**	**°C**
250	½	120
275	1	140
300	2	150
325	3	165
350	4	180
375	5	190
400	6	200
425	7	220
450	8	230
475	9	240
500	10	260
550	Broil	290

Contributors

Bruce Aidells is the author of nine cookbooks, including *Bruce Aidell's Complete Book of Pork*.

Amy Albert is a former editor at *Fine Cooking*.

Katherine Alford is the test kitchen director at the Food Network and is a judge on the network's show *Ultimate Recipe Showdown*.

Ayla Algar is the author of *Classical Turkish Cooking*.

Pam Anderson is a contributing editor to *Fine Cooking* and the author of several books, including her latest, *Perfect One-Dish Dinners: All You Need For Easy Get-Togethers*. Her website is www.threemanycooks.com.

Jennifer Armentrout is senior food editor at *Fine Cooking*.

John Ash is the founder and chef of John Ash & Co., in Santa Rosa, California. He teaches at the Culinary Institute of America at Greystone and is a cookbook author.

Dan Barber is the chef and co-owner of Blue Hill in New York City and Blue Hill at Stone Barns in Pocantico Hills, New York.

Jessica Bard is a food stylist, food writer, and recipe tester who teaches cooking classes at Warren Kitchen and Cutlery in Rhinebeck, New York.

Karen Barker is a pastry chef and cookbook author. She co-owns Magnolia Grill in Durham, North Carolina, with her husband, Ben. She won the James Beard Outstanding Pastry Chef Award in 2003.

Lidia Bastianich is co-owner of four restaurants and is the star of *Lidia's Italian American Kitchen* and *Lidia's Italian Table*. She is also the author of four cookbooks.

Peter Berley is a chef, cookbook author, and culinary instructor.

David Bonom is a food writer in New Jersey.

Julie Grimes Bottcher is a recipe developer and food writer.

Flo Braker is the author of numerous cookbooks; her most recent book is *Baking for All Occasions*.

Sarah Breckenridge is the senior web producer for finecooking.com.

Georgeanne Brennan is an award-winning cookbook author who lives in northern California, where she teaches seasonal cooking classes.

Michael Brisson is the chef-owner of l'etoile restaurant on Martha's Vineyard, Massachusetts.

Bill Briwa is a chef-instructor at Culinary Institute of America at Greystone in California.

Andrew Carmellini trained at the Culinary Institute of America. In 1998, he took over the stoves as chef de cuisine at Café Boulud. He and his wife Gwen are authors of *Urban Italian: True Stories and Simple Recipes from a Life in Food*.

Robert Carter, executive chef and partner of Peninsula Grill in Charleston, South Carolina, has received widespread acclaim for his sophisticated southern cuisine.

Lauren Chattman has written twelve cookbooks. Her latest are *Simply Great Breads* and *Cookie Swap*.

Andrea Chesman is the author of numerous cookbooks, including *Serving Up the Harvest*.

Rosetta Costantino is a cooking instructor in the San Francisco Bay area.

Regan Daley is a food writer from Toronto, Canada. Her cookbook, *In The Sweet Kitchen*, won several awards, including the IACP's Awards for Best Baking and Dessert Book and Best Overall Book.

Robert Danhi runs Chef Danhi & Co., a food consulting firm based in Los Angeles. He is the author of *Southeast Asian Flavors*.

Tasha DeSerio is a cooking teacher and food writer, and the co-owner of Olive Green Catering in Berkeley, California. She is the co-author of *Cooking from the Farmer's Market*.

Darren Deville is a freelance chef and consultant to restaurants, catering companies, and weddings. His desserts have won acclaim, including Best Dessert in Dallas in 1995 and 1997.

Bill Devin was an exporter of Spanish products and resided in Tarragona, Spain.

Paula Disbrowe was the chef at Hart & Hind Fitness Ranch in Rio Frio, Texas, from January 2002 to December 2005, and also spent ten years working as a food and travel writer. Her latest cookbook is *Cowgirl Cuisine: Rustic Recipes and Cowgirl Adventures from a Texas Ranch*.

Abby Dodge, a former pastry chef, is a food writer and instructor. She studied in Paris at La Varenne and is the author of seven cookbooks, including, *Desserts 4 Today*.

Beth Dooley is the restaurant critic for *Mpls.St.Paul Magazine*, a columnist for the *Minneapolis StarTribune,* and a reporter for the NBC affiliate KARE-11 TV, covering farmer's markets and the local food scene.

Tom Douglas has been featured by the media as the Seattle chef who has helped to define the Northwest Style. He was awarded the James Beard Award for Best Northwest Chef in 1994.

Maryellen Driscoll is a *Fine Cooking* contributing editor. She and her husband own Free Bird Farm in upstate New York.

Kay Fahey, a former restaurateur, lives in Reno, Nevada, and writes about food.

Eve Felder is associate dean for new culinary faculty and special programs at The Culinary Institute of America in Hyde Park, New York, and was recognized with the first Educator of the Year Award from Women Chefs & Restaurateurs in 2007.

Janet Fletcher is a Napa Valley food writer and the author of *Fresh from the Farmers' Market* and *Cheese & Wine: A Guide to Selecting, Pairing, and Enjoying*.

Larry Forgione is a James Beard Award-winning cookbook author, food revolutionary, and chef-owner of An American Place Restaurant in Saint Louis.

Fran Gage is the author of six books; her latest is *The New American Olive Oil: Profiles of Producers and 75 Recipes*. She is a member of the California Olive Oil Council, the University of California Extension, and the UC Davis Olive Oil Center.

Dabney Gough worked in the test kitchen at *Fine Cooking*.

Aliza Green is a cookbook author, journalist, and chef. She lives near Philadelphia.

Gordon Hamersley is chef-owner of Hamersley's Bistro in Boston.

Lisa Hanauer is a former chef-restaurateur who now writes about food and teaches preschool. She lives in Oakland, California.

Robert Hellen is the executive chef at Resto restaurant in New York City, where he specializes in rustic Belgian cuisine and charcuterie.

Amanda Hesser is a food columnist for *The New York Times Magazine*, author of *The Essential New York Times Cookbook*, and co-founder of food52.com.

Janie Hibler is an award-winning cookbook author, cooking teacher, and magazine contributor. She was a founder of the International Association of Culinary Professionals and served as its president from 1999-2000.

Greg Higgins is chef-owner of Higgins Restaurant & Bar in Portland, Oregon. He won the James Beard award for Best Chef Northwest in 2002.

Peter Hoffman is the chef-owner of Savoy restaurant and Back Forty, both in New York City. He is also a cooking teacher and leader in the culinary community.

Martha Holmberg is the former editor-in-chief of *Fine Cooking* and a food writer and cookbook author.

Jill Hough is a cookbook author, food writer, recipe developer, and culinary instructor from Napa, California. Her first cookbook is *100 Perfect Pairings: Small Plates to Enjoy with Wines You Love*.

Irit Ishai is Head Pastry Chef and co-founder of Sugar Butter Flour, a well-known bakery in Sunnyvale, California.

Raghavan Iyer is the author of three cookbooks, most recently *660 Curries*.

Rosa Jackson divides her time between Nice and Paris, where she writes about food for major magazines and guidebooks, teaches Niçoise cooking, and runs the custom itinerary company Edible Paris.

Arlene Jacobs is a former chef at Bette restaurant in New York City.

Sara Jenkins is co-author of *Olives and Oranges: Recipes and Flavor Secrets from Italy, Spain, Cyprus, and Beyond*. She is the owner of Porchetta, a takeout restaurant in New York City.

Wendy Kalen is a food writer who has contributed recipes to *Fine Cooking, Cooking Light, Food & Wine*, and many other magazines.

Stephen Kalt is a chef, restaurateur, and consultant with a primary focus on Mediterranean food and culture. He is the principal of Food Think, Inc., a company that develops and operates restaurants primarily in Las Vegas and Atlantic City.

Jeanne Kelley is a food writer, recipe developer, and food stylist. She is the author of *Blue Eggs and Yellow Tomatoes*.

Elinor Klivans has written 13 cookbooks; her latest is *Fast Breads: 50 Recipes for Easy Delicious Breads*. Klivans also writes for the *Washington Post, Real Food, Fresh*, and *Cooking Pleasures*.

Genevieve Ko is a cookbook author and the senior food editor at *Good Housekeeping*. She was previously an editor at *Gourmet* and *Martha Stewart Living* and co-authored *The Sweet Spot: Asian-Inspired Desserts* with renowned pastry chef Pichet Ong.

Richard Leach leads the pastry program for Park Avenue Summer. He was recognized as Pastry Chef of the Year (1997) by the James Beard Foundation and was twice named among the ten best pastry chefs in America by *Chocolatier* magazine.

Seen (Christine) Lippert was a chef at Chez Panisse for 11 years. Currently a resident of Connecticut, her focus is on cooking with locally grown foods.

ANDREW MACLAUCHLAN is the author of *The Making of a Pastry Chef, Tropical Desserts*, and *New Classic Desserts*.

IVY MANNING is a cooking teacher, food writer, and cookbook author; her most recent book is *The Farm to Table Cookbook*.

DOMENICA MARCHETTI is a food writer and cooking instructor who focuses on contemporary Italian home cooking. She is the author of *The Glorious Soups and Stews of Italy* and *Big Night In*.

JENNIFER MCLAGAN is a chef, food stylist, and cookbook author; her most recent book, *Fat: An Appreciation of a Misunderstood Ingredient, with Recipes* was named the 2009 James Beard Cookbook of the Year.

ALICE MEDRICH is a three-time Cookbook of the Year Award winner and teacher. Alice's most recent book, *Pure Dessert*, was named one of the top cookbooks of 2007 by *Gourmet, Bon Appetit*, and *Food & Wine* magazines.

WILL MOYER is a former *Fine Cooking* contributor.

MELISSA MURPHY is the executive chef and owner of Sweet Melissa Patisserie and Sweet Melissa Cremerie.

JAN NEWBERRY has been the food and wine editor of *San Francisco Magazine* for the past 10 years and contributes regularly to *Sunset* and *Food & Wine Magazine*.

DAVID NORMAN is a former *Fine Cooking* contributor.

NANCY OAKES is chef and co-owner of Boulevard and Prospect restaurants in San Francisco. She is the author of *Boulevard: The Cookbook*.

DAVID PAGE is the co-owner of Shinn Estate Vineyards, located on Long Island, New York, with his wife Barbara Shinn. Previously, David co-owned Home Restaurant in New York City.

GREG PATENT was a national spokesperson for Cuisinarts, Inc., teaches cooking classes all over the country, and hosted a TV series on The Learning Channel. He is also an award-winning cookbook author and co-host of the "The Food Guys," a weekly Montana Public Radio show.

LIZ PEARSON is a food writer and recipe developer based in Austin, Texas.

MELISSA PELLEGRINO, former *Fine Cooking* assistant food editor, studied bread baking at Sullivan Street Bakery after graduating from the Institute of Culinary Education. She co-authored *The Italian Farmer's Table*.

LESLIE GLOVER PENDLETON is the author of *Simply Shellfish; Simply Shrimp, Salmon, and (Fish) Steaks;* and *One Dough, Fifty Cookies*. A former food editor for *Gourmet*, Leslie has contributed to many food publications and newspapers.

JACQUES PEPIN is an internationally acclaimed French chef and author of 26 books. He is the Dean of Special Programs at The French Culinary Institute in New York City and a founder of The American Institute of Wine and Food.

JAMES PETERSON worked in a number of restaurants in France and owned a restaurant in New York. He has published 14 books and has been the winner of six James Beard Awards.

JAMES PEYTON is the author of four cookbooks, and also writes for *Food & Wine* and *Southern Living*.

NICOLE PLUE is the pastry chef at Redd in San Francisco. She won the James Beard Award for Outstanding Pastry Chef in 2010. Her desserts have been featured in *Gourmet, Fine Cooking, Food Arts,* and *Food & Wine* magazines.

MICHELLE POLZINE is a pastry chef at Range Restaurant in San Francisco. She was named 2010's Best Pastry Chef by San Francisco Weekly.

NICOLE REES, author of *Baking Unplugged* and co-author of *The Baker's Manual* and *Understanding Baking*, is a food scientist and professional baker.

ANDREA REUSING is chef-owner of Lantern in Chapel Hill, North Carolina. It was named one of America's Top 50 Restaurants by *Gourmet*. Her first book is *Cooking in the Moment: A Year of Seasonal Recipes*.

LESLIE REVSIN was the first-ever woman chef at the Waldorf-Astoria Hotel in New York City. She was an esteemed restaurant chef, television cook, and cookbook author.

ADAM RIED is a cooking columnist, cookbook author, recipe developer, and tester of all things kitchen-related. His latest book is *Thoroughly Modern Milkshakes*.

TONY ROSENFELD, a *Fine Cooking* contributing editor, is also a food writer and restaurant owner based in the Boston area. His second cookbook, *Sear, Sauce, and Serve*, is due out in 2011.

MITCHELL ROSENTHAL is chef/proprietor of Town Hall restaurant in San Francisco. He has cooked alongside Seppi Renggli at The Four Seasons in New York City and was executive chef at Wolfgang Puck's Postrio in San Francisco.

ERIC RUPERT is executive chef at Sub-Zero and Wolf Appliance in Madison, Wisconsin.

SUVIR SARAN, chef-owner at Devi in New York City and American Masala restaurants, is a chef, consultant, and cookbook author. His books include *American Masala* and *Indian Home Cooking*.

LESLIE LEONA DALAVAI SCOTT is a busy mother and spends time in the kitchen cooking healthy and delicious meals in Bedford, Texas.

KATHERINE SEELEY runs a catering company, *Sweet & Savory*, and does regular recipe testing and developing.

SAMANTHA SENEVIRATNE is an editor for *Fine Cooking*.

BARBARA SHINN is the co-owner of Shinn Estate Vineyards with her husband David Page. Barbara is the viticulturists and soil agronomist of the estate. Previously she co-owned Home Restaurant in New York City with her husband.

TANIA SIGAL is a food writer and chef/restaurant owner/caterer in Miami.

MARIA HELM SINSKEY is a chef, cookbook author, and the culinary director at her family's winery, Robert Sinskey Vineyards, in Napa Valley, California. She is a frequent contributor to *Food & Wine, Bon Appetit*, and *Fine Cooking* magazines. Her book *Family Meals* was a 2010 IACP Cookbook Award Winner.

JOANNE MCALLISTER SMART co-authored two Italian cookbooks with Scott Conant as well as *Bistro Cooking at Home* with Gordon Hamersley.

MOLLY STEVENS is a contributing editor to *Fine Cooking*. She won the IACP Cooking Teacher of the Year award in 2006; her book *All About Braising* won the James Beard and International Association of Culinary Professionals awards.

KATHLEEN STEWART runs the Downtown Bakery in Healdsburg, California.

CRAIG STOLL is chef and co-owner of Delfina and Pizzeria Delfina in San Francisco.

ALAN TANGREN, a food writer, was a pastry chef at Chez Panisse and collaborated on *Chez Panisse Fruit* with Alice Waters.

DAVID TANIS is head chef at Chez Panisse, as well as the author of *A Platter of Figs and Other Recipes*.

ALAN TARDI began his cooking career at Chanterelle and Lafayette, working with Jean-Georges Vongerichten. He was chef-owner of Follonico for almost ten years. His latest book is *Romancing the Vine*.

JOHN MARTIN TAYLOR is the author of four cookbooks and a writer, speaker, cooking instructor, heirloom corn product supplier, and consultant to the food industry. He blogs at HoppinJohns.net.

BILL TELEPAN is chef-owner of Telepan in New York City and the author of *Inspired by Ingredients*.

POPPY TOOKER is a food personality, culinary teacher, author, and host of a weekly radio show, "Louisiana Eats," which airs on NPR's affiliate station in New Orleans.

JERRY TRAUNFELD is the chef-owner of Poppy in Seattle and the former executive chef of The Herbfarm in Woodinville, Washington. He was the recipient of the James Beard Award for Best Chef/Northwest in 2000. He is also the author of *The Herbfarm Cookbook* and *The Herbal Kitchen*.

JULIA USHER is a pastry chef, writer, and stylist whose work has appeared in *Vera Wang on Weddings, Bon Appétit, Better Homes and Gardens*, and more. She is a contributing editor at *Dessert Professional* as well as a director of the IACP.

ROBB WALSH is former editor of *Chile Pepper* magazine, restaurant critic for the *Houston Press*, and author of several cookbooks, including *The Texas Cowboy Cookbook* and *Sex, Death, and Oysters*.

ANNIE WAYTE was the executive chef of Nicole's and 202 in New York City. Her first cookbook is *Keep It Seasonal: Soups, Salads, and Sandwiches*.

KATHY WAZANA is a food writer and cooking instructor.

BRUCE WEINSTEIN AND MARK SCARBROUGH are award-winning cookbook authors, columnists, and contributors to national food publications. Their work has appeared in *Eating Well, Cooking Light, The Wine Spectator*, and *The Washington Post*, among others. Their latest book is *Real Food Has Curves: How to Get Off Processed Food, Lose Weight, And Love What You Eat*.

JAY WEINSTEIN is a New York City–based food writer and former chef. His latest book is *The Ethical Gourmet*.

JOANNE WEIR is a cooking teacher, cookbook author, and host of the PBS show *Joanne Weir's Cooking Class*.

BARBARA WITT is the former owner and executive chef of a nationally acclaimed Washington, D.C., restaurant, a private chef, and the author and coauthor of several cookbooks.

PAULA WOLFERT, a resident of San Francisco, is the award-winning author of five cookbooks, including *Couscous and Other Good Food From Morocco, The Cooking of Southwest France*, and *Cooking of the Eastern Mediterranean*.

SU-MEI YU is the chef-owner of Saffron restaurant in San Diego, California. Her latest cookbook is *The Elements of Life, A Contemporary Guide to Thai Recipes and Traditions for Healthier Living*. She is the founder of The Organic Cooking Academy by Su-Mei Yu in Mae Rim, Thailand.

Index

Numbers in **bold** indicate pages with photographs